# Korea's New Economic Strategy in the Globalization Era

# Korea's New Economic Strategy in the Globalization Era

*Edited by*

O. Yul Kwon

*Korea Foundation Chair in Korean Studies and Director, Australian Centre for Korean Studies, Griffith University, Australia*

Sung-Hee Jwa

*President, Korea Economic Research Institute, Seoul*

Kyung-Tae Lee

*Korean Ambassador to the OECD, Paris and former President of the Korea Institute for International Economic Policy, Seoul*

**Edward Elgar**

Cheltenham, UK • Northampton, MA, USA

Published by
Edward Elgar Publishing Limited
Glensanda House
Montpellier Parade
Cheltenham
Glos GL50 1UA
UK



Edward Elgar Publishing, Inc.
136 West Street
Suite 202
Northampton
Massachusetts 01060
USA

A catalogue record for this book is available from the British Library

**Library of Congress Cataloguing in Publication Data**
Griffith University. Australian Centre for Korean Studies. Biennial Conference (3rd : 2001 Brisbane, Qld.)
Korea's new economic strategy in the globalization era / [edited by] O. Yul Kwon, Sung-Hee Jwa, Kyung-Tae Lee.
p. cm.
"A collection of papers that were presented originally at the Third Biennial Conference of the Australian Centre for Korean Studies held at Griffith University, Brisbane, Australia, 20–21 September 2001" —P. .
Includes bibliographical references.
1. Korea (South)—Economic policy—1960—Congresses. 2. Globalization—Economic aspects—Korea (South)—Congresses. 3. Korea (South)—Economic conditions—1960—Congresses. 4. Korea (South)—Foreign economic relations—Congresses. I. Kwon, O. Yul, 1936– II. Chwa, Sung-hui. III. Yi, Kyong-t'ae. IV. Title.

HC467.95.G75 2001
330.95195—dc22

2003049443

ISBN 1 84376 045 2

Printed and bound in Great Britain by MPG Books Ltd, Bodmin, Cornwall

# Contents

# Figures

# Tables

# About the Editors

**Professor O. Yul Kwon** has held the Korea Foundation Chair in Korean Studies at Griffith University since 1996. He is also the Director of the Australian Centre for Korean Studies at Griffith University. Before joining Griffith University, Dr Kwon was Professor at the University of Regina, Canada, and was the Director of the University's Institute for Northeast Asian Studies. Professor Kwon has published a number of books and articles in refereed journals and business magazines, chapters of books and special columns in newspapers. His recent research interest focuses on the Korean economy, international economic relations and international business.

**Dr Sung-Hee Jwa** is President of the Korea Economic Research Institute (KERI), a leading private think tank based in Seoul, Korea. He has also worked many years with the Korea Development Institute (KDI) and has been an advisory member of various presidential committees. Dr Jwa has published extensively on the Korean economy including a number of books, chapters of books, journal articles and special columns in newspapers. He holds a PhD degree in economics from UCLA.

**Dr Kyung-Tae Lee** has been Korean Ambassador to the OECD, Paris, France since 2001. Prior to his current ambassadorial position, Dr Lee served as President of the Korean Institute for International Economic Policy and Vice-President of the Korea Institute for Industrial Economics and Trade. He also worked for the Ministry of Finance and Economy of the Korean government, and served as an advisory member of various presidential and ministerial committees. Dr Lee has published a number of books, chapters of books, and journal articles on the Korean economy. He holds a PhD degree in economics from George Washington University.

# Contributors

**Chong-Bum An** is a Professor of Economics, Sungkyunkwan University, Korea.

**Ki-Yual Bang** is a Senior Research Fellow, Korea Energy Economic Institute, Korea.

**Bernie Bishop** is a Senior Lecturer, Griffith University, Australia.

**Suk-In Chang** is a research fellow, Korea Institute for Industrial Economics and Trade, Korea.

**Kwang Choi** is a Professor of Economics, Hankuk University of Foreign Studies, Korea.

**Nakgyoon Choi** is a Senior Research Fellow, Korea Institute for International Economic Policy, Korea.

**Woo-Jin Chung** is a Research Fellow, Korea Energy Economic Institute, Korea.

**Guangsug Hahn** is a Research Fellow, Korea Economic Research Institute, Korea.

**Jun-Gu Kang** is a Research Fellow, Korea Institute for International Economic Policy, Korea.

**Jong-Il Kim** is a Professor of Economics, Dongguk University, Korea.

**June-Dong Kim** is a Research Fellow, Korea Institute for International Economic Policy, Korea.

**Byoung-Hoon Lee** is a Professor of Sociology, Chung-Ang University, Korea.

**Won-Duck Lee** is President of the Korea Labour Institute, Korea.

**Young-Sun Lee** is a Professor of Economics, Yonsei University, Korea.

**Jong-Chul Lim** is a Professor Emeritus, Seoul National University, Korea.

**Kwang Sun Pai** is President of the Korea Institute for Industrial Economics and Trade, Korea.

**Ki-Hong Park** is a Senior Research Fellow, Korea Institute of Industrial Economics and Trade, Korea.

**Jaebong Ro** is a Senior Research Fellow, Korea Institute for International Economic Policy, Korea.

**Sang-Young Sonn** is an Executive Director, Korea Information Society Development Institute, Korea.

**Chul Ho Yoo** is a Senior Research Fellow, Korea Rural Economic Institute, Korea.

**Chang-Bun Yoon** is President of the Korea Information Society Development Institute, Korea.

**Deok Ryong Yoon** is a Research Fellow, Korea Institute for International Economic Policy, Korea.

# Preface

The economy of South Korea (hereafter referred to as Korea) has been transformed dramatically. It performed exceptionally well over the three decades from the mid-1960s to mid-1990s, recording an annual growth rate of about 9 per cent. This exceptionally strong performance stimulated a broad international discussion of Korea's development model and its applicability to other developing countries. Towards the end of 1997, however, an unprecedented financial crisis plunged the nation into its worst ever economic crisis. Output contracted by 6.7 per cent in 1998, precipitating serious unemployment and social problems. To the surprise of most observers, the economy recovered the following year, achieving a growth rate of 10.9 per cent. As a result, the Korean economy has again stimulated international discussion, this time concerning diagnosis of the crisis, remedial measures, rapid recovery from the crisis, and the implications for neighboring countries.

As the Korean economy recovers further from the crisis, Korean policymakers have faced a new set of challenges adjusting to the demands of globalization and the information era. Both the internal and external policy environments have been changing rapidly, and the nation's policymakers have been gearing towards an economy based on knowledge and information. Under these circumstances, the economic policy paradigm that was used to guide Korea's development for 30 years will no longer work. Thus, the central question that confronts the nation is how to cope with the arduous task of setting up a new economic strategy to meet the emerging challenges of this era.

To discuss the complex issues surrounding Korea's new strategy in the globalization and information era, a conference was held in September 2001. A broad sweep of topical issues was discussed comprehensively among eminent scholars, policy analysts and advisors, and an engaging audience over two days. This volume comprises a selection of the papers that were presented at the conference and revised in light of discussion and further advanced thought.

There are numerous published studies of Korea's post-war economic development and 1997 financial crisis. Very few studies have attempted to explore the broad spectrum of issues associated with Korea's new economic strategy to meet the emerging new challenges as the economy recovers from its financial crisis and moves on in the globalization and information era. This book helps to fill this void in the literature.

The chapters in this book cast a critical lens across the issues deemed most important in establishing Korea's new economic strategy. These issues include recent developments in the Korean geopolitical economy and North–South Korean economic relations, Korea's basic overall policy framework, and specific strategies for key areas such as international trade of commodities and services, business, finance and investment, primary industries, labor and social welfare, and preparing for an information- and knowledge-based economy. The authors are renowned for their expertise on the subjects about which they have written in this volume and were carefully selected from the academic community and economic research organizations. Most of the 25 authors who have contributed to this volume have been involved in strategy formulation as policy advisors for the Korean government and so provide fresh, rich insights into the Korean economic policy environment.

# Acknowledgments

This volume is a collection of papers that were presented originally at the Third Biennial Conference of the Australian Centre for Korean Studies held at Griffith University, Brisbane, Australia, 20–21 September 2001. We are grateful to all who participated in this conference since their comments and discussion have contributed to revision of these papers for publication in this volume.

The success of the conference relied on generous financial support from numerous organizations, to which we express our sincere gratitude. These include in particular the Asia Pacific Council of Griffith University, Department of State Development of the Queensland Government, Korea Research Foundation, Australia–Korea Foundation, School of International Business of Griffith University, International Centre of Griffith University, Korea Institute for International Economic Policy, Korea Labor Institute, Korea Economic Research Institute, Korea Rural Economic Institute, Korea Information Society Development Institute, Korea Energy Economic Institute, the Gold Coast City Council, the Brisbane City Council and LG Electronics Australia. The editors gratefully acknowledge financial support from these institutions.

Twenty-five authors, including ourselves, have contributed to this volume in single and co-authored chapters. We thank the authors for their timely submission of manuscripts. Despite their heavy commitments, they have cooperated readily with our requests. Without their support and cooperation, we could not have assembled this book.

We gratefully acknowledge editorial assistance by Kevin Plastow. His painstaking efforts in polishing papers by authors whose first language is Korean were invaluable in meeting the specifications of the publisher. We thank Robyn White for her careful attention and patience with word processing support. We are also grateful for publication assistance from Edward Elgar Publishing Ltd. As editors, we accept responsibility for the editorial content of this book.

# Introduction: Korea's Response to Globalization

**O. Yul Kwon, Sung-Hee Jwa and Kyung-Tae Lee**

The Korean economy has experienced a variety of transformations in the recent past. During the economic success period from 1963 to 1996, the economy recorded an exceptional annual growth rate of 8.8 per cent (NSO 2002), providing a classic example of successful economic development. As a result, the Korean economy ascended from one of the poorest in the world to one of the richest in just one generation and gained the OECD membership in 1996. This performance stimulated serious international discussion of the Korean development model and the extent of its relevance for other countries.

Abruptly drawing the curtain on this so-called economic miracle, however, the Korean economy was swept dramatically into a financial crisis in 1997. Although the IMF provided a bailout, the economy experienced its worst ever setback. In 1998, the economy contracted by 6.7 per cent, the currency value depreciated by about 50 per cent, and interest rates soared above 30 per cent. The unemployment rate surged from 2.6 per cent in 1997 to 6.8 per cent in 1998, while the inflation rate leaped from 4.4 per cent to 7.5 per cent (NSO 2002).

But perhaps just as remarkable as this swift descent has been this economy's extraordinary reascent. Korean economic recovery took off wholeheartedly in 1999, and recorded 10.9 per cent growth in that year, followed by 9.3 per cent and 3.0 per cent growth in 2000 and 2001 respectively. This recovery from crisis was exceptionally fast in comparison to other countries with similar experiences. The Korean economic experience has thus once again stimulated broad international discussion, this time as a model for overcoming national financial crisis. The significance of Korean economic experiences transcends the issue of guidance that Korea may provide as a model for economic development and for recovery from financial crisis. A raft of structural reforms were undertaken in the business, finance, labor and public sectors as part of the IMF bailout conditions. Indeed, the Korean response to the demands induced by globalization and technological revolution has been so far-reaching as to require a profound shift in the nation's economic policy paradigm. This involves dramatic reorientation from extensive government intervention to market-based liberalization.

As the Korean economy recovers from the financial crisis and moves on in the globalization and information era, it faces new challenges. Ongoing structural reforms of the economy that incorporate a drive toward a knowledge-based economy have changed drastically the internal policy environment. Concomitantly, the external policy environment has also been changing rapidly, particularly under the pressure of globalization and the information technology revolution. These circumstances have rendered the previous paradigm of economic strategy no longer viable. They have thus beset the nation's leader and policymakers with an arduous task: devising and implementing a new economic strategy so that the nation is best placed to succeed in the globalization and information era.

Given the international and regional interest in this matter, a number of Korean specialists – policy advisors and academics – were brought together to share their ideas at a conference in September 2001. The themes for discussion were prospective geopolitical and economic developments in the Korean peninsula, Korea's basic economic policy framework, and specific strategies for key policy areas. These key areas included international trade in commodities and services, the financial and business sectors, foreign direct investment, primary industries, labor and welfare, and an information- and knowledge-based economy. Presenters and discussants were drawn from the academic and business communities, research centers, and the governments of Korea and Australia. Each presentation was followed by comprehensive discussion among these eminent scholars, business managers, policy analysts and advisors, and other audience participants.

This volume brings together a number of the papers that were presented at the conference. Authors have revised their papers extensively in light of conference discussion and further advanced thought. As chapters in this volume, the breadth of the relevance has been extended to meet the interests of an international readership. Most of the 25 authors included here have been involved in strategy formulation as policy advisors for the Korean government, attesting to the validity of their policy analyses and proposed strategies, and richness of the insights they offer.

The authors present a range of views as they traverse an extensive range of issues concerning the contemporary Korean economy. At the heart of much of the discussion in these studies are the policy implications of the ongoing structural reforms of the economy as it is reshaped to respond to globalization, and a national drive to develop an information- and knowledge-based economy. Each of these studies also considers what lies ahead as the Korean economy moves on in a new terrain of the globalization and information era, and proposes strategies to meet the emerging challenges in each key area.

Readers will find general consistency in the views expressed here about appropriate strategy for each strategic area. There is general agreement among the authors about the nature of the internal and external policy environments and how to respond most effectively to them as both environments are pulled by the powerful, ineluctable forces of globalization and the information technology revolution. The tenet of the strategies proposed here derives from the thrust of policy shift from extensive government intervention to a market-oriented paradigm. It argues for further liberalization and internationalization of the economy as a way of securing Korea's international competitiveness, which is prerequisite for economic prosperity in the new era.

The chapters in this volume are arranged thematically across six parts. Part I begins with a consideration of prospective developments in the Korean Peninsula and North–South Korean economic relations. In Chapter 1 Jong-Chul Lim and Jaebong Ro examine the geopolitical and economic roles of the Korean Peninsula in the new millennium. They proceed with a premise that unification of the two Koreas is South Korea's ultimate objective. They provide the view that the new emerging international order after the end of the Cold War is characterized by globalization and regionalism with economic power at the apex. They examine the impact of the post-Cold War international order on the Northeast Asian region where, they argue, Russia, China, Japan and the United States compete for hegemony. They argue that to attain the unification objective, South Korea needs to respond astutely to the international and regional developments, and to make persistent efforts with support from their neighbors. From a geostrategic perspective, they propose a forum or security system involving both Koreas and the region's four competing powers. From an economic perspective, they emphasize the usefulness of continual inter-Korea economic exchanges, the establishment of a regional business center on the peninsula and a regional economic integration. Cooperation and collaboration on the peninsula will help to facilitate Korean unification, which will in turn generate economic benefits not only for the unified Korea but also for Northeast Asian neighbors and the international community.

In Chapter 2 Young-Sun Lee and Deok Ryong Yoon examine North–South Korean economic relations, which have an important bearing on economic development in South Korea, and assesses their future development. Lee and Yoon argue that the most important task of inter-Korean relations has been to escape the culture of confrontation and hostility, and to this end economic relations play a critical role. Inter-Korean economic relations have expanded rapidly in the recent past such that South Korea has become the second-largest trade partner of North Korea and one of its most important sources of investment and humanitarian aid. Yet since inter-Korean economic relations are largely driven not by economic interests but by political factors, they are in many ways hostage to politics and remain unstable. The authors argue that economic interests and motives should be the driving force of the economic relationship. According to Lee and Yoon, inter-Korean economic relations will advance further in the future because of strong political and economic interests between South and North Korea. South Korea sees greater economic interaction as a way of ensuring peace and stability on the peninsula and an opportunity for South Korean companies to take advantage of cheap labor in the North. For the North, strengthening inter-Korean economic relations are the principal way for the country to escape its poverty trap, because South Korea has greater political and economic interest in North Korea than any other nation.

Part II considers the basic strategic direction for the Korean economy and specific strategies for international trade in commodities and services. O. Yul Kwon proposes a basic policy framework for Korea over the medium and long term in Chapter 3. Kwon reviews the policy paradigm before the 1997 financial crisis that guided the economy to greater strength, and identifies the direct linkage between past policy and the causes of the financial crisis. He then examines the shift in the policy paradigm in the wake of the crisis. Since a policy framework is predicated on policy environments, Kwon assesses trends in both the internal and external policy environments, noting the emergence of the globalization and information era, the rising importance of the Chinese economy, demographic changes from declining population growth and aging population structure, declining saving and investment rates, rising economic influence of foreign capital, and widening of the digital divide. Kwon argues that the government should play a complementary role to the private sector, guaranteeing the freedom of the private sector and providing an environment conducive to its development. To this end, the Korean economy must embrace market principles, pursue an across-the-board liberalization policy, and provide comprehensive and robust infrastructure to safeguard the private sector's sources of success and attract mobile resources from abroad. Kwon also argues that a judicious science and technology development policy, an appropriate human resource policy consistent with demographic change, and more emphasis on equity should be integral to the new policy framework.

In Chapter 4, Kyung-Tae Lee, Nakgyoon Choi and Jun-Ku Kang examine future strategies for international trade that will help Korea to achieve a globally competitive market-oriented economy. They argue that Korea's economic success since 1960 is attributable to externally-oriented development strategies and that the Korean economy recovered quickly from the 1997 crisis not by closing domestic markets but by accelerating globalization efforts. The rapid liberalization of domestic markets has also enabled Korea to record annual trade surpluses since 1998. These authors argue for more effective liberalization and deregulation through a multi-track approach toward the WTO's new round, FTAs (free trade agreements), and BITs (bilateral investment treaties). The current strength of the Korean economy owes much to a judicious and carefully implemented foreign trade strategy. If this trade strategy can be adjusted again judiciously to the evolving international trade environment, foreign trade will remain as one of the most vital spheres in sustaining the nation's economic strength.

June-Dong Kim and Jong-Il Kim in Chapter 5 examine the liberalization of the trade in services, arguing for further liberalization and deregulation in the service sector and improvement in the discriminatory regulations against foreign service suppliers. Korea's intensive industrialization during the 1970s and 1980s was achieved at the expense of services, rendering the service sector grossly underdeveloped prior to the early 1990s. Regulations and restrictions on the service sector prevented competition and stifled efficiency and development. Since the mid-1990s, the Uruguay Round of the WTO and Korea's accession to the OECD in 1996 have forced Korea to gradually open its service sector to foreign suppliers, and the 1997 financial crisis accelerated the liberalization. Kim and Kim point out, however, that there are still some remaining sectoral restrictions and *de facto* discrimination against foreign service providers operating in Korea. The authors have estimated productivity gains arising from the service sector liberalization, not only within the sector but also in the manufacturing sector that used liberalized services as inputs over the period 1970–97. They found it difficult to conclusively prove productivity gains as a result of trade liberalization of services, but found that some sub-sectors of services such as distribution, transport and communication, showed significant improvements in productivity.

Part III turns to Korea's new strategy for the business and finance sectors, and incoming foreign direct investment. In Chapter 6, Sung-Hee Jwa analyzes government policy towards the corporate sector in Korea and suggests a new model of the government–business relationship. Given the importance of *chaebols* (business conglomerates) for the economy, and inveterate criticism of them as the main source of both the financial crisis and social injustice, Jwa overviews the formation, growth and characteristics of *chaebols*, and reviews government regulations and reform efforts in relation to the corporate sector. Jwa argues that since these regulations and reform efforts are based on a weak theoretical foundation, they are ineffective in influencing corporate behavior. He advocates development of a coherent framework to guide government–business relations based on the principles of a market economy, and changing the focus of government policy from direct control of the corporate sector to indirect management of the overall economic environment and its institutions. Chapter 7 by Bernie Bishop examines Korea's foreign direct investment policy and addresses the question of whether East Asian neighboring countries will follow Korea's policy. In Bishop's analysis, Korea's foreign direct investment policy has evolved from a relatively restrictive regime towards a much more liberal and open stance from the 1990s.

Korea has transformed its formerly complex approval processes in most industries into mere formalities, reduced the range of restricted industries to barely a handful, and abolished almost all limitations on foreign equity. As a result, Korea's foreign direct investment policies are now more liberal than those of other countries in the East Asian region. Bishop argues that despite some progress towards more liberal investment regimes elsewhere in the region, further liberalization may take some time due to political constraints and concerns about economic development.

In Chapter 7, Sung-Hee Jwa and Guangsug Hahn examine Korea's financial system through a new-institutional economics perspective. They review the evolution of the financial system, its relationship with a country's institutional setting, and its effect on the corporate sector, and identify various types of weaknesses in the Korean financial system that are, they argue, attributable to extensive government intervention. Jwa and Hahn argue that due to Korea's salient institutional setting, neither the Anglo-Saxon system nor the bank-dominated financial system are appropriate for Korea. They propose instead a universal banking system through which banks provide a broader array of financial products including equity investment, underwriting, securitization and insurance services, so that banks take a more active role in both the securities and banking markets. The authors argue for greater autonomy for financial institutions to improve their monitoring functions in loan and securities markets. They also highlight the necessity of properly implementing prudential regulations in this sector to ensure its stability.

Part IV turns to primary industries, focusing on Korea's perennial tasks of maintaining the viability of its agricultural sector and securing overseas energy supplies to meet the ever-rising domestic demand. Chapter 9 by Chul Ho Yoo examines the new challenges faced by Korean agriculture in reference to globalization, China's accession to the WTO, the Doha negotiations of the WTO, and the materialization of free trade agreements with other countries. Yoo reviews the complex changes in the Korean agricultural sector in the decade of 1990–2000. He argues that changes in the number of farms, crop mix, food balance and imports of food products will accelerate under the process of globalization. Under these circumstances, survival of the Korean agricultural sector depends on how effectively national policy promotes the competitiveness of the sector so that it can compete against other countries that have strong agricultural sectors. Yoo critically reviews the attempts made so far to strengthen the sector's competitiveness. Yoo also offers suggestions to enhance competitiveness in this sector, including reducing production costs, upgrading product quality, revamping regulations that restrict efficient use of agricultural land, enforcing product standards, improving the compatibility of domestic products standards with those among major trade partners, and enhancing food safety. In addition, he critically reviews the Korean government proposals for the ongoing WTO negotiations with regard to two key areas – market access and domestic support – and assesses the implications of the proposals for the Korean agricultural sector.

Chapter 10, by Ki-Yual Bang and Woo-Jin Chung, reviews government policy on the energy industry, a mainstay of Korea's economic growth, and examines the shift in the energy policy paradigm since the 1997 crisis. Since Korea has to rely solely on imported energy supplies to meet its ever-rising energy demand, the government has been involved extensively in the energy sector from securing foreign energy sources to domestic energy supplying industries. The government has also controlled end-user pricing of energy as an integral part of its anti-inflation policy. In recent years, however, government policy has been liberalized to promote competition and efficiency in the industry based on market principles. Structural reform of the energy sector is dismantling the vertically integrated monopoly, and state-owned energy companies are being privatized. Bang and Chung anticipate that along with the structural change in the energy industry, Korean companies will change their energy procurement strategies from long-term contracts for stable energy supply to short-term and flexible supply contracts that are more appropriate in competitive and deregulated markets. These authors also speculate on the possibility that major energy consumption countries in Northeast Asia could establish an inter-regional cooperative scheme for their energy procurement.

Part V turns to some of the major social issues consequent to shift in economic policy: industrial relations, labor standards and social welfare. In Chapter 11, Won-Duck Lee and Byoung-Hoon Lee examine the transformation of Korea's industrial relations system from the pre-1987 authoritarian model to a new model of negotiated partnership in conjunction with political democratization in 1987. Since 1987, globalization and the 1997 financial crisis have inspired profound changes in industrial relations. The authors have identified four phases:

1. expansion of organized labor (1987–89);
2. a neo-interventionist policy approach (1990–92);
3. a tripartite approach – workers, employers and government – to labor reforms (1993–97); and
4. economic restructuring (1998–).

They review the historical development and legislative framework of Korea's labor standards and examine existing labor standards such as employees' basic rights, dismissal for managerial reasons, compensation and working hours. Finally, this chapter discusses the thorny issues in industrial relations and labor standards facing Korea today, including reduced working hours, an increase in the non-standard workforce, a shift in the organizational structure of unions from enterprise-based to industry-based unions, and the unionization of civil servants and the unemployed.

In Chapter 12, Chong-Bum An and Kwang Choi critically review Korea's social welfare system and propose an alternative strategy. Korea maintained a policy emphasis on 'maximum growth first, then welfare' over three decades until the end of the 1980s, disabling development of a proper social welfare system. However, swift political democratization at the end of the 1980s intensified public demands for an adequate social welfare system, and the 1997 financial crisis further accelerated the paradigm shift in social welfare policy.

An and Choi argue that there are two distinctive types of demands for welfare in Korea: short-term demands for welfare programs to reduce hardship arising from unemployment, poverty and inequality, and long-term demand for welfare measures that aim to enhance quality of life. An and Choi criticize the existing welfare policy particularly on the grounds of cost-effectiveness and target efficiency. They argue that the welfare policy under the Kim Dae-jung government should be replaced by a new system that distinguishes between the two types of welfare demand, enabling more efficient allocation of welfare funds and ability to address real welfare needs.

Part VI is concerned with strategy to develop Korea's information- and knowledge-based economy. With experience of the 1997 financial crisis, Korea has realized that an input-driven growth strategy is no longer viable in the face of globalization and the information technology revolution, and has shifted its strategic thrust towards development of a knowledge-based economy. In Chapter 13, Kwang Sun Pai, Ki-Hong Park and Suk-In Chang assess Korea's drive towards a knowledge-based economy. In their proposed policy framework for development of a knowledge-based economy, they argue that the government should play a critical role – providing information infrastructure, upgrading the education system, improving incentives for innovation, and implementing institutional reforms. In their evaluation of the government policy in place, they argue that further improvements are required for each of these areas, although they acknowledge the substantial progress that has been made. The new approach requires a shift of strategy from the earlier interventionist policies to fostering a flexible, market-based and networked economy. Under the proposed paradigm, the central role of government is to promote competition, entrepreneurship and especially 'technopreneurship'.

Korea has already drawn international attention for its success in constructing a national information infrastructure. In Chapter 14 Chang-Bun Yoon and Sang-Young Sonn examine the major policies and strategies to develop an information society in Korea. In 1999 the government put forward a proposal for Cyber Korea 21, as a blueprint for Korea's development of an information society in the 21st century. Yoon and Sonn claim that much has been achieved in establishing the infrastructure of information technology since the blueprint was adopted. They argue, however, that further progress in the information infrastructure is needed so that Koreans can adapt smoothly to the development of new information technology, which has moved at tremendous pace over the past decade. The authors argue that economic benefits of informatization such as enhancement of productivity and transparency have not fully materialized because legal and institutional reforms are not complete and not everyone in Korean society can fully utilize the technologies. They highlight that, with the growing risk of cyber-terrorism, more efforts should be made to secure the safety and reliability of cyberspace.

Clearly, the 1997 financial crisis and the ensuing metamorphosis in economic structure and policy environments has rendered the existing economic strategies untenable for sustainable growth of the Korean economy. These developments have inspired considerable exploration for a new economic strategy for the Korean economy. Much of the English language literature has constrained analysis to specific issues and policy areas. As a comprehensive single source that presents in the English language the expertise and experience of authors involved in Korean policymaking, this volume provides a more complete analysis of the broad spectrum of the issues associated with Korea's new economic strategy, as the Korean economy launches into the new terrain of further globalization and information technology revolution.

## REFERENCES

National Statistical Office (NSO) (2002), *Major Statistics of Korean Economy*, Seoul: Korea National Statistical Office.

# Part I

# Korean Geopolitical Economy in the 21$^{st}$ Century

# 1. Geopolitical and Economic Role of the Korean Peninsula for the 21st Century

**Jong-Chul Lim and Jaebong Ro**

## 1. INTRODUCTION

Following the collapse of the Soviet Union in 1990, a new international order has taken shape in the early 21st century. This new order is characterized by the absence of the Cold War, the emergence of a new international economic system represented by inauguration of the World Trade Organization (WTO) and deepening regionalism accelerated by the European integration. These developments have resulted from the destruction of ideological confrontation and the dynamics of the market economy, especially the deepening of economic interdependence across ever more porous national boundaries.

In the new international order, power is cast in terms of hegemony rather than ideology, and depends on the ability to wield economic and diplomatic as well as military muscle. Numerous studies through the 1990s have examined the geopolitics of regional blocs as well as global and bilateral concerns, recognizing the growing significance of economic power. The Korean Peninsula is inevitably influenced by the geopolitics of regional blocs since it is surrounded by three powerful nations – Japan, China and Russia, who with the US have competed for hegemony under the pretext of filling the political vacuum in the region. While the absence of national leadership continues in Northeast Asia, this trend among the four powerful competitors is expected to continue and the Korean Peninsula will need to respond astutely

The division of the peninsula into North and South Korea was a clear product of Cold War tensions played out in Northeast Asia. Despite the end of the Cold War, however, the peninsula remains partitioned amidst a complex mix of geostrategic interests that are quite different from those that produced the ideological divide. A high level of diplomacy will be needed to achieve unification, while also managing the complicated international relations of the region.

This chapter argues that while simultaneously responding to globalization and regionalism, Korea should try to connect the issue of security to its economic policy. One constructive way to make this engagement is by establishing the Korean Peninsula as a business center in Northeast Asia and pursuing the economic integration of the region, as a strategy of diplomacy.

This chapter also examines the geopolitical and economic roles of the Korean Peninsula in the 21st century. It consists of four sections. Following the introduction, section 2 examines the new international order in the post-Cold War era and its impact on the

Northeast Asian region, analyzing the foreign policies of the region's key strategic players. This examination provides the context for discussion in section 3 which considers the position of the Korean Peninsula within the Northeast Asian region and explores possible political and economic roles for a reunified peninsula in the 21st century. The chapter is concluded in section 4.

## 2. NORTHEAST ASIA AND THE NEW INTERNATIONAL ORDER IN THE 21ST CENTURY

The new international order as the world entered the 21st century has had a great impact on the circumstances of Northeast Asia thereby forcing the nations in the region to change their foreign policies.

Indeed, there has never been a period in Northeast Asia when tensions were as high as they were in the late 20th to the early 21st century. These tensions resulted in the wake of deep uncertainties in this region ensuing from the end of the Cold War with new severe struggles among the three powerful countries around the Korean Peninsula and the US which maintains strategic interest in East Asia.

With the end of the Cold War, the order in Northeast Asia has tended to take the form of a mix of bipolarity and Pax Consortis. The US, Japan, China and Russia have put a priority on maintaining stability in the region, deepening regional interdependence through both cooperation and tension. The changed international environment has positively affected the security of the Korean Peninsula by coaxing North Korea into international talks.

### 2.1 The Evolving Order in Northeast Asia

Several possible scenarios have been put forward on the future order in Northeast Asia. Some foresee an order in which a specific country plays a leading role in the region: Pax Americana, Pax Sinica, Pax Nipponica and Pax Koreana. Others foresee an order with more than one country involved in leadership. Under bigemony, the order is maintained by cooperation between the US and Japan, based on the principle of burden sharing. In this scenario China is eliminated from the competition for hegemony in the region or endorses the leadership of the US and Japan. Another possibility is a troika, an order maintained through cooperation between the US, Japan and China, which is appropriate during a transition period. This form is highly possible in that China, hoping to become a world superpower, needs time, and that the US and Japan, because of their political and economic power, cannot exclude China in the contention for hegemony. Another possibility is bipolarity similar to that during the Cold War. Here the two possible poles are as follows: one consisting of the US and Japan against China; the other of China and Russia against the US and Japan. This form implies the advent of a 'New Cold War' in the Northeast Asian region. Pax Consortis is a multi-polar order, maintained through mutual cooperation and checks among Northeast Asian countries, with the US and Russia, all contributing to maintaining order in the region (Hwang 1999).

## 2.2 Foreign Policies of the Nations Concerned

It is useful here to consider the foreign policies of the nations particularly concerned with the Korean Peninsula. First we consider inter-Korean relations, then turn to the policies of the three countries in the vicinity of the Korean Peninsula and the US, which maintains an active strategic interest in the region.

### 2.2.1 Inter-Korean relations

The collapse of the Soviet Union in 1990 had a significant political influence on inter-Korean relations. Of note, the high-level South–North talks between the two Korean leaders started in 1990 and produced the South–North Basic Agreement in 1991.[1] The agreement recognized South and North Korea in a 'temporary special relationship' in the process toward reunification. In February the following year, both sides signed the Joint Declaration of Denuclearization. However, even before the Basic Agreement or the Joint Declaration could bear tangible fruit, North Korea's attempt to arm itself with nuclear weapons revived tensions on the Korean Peninsula.

On 15 June 2000, South Korean President Kim Dae-jung and North Korean Chairman Kim Jong-il met in Pyongyang. The Pyongyang Summit of 2000, as the meeting became known, was groundbreaking as both the first meeting between the leaders of the two Koreas and the forum that officially introduced Kim Jong-il to the international community. The summit was different from past exchanges in two significant ways.

First, unlike earlier prime ministerial-level talks, the main actors in the summit were the highest authorities of South and North Korea. Here, President Kim and Chairman Kim reached agreements on some highly significant points: the two leaders arrived at an understanding on the issue of Korean unification and agreed to engage in inter-Korea exchanges and cooperation; the leaders decided that Chairman Kim Jong-il would pay a return visit to Seoul; and North Korea accepted the condition of stationing of US forces in South Korea after unification. Such agreements were possible only with the direct participation of the two leaders. Second, given the past Cold War geostrategic climate, the two leaders were freer than in Cold War times from external pressures, and asserted that the issue of unification should be resolved independently by Seoul and Pyongyang. This was possible because both Koreas maintained close ties with interested parties such as Russia, China and the US.

With the Pyongyang Summit as a backdrop, a number of landmark developments have occurred. These include the first meeting between the defense ministers of South and North, an agreement to facilitate inter-Korean trade and investment, an agreement on reconnecting the rail and road links through the demilitarized zone and cross-border family reunions involving 3600 people. Particularly noteworthy here is that inter-Korean trade has increased to such an extent that South Korea has become the second-largest trading partner of North Korea.

The success of the Pyongyang Summit has removed much political uncertainty. Moreover, it has greatly improved conditions for economic cooperation, spreading from the private to the governmental level. North Korea is expected to take a more active economic stance as set out in the fourth section of the Joint Declaration of 15 June 2000, whose fourth goal is 'balanced development of the inter-Korean economy'. In addition, the mutual trust built at the summit has helped as a safeguard against backsliding in the process of further reconciliation between South and North Korea. Although official talks have slowed somewhat since March 2001, it is clear that business activities and exchanges will continue in the private sector at unprecedented levels.

### 2.2.2 Northeast Asia policies of the four strategically interested nations

The direction of policies of the three powerful countries around the Korean Peninsula plus the US has been the most important variable in the formation of order in Northeast Asia.

This region currently has two axes -- one formed by the US and Japan and the other by China and Russia. The US has attempted to affirm its status as a superpower through maintaining its hegemony in the region. According to the East Asian Strategic Report (EASR) (Lee 1999a), the US intends to continue intervening in Northeast Asia to play a central role as a regional security guarantor. For this reason, the US has strengthened its alliance with Japan and held in check its potential enemies, China and Russia. US policy towards the region is based on the principle of 'burden-sharing', under which the US shares military costs with Japan and strengthens Japan's political and military roles in the region. This strategy is evident in the Guide to Cooperation and Defense between the US and Japan of November 1997, which allows Japan to provide weapons to neighbors in emergency situations. At the same time, the US checks and appeases China, a potential political and economic threat (Lee 2000b), through another strategic alliance.[2] Nye, who has been influential in the US foreign policy elite, has argued that the US must play a more substantial role in East Asian security in order to cope with China's expansion policy and continuous tension on the Korean Peninsula. US hegemony appears to be firming as reflected in its plans to establish missile systems in Japan and Taiwan and against North Korea and Iran.

The post-Cold War period provided favorable conditions for Japan to emerge as a significant military power in Northeast Asia. Although Japan's so-called constitution has effectively limited the nation's military involvement to national self-defence, Japan has in fact built up a substantial military, ranking second in the world in terms of military spending.[3] Given that Japan's principal security partner is the US, as set out in the Guide to Cooperation and Defense between the US and Japan of November 1997, the role of Japan in the security of this region is sure to expand in the 21st century.

China also has ambitions of being a world superpower, in the wake of its rapid economic growth from the 1980s. However, China in the short run needs time to modernize, and recognizes both the strategic and economic benefits for China of stability on the Korean Peninsula. For this reason it has evaded involvement in conflicts in the region. Russia, the US nemesis during the Cold War period, has struggled to find a new strategic role after the Cold War. Its current objective is mainly to prevent anti-Russian offensives by neighbors through stabilizing its border problems with Japan and promoting the multi-polarization of order in the Northeast Asian region.

China and Russia have been strengthening their alliance *vis-à-vis* the US and Japan. When Russian President Boris Yeltsin visited China in April 1996, the leaders of the two countries expressed their hopes of establishing a strategic alliance in order to contend with the US pursuit of a new hegemony in the region. At a summit-level conference in Moscow in April 1997, Russian President Yeltsin and Chinese President Jiang Zemin agreed to cooperate to check the unrestrained powers of the US. At the summit-level conference in Beijing in November 1997, the presidents of the two countries reiterated the need for deterrence against the growing powers of the US and Japan. Moreover at a summit-level conference in December 1999, China and Russia recognized the US missile plan as a strategy threatening to them (Lee 1999a).

Recognizing the stance of these four key players, it is likely that order in the Northeast Asian region will be maintained in the form of a mix of bipolarity and Pax Consortis for the time being. The US appears to be able to maintain its leadership, while the regional status of Japan and China will be enhanced.

## 3. ROLES OF THE KOREAN PENINSULA IN THE 21ST CENTURY

While the two Koreas remain divided, the most important objective to be achieved on the Korean Peninsula is Korean unification. However, present indications suggest this is possible only in the long run. Here we will focus on more feasible short-run options. Korean unification can be achieved only through the persistent efforts of both South and North, along with the support of the key regional players. Thus, in considering the possible roles of the Korean Peninsula within Northeast Asia in the 21st century, management of political and economic relations in Northeast Asia is the most important concern.

To be sure, the evolving geostrategic order will impact substantially upon the Korean Peninsula in all foreign policy respects. Will it facilitate or impede Korean unification? On the one hand, with the multi-polarization of order in the region both Koreas appear to be developing a more influential role in regional and international affairs, which may enhance the possibility of unification. On the other hand, the actions of the region's four key player nations indicate their resistance to even the smallest changes on the Korean Peninsula. As globalization progresses, the economic importance of the Korean Peninsula within both regional and international contexts will grow, due to the geographical importance of the peninsula in linking the Eurasian continent and the Pacific Rim. South Korea already provides a platform for multinational corporations (mostly Western firms) planning to tap into the Chinese market.

Thus, economically and geostrategically, the potential of the Korean Peninsula to play an increasingly important role in the Northeast Asian region increases as the process of reconciliation gains momentum.

### 3.1 A Political Geostrategic Perspective

Northeast Asia has special significance in international politics – a region in which the diverse interests of powerful previously adversarial countries are entangled. The region comprises two neighboring nuclear powers – China and Russia; it is heavily influenced by another nuclear power – the US with North Korea appearing to be nuclear aspirant. On the region's eastern flank sits an economic giant, Japan. China and Russia are continental powers while Japan is an insular power. The US, although it has military bases in Japan and forces stationed in South Korea, is geographically remote from Northeast Asia, on the other side of the Pacific Rim. Given the geopolitical diversity of the region, it will be extremely difficult to establish a multilateral security regime similar to the North Atlantic Treaty Organization (NATO) in the near future. However, a multilateral forum for security dialogues including the US, Russia, China, Japan and the two Koreas can be a realistic alternative.

Such a forum for regional security will need to embrace the concept of comprehensive security, including a broad range of economic, political and cultural cooperation among the nations of the region as the foundation for a common 'security culture'. To even begin, the forum will need to accommodate the existing systems of bilateral arrangements between regional players and with the US, in order to lay a foundation for continued peace and stability in the region.

In implementing this forum or security system, the role of the Korean Peninsula will be essential. First, for the proposed forum or security system to be viable, North Korea must be included. Regional cooperation without North Korea is meaningless, since this nation purveys the highest probability of threatening the peace and security of the region. Here, the support of its neighbors is crucial. Therefore, the South Korean government, aiming to include North Korea in the dialogue, should focus on inducing consensus in the region on the nature of the region's security issues. To this end it will be essential for the South Korean government to understand and acknowledge the complex power structures established among the various participants.

The improvement of inter-Korean relations also can lead to progress in North Korea's relations with the US, Japan and other regions. Regional cooperation including North Korea will improve the prospects for obtaining funds from international institutions or for successfully negotiating reparations from Japan. If the North Korean government is able to use whatever means possible to inject funds into the economy, this will make the North more attractive to firms from around the world seeking rewarding investment locations. In particular, if normalization of North Korea's relations with Japan results in large-scale reparations, this would provide substantial seed money to revive the North's economy. Such reparations are not likely to be in cash, but in economic development projects by Japanese firms that will focus on infrastructure projects such as roads, railways and ports. This would be a catalyst for South–North economic cooperation by stimulating consortium-style investment in the North.

Second, in the proposed security forum South Korea is well placed to take initiatives. US or Japanese leadership of the forum would make China uneasy and vice versa. A feasible solution to this problem is for both the Koreas to take the initiative, especially in regard to the unification issue. Since North and South Korea have neither the will nor the capability to threaten any of the major powers in the region, the Koreas can serve as a neutral mediator of the forum. Regardless of whether the Koreas are formally designated to lead the forum, the attitude of the two Koreas will be important for its success.

### 3.2 An Economic Perspective

As recognized in the concept of comprehensive security, economic stability is an essential component of national or regional security. Economic stability on the Korean Peninsula is significant for Northeast Asian regional security, recognizing that if the economic interests of the countries in the region are closely intertwined, these countries will make more effort to maintain security in the region to protect their own economic interests. As globalization proceeds, the Korean Peninsula can take advantage of its geographical position linking the Eurasian continent and the Pacific Rim to facilitate flows of goods, people, and ideas between the continent and the Pacific Rim. Therefore, the security of the region could be protected or enhanced through an appropriate economic strategy that fosters greater economic interdependence within the region and equips the peninsula to serve as the ideal linkage or access platform between the Pacific and the Eurasian continent. So that the Korean Peninsula can play a positive role in managing the strength and economic stability of the region, both South and North will need to agree on a practicable strategy and work cooperatively to implement this strategy. Here we consider three possible strategies.

First, South Korea can promote inter-Korean economic exchanges to build trust between North and South Korea and coax North Korea into the international arena. At the end of 1990s, a time of considerable increases in North–South mutual exchanges, North Korea became more willing to cooperate in regional security. Increased economic interaction between the two Koreas, by helping to create trust and transparency and enhancing the business environment, will induce more opportunities for trade and investment from abroad. This in turn would heighten the need to resolve differences in national policies and practices among all Northeast Asian countries as well as North and South Korea. In recent years, the influence of large economic powers in the international community has been significantly weakened. On the other hand, middle powers are seeking collectively to strengthen their influence internationally. Although each middle-power country cannot exert significant influence individually, a caucus of like-minded nations could be very effective for generating a multi-polar approach to regional economic management. The Korean Peninsula is likely to have sufficient geostrategic and economic clout to join other middle powers working towards this objective.

A second potential strategy is to establish and maintain a business center on the Korean Peninsula that would serve the Northeast Asian region. In such a business center, various economic actors, particularly multinational corporations, would conduct businesses providing a high level of value-added services (in trade, finance, technology and information) to regional neighbors. When we consider examples of countries providing a business center function to a regional community, we find that the GDP per capita of such a country tends to be much higher than that of its neighbors. Singapore is a consummate example. Functioning as a trade and business center in Southeast Asia, Singapore had a per capita GDP of $27 000 in 2000, while the per capita GDPs of Malaysia and Indonesia were one-seventh and one-fiftieth of that figure, respectively (Kim 2002). If the Korean Peninsula becomes a business center for the region, this will also raise the international economic status of the Peninsula. It is likely to enhance the security of the region since Northeast Asian countries whose corporations have established subsidiaries in Korea would have more interest in maintaining peace on the Peninsula as well as within the region. Therefore, for the facilitation of business, so that such a business center can be nurtured, policy and structural reforms will be required in South and North Korea, not only in the four main areas of finance, corporations, trade and labor, but also in education and taxes.

A third possible strategy is a trial of regional economic integration. Parallel with multilateralism, regionalism has tended to spread rapidly since the early 1990s, gaining significant momentum as evidenced by the launching of the EU, NAFTA and other regional agreements.[4] Even Northeast Asian countries, which had previously avoided the regional approach, have come to recognize its merits and are hurrying to join the trend. Here, the danger brought about by overlapping regional contracts has played a role in facilitating the phenomenon. According to Baldwin's (1995) Domino Theory of Regionalism, the intention of non-members to evade the negative effects of the formation of a new regional bloc or enlargement of an existing one facilitates the spread of integration. South Korea, in participating in multilateral trade negotiations, has been trying to establish regional arrangements with several countries and has been negotiating free trade agreements with Japan, the US and several developing countries. South Korea is also considering economic integration in the Northeast Asian region, and even extending a drive to deepen and strengthen the ASEAN+3 alliance. These efforts towards economic integration will bring large-scale economic benefits to South Korea through synergy effects and by averting the trade diversion effects from existing regional blocs. In addition, it will help converge the political and economic interests of North and South Korea, which will eventually improve substantially the security of the region. Considering recent examples in which regionalism extends into various issues beyond economic integration, moves towards formation of a Northeast Asian economic bloc may help produce regional integration in security and other areas.

## 4. CONCLUSION

With the advent of the 21st century, international relations in Northeast Asia are complex and in transition, and the evolving order in Northeast Asia presents a unique opportunity for the Korean Peninsula to play important geopolitical and economic roles in this region.

In this chapter we have examined the new international order in the 21st century and its impact on the Northeast Asian region, analyzing the geostrategic positioning of the 'four influential countries' (Russia, China, Japan and US) to argue that stabilization of the Korean Peninsula cannot be achieved by the two Koreas alone. While South and North Korea can and should take the initiative themselves to move towards unification, the strategic interests of the surrounding countries have always influenced the Korean Peninsula and will continue to do so in the future, especially if some form of regional integration is achieved.

In considering the geopolitical and economic roles of the Korean Peninsula in the 21st century, we have noted the overriding importance of Korean unification as a long-term objective of both Koreas. We have argued that this objective should be attained by the persistent efforts of both Koreas, with support from their neighbors. Thus we claim that management of geostrategic and economic relations in Northeast Asia is the most appropriate objective in the short run as a means towards the ultimate goal of unification.

From a geostrategic perspective, we have proposed a forum or security system involving both Koreas, their three neighbors and the US. From an economic perspective, we have emphasized that the security of the region should be assisted using economic options such as inter-Korean economic exchanges, the establishment of a regional business center on the peninsula, and a trial of regional economic integration.

Security and economic stability remain vitally important concerns for both South and North Korea. We have argued for pursuing cooperative possibilities between North and South in the interests of both Koreas and the Northeast Asian region at large. Cooperation and collaboration on the peninsula and within the Northeast Asian region will help to facilitate Korean unification, with consequent benefits for the reunified Korea, its Northeast Asian neighbors, and for the international community.

## NOTES

1. Bluehouse (http://www.bluehouse.go.kr/english/korea_info/inter).
2. A. Mahan (1997) selected Russia, China, and Germany as the most dangerous countries among marine civilizations. N. Spykman (1944), predicting Japan's failure at the end of the WWII, foresaw that China would emerge as the biggest and most powerful country in the world, and recommended implementing a protection policy for Japan (Quoted from Lee [2000b]).
3. *Military Power of Northeast Asian Countries*

| | Military power (1998) | | | Military power | (2010, prospects) |
|---|---|---|---|---|---|
| | GDP (US$ billion) | Military cost (US$ billion) | Army (1000) | GDP (US$ billion) | Military cost (US$ billion) |
| US | 8416 | 259 | 1400 | 10 844 | 333 |
| Japan | 4067 | 35 | 240 | 4865 | 42 |
| China | 976 | 37* | 2820 | 2110 | 79 |
| Russia | 441 | 34 | 1150 | 626 | 48 |
| South Korea | 419 | 10 | 670 | 775 | 19 |
| North Korea | 18 | 2 | 1060 | – | – |

*Note*: * Estimation.
*Source*: Hwang (1999), 'The Policies of Four Neighbors towards the Korean Peninsula', in Kim et al., 1999.

4. The emergence of regional blocs has raised concerns about the global trading system as they implicitly discriminate against non-member countries.

## REFERENCES

American Chamber of Commerce, Korea (2000), *Annual Review 2000*.
Anderson, K. and R. Blackhurst (1997), *Regional Integration and the Global Trading System*, New York: Harvester Wheatsheaf.
Baldwin, R. (1995), 'A domino theory of regionalism', *NBER Working Paper* 4465.
Bluehouse (http://www.bluehouse.go.kr/english/korea_info/inter/).
Cheong, In-Kyo (1999), *Economic Integration in Northeast Asia: Regional Economic Cooperation*, Korea Institute for International Economic Policy (in Korean).
Demko, G.J. and W.B. Wood (1994), *Recording the World: Geopolitcal Perspectives on the Twenty-first Century*, Boulder, CO, San Francisco, CA, Oxford: Westview Press.
Fifield, R.H. and G.E. Etzel (1944), *Geopolitics in Principle and Practice*, Boston: Ginn and Company.
Gong, G.W. (1999), 'The Korean Peninsula on the eve of the 21st century: "Remembering and forgetting" as strategic issues', *Korea and World Affairs*, **23** (2), 241–54.
Huntington, S. (1993), 'The clash of civilization', *Foreign Affairs*, **72** (3), 22–50.
Hwang, Eui-Suh (1999), 'The policies of four neighbors towards the Korean Peninsula', in Kim et al. (eds), *International Relations in the 21st Century and the Korean Peninsula*, Seoul: Bum-hak-sa (in Korean).
Kim, Gi-Whan (2002), 'Strategy for the establishment of a business center', *The World Economy*, **3**, Korea Institute for International Economic Policy, pp. 4–5 (in Korean).
Kim, Hee-O, Chul-Gi Lee, Eui-Suh Hwang, O-Yoon Kwon, Byung-Wook Kim, Byung-Hyo Kim, Kwon-Ho Lee and Sung-Sik Lee (eds) (1999), *International Relations in the 21st Century and the Korean Peninsula*, Seoul: Bum-hak-sa (in Korean).

Krause, L.B. (1997), *Korea's Economic Role in East Asia*, Asia-Pacific Research Center, Stanford University.

Lee, Chang-Jae, Sang-Soo Park and Ik-Pyo Hong (1999b), *Economic Integration in Northeast Asia: Study on Strategy*, Korea Institute for International Economic Policy (in Korean).

Lee, Chul-Gi (1999a), 'Changes in order in northeast Asia and environment of unification and security on the Korean Peninsula', in Kim et al. (eds), *International Relations in the 21st Century and the Korean Peninsula, Seoul*: Bum-hak-sa (in Korean).

Lee, Sun-jin (2001), 'Recent developments on the Korean Peninsula: Seoul's perspective', *IFANS Review*, **9** (1), Institute of Foreign Affairs and National Security, pp. 37–46.

Lee, Sung-Kon (2000a), 'Korea's foreign policy in the 21st century', *IFANS Review*, **8** (1), The Institute of Foreign Affairs and National Security, pp. 1–11.

Lee, Young-Hyung (2000b), 'The geographical interpretation of international relations in the northeast Asian region', *The Journal of Northeast Asian Studies*, **5**, The Institute for Far Eastern Studies, pp. 251–72 (in Korean).

Lilley, J. (1997), *The 'Great Game' on the Korean Peninsula*, Asia/Pacific Research Center, Stanford University.

Park, Doo-Bok (2000), 'Prospects of North Korea-China relations: Inter-Korean summit and thereafter', *IFANS Review*, **8** (2), The Institute of Foreign Affairs and National Security.

Yoo, J.H. and J.S. Lee (1995), *'The Principle of Open Regionalism: Unilateralism or Concerted Unilateralism'* presented at the 11th Annual Meeting of the Korea-America Economic Association.

# 2. Inter-Korean Economic Relations: Past, Present and Future

**Young-Sun Lee and Deok Ryong Yoon**

## 1. INTRODUCTION

Economic relations between North Korea and South Korea began in 1989. During the period to 2001, inter-Korea economic relations continued to strengthen. By 2001, South Korea had become the second-largest trade partner of North Korea and one of its most important sources of investment and humanitarian aid.

Yet despite the rapid growth, economic relations between North and South Korea are in many ways hostage to politics. The continuous prospect that tensions in political relations will spill across to disrupt the economic relationship ensures that this relationship cannot be fundamentally stable. This bilateral economic relationship can be stabilized only when it is driven by economic rather than political interests. Yet almost half of the total trade between the two Koreas has been driven by non-economic motives, and the economically motivated trade has stagnated or is decreasing, as explained later in this chapter.

Investment has also grown rapidly over time, even though the flow has been exclusively unilateral, from the South to the North. However, in 2002 this investment is no longer expanding. South Korean investors are dissuaded because the North has been negligent in providing South Korean investors with institutional security in the form of investment guarantees, dispute settlement mechanisms and means of preventing double taxation, as are usual in foreign investment arrangements.

The South Korean government offered the government of North Korea diverse forms of economic aid including food, medicine and fertilizers. However, public support in the South for such efforts has been decreasing, making it increasingly difficult for the South Korean government to expand economic aid to the North. Other factors such as North Korea's declining production capacity, and economic sanctions imposed by the US, further limit development of inter-Korean trade.

All these issues raise questions about the future of inter-Korean economic relations. This chapter will survey the past and present situation of these relations and attempt to assess the prospects for future development. In the second section we analyze inter-Korean trade and investment, identifying its main characteristics and suggesting some possible measures to overcome present problems. In the third section we offer a forecast on the development of inter-Korean economic relations in terms of the complex motives that drive them. In section 4 we summarize our discussion and draw conclusions from it.

# 2. INTER-KOREAN ECONOMIC RELATIONS

## 2.1 Brief History

After almost 40 years of division, the two Koreas began economic relations with each other under the 'Special Declaration in the Interest of National Self-Esteem, Unification and Prosperity', announced on 7 July 1988 by then South Korean President Roh Tae-woo. To bring life to the declaration, the South Korean government published the 'Basic Guide for Cooperation and Exchange between South and North Korea' on 21 July 1988. While the declaration was enacted in 1989, economic relations became vigorous from 1991 when economic disaster overshadowed the North and trade with the South took on a new sense of urgency.

Inter-Korean economic relations have been steered mainly by trade. With rapid growth since 1991, South Korea became the North's third-largest trade partner only after three or four years. The trade volume in 2000 (including both transactional and non-transactional trade) reached a record high of $425 million, a rise of 27.5 per cent on the previous year (Table 2.1).

Investment, however, did not grow as rapidly as trade due to political and practical restrictions. From the outset the South Korean government limited the volume of investments and the sectors in which South Koreans could invest in the North. These restrictions were removed by the Kim Dae-jung government on 30 April 1998 as part of a new campaign to promote economic cooperation. The North Korean government also imposed restrictions on investment from the South, such as a high minimum wage level for workers in investment projects, and limits on the legal form of foreign companies.[1] In addition to poor infrastructure in the North, the lack of an institutional framework in particular blocked the expansion of inter-Korean economic cooperation. The main obstacles were the lack of government agreements concerning investment protection, taxes, dispute settlement and payment systems. All of these problems restricted investment from the South in the North, and led investors to concentrate on commission-based processing trade, which has practically the same effect as investment.

The historic summit talks of June 2000 opened a new era of inter-Korean economic relations, with leaders of North and South agreeing to strengthen economic cooperation. Specific projects include rebuilding the Kyungeui railway that runs from Pusan at the southern end of the peninsula to Shineuiju at the northern end, and building a huge industrial complex in the North Korean city of Gaesung located just 40 kilometers from the South Korean capital of Seoul.[2] The two Korean governments agreed to establish an institutional framework for investment at the fifth ministerial dialogue in December 2000.[3] Humanitarian aid at the governmental level has also increased significantly. These various developments suggest that the two governments have become active players in inter-Korean economic relations.

## 2.2 Inter-Korean Trade

Inter-Korean trade is composed of transactional and non-transactional trade, distinguished according to the trade motive. Transactional trade refers to normal buying

*Table 2.1* *Classified Inter-Korean Trade*

(Unit: $1 million)

| Year | Transaction trade | | | | | | Non-transactional trade | | | | | | | |
|---|---|---|---|---|---|---|---|---|---|---|---|---|---|---|
| | Exports | | Imports | | Total | Trade balance | Exports | | | | | | Imports | Total |
| | Commercial | CPT | Commercial | CPT | | | KEDO | Aid | Heavy oil | Mt Kumkang | Cooperation | Sub-total | | |
| 1989 | 0.1 | – | 18.7 | – | 18.7 | 18.6 | – | – | – | – | – | – | – | – |
| 1990 | 1.2 | – | 12.3 | – | 13.5 | 11.1 | – | – | – | – | – | – | – | – |
| 1991 | 5.5 | – | 105.7 | – | 111.3 | 100.2 | – | – | – | – | – | – | – | – |
| 1992 | 10.4 | .2 | 162.2 | 0.6 | 173.4 | 152.3 | – | – | – | – | – | – | – | – |
| 1993 | 4.4 | 4.0 | 175.2 | 3.0 | 186.6 | 169.8 | – | – | – | – | – | – | – | – |
| 1994 | 6.9 | 11.3 | 162.0 | 14.3 | 194.5 | 158.0 | – | – | – | – | – | – | – | – |
| 1995 | 28.7 | 24.7 | 201.7 | 21.2 | 276.3 | 169.4 | – | 0.2 | 10.8 | – | – | 11.0 | – | 11.0 |
| 1996 | 17.2 | 38.2 | 146.2 | 36.2 | 237.8 | 127.0 | – | 1.5 | 12.8 | – | – | 14.3 | – | 14.3 |
| 1997 | 23.8 | 36.2 | 147.4 | 42.9 | 250.3 | 133.0 | 17.8 | 8.4 | 29.0 | – | – | 55.3 | 2.8 | 58.0 |
| 1998 | 21.9 | 29.6 | 50.8 | 41.4 | 143.6 | 40.6 | 4.0 | 15.6 | 19.9 | 37.6 | 1.2 | 78.1 | .1 | 78.3 |
| 1999 | 21.7 | 43.9 | 67.8 | 53.7 | 161.8 | 26.7 | 14.4 | 43.4 | 39.5 | 40.6 | 6.3 | 144.3 | .1 | 144.4 |
| 2000 | 36.5 | 57.2 | 78.6 | 72.0 | 244.2 | 56.8 | 35.6 | 104.5 | 7.2 | 14.6 | 17.2 | 170.1 | 1.9 | 180.9 |
| 2001 | 10.5 | 52.3 | 100.9 | 72.6 | 236.3 | 110.6 | 33.7 | 110.6 | 3.5 | 5.8 | 10.4 | 164.0 | 2.7 | 166.7 |
| Total | 188.8 | 297.7 | 1429.3 | 358.0 | 2248.4 | 1300.7 | 105.6 | 284.2 | 122.6 | 98.5 | 35.1 | 482.0 | 7.6 | 486.9 |

*Source*: Unpublished data prepared by the Ministry of Unification (2002).

and selling to meet commercial objectives and explains mainly commission-based processing trade. Non-transactional trade is motivated by non-economic factors and has two main components: trade for economic cooperation like the KEDO (Korean Peninsula Energy Development Organization) project and trade for aid.[4]

### 2.2.1 Characteristics

The main characteristics of inter-Korean trade can be summarized as follows. First, the portion of non-transactional trade is high, as we see in Figure 2.1. While inter-Korean trade was initially motivated by mainly economic factors, the weight of non-transactional trade has grown steadily and in 2001 accounted for the main part of the rapid growth of inter-Korean trade. In 2001, transactional forms of trade, such as commercial trade and commission-based processing trade (CPT) amounted to $236 million (Table 2.1). This accounted for 58.6 per cent of the total trade and represented a 1.4 per cent fall from the previous year. Non-transactional trade that year amounted to $167 million, accounting for 41.4 per cent of all inter-Korean trade (Table 2.1). As discussed below, the recent rapid growth of inter-Korean trade in the recent past has been caused mainly by the acceleration of non-transactional trade. Although transactional trade has grown at a rapid pace, it has fluctuated since the mid-1990s and by 2001 remained below its peak of 60 per cent recorded in 1995.

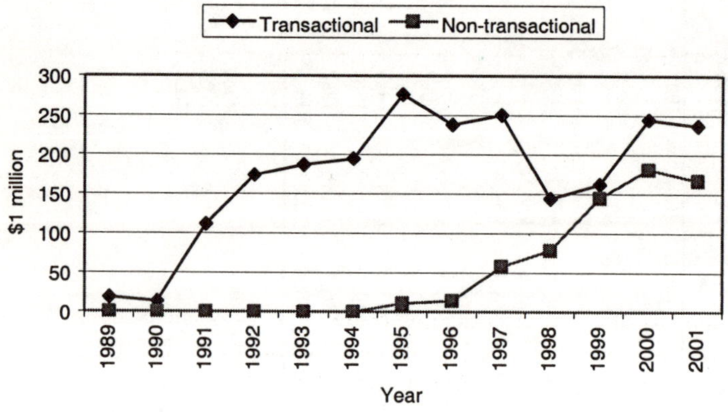


*Source*: Derived from Table 2.1.

*Figure 2.1 Transactional and Non-transactional Trade*

The high proportion of non-transactional trade poses some problems. It leads to a trade flow that does not create mutual benefits but rather increases the economic gains of the North at the expense of the South. If this trend continues, the South Korean public may resist further strengthening economic relations with the North, which will create another obstacle to the integration process. Non-transactional trade should therefore be reduced as much as possible, while trade motivated by economic interests should be expanded.

Another disadvantage is that non-transactional trade creates greater dependency on non-economic factors, making trade vulnerable to a variety of forces including, in particular, political factors. Expansion of trade with economic objectives can sustain long-term trade, while trade with political objectives does not deepen the roots of trade to sustain enduring, mutually rewarding trade development.

A second characteristic of inter-Korean trade is the notable shrinkage of import volume (Figure 2.2). South Korea's imports from North Korea peaked at $223 million in 1995, but dropped to just $176 million in 2001 (Table 2.1). This reduction has resulted from the contraction of production capacity in North Korea. The North's withering production capacity is evident in declining production volume, decreasing diversity and deteriorating quality of goods. Imports from the North are now concentrated in just a few types of products. In 2001, these were mainly agricultural and fishery products (51.0 per cent), textiles (31.2 per cent) and steel and metal products (5.6 per cent).

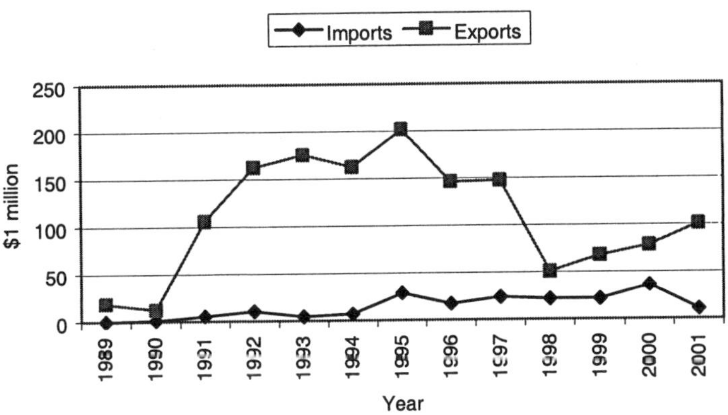


*Source*: Derived from Table 2.1.

*Figure 2.2 Commercial Trade*

When commission-based processing trade is excluded from transactional trade, the trend towards concentration on just a few types of products becomes even clearer: agricultural and fishery products account for 85.8 per cent and steel and metal products for 9.2 per cent of total imports by the South from the North in 2001. Almost all the textile products from the North are imported through commission-based processing trade. These characteristics show clearly that the North's highly limited production capacity seriously restricts inter-Korean trade in various ways, particularly because it narrows the choice of products that can be bought from the North.

Third, inter-Korean trade is characterized by South Korea's continued trade deficit. North Korea has never had a deficit since the inauguration of inter-Korean trade in 1989. In the period from 1991 to 1997, the North enjoyed a trade surplus exceeding $100 million in some years (Table 2.1). South Korea has therefore become the greatest provider of hard currency to North Korea. Even though data on nominal trade show that South Korea had a surplus of $51 million in 2001, if the non-transactional trade is excluded North Korea has a trade surplus of $111 million (Table 2.1). North Korea makes use of the hard currency from its trade with South Korea to settle accounts for indispensable imports. South Korea is the most important buyer for the North, although the North also buys products from other countries. Its trade relationship with the South functions as an incentive for North Korea, because the North has no other trade partner from which it can reap such a lucrative trade surplus. However, this situation implies that the benefits of trade are lopsided in favor of the North. Should this situation continue, further economic integration could be hampered.

The fourth characteristic of inter-Korean trade is a high proportion of commission-based processing trade (CPT). As Figure 2.3 indicates, the volume of CPT grew continuously except in 1998 on account of the 1997 economic crisis. However, the general trend of CPT growth has been somewhat stagnant since 1996. In 2001 CPT decreased again by 3.3 per cent on the previous year. This trend implies that CPT has reached its limit of growth and that total trade with North Korea cannot expand further under prevailing conditions. Despite the slowing growth trend, CPT increased by 40 per cent in 1999 after its fall in response to the economic crisis, and accounted for 53 per cent of total inter-Korean transactional trade in that year. In 2001 CPT still comprised 31.0 per cent of total inter-Korean trade and 52.9 per cent of inter-Korean transactional trade (Table 2.1).

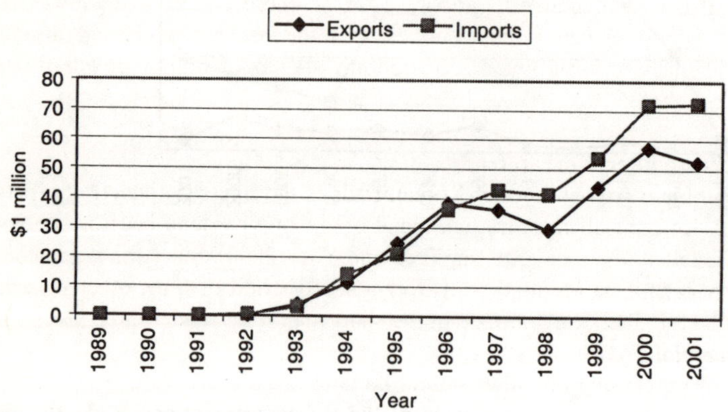


*Source*: Derived from Table 2.1.

*Figure 2.3 Commission-based Processing Trade*

### 2.2.2 Why is inter-Korean trade stagnating?

As data in Table 2.1 indicate, the volume of inter-Korean trade experienced phenomenal growth in 1991 and in 1992, and again in 1995, then the first decline in 1996. We see growth and decline has registered alternately since 1995. A number of reasons help explain the stagnating trade growth from the mid-1990s. First, as mentioned above, the North's production capacity has been shrinking steadily. Continuously decreasing capital has reduced the extent of available production facilities. The present capital volume engaged in the production process was estimated to be around 30 per cent of the 1989 level. Consequently, 70 per cent of the North Korean products in the South Korean market imported as commercial trade in 2001 were agricultural and fishery products. Producing and harvesting primary-industry products are becoming increasingly difficult due to the lack of energy and other resources available for industrial production. Inter-Korean trade will therefore decrease further if there is no investment from outside North Korea to improve North Korea's production capacity.

The second reason for the overall stagnation in trade is the weak purchasing power of the North. Given the priorities of the North Korean government, the North can pay foreign currency only for the products necessary to sustain its the ruling regime. North Korea cannot even feed its own people and a considerable amount of food has to be provided through international humanitarian aid to sustain the North Korean population. Weak purchasing power and the particular funding priorities of the ruling regime naturally present a great obstacle to promoting inter-Korean trade.

A third key reason behind the stagnation is the lack of institutional cooperation. North Korea never agreed to cooperation at government level before the June 2000 summit and even though at the summit both governments agreed to settle some problems in the institutional field, there has been no action following the agreement. This has meant that disincentives such as double taxation and the indirect payment system for the South raise the cost of trade with the North. Currently in 2001, 85 per cent of trade was still carried out indirectly. The South applies import-control rules on North Korean products, especially primary products. It does not, however, impose a tax on these products, acknowledging them as domestic goods. Because disincentives to trade are not addressed at inter-government level, the lack of institutional cooperation works to inhibit the growth of inter-Korean trade.

### 2.2.3 Ways to increase inter-Korean trade

The fundamental problem restricting inter-Korean trade is the limited production capacity of the North. North Korea itself must try to expand production capacity but it is unable to do so because it has fallen into a poverty trap (Lee and Yoon 2000). Since the expansion of production capacity cannot be accomplished over a short period of time, other measures are necessary to increase inter-Korean trade in the short run. We consider three practicable measures below.

First, a system of purchasing on credit should be introduced to increase North Korea's purchasing power. Prior to German reunification, West Germany introduced the so-called SWING system, which made dealings 'on book' and accepted East Germany's buying over selling to West Germany within a certain range. This kind of payment system could enable North Korea to buy goods from South Korea without foreign currency and ease the financing bottlenecks. North Korea may oppose the introduction of a 'dealing-on-book' system because North Korea currently enjoys an annual surplus from inter-Korean trade of over $100 million. To introduce the new payment system, the South should allow selective use of the dealing-on-book system, which could encourage North Korea to buy on credit and sell for cash. This would contribute to the expansion of North Korea's imports from South Korea.

Second, a direct trade system and direct transport system should be introduced. North Korea has insisted on an indirect trade system at least officially. This has raised the costs of inter-Korean trade. A simple agreement between the two Koreas would remove these costs. When the Kyungeui railway and a new road to Gaesung are constructed, as both governments have agreed, direct land transport will be possible. A direct transport connection may lead to a direct trade system physically and administratively. This will reduce the costs of inter-Korean trade and expand trade volume.

Third, both Koreas should fully acknowledge inter-Korean trade as domestic trade. The South should not apply the rules for trade control to North Korean products and the North should abandon all institutional restrictions on products from South Korea. Institutional cooperation alone will help increase the production capacity of the North and expand inter-Korean trade without extra costs.

#### 2.2.4 The future of inter-Korean trade

Noland et al. (1996) used the gravity model to predict which countries would become North Korea's major trade partners if the North Korean economy normalized. The analysis estimated the potential extent of inter-Korean trade to be around 35 per cent of North Korea's total trade volume. The GDP share of North Korea's trade stands far below the international average, accounting for just 11.7 per cent in 2000. South Korea accounts for around 20 per cent of North Korea's total trade volume. This implies that normalization of the North Korean economy and high cooperation between the two sides could further extend inter-Korean trade.

### 2.3 Inter-Korean Investment

#### 2.3.1 Problems and proposals for improvement

With the launching of the Sunshine Policy, the Kim Dae-jung government took measures to promote investment in North Korea on 30 April 1998[5] These measures removed many investment restrictions to ease investment in the North by investors in the South. The upper limit on investment was removed and the list of restricted investment fields was changed from a positive list to a negative list, which means that all investment activities not explicitly prohibited on the list are permitted. The approval process for cooperative companies was simplified considerably. Even though these measures have almost fully liberalized investment from the South into North Korea, this investment has not increased significantly. Many companies from the South have given up on investing in the North, since most have been unable to make profit from their investments. Even though 39 companies have been approved as cooperative partners and 18 projects have been authorized by the Ministry of Unification, the plans are not being put into practice actively.[6]

There are two reasons for inactivity in investment. One is the lack of an institutional framework and the other is North Korea's lack of appeal to the South as a destination for investment.

In an FKI (Federation of Korean Industries) survey in August 2000, most respondents (South Korean companies) pointed to the lack of an institutional framework as the most important obstacle to economic cooperation with the North. They especially emphasized the problem of investment guarantees and double taxation as the most urgent obstacles to address. Poor social overhead capital (SOC), uncertainty in the political situation, poor information and high transport costs, in that order, were mentioned as the next major obstacles. The companies that responded to the survey also gave their ideas on improving the conditions for investment. The largest group proposed shaping an institutional framework for investment guarantees as the first task to increase investment in the North.

Introducing a guarantee system for investment will not only make investments more secure but also enhance political stability. They recommended improving SOC through the construction of railways, roads and electricity facilities, introducing better information systems, and providing government subsidies. All of these proposals centered on tasks for the government, not private companies. These recommendations imply that in the view of the survey respondents, the limits to economic cooperation stem from institutional problems and therefore future development will depend largely upon the role of government.

### 2.3.2 The tasks for North Korea

If North Korea had other points of attraction as an investment destination, problems with the institutional framework would have been less of a deterrent for investors. However, it is clear that North Korea has a wide range of tasks that must be carried out in order to attract external investment. Below we discuss some of the most urgent measures needed to enhance the North's attractiveness as an investment destination.

First, North Korea should undertake systemic reform. Returns on investments in socialist countries are around two-thirds of those from market economies.[7] If the North does not improve investment efficiency through systemic reforms, investments will not flow into the country.

Second, North Korea must guarantee a certain level of limits on wages since its main appeal for investors in the South is its relatively cheap labor. North Korea has set the minimum wage level too high, above what investors in the South are willing to pay, and a labor strike at KEDO is contributing to even more uncertainty over the development of wages in North Korea. If wages increase faster than productivity, the invested capital will lose competitiveness and be rapidly destroyed, causing investors to incur losses. For these reasons, it is better for the North to guarantee a wage limit related to the development of productivity. Otherwise the uncertainty over wages will prevent capital from coming into the North.

Third, North Korea should do its best to induce capital, especially in the first phase of economic development. If capital stock grows over a certain level, profits from economies of scale can be realized. North Korea will become more attractive to investors if capital stock extends beyond a certain set amount. North Korea should, therefore, take great steps to improve investment conditions, especially at the beginning of implementing the market opening and reform policy.

## 3. PROSPECTS FOR INTER-KOREAN ECONOMIC RELATIONS

### 3.1 North Korea in a Poverty Trap

An economy's production decreases when its capital stock is reduced, the quantity of labor decreases, or technology is downgraded. Lack of infrastructure, inappropriate policy measures and an inefficient institutional framework can also cause negative economic growth. What was the main cause of North Korea's economic downturn? The economic trouble began to intensify with the decline of the North's capital stock, caused mainly by the collapse of the international cooperation network among socialist countries. The most severe shock came from the abrupt break in economic relations with the Soviet Union when it collapsed in 1990.

The sustained negative economic growth in North Korea after the abrupt initial downturn can be explained by the continuous decrease of capital stock. Capital has a limited lifetime because of natural decay and technical deterioration. Since change in capital stock is determined by GDP minus consumption and depreciation, production must be greater than the sum of depreciation and consumption, if the national production is not to decrease. If domestic production is not large enough to cover depreciation and consumption, foreign capital must flow in to compensate for the capital deficiency. Otherwise, capital volume will decline and so too will domestic production.

The present severe famine situation in the North in the early years of the 21st century reveals that North Korea's production cannot even cover its basic consumption needs. This means that the country cannot save any more, and capital stock diminishes by the depreciation rate every year. The diminishing capital stock is the main reason for the continuous negative economic growth in North Korea. This economic situation seems to fit into what has been called the 'poverty trap'. In a poverty trap, the supply of domestic and foreign savings is so low that the depreciation of physical stock cannot be replaced.

North Korea's economic growth in 1999 and 2000 was boosted by external capital inflow, especially from South Korea. The Hyundai Group of South Korea invested over $200 million in the Mt Kumkang tourism project in 1999.[8] Hyundai agreed to pay North Korea $150 million annually as an entrance fee to Mt Kumkang. Furthermore, China and Russia increased their economic assistance to maintain their influence over North Korea. Humanitarian assistance from the US and other countries also increased. All of these developments contributed to the economic growth of North Korea in 1999 and 2000. However, the country does not have a large enough production capacity to satisfy domestic consumption and to compensate for capital depreciation. This suggests that the recent positive economic growth of North Korea may come to a halt at any time, particularly if external capital inflow ceases. External aid is the only way to survive for an economy in a poverty trap. It is indispensable, therefore, that North Korea open its economy in order to escape from the trap.

### 3.2 Economic Cooperation as a Main Motor of the Sunshine Policy

The Sunshine Policy is based on the conviction that economic interests can forge the way to peace on the Korean Peninsula. The strategic framework of the Sunshine Policy lies in maximizing economic interaction between the two Koreas so that common interests can force North Korea to cooperate with the South because non-cooperative behavior will result in the destruction of its own economic profits. Economic cooperation will, therefore, play a central role in the Sunshine Policy.

South Korea's strategy can be regarded as a tit-for-tat strategy as seen in game theory. The basic principle of this strategy is to reward the cooperative player and punish the non-cooperative player. If players learn the principle of the game by repeated participation, the game will turn out in the long term to be a cooperative one.

The main objective of the Sunshine Policy is to change the paradigm in relations between the two Koreas. The policy assumes that transforming the long-dominant paradigm of non-cooperation into a cooperative paradigm will automatically extinguish the possibility of military confrontation. Several preconditions are required to make this strategy successful.

First, North Korea must participate in this game. Non-participation is the simplest way for North Korea to reject the attempt to change the paradigm. In reality, North Korea refused to participate in any official dialogue with the South Korean government until the inter-Korean summit talks in June 2000. North Korea allowed businesses to operate at the private level only to avoid any attempt at a paradigm change. South Korea therefore had to provide many more rewards to induce the North to play the game. The Mt Kumkang tour project is a good example of this.

However, when business on the private level reached its limit, North Korea was forced to acknowledge the reality that it could not survive in the long run without cooperating with the South Korean government, and accepted the paradigm change. This was manifested in the summit talks between President Kim of the South and Chairman Kim of the North in 2000. The summit talks imply, therefore, that North Korea has begun to participate in the new game initiated by South Korea in an effort to change the paradigm. But it is just the beginning of the new game.

The second precondition for the tit-for-tat strategy to work is that the prize and punishment must be large enough to ensure continued participation. The prize should be attractive enough to motivate the North to continue to cooperate, and the punishment should be deleterious enough to force the North to give up its hostile stance. However, South Korea lacks the capacity to reward and punish to such an extent that the North is compelled to participate. The South should therefore enlarge this capacity. It is impossible to change the paradigm when North Korea can easily give up the prize and bear the punishment without difficulty. The diverse projects of South Korea in the form of non-transactional trade can be understood as operations to expand the capacity to reward and punish.

The prize and the punishment cannot always be clearly separated. The enlargement of economic cooperation can be a prize for North Korea, although the dependence that this creates for North Korea can be seen as a simultaneous cost since it leaves the North vulnerable to punishment if the South chooses to stop the cooperation. On account of this double-edged character, it is necessary to make the North as dependent on the South as possible, so that the North will find the prospect of punishment too expensive to justify withdrawal. The diverse projects being planned – a deal for the South to supply electricity to the North, the reconstruction of the Kyungeui railway, and the establishment of an industrial complex in Gaesung – are being considered for this reason. Once addicted to the resources from the South, the North would suffer severely in case of a break in inter-Korean economic relations. If we take these preconditions into account, South Korea is not yet ready to follow the tit-for-tat strategy. It is merely in the preparation stages. This means that the South needs more time to improve its capacity to reward and punish by expanding economic relations.

### 3.3 Prospects for the Tit-for-Tat Strategy from an Economic Perspective

South Korea's tit-for-tat strategy based on economic profit has a high chance of succeeding insofar as its capacity to play the game with the North is large enough. A number of reasons point to this conclusion.

First, North Korea is in a difficult situation after a ten-year economic downturn. This has raised the marginal utility of economic profit to a very high level, causing the North's interest in the economic profit provided by South Korea to peak. Therefore, the South can reward the North largely with relatively small payments.

Second, South Korea's investment in North Korea has the greatest potential of any country investing in the North to improve circumstances in North Korea. No other country provides as much economic support to the North as South Korea does and North Korea is increasingly coming to expect more economic aid from the South because few other countries show an interest in North Korea economically. There is strong potential that economic cooperation between the two Koreas will also bring profits to the South because of the two countries' shared cultural and national identities, their shared history as a single nation, and geographical proximity. In terms of economic cooperation, North Korea's interests can be harmonized more easily with those of South Korea than with those of any other country. This means that private investment can be activated without any governmental assistance as long as the basic conditions of infrastructure such as the transport system and electricity are maintained.

Third, South Korea can provide North Korea with a niche market for regional goods. As a market that uniquely shares its culture, South Korea can be a profitable market for a diverse range of culturally specific products from North Korea such as dried medicinal herbs and special foods. In this sense, North Korea can have exclusive access to the South Korean market for ethnic Korean goods.

However, a number of factors could destabilize economic relations between the two Koreas. First, inter-Korean trade can be influenced by political circumstances, because the proportion of non-transactional trade is so high. South Korea has rapidly expanded non-transactional trade, aiming to use economic relations as an instrument for its carrot-and-stick scheme. This has made it possible for governmental negotiations and even the summit talk between the two Koreas to take place. However, this type of economic relationship can also be prone to abrupt setbacks, depending on political conditions. This was evident when disagreements over the Sunshine Policy within South Korea and with the US negatively affected inter-Korean economic relations in 2001. As internal and external pressure for a change in South Korean policy increased, non-transactional trade decreased in 2001 for the first time since its launch. The Mt Kumkang project – the symbolic project of inter-Korean economic cooperation – struck difficulty because Hyundai could not obtain government support.

A second problem is that the incentive for North Korea to shift paradigms is undermined by South Korea being unable to ensure political and economic stability for the North. According to estimates by Yoon and Park (2000), it would cost at least $5 billion to stop North Korea's negative economic growth. North Korea needs over $20 billion to grow as it did in the 1980s. These costs are too great for South Korea to carry alone, because the country is itself just recovering from the economic crisis of 1997. In addition, South Korea does not have the power to control the military in case of a war in the region since this power belongs to the US army stationed in South Korea as the representative of the UN allied powers in accordance with the cease-fire agreement. Thus, lacking the power to guarantee both political stability and economic recovery, the South's ability to provide sufficient incentives to coax North Korea into cooperation is limited.

### 3.4 Prospects for Inter-Korean Economic Relations

Economic relations are expected to be strengthened further because there are demands for economic change on both sides. The South wants to ensure peace and stability on the peninsula and greater economic interaction to make the tit-for-tat strategy function. On the private level, enterprises in the South can reduce production costs by using cheap North Korean labor. The Kyungeui railway will open to South Korea a new means to reach the markets and resources in China and Russia.

For the North, finding a stable partner to provide economic assistance is necessary. Strengthening inter-Korean economic relations seems to be the only way to get out of the poverty trap because South Korea has the greatest political and economic interest in the North. Although the South cannot guarantee the full economic recovery of the North, it could improve the North's economic conditions. Enhancing economic relations is the main instrument to bring the two Koreas together to establish a new cooperative paradigm on the Korean peninsula. This underscores the importance of strengthening inter-Korean economic relations.

## 4. SUMMARY AND CONCLUSION

South and North Korea are entering a new era. Since the end of the Cold war the most important task of inter-Korean relations has been to escape from confrontation and hostility and thaw the Cold War structures so that more cooperative relations can be developed. The paradigm of inter-Korean relations is being changed from a non-cooperative one to a cooperative one largely through economic cooperation. The South has been actively pursuing the Sunshine Policy, which can be explained by the theoretical framework of 'tit-for-tat' strategy. Summit talks and several ministerial meetings have shown the possibility of a paradigm change. Even though governmental negotiations have been suspended for the time being, they will be resumed because they bring benefits for both Koreas.

Economic interaction between the two Koreas inspired by economic motives has stagnated or decreased in the recent past, while economic relations motivated by non-economic interests have expanded rapidly. With growing criticism of the South's economic assistance to the North, there are concerns about the future of inter-Korean economic relations. However, there is enough demand and motives for the South and the North to solve the institutional problems that currently hinder development of stronger bilateral economic relations. North Korea cannot avoid opening its doors, especially to South Korea, since it has fallen into a poverty trap that is unsustainable. South Korea is the most likely investor to help North Korea free itself from the poverty trap. Agreements in the ministerial dialogue are evidence of improvement in the bilateral relationship at the government level. If the two Koreas cooperate closely with each other, their economic relationship will advance further since the two share many potential economic interests that mutual cooperation can address.

## NOTES

1. The North Korean government does not allow South Korean companies to establish an enterprise as a foreign company. The one exception to this regulation is Hyundai's Mt Kumkang project discussed later in this chapter.
2. See the information about summit on the website of the Ministry of Unification (http://www.unikorea.go.kr/).
3. See the agreements of Ministerial talks on the website of the Ministry of Unification.
4. KEDO was created in 1995 to advance the implementation of the Agreed Framework between the United States and the Democratic People's Republic of Korea (DPRK), under which the DPRK agreed to freeze and ultimately dismantle its existing nuclear program. In return, KEDO is providing the DPRK with alternative sources of energy in the form of heavy fuel oil and a modern nuclear power plant that will be built, operated and regulated in accordance with international standards of safety. For more information see the official website of KEDO (http://www.KEDO.org).
5. The term 'sunshine policy' has been used as a description of engagement policy with North Korea. President Kim Dae-jung launched his 'sunshine policy' just after taking office in February 1998 to induce North Korea to implement policies of openness and reforms.
6. For details see the information about inter-Korean Cooperation on the website of Ministry of Unification.
7. This is the result of empirical analysis performed by Gregory and Stuart (1985), who compared the productivity growth of GDR (East Germany) and FRG (West Germany) in the period from 1960 to 1981.
8. The value of this capital injection was more than 20 per cent of North Korea's total export volume of $1480 million in 1999.

## REFERENCES


Barro, Robert and Xavier Sala-i-Martin (1995), *Economic Growth*, New York: McGraw Hill.

Choi, Jean Ah (2000), 'Changes in North Korea's trade structure and revealed comparative advantage (RCA)', Mimeograph, Graduate School of International Studies, Yonsei University, June.

Deutsches Institut Für Wirtschaftsforschung (DIW) (1998), *Finanzkrise in Asien: Realistiche Waerungspolitik erforderlich, Wochenbericht*, No. 26/98, Berlin.

Falk, Martin and Martin Raiser, Holger Brauer (1996), 'Making sense of the J-Curve: Capital utilization, output and total factor productivity in Polish industry 1990–1993', Kiel Working Paper No. 723, Kiel: Kiel Institute of World Economics.

Folders, Federico (1998), 'A note on economic growth and human capital in Eastern Europe', Kiel Working Paper No. 864, Kiel: Kiel Institute of World Economics.

Gregory, Paul and Robert Stuart (1985), *Comparative Economic Systems* (2nd edn), Boston: Houhton Mifflin Company.

Korea Trade Investment Agency (KOTRA), web site (http://www.kotra.or.kr/main/ info/nk).

Lee, Young Sun (1994), 'Economic integration of the Korean Peninsula: A scenario approach to the cost of unification', in Kwack, Seung Yung (ed.), *The Korean Economy at a Crossroad*, Praeger: Westport, CT.

Lee, Young-Sun and Deok Ryong Yoon (2000), 'Inter-Korean economic cooperation as a way out of the poverty trap', *Journal of Comparative Economics* (Bigyo Gyungje Yeon Gu).

Ministry of Unification (1998), 'Monthly report on intra-Korean interchange and cooperation', no. 90, Seoul.

Ministry of Unification (2002), 'The general report on the exchange and cooperation between the South and the North 2001'.

Noland, Marcus, Sherman Robinson and Monica Scatasta (1996), *Modeling Economic Reform in North Korea*, Washington: Institute for International Economics.

Siebert, H. (1995), *Aussenwirtschaft (International Economics)* (5th edn), München: UTB, Gustav Fischer.

Yoon and Park (2000), *Capital Needed for North Korea's Economic Recovery and Optimal Investment Policy*, Policy Analysis 01–08, Seoul: Korea Institute for International Economic Policy.

# Part II

# Strategy for International Trade

# 3. Korea's Economic Policy Framework in the Globalization Era

## O. Yul Kwon

### 1. INTRODUCTION

The objective of this chapter is to propose a policy framework for the Korean economy in the globalization and information era. Economic policy is not path-independent; the past policy path has important bearings on future policy developments. Hence, Korean economic policy over the last three decades will be briefly reviewed. No one would repudiate the thesis that the government has played a pivotal role not only in the prodigious growth of the Korean economy since the mid-1960s, but also in the 1997 financial crisis and the ensuing restructuring process. A few key questions have therefore arisen, including the following. Why did Korean economic policy work well over the three decades of economic success? Why did the economic policy that had worked well in the past suddenly fail, thereby resulting in the financial crisis? How has the Korean policy paradigm changed in the wake of the financial crisis? Addressing these questions will help set up the basic policy framework to produce economic prosperity in the emerging knowledge-based economy in the globalization era.

There are numerous studies in the literature on Korea's economic growth, its financial crisis (Kwon 1998; Cha 2001; Jwa and Yi 2001), its economic recovery and restructuring after the crisis (Kim K. 2002; Krause 2002; Jung 2002; Jwa 2001; Ahn 2001), and its future policy direction (Kim K. 2002; Krause 2002; Jwa 2001; Kim J. 2002).[1] However, it appears that the existing studies have not paid adequate attention to the specific questions raised above. Kwon's (2001a) study has attempted to address those questions, but it has not dealt with the future policy framework systematically and comprehensively.

In order to address those specific issues this chapter is organized as follows. Section 2 examines the policy paradigm during the economic success period. Section 3 relates the failure of economic policy to the causes of the 1997 financial crisis. Section 4 then examines the shift in the economic policy paradigm after the financial crisis. By inquiring into the workings of economic policy during the economic success period, its relationship with the 1997 financial crisis, and the policy shift required by the IMF rescue package, an attempt will be made in section 5 to propose a policy framework appropriate to the emerging economic policy environment. The final section, section 6, contains concluding remarks.

## 2. THE KOREAN ECONOMIC POLICY PARADIGM PRIOR TO THE 1997 FINANCIAL CRISIS[2]

### 2.1 Extensive State Intervention in the Economy

There is a general consensus that Korea maintained a state-led economy during its economic success period (1962–97). Since 1962, national economic activities had been geared to the achievement of targets set by the government's consecutive five-year economic plans. The economy was thus tightly controlled and subject to extensive intervention by the central government. It was therefore the government, not market forces, which controlled the direction and pace of industrialization under the successive authoritarian regimes until the late 1980s. By the end of 1980s, economic policy became less industry-specific and followed an economic liberalization program towards a market-oriented economic system under the pressure of economic partners. The Kim Young Sam regime, which held power from 1993 until 1997, further attempted to liberalize and internationalize the economy to meet the admission requirements of the OECD, which Korea subsequently joined in 1996. However, a strong sense of *dirigisme* remained in the mindsets of policymakers, and Korean society took it for granted.

The government mobilized all possible policy tools in the process of intervening in the economy, and they may be classified into incentive schemes and domestic market protection. The former included tax, credit, foreign exchange allowances and interest rate policies. Market protection measures included trade policy, foreign direct investment policy and other forms of intervention with a plethora of regulations.[3] Among the incentive schemes, the most powerful tool was the allocation of credit at preferential interest rates for specific purposes such as promoting exports and investments in specific target industries or projects during the 1960s and 1970s.[4]

The Korean government protected domestic producers in strategic manufacturing sectors – including heavy and chemical industries – by erecting high barriers to imports through regulations, tariffs and non-tariff barriers. At the same time, the government used a licensing procedure to block the entry of domestic and foreign competitors into the target industries. For instance, the government implemented a singular foreign direct investment (FDI) policy that discouraged and restricted inward FDI in order to protect domestic firms from foreign competition. This resulted in an amount of FDI in Korea far below that of its competitor countries (Kwon 2001b).[5]

The Korean government intervened extensively in the labor market until the late 1980s. The focus of government labor market policy was directed at the maximum generation of employment in line with its maximum growth policy. As part of the manpower policy, the government promoted the rights of management at the expense of labor, suppressing union activities and intervening in labor disputes. Management, taking advantage of government policy and intervention, applied an authoritarian method of labor management. Whenever labor disputes occurred, management often relied on the government to resolve the disputes, instead of learning and practising appropriate methods of dispute resolution. Therefore, the labor market did not progress towards the sort seen in advanced countries, and remained inflexible with regard to retrenchment of workers for business reasons.

The government kept the financial sector under tight control in order to utilize it as a conduit through which to allocate credit to targeted policy sectors and to increase domestic savings. The government maintained the stability of the financial sector through direct involvement in appointing senior managers of the banking institutions and holding significant portions of the shares of banks. It also controlled interest rates for deposits in the financial institutions. By maintaining the stability of the financial sector and interest rates for deposits in the banking institutions, Korea was able to maintain high domestic saving rates. In addition, the government implemented a foreign exchange rate policy as an important tool for promoting exports, and managed to maintain stable effective exchange rates over time in the presence of a relatively high inflation rate in Korea and variations of official exchange rates with trading partners.

## 2.2 Why Was the Policy Successful?

Extensive state intervention in the Korean economy raises a critical question: did the intervention contribute to economic development? This question has been discussed extensively in the literature, and comprehensive analyses of Korea's state intervention have been undertaken in recent years by Pack and Westphal (1986), Westphal (1990), Chang (1993), the World Bank (1993), Smith (1994), Stern et al. (1995), Cha et al. (1997) and Kwon (1997). However, these analyses were all undertaken before the 1997 financial crisis, and failed to fully comprehend the problems this economic strategy generated over time, lurking behind the veil of the opaque operations of government, business and banks, and the euphoric and inertial attitudes of policymakers. It appears necessary to reassess Korea's state intervention in this light.

State intervention beyond rectifying neoclassical market failure could be easily justified at the initial stage of Korean post-war economic development. The market size was too small and too primitive, and without requisite structures to function efficiently, and the institutions required for information and efficient market operation had not been developed. Korea's economic growth required overseas knowledge and technology, for which international markets were imperfect and characterized by pervasive inequality of bargaining power. These features of underdevelopment, as well as technological externalities and economies of scale, justified state intervention in the Korean economy.[6]

Although the efficacy of state intervention could have abated over time, international and domestic environments and institutional infrastructure were all conducive to the success of state intervention until the mid-1980s. The consecutive authoritarian military regimes, which held political power until then, maintained visions and objectives consistent with the national interest of rapid economic development as a way of legitimizing their political power. Nationalism, which has always been strong in Korea, generated a powerful incentive for all citizens to assign high priority to national economic growth. In this context, predatory behavior of state officials for their own self-interest was not a serious concern in Korea.

The international environment was also conducive to the Korean economic strategy of state intervention. Korea played an important role for the Western allies in the Cold War because of its strategic location. Also, the Korean economy was relatively small in size and underdeveloped until the mid-1980s. Hence, Korea's export-led economic development strategy together with state intervention and the protection of domestic industries did not raise serious objections from advanced countries. This enabled Korean products to penetrate advanced countries, thereby rendering Korea's export-led industrialization strategy successful.

From the early stages of its economic development, Korea established the appropriate institutions required for economic development and operated them effectively. A powerful Economic Planning Board, established in 1962, was assigned the central economic policymaking role and served as a broad budgetary authority. Integration of planning and budgeting eliminated possible conflicts of interest among different ministries. The government secured competent economic technocrats through highly competitive civil service examinations. Almost every ministry of the government established its own research institution staffed by academics, most of whom had earned doctorates from abroad.

A bureaucracy staffed with talented technocrats ensured a high degree of autonomy from political interference under the authoritarian regimes. Shielded by their powerful, prestigious and highly reputable organizations of economic policy-related ministries and affiliated research institutions, and guarded by the respect of society, the core technocrats were able to formulate and implement policies in pursuit of national goals. They were to answer directly to the top authoritarian leader, maintaining significant independence from the legislature and other sources of political pressure. In order to maintain close interactions between the public and private sector, the government established a number of deliberation councils under various ministries and for special policy tasks. These councils were fora for government officials, relevant industrial representatives and experts from the academic community to discuss policy issues and to exchange views and information.

In summary, state intervention was justified at the initial stage of Korean economic development during the 1960s and 1970s. It worked well until the end of the 1980s because of a clear social consensus on policy goals, high organizational capabilities and a cooperative external environment.[7]

## 3. STATE INTERVENTION AS THE MAJOR CAUSE OF THE FINANCIAL CRISIS

### 3.1 Why Did State Intervention Become Unsuccessful?

The effectiveness of state intervention changes with environments and institutions. State intervention in Korea, which was effective during the 1960s and 1970s, might produce different outcomes under different international and domestic environments. In the early 1990s after the end of the Cold War, the world economy in general became less receptive to the industrial policies of individual countries. In particular, Korea was no longer treated in a preferential way by advanced Western countries. The pull of globalization with increasing economic integration and competition made the use of state intervention to protect the Korean domestic market and industries increasingly difficult and infeasible.

Domestically, the high organizational capabilities under the old authoritarian regimes could not be maintained under the new internal environment. Since the late 1980s, Korea has been undergoing rapid political democratization. The government has also lost its strong policy direction sanctioned by the whole of society, as attested by the 7th Five-Year Economic Plan (1993–97) being left unattended. Political changes have altered the government–business interface, leading the balance in the relationship to swing markedly toward business. As the world economy has become increasingly competitive, interdependent and complex due to emerging globalization, the government has lost its advantage over the business sector in collecting and understanding the information required to pursue appropriate economic strategy. These changes in government–business relations have rendered government control over the private sector less effective. With the advent of political democratization in the late 1980s, the government liberalized the labor market in which it had extensively intervened under the authoritarian period. This had led to the flare-up of labor disputes, and state intervention in the labor market had now become politically impossible. Under these developments of the policy environment, state intervention across the economy could not be successful.

### 3.2 State Intervention as a Cause of the Financial Crisis

Over time not only did state intervention lose its efficacy, but it also sowed the seeds of the 1997 financial crisis in Korea. The causes of the Korean financial crisis, which have been extensively investigated in the literature (see, for example, Cha 2001; Jwa and Yi 2001; Kwon 1998), include:

1. excessive expansion and diversification of *chaebols* using debt capital;
2. an inefficient financial sector afflicted with moral hazard;
3. lack of transparency in business operations;
4. low productivity and loss of international competitiveness; and
5. rigid labor market practices. Each of these causes of the Korean financial crisis was directly related to state intervention.

Korea developed its own unique government–business relations from the beginning of its export promotion and industrial policy. In order to pursue its economic development strategy, the government nourished a limited number of *chaebols* by providing protection, a variety of incentives and institutionalized privileges. These privileges included cross-subsidiary loan guarantees, cross-subsidiary ownership, prevention of *chaebol* takeover through hostile M&A by domestic and foreign firms, and a skewed corporate governance system that favored majority shareholders. This process fostered intensive collusion between the government and *chaebols*, and generated a widely held perception that *chaebols* were 'too important and too big to fail', implying a guarantee of government bailout if needed.[8] Taking advantage of these privileges and government protection against not only potential domestic and international competitors but also minority shareholders, *chaebols* expanded and diversified excessively. In doing so, they relied on debt capital for investment purposes, because of perceived low risk together with readily available loans at preferential interest rates. This reliance on debt was reflected in the high debt–equity ratio of 519 per cent held by the top 30 *chaebols* in 1997 (Joh 2001). It follows that collusion with the government and the skewed corporate governance system led to a lack of transparency in *chaebol* operations.

The unhealthy structure and financial weaknesses of *chaebols* rendered them vulnerable to a financial crisis. In 1997, a number of the major *chaebols* became insolvent because of their excessive expansion and diversification with debt capital together with their operational inefficiency. By allowing a number of *chaebols* to go bankrupt, the government signaled that it would no longer bail out large companies, a signal that caused their creditworthiness to crumble. These bankrupt companies eventually dumped their non-performing debt on domestic financial institutions, thereby further damaging the already weak financial system. This was the genesis of the financial crisis.

The inefficiency and lack of transparency and accountability of financial institutions, which were major causes of the 1997 financial crisis, were also attributable to government intervention. To control credit allocation for its own purposes of industrial policy, the Korean government controlled and protected financial institutions as the owner and the legitimate regulator. From the 1960s until the mid-1980s, the government was the major shareholder in a number of banks and intervened extensively in bank management. The government imposed protective measures on the financial sector to safeguard this sector from domestic and international competition. *Chaebols* were prohibited from being controlling shareholders of commercial banks. This ensured that the ownership of banks was widely diversified, and minority shareholders had little power in terms of corporate management. Accordingly, Korean banks were regarded as 'entities without owners'. Banks were therefore accountable to no one except their political masters, and thus their operations lacked transparency and accountability.[9] The strong prevailing perception that 'banks will never fail' because of government protection generated moral hazard. As a result, the banking sector was inefficient, inexperienced in risk assessment, and under-capitalized.

In 1993 the government started to liberalize and internationalize its financial markets, and sped up the liberalization process to fulfill the membership requirements for admission into the OECD in 1996. As a consequence, banks were allowed to access international financial markets. However, the supervisory structure of banks did not adapt to the liberalization of the financial sector, and appropriate restraints on the risk-taking behavior of banks were not in place. The lack of prudential regulation on banks left them free to borrow excessively from offshore financial markets as soon as they were allowed to access them. In the presence of mounting short-term foreign debt, foreign reserves held by the Bank of Korea dwindled quickly. Meantime, state intervention in the foreign exchange market maintained an overvalued Korean currency. The financial situation in Korea was therefore certainly ripe for speculative financial attack, thereby propagating financial panic.

The inflexibility of the Korean labor market also contributed to the 1997 financial crisis. Under government interference and repression until the late 1980s, labor management skill in conciliation did not develop. A proper workforce retrenchment mechanism could not develop because of the continuously rising demand for labor over time resulting from sustained rapid economic growth and lifetime employment practices. The labor market liberalization at the end of the 1980s brought on rampageous and militant union activities. This raised labor costs rapidly, and by 1995 Korea had the most expensive labor among Asian countries, with the exception of Japan (Kwon 1998). This helped to induce a loss of international competitiveness for Korean firms, which contributed to economic recession from the beginning of 1996, and to a current account deficit that was an important source of the financial crisis.

A paradox of domestic market protection against international competition materialized in Korea. As mentioned earlier, to protect the domestic market and industries as part of its industrial policy, the Korean government imposed a variety of restrictive measures against imports of consumer goods, inward FDI and business takeover by means of M&A. This policy contributed to the rapid growth of target industries and banks until the late 1980s. However, this protection generated excessive economic power concentration in a limited number of *chaebols*, which practiced monopolistic business operations domestically. This in turn meant *chaebols* and banks missed the opportunity to equip themselves with the skills needed to be competitive internationally. The protectionist policies also led to slow growth in productivity and eventually to the loss of national competitiveness, a key cause of the financial crisis.

Another important cause of the Korean financial crisis was the failure of the government to take appropriate action in advance. The critical factor underlying the causes of the financial crisis, as examined above, appeared to be the failure of economic institutions and structures to adapt to emerging changes in the domestic and international environments. Institutional and structural impediments had developed over a long period of time though collusion between the government, *chaebols* and banks. However, although these institutional and structural problems had been analyzed extensively, the government failed to take appropriate action to remedy them. Instead, the government maintained its policy of excessive intervention and multitudinous regulations over business and banks, indicating the structural and institutional dysfunction of the policy process.[10]

The outbreak of the November 1997 financial crisis enables one to draw a couple of conclusions about Korea's policy apparatus. First, the Korean government did not realize that state intervention was creating circumstances that would render the national economy highly vulnerable to financial crisis. Second, the government did not introduce appropriate measures in time to stem the financial crisis despite the presence of numerous emerging symptoms and other instructive evidence. This clearly signified the demise of the old paradigm of economic policy. The actual financial crisis in November 1997 and the ensuing economic damage have made the government and other economic actors comprehend the multiple problems of moral hazard, political cronyism and the resulting institutional and structural dysfunction. The crisis has also forced all Koreans to realize the need for a dramatic shift in policy paradigm. This realization was reinforced by the IMF's rescue package that was conditional upon the nation discarding the old interventionist paradigm and undertaking a new free market paradigm of economic policy.

## 4. SHIFT IN THE ECONOMIC POLICY PARADIGM

At the Korean government's request, the IMF agreed to provide financial assistance of $58 billion to save Korea from foreign debt default on the condition that Korea adhered to its strict policy prescriptions. The IMF policy package consisted of three components:

1. macroeconomic policy,
2. financial sector restructuring, and
3. other structural reform measures.

The objectives of macroeconomic policy were to restrain aggregate demand, maintain a flexible exchange rate without state intervention, and build up foreign reserves. These objectives were achieved in that interest rates were lowered below the crisis levels, the exchange rate stabilized under a flexible exchange rate system without state intervention, and foreign reserves were accumulated beyond the agreed level.

In accordance with the IMF policy package, the restructuring of the financial sector was intended to increase the independence of the banking sector from the government, to consolidate and strengthen the supervision of all financial institutions, to liquidate and restructure insolvent financial institutions and to recapitalize viable ones. Added to this was the liberalization of the financial sector, thereby allowing competition from abroad and M&A of banks.

The Korean government has been quite successful in remaining true to the conditions of the IMF bailout. The government has changed quite dramatically from the control, interference, protection and fragmented supervision that characterized its former policy approach toward the financial sector. New financial bills, passed in December 1997, have firmly enhanced the independence of the Bank of Korea (the central bank) from the government. The new bills have also strengthened and consolidated all the supervisory functions of the financial sector (including banks, insurance and trust companies) under the new Financial Supervisory Commission, thereby improving the prudential supervision of the financial sector.

The banking sector has been restructured substantially. In the course of restructuring, 631 non-viable financial institutions were closed, while the remaining ones were recapitalized with the support of 157 trillion won of public money. This public money was used to purchase non-performing loans (NPLs) from the viable financial institutions, and greatly assisted them in obtaining 'sound bank' status according to the BIS ratios (MOFE 2002: 7). As a result, the value of NPLs in the banking sector dropped from 61.0 trillion won at the end of 1999 to 14.2 trillion won by the end of June 2002 (MOFE 2002: 7).

In contrast to the past practices of protecting the banking sector from foreign competition, the new financial framework has introduced greater competition into the financial sector by opening the sector to foreign capital and allowing M&A of banks by foreign investors. Since foreign ownership of banks was permitted with a few nominal restrictions in March 1998, foreigners' participation in domestic banks' equity capital has increased remarkably. As a result, for two banks, the number one majority shareholders are foreigners, and for three banks foreigners participate in management (SERI 1999a). In September 1999 the decision was made to sell a troubled bank (Korea First Bank) to Newbridge Capital of the US, marking a watershed in the Korean financial sector.

As some control over major financial institutions is transferred to foreigners, the government will find it more difficult to directly intervene in the management of the nation's financial institutions, signifying the end of the old practice of government control over finance. In particular, putting one bank (Korea First Bank) in the hands of experienced foreign managers will help this sector discard the traditional practice of lending on the basis of the borrower's size or political connections rather than sound credit analysis. As Korea First Bank is transformed so that it lends on objective criteria and shows strong profitability, the rest of the financial industry will have little choice but to follow its lead.

In the past, the Bank of Korea maintained the money supply as the target of its monetary policy. Since the financial crisis, however, the overnight call rate has become the key target of the central bank's monetary policy. The government began interest rate liberalization in 1991 and by July 1997 the task was completed for all lending and borrowing rates (SERI

1999b: 15). This has allowed interest rates to recover their market function of allocating funds and balancing supply and demand in the financial market. With the role of interest rates restored in the financial market, the primary tool of monetary policy shifted from controlling the money supply to adjusting interest rates, as in advanced countries.

The Korean government has also made a marked shift in its policy toward *chaebols* in the process of complying with the IMF rescue package. This policy shift was reflected in the *chaebol* reforms enforced by the government. The reforms were intended to eliminate institutionalized privileges bestowed on *chaebols*, as mentioned above, in order to improve financial structure, corporate governance, transparency and accountability in their operations, and to focus *chaebols* on their core areas of competence.

In the course of *chaebol* restructuring, 16 of the 30 biggest conglomerates were sold, merged or liquidated, including Daewoo, the second-largest *chaebol* in terms of asset size (MOFE 2002: 5). This has discredited the perception of *chaebols* being 'too big to fail'. In the absence of the earlier privileges for *chaebols*, financial institutions will lend to them only if they have evidence of sound business operations. The newly liberalized market allows 100 per cent foreign ownership of Korean companies listed on the stock market and hostile takeovers of domestic companies by foreigners.

As *chaebol* restructuring proceeds amidst changing international and domestic circumstances, government interference in business is bound to decline. As a way to improve their financial soundness, Korean companies have begun to attract foreign capital. For instance, the four largest *chaebols* alone had attracted US$10.8 billion foreign capital by the end of March 1999 (SERI 2001: 105). By the end of January 1999, the number of listed firms whose combined foreign ownership exceeded the share of the largest domestic shareholder increased to 42 (*Newsreview* 1999: 26). Once companies that are influenced by foreign investors become uncooperative with government's attempts at intervention, the government will have little choice but to give up its intervention in the business sector. Besides, the government no longer provides protection of businesses from overseas competition and takeover by M&A. Nor does the government allocate credit to special sectors of the economy. Loss of the credit allocation power together with waning influences on business will also help to erode the government–business nexus that gave rise to moral hazard and the collusive relationship between the government and *chaebols*. It is thus safe to conclude that the old paradigm of state intervention in the business sector will continue to shift toward an economic policy based on market principles, as considerable progress is this direction is already observable.

As discussed earlier, another important facet of the former Korean policy paradigm was to protect the domestic market and industries by restriction and intervention on imports, capital flows and FDI. This protective approach has also changed since the crisis, as the IMF reform package has required liberalization of trade and the capital account. Substantial progress has been made in these areas as well. The government fulfilled the trade liberalization requirements by the end of 1998 (MOFE 1998: 27). To increase Korea's access to foreign capital, the government has complied fully with the IMF requirements of capital account liberalization. All controls on capital movements, including Koreans' overseas investment and borrowing, incoming FDI, and the establishment of financial institutions, have already been abolished. Foreign exchange transactions were fully liberalized on 1 April 1999. Foreign equity ownership ceilings have been eliminated, and foreigners are now able to purchase real estate and invest in local bonds and short-term money market instruments without restrictions. These concrete moves also signal the marked shift that has been undertaken in the policy paradigm.

Finally, another important shift in the policy paradigm is evident in the labor market. Under government repression and interference, the Korean labor market lacked flexibility in adjustment of the workforce, which contributed to the financial crisis. To comply with a requirement of the IMF policy package for labor reform, a Tripartite Commission with representatives of labor, government and business was established in February 1998, facilitating revision of the labor laws. The revised laws instituted labor market flexibility by allowing lay-offs for the first time in Korean history in the event of urgent management needs, such as business transfers and M&A caused by extreme financial difficulty. This amendment has facilitated the necessary corporate sector restructuring and allowed firms to function more competitively.

## 5. KOREAN ECONOMIC POLICY FRAMEWORK IN THE GLOBALIZATION ERA

### 5.1 Policy Objectives and Emerging Environments

As examined above, in the wake of the 1997 financial crisis the paradigm of Korean economic policy has been shifted from a government-led economy with extensive state intervention toward a market economy. This shift has been reflected in the ongoing institutional and structural reforms of financial institutions, *chaebols* and the labor market. The Korean economy is thus in transition. Even though the economy has recovered substantially from the crisis since 1999, the transition period will probably take a few more years until the reforms are completed and the economy recovers fully.[11]

At this juncture, an important question arises as to the basic economic policy framework during the transitional period and beyond. More specifically, what type of policy should the government take up from here? In light of the past experiences of Korean economic policy examined above, this section attempts to address this specific question.

A policy framework would be predicated on the main objective that a society attempts to achieve, and on emerging national and international policy environments. Although it is difficult to identify a social consensus on the nation's principal economic objective, sustainable and equitable economic development under market principles will be assumed to be the main economic objective of Korea for the purpose of this chapter. During the 1960s and 1970s Korea pursued an overriding objective of maximum growth, and soon after the 1997 financial crisis the whole of Korean society was mobilized by a burning desire to achieve swift economic recovery from the crisis. Because of the bitter experience of the 1997 crisis and the ensuing economic setback, together with a strong feeling of economic injustice, the importance of both sustainability and equity should be emphasized in the process of economic development. It also appears that Korean society has taken a market economy for granted since the onset of the financial crisis.[12]

With regard to the emerging economic policy environments, one of the most salient trends is that since the end of the Cold War the world economic order has rapidly been reorganized into a global market economy. Under the rising globalization, not only goods and services but also factors of production such as capital, technology, information and labor move easily across national borders. As a result, the world economy is becoming further interrelated, integrated and more competitive. The globalization trend will strengthen continuously and forcefully with improvements in transportation, telecommunications and information technology and with advances of international institutions such as the WTO and free trade agreements (FTA).

Another salient trend is that the basis of the world economy is moving toward knowledge and information. In a knowledge-based economy, high value-added industries based on new technology and innovation will become the basis for economic growth, and human creativity will become increasingly important as a source of value-creation. Continuous invention of new information technology and technological innovation accelerate changes in economic activities and accentuate competition, thereby increasing economic uncertainty. The Korean economy is surely evolving toward a knowledge-based economy as attested to by the rising contribution of the information technology industry to GDP from 7.7 per cent in 1997 to 15.6 per cent in 2001 (MOFE 2002: 14). Since 1977, the growth of the information industry has contributed more than one-third to the overall growth of the economy (Hong 2002).

The rising importance of the Chinese economy is another highly influential factor. China has achieved extremely rapid economic growth over the last two decades. So far, the Chinese economy has grown largely through industrialization in low value-creation areas using cheap labor and FDI. However, it is likely that China will move toward an economy of high value creation. If the Chinese economy continues its recent rapid growth, it will become equivalent in size to the US economy in terms of purchasing power by 2015 (Kim J.H. 2002). Regardless of the relative size of the Chinese economy in the world, it is very likely that China will become the paramount economic player in Asia, surpassing Japan, and will therefore be a formidable competitor against Korea. With the booming Chinese economy, Northeast Asia will be an important economic bloc, comparable to those of North America and the EU.

Domestically, there are clear trends in Korea's demographic development. The rate of population growth has slowed, and the population is aging quickly. The population grew at 1.75 per cent per year during the 1970s, but the growth rate declined to 1.24 per cent and then to 0.99 per cent per year during the 1980s and the 1990s respectively. During the three-year period from 2000 to 2002, the Korean population grew at 0.73 per cent per year (National Statistical Office 2002). The proportion of citizens older than 65 was 3.8 per cent at the beginning of the 1980s, and increased to 5.1 per cent at the beginning of the 1990s. The proportion reached 7.6 per cent in 2002 (National Statistical Office 2002). It is estimated that the share of the population aged over 65 will reach 20 per cent by 2026 (*Chosun Ilbo* 2002a). This indicates that the growth rate of the labor force will decline and the social burden of support for the elderly will increase.

As people's disposable income further increases alongside globalization, their preference for quality of life and for leisure will rise. This development has two important implications. First, Koreans will reduce the number of hours they work each year, and five days of work per week will become a normal practice rather than the exception, as in advanced countries. Second, the national saving rate will decline. During the 1980s and 1990s, the gross national saving rate was above 35 per cent, but it fell below 30 per cent in 2001 (National Statistical Office 2002).

The national investment rate will also decline. During the high economic growth period, *chaebols*, the major undertakers of investment, were provided with institutionalized privileges that lowered business risk. The government provided *chaebols* with protection from domestic and international competition, and loans at preferential interest rates. These policies helped maintain a high national investment rate. However, as examined above, the environment conducive to investment by *chaebols* has been progressively dismantled since the 1997 financial crisis. Furthermore, economic uncertainty has increased in the era of globalization and information. These developments will lead to a reduction of the national investment rate, a trend that has taken hold. While the national investment rate was over 35 per cent during the 1980s and 1990s, it has decreased to below 30 per cent since 2001 (National Statistical Office 2002).

The influence of foreign capital on the Korean economy will rise. Since the liberalization of the FDI regime in the wake of the 1997 crisis, FDI in Korea has increased remarkably, as reflected in the increase in the ratio FDI stock to GDP in Korea from 2.1 per cent in 1995 to 7.9 in 1999 (UNCTAD 2001). FDI has penetrated every sphere of the Korean business sector. The number of Korean companies with a foreign-owned equity stake of more than 10 per cent increased from 4419 in 1997 to 11 515 in 2001 (KOTRA 2002: 19). Portfolio investment has also increased substantially. Net portfolio inflow, which varied between one and US$5 billion annually from 1992 to 1999, leapt to almost US$12 billion in 2000 (Crotty and Lee 2002). As a result, the percentage of Korean market capitalization owned by foreigners increased from 2.7 per cent in 1992 to 12.3 per cent in 1997, and leapt to 36.2 per cent in January 2002 (Crotty and Lee 2002). The rising presence of foreign capital, business firms and ideas will propel Korea's drive toward transformation into a more open, liberal economy as well as the adoption of international norms and practices by all segments of society.

In the information- and knowledge-based economy, the so-called digital divide will be an emerging phenomenon in Korea and elsewhere in the world. The digital divide, if left unchecked, will aggravate income inequality and lead to bipolarization of society. This will heighten conflict between the underprivileged and the mainstream of society.

National tradition and culture will also play a significant role. Each country has its own deep-rooted traditions and culture. Korea is no exception in this regard, and its culture is quite different from Western culture. It is well known that national culture dies hard. Thus, conflicts are highly likely to arise between on the one hand the fast process of globalization and informatization of the economy and on the other hand the laggard adjustments of Korean society and culture to the ensuing new systems and institutions under globalization.

### 5.2 Policy Framework for Sustainable and Equitable Development

Under the emerging domestic and international policy environments as examined above, the basic policy framework most appropriate for the Korean economy in the globalization and information era transpires quite clearly. In this chapter we have considered how Korea's dirigist approach to national economic policy up to the mid-1990s could no longer work effectively because of changes in the policy environment, as shown above. In the process of structural reforms after the 1997 crisis, the policy paradigm of the Korean economy has already shifted from a government-led to a market-oriented economy.

There has been much debate in the literature about what governments should do under economic situations similar to that in Korea, where *dirigisme* has been abandoned and market principles adopted. According to the Washington consensus, there is little scope for government action as it has more or less fulfilled the policy prescription of liberalization, privatization and macroeconomic stabilization (Williamson 1990). However, the World Bank (1993) and Stiglitz (1997, 1998 and 1999) argue for a complementary role for the government beyond the policy prescriptions of the Washington consensus. As Krause (2002) points out, Korean society, having been under the strong influence of Confucian tradition and extensive government interference until recently, is not ready to rely exclusively on the market mechanism. Korean society still looks to the government to take charge and solve problems. Furthermore, the government should play an important role in improving economic equity, although a too intrusive role is not consistent with globalization. In this respect, a complementary role for the public sector appears to be appropriate. The essence of the complementary role should be to guarantee the economic freedom of the private sector and to create an environment conducive to the development of a strong, competitive and efficient private sector.

It should be noted that a complementary role for government is constrained by globalization. Under the emerging global economic integration, Korea, like any other country, wishes to take advantage of the benefits of globalization in the form of foreign technology, capital and other mobile resources. At the same time, Korea wishes to regulate the domestic economy and to maintain national sovereignty. Summers (1999) points out that the three goals are incompatible. If Korea wishes to maintain sovereignty and yet allow international economic integration, it must accept an entirely free market at the global level, which requires abandoning its regulatory powers over the domestic economy, as the member countries of the EU have done. If Korea embraces economic integration and its own economic regulation, it will end up forfeiting sovereignty. Finally, Korea will not be able to enjoy the full benefits of international economic integration by maintaining its sovereignty and regulatory power over its economy. Under these circumstances, Korea has little choice but to align domestic policy with international standards – including the WTO and OECD standards. Under the basic policy framework that accommodates these constraints, what specific policies should the Korean government undertake to achieve the objective of sustainable and equitable development?

First of all, the underpinning principle of the policy framework should be to embrace market principles and global standards geared towards the emerging globalization and information era. The sources of economic growth are in essence labor, capital and advancement of total factor productivity. In the globalization era, available resources and technology are no longer limited to those within a nation's boundaries. Hence, to achieve economic growth the critical issue is how to attract and retain relatively mobile resources. This will be done by providing fertile soil for mobile resources which requires improving relatively immobile resources and factors. Relatively immobile resources of a nation include its social infrastructure, political, social and economic institutions, and social norms and culture. Korea is therefore in need of an across-the-board liberalization policy. This includes opening not only the economy and institutions, but also Korean society.

Second, under the basic policy framework, openness, transparency and accountability are required in the policymaking process as well as policy contents to measure up to the level of global standards. The lack of openness and transparency in policy content and the policymaking process increases the influence and rents that government officials and special interest groups can share, as evidenced in Korea's recent past. Accountability will improve when the level of secrecy is reduced so that errors made by officials can be corrected and their work performance can be easily evaluated. All this will discourage political cronyism and enhance the efficiency of the public sector.

Third, as Korea has learned painfully from the onset of the financial crisis, the private sector prospers under the emerging global environment by enhancing its transparency, accountability and competition. This requires the Korean accounting systems, corporate governance, and competition and bankruptcy laws to be aligned with international standards. To this end, the government needs to establish the required comprehensive and transparent regulatory infrastructure (incorporating legal and institutional frameworks). This infrastructure needs to be consistent with market principles and global standards, and be imposed on all players fairly and impartially. These changes would serve to reshape the relationship between government and the private sector. Coupled with transparent and democratic oversight of *chaebols* and banks, they would also serve to minimize political cronyism.

Fourth, the government should complete the ongoing restructuring of the financial, corporate, labor and public sectors to bring them in line with global standards. As Ahn (2001) and Jung (2002) point out, restructuring of the financial and corporate sectors has not been completed. From mid-2000, the economy was so fragile that the Kim Dae-jung government shifted its policy focus to growth rather than strengthening the foundation of the Korean economy through structural reforms. For the financial sector, the government should privatize those banks that were nationalized in the process of bailing them out after the crisis, thereby reducing the chances of bureaucratic interference. Most Korean banks are too small by international standards to take advantage of economies of scale which is the main source of efficiency in the banking sector. Hence, the government should further encourage amalgamations of small-sized banks.

The financial structure of a number of *chaebols* is still unhealthy. Even though their debt–equity ratio has decreased below the required level of 200 per cent, this was achieved not by decreasing debt but by new stock issues, assets sales and asset revaluations. Corporate governance has not been greatly improved so that the degree of founding-family control over the large *chaebols* has not significantly diminished. The government has attempted to rescue the ailing Hyundai group, running counter to its reform track. Despite laws banning *chaebols* from controlling banks, they can still own insurers and brokerages. Finally, unless the labor market becomes further flexible, and union militancy and illegal union activities decline, structural reforms of banks and *chaebols* cannot be completed.

During the restructuring period of the Kim Dae-jung regime, government interference and intervention in the market have actually increased due to the bailing out of debt-ridden financial institutions with public funds, the wielding of discretionary power in corporate restructuring, and deciding whether to assist or dismantle particular companies. In effect, the government nationalized a number of banking institutions by purchasing their non-performing loans with public funds. These structural reforms were enforced on the private sector, relying not on market principles but on administrative power. Now that the transitional period of structural reforms is over, future restructuring should rely on market forces.

Fifth, the government should improve the domestic business and investment environment by improving social infrastructure, labor relations, and political, social and economic institutions in order to attract relatively mobile resources from abroad and in particular FDI. FDI is needed to attract foreign technology and to supplement declining domestic investment. FDI has significantly increased in the recent past and the ratio of FDI stock to GDP in Korea increased from 2.1 per cent in 1995 to 7.9 per cent in 1999 (UNCTAD 2001). However, the magnitude of FDI in Korea is still small as compared to in other countries. In 1999, the ratio of FDI stock to GDP was 17.3 per cent, 20.0 per cent, 85.8 per cent and 27.6 per cent, respectively, for the world, developing countries as a whole, Singapore and China (UNCTAD 2001). To attract FDI, not only entry restrictions but also operational restrictions should be abated, and a public campaign may be needed to make the general public more receptive toward foreign customs and cultures.

Sixth, the government should set up a strategy in the face of the slowing population growth and an aging population. Mandatory early retirement and early dismissal practices result in waste of human resources, and run counter to what policy requires to cope most effectively with these demographic trends. There were 850 000 unemployed people in the age range of 40–60 in 2002 (*Chosun Ilbo* 2002b). A strategy has to be implemented to stem early retirement and dismissal, and retraining systems have to be developed to enable early-retired workers to find new jobs. Institutional arrangements are also needed to incorporate the potential female members of the population in knowledge- and information-based industries. Human resources from abroad are required for jobs shunned by domestic workers, and in science and technology areas. To this end, the exclusive and xenophobic provisions in Korea's immigration laws needed to be abolished to facilitate inflows of foreign labor as required.

Seventh, Korea is far behind advanced countries in many areas of science and technology. To improve technology, developing countries including Korea relied in the past on technology purchased, rented and sometimes stolen from abroad. These options are no longer available for emerging industrialized countries like Korea. Rather, the available options that Korea can take up to narrow the gap in science and technology are attracting FDI, hiring foreign scientists and engineers, and developing scientific and technological capability domestically through research and development and education.

It is well known that the Korean education system does not measure up to those of advanced countries. Hence, reform of the Korean education system is required to nurture the necessary human resources for the development of science and technology. This will include liberalization of the education system and opening it to international competition. Eighth, Korean society and culture have to open up. Korean society is homogeneous in terms of the ethnic background of the population, and mono-culturalism and strong nationalism have prevailed over the nation's long history. Korean tradition and culture are not fully compatible with globalization, in that multiculturalism is the prevailing cultural mode in global society. As members of the global village, Korean people have to be open and receptive to international cultural norms and develop their society and culture accordingly. This also requires a social campaign to enable multiculturalism to take root in Korea.

Finally, social development programs should be an integral part of the new policy framework. This is a policy area to which the Korean government has paid minimal attention over the three decades of economic success. Korea has carried on its economic development strategy based on a 'growth first then equity' ideology since the early 1960s. Thus, social development programs have not developed in parallel with economic growth. In particular, social safety nets such as unemployment insurance have not been developed, not only because of the low priority that the government has attached to these programs but also because of the cultural heritage of supporting family members during difficult times. A constant high demand for workers and a minimum level of unemployment over the long period of economic success, coupled with lifetime employment practices, have minimized the necessity of safety net systems. The low priority attached to social development programs is reflected in the small portion of the government budget allocated for social development programs, which was well below those of advanced countries. In Korea, the portion was consistently below 10 per cent throughout the three decades up to 1997, except for 1991 with a ratio of 10.2 per cent, and increased to 13.1 per cent in 2002 (National Statistical Office 2002).

The circumstances surrounding equity issues have changed remarkably, particularly since the 1997 financial crisis. Since the crisis, income distribution has substantially deteriorated. The household poverty rate has increased from 3.0 per cent in 1997 to 6.4 per cent during the first three quarters of 1999. The Gini coefficient increased from 0.28 in 1997 to 0.32 in 2000, and during the same period the ratio of the income of the highest quintile of households to that of the lowest quintile rose from 4.49 to 5.32 (An and Choi 2003). The social fabric has been changing to such a discernible extent that the culture of family safety nets has eroded substantially. Furthermore, as the lay-off system takes root, the long-cherished lifetime employment practices are disappearing. The digital divide is also becoming wider in the information era, and expands the income gap between rich and poor. Therefore, it is increasingly incumbent on the government to provide support for the rising number of people who cannot support themselves.

Equitable development with advanced social development programs will be justified not only for equity purposes but also on efficiency grounds. Not only do social safety nets protect those who have been affected adversely by macroeconomic shocks like the financial crisis, but they also play the so-called built-in stabilizer role against economic fluctuations. It is argued that redistribution may enhance growth, because redistribution improves human capital accumulation which has in turn positive externalities, and this positive relationship between more redistribution for equity and high growth was found to be empirically robust (Drazen 2000: 460). It is also argued and empirically robust that more equal societies have significantly lower fertility rates which is in turn associated with higher rates of growth (Drazen 2000: 521).

Although social spending increased substantially after the crisis, the level of social protection is still woefully inadequate. The ratio of social welfare expenditure to GDP in 1998 was 5.94 per cent in Korea as compared to 14.66 per cent, 14.59 per cent and 27.29 per cent respectively in Japan, the US and the UK (An and Choi 2003). Since the crisis, the government has expanded unemployment insurance coverage, shortened the contribution period required for eligibility, and extended the duration of unemployment benefit. However, only 10 per cent of unemployed workers received the benefits, and such benefits amounted to about 50 per cent of the previous wages, and the maximum duration of benefits is three to eight months. Moreover, only a quarter of those of retirement age receive a pension of any kind (Crotty and Lee 2001). An and Choi (2003) argue that the overall social welfare system in Korea is fragmented and inadequate, and they also point out that the national pension system is actuarially unsound and does not cover persons without income. Finally, public education has to be reformed and improved as part of the social development program. Government expenditure for education as a percentage of GDP declined after 1997 for three consecutive years (NSO 2002) and is still far below those of other advanced countries. Hence, there is a rising imperative to reform and improve the current social welfare programs to a considerable extent. Politically, adequate social protection is required to ensure political support for the ongoing reform, particularly in the labor market.[13]

## 6. CONCLUSIONS

This chapter has recognized the overriding importance of economic policy for shaping the Korean economy not only over the three decades of economic success but also in the present era of globalization and information. The objective of this chapter was to propose an appropriate economic policy framework for the medium- and long-term future, and in doing so Korea's past policy practices were reviewed for guidance. The Korean economic policy paradigm from the mid-1960s up until the 1997 crisis involved extensive state intervention in implementing its industrial policy and consecutive five-year economic plans. State intervention worked well until the late 1980s because of a clear social consensus on a national vision of maximum growth, strong organizational capabilities and cooperative external environments. From the late 1980s, however, adverse changes in the internal and external policy environments eroded the effectiveness of state intervention, which became the major underlying cause of the financial crisis that suddenly knocked the Korean economy late in 1997.

Government control and protection of *chaebols* led to a lack of transparency and accountability, and encouraged excessive expansion with debt capital. State intervention in financial markets resulted in financial institutions being inefficient, undercapitalized and inflicted by moral hazard. Government protection of domestic industries from international competition resulted paradoxically in their loss of efficiency and competitiveness. Government intervention in the labor market resulted in inefficiency in labor management and labor-market inflexibility. Finally, the government failed to introduce appropriate measures in time to stem the financial crisis, despite the presence of emerging symptoms that were evidence of the looming crisis. The 1997 crisis brought the demise of the old paradigm of dirigist economic policy.

Since the financial crisis drove home to Koreans the limitations of the old policy paradigm, national economic policies have been shifted from state intervention towards the development of a market economy. This policy shift has been reflected in the ongoing institutional and structural reforms of the financial, business, labor and public sectors. What policy framework is most appropriate during the transitional period and beyond remains a critical question for Korean policymakers. Since an appropriate policy framework must be predicated on the nation's economic objectives and policy environments, sustainable and equitable economic development was assumed to be the key objective of Korea's economic policy. Then, trend developments in internal and external environments were assessed and policy measures most appropriate under these circumstances were considered.

Key trends in the policy environments include the emergence of the globalization and information era, the rising importance of the Chinese economy, demographic changes from declining population growth and an aging population, declining savings and investment rates, rising influence of foreign capital on the economy, a widening digital divide, and rising conflicts between indigenous cultures and the emerging internationalized culture in the global village. Under these circumstances, the crux of economic development exists in attracting mobile resources from abroad by improving relatively immobile domestic resources, and in developing domestic technology through research and development, FDI and improvements in the Korean education system.

The analysis of Korea's domestic and international policy environments has led to the proposal that the government should play a complementary role to the private sector within the basic policy framework. The government must guarantee the freedom of the private sector and provide an environment further conducive to development, and at the same time ensure transparency, accountability and competition in private sector operations. The Korean economy must therefore embrace market principles, undertake an across-the-board liberalization policy and provide a comprehensive and robust infrastructure to both safeguard the strengths of the private sector and attract mobile resources from abroad. Korea also needs to adopt an appropriate human resource policy that is responsive to demographic changes and to science and technology development. Equity has become a much higher priority than it was during the earlier success period and thus must be incorporated as an important part of the policy framework.

From the present case study of Korea's economic policy paradigm over the last three decades, it is evident that the policy paradigm of a nation continues to evolve over time, responding to changes in domestic and international circumstances and the national priorities and goals. To maintain economic development over time, national policymakers need to be diligent in identifying changes in the policy environment and adapt the nation's policy paradigm to these changes and anticipated future developments. Otherwise, the country may experience economic setbacks as Korea's experience in the late 1990s demonstrates clearly. This chapter has proposed a basic policy framework for the Korean economy as it develops further in the still new terrain of globalization and information, with national aspirations for return to its performance of impressive growth but this time in a more sustainable and equitable manner.

## NOTES

1. For a comprehensive survey of the literature on Korean economic development up to 1996, see Kwon (1997).
2. This section and the following two sections draw in part on Kwon (2001a).
3. State intervention based on these two types of tools was an indirect measure in that it was not reflected in the government budget. As a result, the size of the government, as measured by its expenditure to GNP ratio, was relatively small.
4. For estimates of the extent of incentives in the form of credit allocations with preferential interest rates for target industries and the effective subsidy rates, see Stern et al. (1995), World Bank (1993) and Ahn and Kim (1997).
5. For an estimate of the extent of domestic market protection in terms of the effective protection rate, see Ahn and Kim (1997). As a result of protection of domestic market and industries, Korea has long been regarded as the most difficult market in East Asia (Kwon 2001b).

6. Stiglitz (1997) argues that state intervention contributed strongly to US economic growth in the late 19th century.
7. Stiglitz (1997, 1999) argues strongly that government intervention has had an enormous effect on promoting rapid economic growth in Korea and other countries in East Asia. Likewise, Heo (2001) puts forward a survey of arguments that government intervention – not neoclassical policy – has been the main source of Korean economic development over the three decades from 1960. It appears, however, that Heo (2001) has not paid adequate attention to the reasons for the success of government intervention. He has not mentioned policy failure, which this author sees was one of the causes of the 1997 financial crisis.
8. Since 1972 the government actually bailed out a number of large companies from financial difficulties, and large-scale bankruptcy was almost non-existent until the 1997 financial crisis (Joh 2001).
9. The Korean banking sector generated the typical principal–agent problem. Since the agents (bankers) existed without owners, agents were bound to collaborate with regulators and politicians (the government).
10. According to an executive poll conducted by the *Far Eastern Economic Review*, Korea had the highest degree of government influence over business among Asian countries (*Far Eastern Economic Review* 1998: 36). Also, according to an index compiled by the Canada-based Economic Freedom Network, Korea ranked far behind its Asian rivals, let alone advanced countries, in terms of economic freedom. Korea ranked 44th in 1998 out of 110 countries surveyed. It ranked 39th in 1990 (*Korea Herald* 12 November 1998).
11. From their empirical studies based on a large number of financial crisis-afflicted countries, Khan and Knight (1985) and Conway (1994) argue that it takes several years to complete structural reforms. Stiglitz (1999) submits that the Mexican economy had not fully recovered from its 1994 financial crisis by 1999, even though the Mexico crisis was declared over in mid-1995.
12. It can be argued that to achieve the objectives of a national economic policy, a clear vision is needed to mobilize and motivate economic agents toward the policy objectives (Kim 2002). Identifying a vision for the nation that is accepted by society as a whole is a valuable first step for economic development, however identifying the Korean national vision is beyond the scope of this study. Instead, this chapter proceeds with an objective that seems likely to meet with the underlying social feeling in Korea about the nation's economic development.
13. If one accepts the Kuznets hypothesis of the relationship between the level of income and inequality in the form of a U-shape, with inequality first rising and then falling as a country becomes more developed, now is the time for Korea to improve equity.

## REFERENCES


Ahn, Choong Yong (2001), 'Financial and corporate sector restructuring in South Korea: accomplishments and unfinished agenda', *Japanese Economic Review*, **52** (4), 452–70.

Ahn, Chung Yong and Joo-Hoon Kim (1997), 'The outward-looking trade policy and the industrial development of South Korea', in Cha, Dong-Se, Kwang Suk Kim and D.H. Perkins (eds), *The Korean Economy 1945–1995: Performance and Vision for the 21 Century*, Seoul: Korea Development Institute.

An, Chong-Bum and K. Choi (2003), 'Welfare policy in Korea: issues and strategy', Chapter 12 of this book.

Cha, Dong-Se (2001), 'The Korean economy into the new millennium: reform and revival', in O. Yul Kwon and W. Shepherd (eds), *Korea's Economic Prospects: from Financial Crisis to Prosperity*, Cheltenham: Edward Elgar.

Cha, Dong-Se, Kwang Suk Kim and D.H. Perkins (eds) (1997), *The Korean Economy 1945–1995: Performance and Vision for the 21 Century*, Seoul: Korea Development Institute.

Chang, Ha-Joon (1993), 'The political economy of industrial policy in Korea', *Cambridge Journal of Economics*, **17** (2), 121–57.

*Chosun Ilbo* (2002a), 'Life in Korea in 2002', 26 December.

*Chosun Ilbo* (2002b), 'Hidden unemployment', 17 December.

Conway, Patrick (1994), 'IMF lending programs: Participation and impact', *Journal of Development Economics*, **45**, 365–91.

Crotty, J. and K.-K. Lee (2001), 'Economic performance in Post-Crisis Korea: a critical perspective on neoliberal restructuring', *Seoul Journal of Economics*, **14** (2), 183–242.

Crotty, J and K-K Lee (2002), 'A political-economic analysis of the failure of neo-liberal restructuring in post-crisis Korea', *Cambridge Journal of Economics*, **26**, 667–78.

Drazen, Allan (2000), *Political Economy in Macroeconomics*, Princeton, NJ: Princeton University Press.

*Far Eastern Economic Review* (1998), 'Asian executives poll', 18 June, **36**.

Heo, Yoon (2001), 'Development strategy in Korea re-examined: an interventionist perspective', *Social Science Journal*, **38**, 217–31.

Hong, Dong-pyo (2002), 'IT policies in Korea to establish a KBE: outcomes and future directions', in Korea Institute for International Economic Policy (ed.), *Korea's Road to a Sound and Advanced Economy,* Seoul: Korea Institute for International Economic Policy.

Joh, Sung Wook (2001), 'The Korean corporate sector: crisis and reform', in O. Yul Kwon and W. Shepherd (eds), *Korea's Economic Prospects: from Financial Crisis to Prosperity*, Cheltenham: Edward Elgar.

Jung, Ku-hyun (2002), 'The Korean model: can the old and new economies coexist?', in *The Challenges of Reconciliation in Korea*, Joint US-Korea Academic Studies, vol. 12.

Jwa, Sung Hee and Inshill Yi (2001), 'Korean financial crisis: evaluation and lessons', in O. Yul Kwon and W. Shepherd (eds), *Korea's Economic Prospects: from Financial Crisis to Prosperity*, Cheltenham: Edward Elgar.

Jwa, Sung-Hee (2001), *A New Paradigm for Korea's Economic Development*, Hampshire: Palgrave.

Khan, M., and Knight, M.D. (1985), 'Fund-supported adjustment programs and economic Growth', *IMF Occasional Paper* No. 41. Washington: IMF, November.

Kim, Joo Hoon (2002), 'New vision and strategy required for another takeoff, *Korea Focus*, **10** (4), 130–43.

Kim, Kihwan (2002), 'Korea's new development paradigm: the business and cultural center of Asia,' in *The Challenges of Reconciliation in Korea*, Joint US–Korea Academic Studies (2002), **12**, 1–19.

*Korea Herald* (1998), 12 November.

KOTRA (Korea Trade-Investment Promotion Agency) (2002), "Korea's foreign investment explosion', *Korea Trade and Investment*, **20** (1), 18–23.

Krause, Lawrence B. (2002), 'The Korean economy in the post September 11 environment', in *The Challenges of Reconciliation in Korea*, Joint US–Korea Academic Studies (2002), vol. 12, pp. 21–39.

Kwon, O. Yul (1997), 'Korean economic developments and prospects', *Asian-Pacific Economic Literature*, **11** (2), 15–39.

Kwon, O. Yul (1998), 'The Korean financial crisis: diagnosis, remedies and prospects', *Journal of the Asia Pacific Economy*, **3** (3), 331–57.

Kwon, O. Yul (2001a), 'Paradigm shift in Korean economic policy in the wake of the 1997 financial crisis and future policy directions', in Chowdhury A. and I. Islam (eds), *Beyond the Asian Crisis*, Cheltenham: Edward Elgar.

Kwon, O. Yul (2001b), 'Korea's international business environment before and after the financial crisis', in O. Yul Kwon and W. Shepherd (eds), *Korea's Economic Prospects: from Financial Crisis to Prosperity*, Cheltenham: Edward Elgar.

MOFE (Ministry of Finance and Economy) (1998), *Economic Bulletin*, **20** (12), December.

MOFE (Ministry of Finance and Economy) (2002), *KOREA: A New Model Economy beyond the Crisis*, Seoul: MOFE.

National Statistical Office (2002), *Major Statistics of Korean Economy*. National Statistics Office, Seoul, Korea.

*Newsreview* (1999), 'Corporate raiders looming', 13 February, pp. 26–7.

Pack, Howard and Larry E. Westphal (1986), 'Industrial strategy and technological change', *Journal of Development Economics*, 22 June, 87–128.

SERI (Samsung Economic Research Institute) (SERI) (1999a), 'The advancement of foreign capital into the domestic financial industry and its effects', *Korean Economic Trends*, SERI, 18 September, 13–21.

SERI (1999b), 'The direction of future financial policy', *Korean Economic Trends*, SERI, 22 May, 13–21.

SERI (2001), *Three Years after the IMF Bailout*, Seoul: Samsung Economic Research Institute.

Smith, Heather (1994), 'Korea's industry policy during the 1980s', *Pacific Economic Papers*, (229), March.
Stern, Joseph D., J.H. Kim, D.H Perkins. and J.H. You (1995), *Industrialisation and the State: the Korean Heavy and Chemical Industry Drive*, Cambridge: Harvard University Press.
Stiglitz, Joseph (1997), 'The state and development: some new thinking', Mimeograph, website (http://www.worldbank.org).
Stiglitz, Joseph (1998), 'More instruments and broader goals: moving toward the post-Washington consensus', Mimeograph, website (http://www.worldbank.org).
Stiglitz, Joseph (1999), 'Back to basics: policies and strategies for enhanced growth and equity in post-crisis East Asia', Mimeograph, website (http://www.worldbank.org).
Summers, Lawrence H. (1999), 'Distinguished lecture on economics in government: reflections on managing global integration', *Journal of Economic Perspectives,* **13** (2), 3–17.
UNCTAD (2001), *World Investment Report*, New York: UNCTAD.
Westphal, Larry E. (1990), 'Industrial policy in the export-propelled economy: lessons from South Korea's experience', *Journal of Economic Perspective*, **4** (summer), 44–54.
Williamson, John (1990), 'What Washington means by policy reform), in John Williamson (ed.), *Latin American Adjustment: How Much Has Happened?* Washington, DC: Institute for International Economics.
World Bank (1993), *The East Asian Miracle*, World Bank, Washington, DC.

# 4. Korea's Foreign Trade Strategy in the New Millennium

**Kyung-Tae Lee, Nakgyoon Choi and Jun-Gu Kang**

## 1. INTRODUCTION

Since adopting capitalism about 50 years ago, Korea has accomplished remarkable economic growth. Especially since the 1960s when the government implemented an aggressive economic development plan, Korea has achieved a substantial growth rate of 9 per cent per year on average. As a result, the nation's GDP recently reached $10 000 per capita in 1995. One of the world's poorest countries after the Korean War, it is now about to rank among the advanced countries. The Korean economy has also undergone a sudden structural transformation. Although Korea's development strategy was based on unskilled labor at the early stages, the government has changed this strategy to transform Korea into a highly developed industrial nation whose economy is based on skilled labor, technology and competitive power through the support of an aggressive government economic policy.

Among the many factors that brought about economic growth and structural change in Korea, the most outstanding were an externally oriented policy associated with exports, the Korean people's continuous willingness to implement the systematic policy of the government, and prompt and adequate measures against external shocks. Particularly since the nation emerged from the Korean War with a lack of natural resources and a weak economic base, the export promotion policy and infant industry protection policy through import substitution played a critical role in economic growth and structural transformation. Prompt and appropriate government measures also enabled Korea to overcome the financial crisis in the late 1990s.

Over the last three decades of the 20th century, the global economy experienced a number of recessions and booms. Along with these, cyclical movements of the world economy, liberalism and protectionism have risen in the international trade environment. Such external changes inevitably prompted the Korean government to adopt an externally oriented economic model for national development. It has been argued that the achievement of national economic development in harmony with the global economy was possible because the Korean government succeeded in adapting the national economy to the changing external conditions and pushed forward an economic liberalization policy. Since globalization and the revolution in information technology are expected to greatly influence the global economy, the Korean government needs to carry on a development strategy in harmony with globalization and the information technology revolution.

In this chapter, we will first examine the development of the Korean economy and the transformation in trade structure before looking into the new challenges and opportunities in the 21st century. We will then review the future agenda for achieving a globally competitive market-oriented economy.

## 2. TRADE PERFORMANCE IN THE DEVELOPMENT PROCESS

Although the Korean economy experienced temporary minus growth during the Asian financial crisis from late 1997, over three decades it accomplished such rapid expansion that GDP and GDP per capita in 2000 were respectively 57 and 39 times the figures of 1970 (Table 4.1). Especially in the case of trade volume, which increased during the same period, exports and imports rose more than 200 times and 80 times respectively. Also, the share of trade against GDP jumped from 34.8 per cent to 72.7 per cent during this period.

*Table 4.1 Structure and Trends of the Korean Economy*

| | 1970 | 1980 | 1990 | 1995 | 1996 | 1997 | 1998 | 1999 | 2000 |
|---|---|---|---|---|---|---|---|---|---|
| GDP ($ billion) | 8.0 | 62.2 | 252.5 | 489.4 | 520.0 | 476.6 | 317.7 | 405.8 | 457.4 |
| Per capita income ($) | 249 | 1598 | 5886 | 10 823 | 11 380 | 10 307 | 6723 | 8551 | 9628 |
| Trade | 2.8 | 39.8 | 134.9 | 260.2 | 280.1 | 280.1 | 225.6 | 263.4 | 332.8 |
| Dependence ratio (%) | 34.8 | 65.8 | 53.2 | 57.1 | 53.9 | 58.9 | 71.0 | 64.9 | 72.7 |
| Exports | 0.8 | 17.5 | 65.0 | 125.1 | 129.7 | 136.2 | 132.3 | 143.7 | 172.3 |
| Dependence ratio (%) | 10.3 | 28.9 | 25.6 | 27.5 | 24.9 | 28.6 | 41.6 | 35.4 | 37.7 |
| Imports | 2.0 | 22.3 | 69.8 | 135.1 | 150.3 | 144.6 | 93.3 | 119.8 | 160.5 |
| Dependence ratio (%) | 24.5 | 36.8 | 27.5 | 29.7 | 28.9 | 30.3 | 29.4 | 29.5 | 35.1 |

*Note*: Dependence ratios for each year are measured by dividing the combined values of trade, export and import by the GDP.

*Source*: The Bank of Korea, *Economic Statistics Yearbook*, homepage (http://www.bok.or.kr).

In Table 4.2 we present data on average annual growth rates of GDP, exports and imports. Export volume, which grew more than 30 per cent per year during the 1960s and 1970s, declined so sharply as to record single-digit growth in the late 1990s. Import volume, which once expanded at a rate close to 30 per cent in the 1970s and increased continuously from 1990 to 1996 after a sharp fall during the 1980s, declined sharply before and after the IMF bailout program in response to the crisis.

As the data in Table 4.3 indicates, Korea's export structure has changed markedly over time, shifting away from light industrial products to an ever greater emphasis on heavy and chemical products. In 1970, exports by light industries, based on low-wage labor, dominated with an almost 70 per cent share, while exports from capital and skilled-labor intensive heavy and chemical industries accounted for just over 12 per cent. However, in response to a shift in government policy to favor heavy and chemical industries during the

1970s, the export ratio of the heavy and chemical industries increased rapidly in the 1980s and by 1990 accounted for more than half of total exports. By 2000, exports of heavy and chemical industrial products had increased to 80.8 per cent of all exports, while those of light industries accounted for 16.4 per cent. This is indicative of changes in comparative advantage over time from labor-intensive light industries to capital and skilled-labor intensive heavy and chemical industries. Parallel with these developments in light and heavy industrial production, exports of food and raw materials have also declined considerably as the sector's share of total exports dropped from 17.6 per cent in 1970 to a negligible 2.8 per cent by 2000.

*Table 4.2 Performance of the Korean Economy (annual average growth rates)*

(Unit: %)

| | 1961–70 | 1971–80 | 1981–90 | 1995 | 1996 | 1997 | 1998 | 1999 | 2000 |
|---|---|---|---|---|---|---|---|---|---|
| GDP (real) | 8.4 | 7.7 | 9.6 | 8.9 | 6.8 | 5.0 | –6.7 | 10.9 | 8.8 |
| Exports (nominal) | 32.8 | 35.6 | 14.0 | 16.8 | 30.3 | 3.7 | 5.0 | –2.8 | 8.6 |
| Imports (nominal) | 19.2 | 27.4 | 12.1 | 22.1 | 32.0 | 11.3 | –3.8 | –35.5 | 28.4 |

*Source*: The Bank of Korea, *Economic Statistics Yearbook*, various issues.

*Table 4.3 Industrial Composition of Korean Exports (annual growth rates)*

(Unit: %)

| | 1970 | 1980 | 1990 | 1995 | 1996 | 1997 | 1998 | 1999 | 2000 |
|---|---|---|---|---|---|---|---|---|---|
| Food and raw materials | 17.6 | 9.1 | 6.2 | 4.9 | 7.0 | 7.3 | 7.9 | 4.4 | 2.8 |
| Light industrial products | 69.6 | 49.4 | 38.7 | 22.5 | 21.3 | 20.4 | 18.9 | 18.1 | 16.4 |
| Heavy and chemical products | 12.8 | 41.5 | 55.2 | 72.6 | 71.7 | 72.3 | 73.2 | 77.4 | 80.8 |

*Source*: Korea International Trade Association, *Foreign Trade Statistics*, various issues.

It is instructive to consider the transformation of export structure in connection with concomitant shifts in comparative advantage. According to classical economics, comparative advantage is determined by relative resource abundance; therefore government economic and trade policy during this period of rapid economic development induced changes in factor endowments and in export items in which Korea held or could develop a comparative advantage.[1]

We see that strong concern with education during that period drove the creation of an abundant supply of skilled labor. An export-oriented industrialization policy and private and public determination to implement government policy not only built up the national economic base but also increased capital supply. As capital and skilled labor became abundant, Korea gained a strong comparative advantage in exporting heavy and chemical industries, which are capital and skilled-labor intensive (Song 1996).

The composition of Korean imports reflects another important aspect of the Korean economy. As noted earlier, Korea is poorly endowed with natural resources and thus must rely heavily on foreign sources for the natural resources that it required. This is clearly evident in the composition of imports. As shown in Table 4.4, the share of oil and natural resources has been steady at about 50 per cent of total imports during this high-growth period. As the export share of the heavy industry and chemical products grew, the import share of capital goods also increased, though to a lesser extent. Although Korea succeeded in developing the heavy and chemical industries, it has not overcome its dependence on foreign capital goods and intermediate products. On the other hand, the import share of food and consumer goods stabilized during the 1990s at about 10 per cent.

*Table 4.4 Composition of Korean Imports by Commodity (annual growth rate)*

(Unit: %)

| | 1970 | 1980 | 1990 | 1995 | 1996 | 1997 | 1998 | 1999 | 2000 |
|---|---|---|---|---|---|---|---|---|---|
| Food and consumer materials | 17.3 | 12.1 | 9.6 | 10.2 | 11.1 | 10.7 | 9.9 | 9.8 | 9.3 |
| Capital goods | 29.7 | 23.0 | 36.4 | 39.8 | 39.4 | 36.7 | 36.4 | 39.4 | 40.0 |
| Raw materials (including petroleum) | 50.6 | 65.0 | 53.9 | 50.0 | 49.5 | 52.6 | 53.8 | 50.8 | 50.7 |

*Source*: Korea International Trade Association, *Foreign Trade Statistics*, various issues.

As shown in Table 4.5, exports have been particularly important for many facets of the Korean economy during recovery from the financial crisis towards the end of the 1990s. Estimates by the Korea International Trade Association (2001) for the period 1996 to 2000 provide useful indications. Of the 9.2 per cent growth rate of the total economy in 2000, 5.4 percentage points were attributable to exports, accounting for 58.7 per cent of the total growth. The earning rate of foreign exchange of exports decreased from 69.1 per cent in 1996 to 56.3 per cent in 2000 because imports of capital and intermediate goods and oil rose during the period. Employment creation by exports fell during this period so that exports created employment for only 13 persons per $1 million of exports in 2000, down from 18 persons in 1996, indicating that Korea's export structure has become more capital and technology oriented. Fourth, the import inducement effect of exports increased notably from 30.9 per cent in 1996 to 43.7 per cent in 2000 due to the increasing export share of heavy and chemical industries, especially electric and electronic products, that depend heavily on imported capital and raw materials.

## 3. NEW CHALLENGES AND OPPORTUNITIES FOR KOREAN TRADE IN THE 21ST CENTURY

Korea's trade performance during the three decades of vigorous economic development from the early 1970s indicates that trade will remain critically important to Korea's future economic strength, particularly in the context of a globalizing economy. Indeed the future performance of the Korean economy will depend heavily on how efficiently the Korean trade sector will adjust to the many challenges that globalization presents.

### 3.1 The New Round of the World Trade Organization Negotiations

At the 4th WTO Ministerial Conference in Doha, trade ministers representing 144 countries agreed to a declaration launching a new round of world trade negotiations called the Doha Development Agenda (DDA), to be concluded by 1 January 2005. Through the new round of negotiations, the WTO is expected to recover its standing which has been weakened by the increase in what have been seen as unfair trade practices and expansion of regionalism. For some, the Doha Declaration has helped to ease the political and economic uncertainty that followed the terrorist attacks of 11 September 2001 in the US, reconfirming that a free trade system is the only path for the global economy.

For Korea, the DDA will present great challenges as well as opportunities in that it mandates the Korean government to liberalize all sectors of the national economy including the relatively weak industries. It is well accepted that the growth of the Korean economy has depended on externally oriented development strategies, meaning that the global market is indispensable to Korea's economic strength. In this context, the more open foreign market expected to result from the conclusion of the New Round is welcome. The agricultural sector among others, however, will experience a very painful restructuring process. This will be so because the New Round will deal with three long-term negotiating objectives in agriculture: substantial improvements in market access; reduction of all forms of export subsidies with the final objective of a full phase-out; and substantial reductions in trade-distorting domestic support. All of these will intensify the domestic competition for the Korean agricultural sector that has depended on strong government protection to retain its domestic market.

*Table 4.5 Economic Effects of Exports*

(Unit: $ billion; %)

| | 1996 | 1997 | 1998 | 1999 | 2000 |
|---|---|---|---|---|---|
| Value of total exports | 129.7 | 136.2 | 132.3 | 143.7 | 172.6 |
| Economic growth | | | | | |
| Total of economic growth rate (A) (%) | 6.8 | 5.0 | –6.7 | 10.7 | 9.2 |
| Economic growth rate by exports (B) (%) | 1.8 | 1.8 | 3.9 | 5.2 | 5.4 |
| Contribution of exports to total economic growth (B/A) (%) | 25.0 | 36.0 | n.a. | 48.6 | 58.7 |
| Income inducement effect | | | | | |
| Earning rate of foreign exchange in exports | 69.1 | 61.2 | 58.3 | 59.8 | 56.3 |
| Contribution of exports to GDP (%) | 17.2 | 17.5 | 24.3 | 21.1 | 21.0 |
| Employment inducement effect | | | | | |
| Employment creation effect (persons per million $) | 18 | 17 | 18 | 16 | 13 |
| Contribution of exports to worker engagement (%) | 11.2 | 11.2 | 11.9 | 11.2 | 10.8 |
| Production inducement effect | | | | | |
| Production inducement effect (times) | 1.83 | 1.85 | 1.85 | 1.84 | 1.83 |
| Contribution of exports to total output (%) | 20.1 | 23.1 | 32.0 | 25.4 | 26.6 |
| Import inducement effect | | | | | |
| Import inducement effect (times) | 30.9 | 38.8 | 41.7 | 40.2 | 43.7 |
| Contribution of exports to total imports (%) | 26.7 | 36.5 | 59.2 | 48.2 | 47.0 |

*Source*: Korea International Trade Association (2001).

### 3.2 Expanding Free Trade Agreements (FTAs) and Bilateral Investment Treaties (BITs)

In 2002, over 200 regional trade agreements were notified to the GATT/WTO.[2] The number of regional trade agreements rapidly increased after the launch of the WTO in

1995 (Figure 4.1). This has been especially true in the Asia Pacific region and it is noteworthy that Japan and China, which have never participated in regional trade agreements before, altered their positions to pursue agreements with Singapore (January 2002) and ASEAN, respectively. The US, EU and other regions are also actively searching for new partners. The US had already signed an FTA with Chile in December 2000 and is accelerating the process of establishing the FTAA (the Free Trade Area of the Americas) as the Bush administration has adopted a policy that puts a priority on South America. Also, having integrated its economy through the Maastricht Treaty, the EU is accelerating the integration process by successfully launching the EMU, and by expanding to Eastern and Southern Europe.

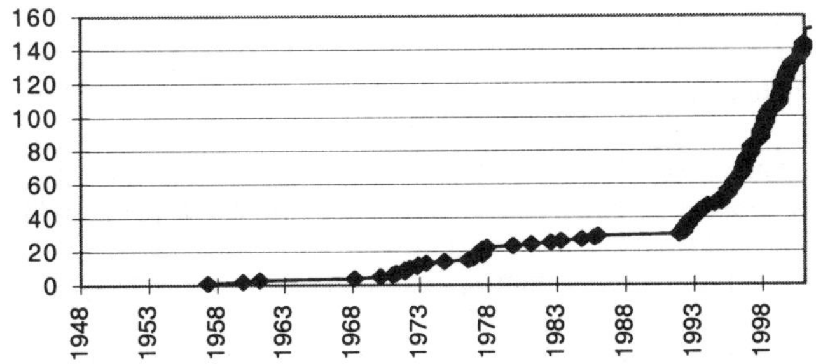


*Source*: The WTO Secretariat (http://www.wto.org/english/tratop_e/region_e/regtac_e.htm).

*Figure 4.1 Regional Trade Agreements, 1948–2001*

Regional trade agreements including FTAs aim at achieving various goals. These include economic efficiency, larger markets and evading regional protectionism. Recent developments reflect the domino effects caused by increasing numbers of FTAs among major economies such as the US and EU. In that regard, the multilateral trade system of the WTO and regional trade agreements can be seen as compatible rather than conflicting. The establishment of the DDA, if achieved, also implies that the liberalization of the global market is unavoidable and contributes to the acceleration of FTAs. Even with the delay in the establishment of the DDA, FTAs will still propagate effectively as insurance policies and thus the number of FTAs is expected to increase, at least during the first decade of the 21st century. The BIT is a bilateral treaty intended to protect and facilitate foreign investment. BITs protect those in investor countries (investors) from non-commercial risks, and enable recipient countries to enhance their investment environments by becoming more attractive to foreign investment through lower-risk returns. The number of BITs increased rapidly in the 1990s to reach 1332 agreements involving 162 countries by the end of 1996 (Kim K.-H. 1998: 14). Much of this increase was a response to the post-Cold War transition economies in Eastern and Central Europe. These economies desperately needed FDI from capital-rich countries, while investors in the capital-rich countries sought protection for their investments. Parallel with this development, investment from high-income developing countries to low-income developing countries has been increasing and

BITs have facilitated this flow by providing investors with a stable business environment in the latter countries. Comparing average investment share for the three years prior to signing a BIT with the three years following the signing, 12 out of 16 countries that had signed BITs with the US since 1990 had seen increased investments. For example, Argentina's share of the world's total foreign direct investment increased from 0.75 per cent to 1.62 per cent, the Czech Republic's from 0 per cent to 0.22 per cent, and Russia's from 0 per cent to 0.3 per cent as investment from the US increased in response to BIT agreements (Kim K.-H. 1998).

## 3.3 Introduction of the Euro and China's Entrance to the WTO

On 1 January 2002, 12 countries of the EU, excluding England, Sweden and Denmark, adopted the euro as their shared national currency. Circulation of the euro in private transactions is expected to increase its role as an international currency. The euro region is expected to gain economic benefit through reduced transaction costs, increased competition and removal of the need for foreign reserves. Low interest rates, stable prices and removal of currency barriers are also expected to increase economic growth as well as create new jobs. The IMF projects an additional 0.3 per cent annual economic growth and 2.0 per cent reduction in unemployment in these countries.

Circulation of the euro will also affect countries outside the euro region. Integration of financial markets and lowered interest rates will increase direct investment in the euro region, and non-member countries' trade with euro members will increase in the long term. The IMF estimates a $67 billion increase in trade for the 12 euro countries over the first decade following the introduction of the euro, as a result of reduced currency risks and costs, and increased investment and trade.

In another part of the world China is undergoing swift economic growth and expansion of trade volume despite the global recession. China's accession to the WTO in 2001 is regarded as the second liberalization for China and is expected to play an important role in catalyzing fundamental change in the Chinese regime. In 2002, China ranks third among Korea's major trading partners. Since 1992, the bilateral trade volume between the two countries increased by an annual average of 21.9 per cent and by 2000 it reached $31.24 billion, accounting for 10.7 per cent of Korea's total trade for that year.[3]

With China's accession to the WTO, Korea's exports to China are expected to increase by $1.3 billion while imports will increase by $0.3 billion.[4] Alleviation of China's non-tariff barriers, increased inflow of foreign investment and overall rapid economic growth are the major factors boosting China's demand for Korea's exports. However, some negative prospects are that increased competition from other countries will lower profitability for Korean companies in China and there is also apprehension about direct competition from China against Korea in the global market. An increase in China's economic size and production capacities, increased competitiveness and concentration of economic resources are expected to follow China's accession to the WTO. Thus China's future economic success will provide both threats and opportunities to Korea. First, multinational enterprises in China will likely expand their exports aggressively, resulting in shrinking market shares for Korean enterprises in China. Second, if Korea's trade surplus with China continues to grow, Korea will possibly face trade disputes with China over the low-cost products that Korea imports from China such as agricultural and floricultural products. Third, China's low labor costs and improving production facilities will become increasingly attractive to foreign investments, consequently damaging Korea's campaign to attract more FDI.

## 4. A FUTURE AGENDA FOR KOREA TO ACHIEVE A GLOBALLY COMPETITIVE MARKET-ORIENTED ECONOMY

Moves in a number of key areas will help to position Korea so that it can respond successfully to the demanding challenges of globalization while developing further as an internationally competitive, market-oriented economy. Below we will consider four strategies that are particularly important for Korea's future economic well-being.

### 4.1 Preparedness for the New WTO Round

Using the Computable General Equilibrium model, researchers at KIEP evaluated how the New Round of WTO negotiations will affect the Korean economy (Choi et al. 2001a). The results showed that in the event of a 1.0 per cent improvement in productivity, real GDP and welfare would increase by 3.43 per cent and 4.31 per cent respectively. Economic gain in accordance with this level of welfare improvement would reach around $17 billion. This analysis hints that the New Round could lead to substantial benefits for the Korean economy. Because the negotiations may be concluded within three years, the Korean government must establish an economic restructuring program for domestic industries as well as a set of carefully considered negotiation strategies as early as possible.

Specifically, the Korean economy needs to be well prepared for the WTO Agricultural Negotiations in light of the 1993 experiences, when Korea failed to build a national consensus on agricultural liberalization even as the Uruguay Round was coming to a close. The negotiation mandate under the Doha negotiations is to substantially reduce subsidies and support in agriculture. In this context, the reduction of tariffs and subsidies is inevitable and will be unavoidably painful for some Koreans, especially Korean farmers.

The Doha negotiations in the field of services are not expected to have much effect on Korea because Korea has already carried out a wide range of self-initiated liberalization measures in this sector since the financial crisis. However, trading partners are expected to demand further liberalization or elimination of remaining restrictions in their particular areas of interest. More than 50 per cent foreign ownership should be allowed in key telecommunications industries, while in the film and television industry it is necessary to ease the screen quota system and quota system for television programs. In the area of legal services and higher education, it is also necessary to plan for liberalization.

The WTO New Round achieved a negotiating mandate to reduce or eliminate tariff and non-tariff barriers on industrial products including high and peak tariffs. Korea must make an effort to secure negotiations on industrial goods based on a tariff reduction formula, while at the same time making careful preparations for the possibility that negotiations will be carried out by item or by sector. To do this, the Korean government must prepare a detailed item-based request-offer negotiation plan based on an item-based analysis of current tariff rates and competitiveness for WTO member countries. Korean negotiators must also be prepared for sector-based negotiations.

Concerning antidumping, trade and environmental protection, and the Singapore issues, including investment, competition, trade facilitation and transparency in government procurement, Korean negotiators will need to select several important points to target for negotiations and to this end should organize a 'Friends' group with other countries in similar situations.

### 4.2 A New Stance Toward FTAs and BITs

Korea has maintained a policy stance emphasizing a multilateral trade system supported by GATT and the WTO. However, as regionalism emerges as a new axis of the global trade system, Korea needs to actively engage in establishing FTAs. FTAs not only evade trade barriers but also catalyze the restructuring of trade and industrial structures. FTAs can be used as a pre-emptive policy to overcome economic slowdown by restructuring domestic economic structures and regulations. The importance of FTAs in trade policy gained momentum in 2000. The Korean government is currently considering FTAs with Chile, Japan, Thailand, New Zealand and the US, as well as economic cooperation with Japan and China. FTA negotiations with Chile are in progress and four meetings have been held since September 1999. The two governments are negotiating the issue of product concessions; while the Korean government is insisting on exceptions for agricultural products, the Chilean government insists on no concessions for any products. It is crucial for the Korean government to reach an agreement to enhance its international reputation in terms of its own trade policies, as well as to attain the economic benefits of the agreements. Research conducted by KIEP (Cheong 2000: 54) projects the positive economic effects of a Korea–Chile FTA to be $660 million in exports, $260 million in imports and an increase in welfare level of $960 million, assuming full liberalization without considering the opportunities of expanding markets to adjacent Latin American countries. As the Korean and Japanese governments also agreed to launch a project on the viability of a Korea–Japan FTA, KIEP and the Japanese IDE (Institute of Developing Economies) presented the project results in Tokyo in 2000. The Korea–Japan FTA is considered a mid to long-term project compared to the Korea–Chile FTA. Through a Korea–Japan FTA, Korea is expected to alleviate at least some of its trade deficit by attracting foreign investment from Japan in the capital goods industry.

Just as FTAs can be used effectively in a globalizing economic environment, so too can BITs. As the key issues of a BIT agreement involve protection of foreign investors' property and non-discrimination against foreigners, the agreement itself enhances the security of foreign investment. By December 2000, Korea had agreed on BITs with 73 countries; 52 were in active status while 21 were in tentative status. Twenty-eight were with countries in Europe and 13 with countries in the American region.[5] After the financial crisis of 1997, Korea has actively pursued BITs with the US and Japan. BIT negotiations between Korea and Japan started in November 1998 and were completed on 22 December 2001. Through this treaty Korea and Japan agreed mutually on equal treatment of investors of both countries, and preservation of current agreements. However, such categories as screen quotas, newspapers and broadcasting, national security, fisheries, transportation, electricity and gas, rice and cattle breeding were on the list of areas to be excluded from liberalization. In June 1998, Korea agreed on the principles of a BIT with the US and as of 2002 negotiations are still in progress. Key issues of this BIT, including the screen quota issue, relate to the performance requirements placed on foreign investors. The current Korean regulation of mandating cinemas to run Korean films for more than 146 days a year remains a problem to be solved in the future.

These two BIT agreements are likely to facilitate investments by the US and Japan, the first- and the second-largest foreign investors in Korea, in terms of both amount and number of investment projects. Korea's BIT agreements with the US and Japan will also increase global investor confidence in the Korean economy since they are highly likely to encourage investors from outside the US and Japan to upgrade their assessments of Korea as an investment destination.

### 4.3 Improving the Trade and Industrial Structure[6]

The Korean government should move to further strengthen Korea's international economic competitiveness through careful adjustment of the trade and industrial structure and improvement of the environment for corporate activities along with macroeconomic approaches. However, it is difficult to implement such policy responses in a timely manner because the vigorous ups and downs of the sunrise and sunset industries are unpredictable, and also because Korea's trade and industrial structure has become unstable. A review of recent trends in the major economic variables, including production, employment, exports and imports, reveals that the share of each in Korean industries has changed very quickly during the period 1997 to 2001. Therefore, an economic adjustment policy aiming to remove obstacles to the smooth movement of economic resources such as capital, labor and technology, thus supporting the harmonious shift of resources among industries, should be implemented urgently. Such an economic adjustment policy should be implemented in the following directions.

First, the knowledge-based industries including IT (information technology) and BT (biotechnology) should be supported in order to cast off excessive dependence on the large-scale equipment industries. To this end, the small and medium-sized corporations should be activated by providing support through venture capital. Furthermore, the manufacturing-related service industries including design, fashion, engineering and tourism should be approached in a new, positive light.

Second, the sunset industries such as light industries should be restructured by increasing the added value of their products. Useful measures have included supporting development of shared brands and technology most appropriate for small and medium-sized companies.

Third, environment-friendly industries should be fostered to minimize the negative consequences of the energy-consuming industrial structure. For this, a system of certification and standardization should be set up, and policy measures to reduce energy consumption should be managed more robustly.

Fourth, the intermediate goods and capital goods industries should be fostered even further to overcome the processing–assembling structure. Such strategies need to be linked to the foreign-investment policy because the technology transfer from advanced sources is rife with difficulties.

### 4.4 More Effective Deregulation

In recent years domestic regulations rather than border barriers have emerged as major obstacles to foreigners' access to the Korean domestic market. Inefficient regulations serve to lower the competitiveness of domestic businesses and block foreign access to, and presence in, the Korean market. Lifting the discrimination against foreign businesses is conducive to efficient competition and hence to heightened quality of products and services along with lowered costs. Thus, further market deregulation will actually help Korean domestic businesses as well as Korean consumers. Since the financial crisis of 1997, the Korean government has carried out extensive deregulation to reduce the operational burden of businesses. Even with the recent intense efforts, many international institutions point to the need for considerable improvement in transparency, accessibility and compliance with international standards and codes, indicating that most foreign business leaders still have negative perceptions of Korea's business environment. To improve this perception in order to encourage entry of foreign businesses, there is an urgent need to substantially eliminate or alleviate domestic barriers such as business practices, government regulations and cultural factors.

Hitherto, Korean domestic regulations focused on *a priori* qualifications before market entry, while there was negligent supervision of businesses within the barriers, causing serious moral hazards. To address this problem, deregulation of entry barriers along with enhanced monitoring to protect consumers is necessary. A transparent and predictable regulatory environment should be established by reducing government intervention and ambiguous red tape.[7]

## 5. CONCLUSIONS

Korea achieved impressive industrialization over the 40 years since 1960 by means of externally oriented development strategies and with the help of an international environment conducive to these strategies. The financial crisis of 1997 brought hard times for the Korean economy but the difficulties were overcome, not by closing domestic markets but by accelerating globalization efforts.

As indicated above, recent trade indicators reveal that Korean globalization efforts have worked very well for the Korean economy. With the drastic liberalization of domestic markets, Korea recorded huge trade surpluses in the four consecutive years since 1998.

In light of future challenges, it will be in Korea's interest to contribute further to global economic integration through more effective liberalization and deregulation. As we have discussed in this chapter the Korean economy will be best positioned to respond to the challenges of globalization through a multi-track approach toward the WTO's New Round, FTAs and BITs, recognizing the pre-emptive value of all three in the inevitable liberalization of Korean markets and institutions. Korea is surely not the only nation experiencing internal dislocation in the process of adjusting to the demands of a globalizing world economy. The current strength of the Korean economy owes much to a judicious and carefully implemented foreign trade strategy. If this trade strategy can be adjusted, both judiciously to the evolving international trade environment, and ideally to help shape this evolution, foreign trade will be one of the most vital spheres in sustaining the nation's economic strength.

## NOTES

1. In the Heckscher–Ohlin model, a country will export the goods that use its abundant factors intensively. Using this logic, net exports of capital-intensive products and skill-intensive products imply that there is abundant capital and skilled labor in Korea. This is why the government has tailored a national economic policy recognizing the areas in which Korea has gained comparative advantages in exports shift.
2. Source from WTO web site (http://www.wto.org/english/tratop_e/region_e/ region_e.htm).
3. Source from Korea International Trade Association, website (http://www.kita.or.kr/).
4. The Computable General Equilibrium (CGE) analysis in Cheong (2001: 101) suggests that Korea's trade balance with China will improve in the short term, but may worsen in the longer term.
5. Source from Ministry of Foreign Affairs and Trade, website (http://www.mofat.go.kr).
6. Refer to Choi (1997), Choi (1998).
7. This position is put forward constructively in Kim, June-Dong, In-Soo Kang (2000: 90–91).

## REFERENCES


Baldwin, Robert (2000), 'Trade and growth: Still disagreement about the relationships', *Economics Department Working Papers*, No. 264, Paris: OECD.

Bank of Korea (1998), *Financial Crisis in Korea – Why it happened and how it can be overcome*, July, Seoul.

Bank of Korea, *Economic Statistics Yearbook*, homepage (http://www.bok.or.kr).

Bank of Korea, *Economic Statistics Yearbook*, various issues, Seoul.

Cheong, Inkyo (2000), *Korea–Chile FTA: Background, Economic Effects and Policy Implication*, Seoul: Korea Institute for International Economic Policy (in Korean).

Cheong, Inkyo (2001), *Economic Effects of China's WTO Accession and Policy Implications for Korea,* Seoul: Korea Institute for International Economic Policy (in Korean).

Choi, Nakgyoon (1997), 'Korea's industrial policy for balancing the current account', *KIET Economic Review*, **2** (6), Seoul: Korea Institute for Industrial Economics and Trade.

Choi, Nakgyoon (1998), 'Korea's trade policy and the negotiated IMF program', *KIET Economic Review*, **3** (2), Seoul: Korea Institute for Industrial Economics and Trade.

Choi, Nakgyoon (2002), 'Globalization in Korea: Assessment and future agenda', Seoul: Korea Development Institute, International Conference.

Choi, Nakgyoon et al. (2001a), *Main Issues in the WTO New Round Negotiations: The Korean Perspective*, Seoul: Korea Institute for International Economic Policy (in Korean).

Choi, Nakgyoon et al. (2001b), *Evaluation of Korea's Economic Openness,* Seoul: Korea Institute for International Economic Policy (unpublished report) (in Korean).

Kim, June-Dong and In-Soo Kang (2000), *Economic Effects of Korea's Liberalization of Trade in Services,* Seoul: Korea Institute for International Economic Policy (in Korean)

Kim, Kwan-Ho (1998), 'Bilateral investment treaties of the United States: Implications and prospects of the BIT between Korea and the US', *KIEP Working Paper* 98–03, Seoul: Korea Institute for International Economic Policy (in Korean).

Kim, Tae-Jun (2000), 'Modifying the regulatory reform structure in Korea', Seoul: Korea's Official Pool of International Economists, Discussion Paper 2000–28 (in Korean).

Korea International Trade Association (2001), 'The economic effects of trade', Korea International Trade Association Web Site (http://www.kita.or.kr).

Korea International Trade Association (http://www.kita.or.kr).

Korea International Trade Association, *Foreign Trade Statistics*, various issues, Seoul.

Ministry of Commerce, Industry and Energy (2000 and 2001), *Consolidated Public Notice for Foreign Investment*, Seoul (in Korean).

Ministry of Finance and Economy (1997), *IMF Stand-By Credit Arrangement*, Seoul.
Ministry of Finance and Economy (1998), *IMF Program Update*, Seoul.
Ministry of Foreign Affairs and Trade (http://www.mofat.go.kr).
Park, Ki-Hong (1997), *Korea's Trade Policy in Transition: From Government-led to Private Sector Initiating*, Seoul: Korea Institute for Industrial Economics and Trade (in Korean).
Park, Seung-Rok (2000), *The Role of Foreign Sources in Korean Economic Growth*, Seoul: Korea Economic Research Institute (in Korean).
Sohn, Chan-Hyun, Jun-Sok Yang, and Yyo-Sung Yim (1998), 'Korea's trade and industrial policies: 1948–1998', *KIEP Working Paper* 98-05, Seoul: Korea Institute for International Economic Policy.
Song, Ligang (1996), *Changing Global Comparative Advantage: Evidence from Asia and the Pacific*, Melbourne: Addison-Wesley Longman.
World Trade Organization (http://www.wto.org).

# 5. Korea's Liberalization of Trade in Services and its Impacts on Productivity[1]

**June-Dong Kim and Jong-Il Kim**

## 1. INTRODUCTION

Korea's economic development from the 1970s has been based on intensive industrialization, with priority on the manufacturing sector at the expense of the service sector. Since the early 1990s, however, the importance of the service sector has been recognized and the government has been forced to liberalize the sector under strong pressure from trade partners and international trade organizations such as GATT and WTO. Many service sub-sectors were liberalized as a result of the Uruguay Round negotiations and Korea's accession to the OECD in 1996. Korea also participated fully in subsequent negotiations at the WTO, including negotiations on financial services and the basic telecommunications negotiations. The Korean government consequently liberalized the related sectors according to concessions made to the WTO.

The 1997 financial crisis in Korea further developed the understanding of the importance of the service sector to the Korean economy and forced recognition of the urgent need for comprehensive reform as a way to restore the crisis-inflicted economy to its previous growth path (McKinsey 1998). As a result, a number of horizontal and sector-specific restrictions on market access in the service sector were eliminated beyond the commitments the government had made to the WTO. For example, restrictions on the foreign acquisition of land and ceilings on foreign equity ownership in most domestic companies except for a few related to national defense were eliminated. The distribution, telecommunications, construction and financial service sectors were the areas where the domestic market was liberalized most significantly after the financial crisis.

This chapter examines the process of liberalization of trade in services in Korea and the effects of this process on productivity in the service and manufacturing sub-sectors from 1970 to 1997. Despite the importance of these issues to understanding the Korean economy and to deepening conceptual knowledge, the literature suggests that no comprehensive study of this issue has been attempted. The chapter will proceed as follows. Section 2 reviews the evolution of the liberalization of trade in services in Korea and section 3 considers recent trends. In section 4 we consider changes in productivity in the service and manufacturing sub-sectors. Here we investigate whether the liberalized service sub-sectors posted relatively higher productivity growth than the sub-sectors that were not liberalized and also contributed to productivity gains in the manufacturing sub-sectors. In section 5 we examine the experience of the liberalization of distribution services, which were liberalized in the 1990s, and its impacts on the operation of wholesale and retail industries. The final section draws conclusions from the discussion in this chapter.

## 2. EVOLUTION OF THE LIBERALIZATION OF TRADE IN SERVICES

Unlike the manufacturing sector, in which foreign direct investment (FDI) has been liberalized since the early 1980s, much of the liberalization of the service sector has taken place only since the mid-1990s. Table 5.1 shows that by 2000 the Korean government completely or partially liberalized 154 business categories (at the Korean Standard Industrial Classification [KSIC] 5-digit level) in the service sector, which it began to open in 1993.

*Table 5.1 Korea's Liberalization of FDI in 1993–2000, as of March 2001*

(Unit: Number of business categories [a])

| Classification | Total | Liberalized[b] | | | | | | | | Remaining restricted |
|---|---|---|---|---|---|---|---|---|---|---|
| | | 1993 | 1994 | 1995 | 1996 | 1997 | 1998 | 1999 | 2000 | |
| Manufacturing | 585 | 2 | 1 | – | 6 | 1 | 2 | 2 | – | 0 |
| Services | 495 | 9 | 23 | 42 | 39 | 16 | 20 | 3 | 2 | 2 (22) |
| Others[c] | 68 | 5 | 6 | 2 | 4 | 10 | – | – | 1 | 2 (2) |
| Total | 1148 | 16 | 30 | 44 | 49 | 27 | 22 | 5 | 3 | 4 (24) |

*Notes*:
[a] Business categories are at the Korean Standard Industrial Classification (KSIC) 5-digit level. Government services and non-profit organizations, where FDI is prohibited by domestic law, are not included.
[b] Includes complete and partial liberalization.
[c] Denotes agriculture, fisheries and mining.
( ) Indicate the number of partially restricted business categories.

*Sources*: Ministry of Finance and Economy, 'Five-Year Foreign Investment Liberalization Plan', various years; and Ministry of Commerce, Industry and Energy, 'Consolidated Public Notice for Foreign Investment', March 2001.

There have been several triggers to this process. First, many of these service sub-sectors were liberalized as a result of the Uruguay Round negotiations and Korea's accession to the OECD in 1996. Second, the economic crisis in 1997 prompted the government to move quickly with further liberalization. Third, since 1998, the Korean government has accelerated the liberalization of the service sector beyond its commitments to the OECD and the WTO as a way of attracting more foreign investment and enhancing efficiency.

A comparison of service sub-sectors in which FDI was restricted in January 1990 (Appendix Table 5.1) and in November 1997 (Appendix Table 5.2) shows distribution services, business services, entertainment and recreational services, and other personal services that have been liberalized since 1990. Transportation services, financial services, and telecommunications services were partially liberalized during this period.

More drastic liberalization has been implemented since the 1997 financial crisis. Business categories in real estate and financial services were opened, and existing ceilings on foreign equity ratios were raised in telecommunications and cable broadcasting after

1998. Wholesale of meat and news agency activities were partially opened in 2000. As a result of these liberalizations, only 24 business categories in the service sector had not been liberalized to some extent as of March 2001 (Table 5.2). In particular, remarkable liberalization was implemented in financial services after the financial crisis. In addition to the liberalization of the stock, bond and foreign exchange markets, foreigners have been allowed to establish subsidiaries of banks and securities firms since 1998.

*Table 5.2 Service Business Categories in which FDI is Restricted, Korea, as of March 2001*

| Wholly restricted | Partially restricted |
|---|---|
| Radio broadcasting | Wholesale of meats |
| Television broadcasting | Publishing (newspapers, periodicals) |
| | Processing of nuclear fuel |
| | Electric power generation and distribution |
| | Coastal water transport (passenger, freight) |
| | Air transport (scheduled, non-scheduled) |
| | Telecommunications (leased line, wired, mobile, cellular, resellers, other) |
| | Domestic banking (special banking) |
| | Investment trust companies |
| | Program supplying |
| | Cable broadcasting, satellite broadcasting |
| | News agency activities |
| | Radioactive waste disposal |

*Source*: Ministry of Commerce, Industry and Energy, 'Consolidated Public Notice for Foreign Investment', March 2001.

It should be noted that some sub-sectors still remain closed legally or practically to FDI. Table 5.2 lists sub-sectors where FDI is wholly and partially restricted. Yet we should also note some other services not on this list, in which FDI is effectively restricted partially or fully. For instance, FDI in elementary, secondary and higher education is prohibited on the grounds that the final responsibility for education rests with the government. Some other services have requirements on licenses and qualifications that in fact make it impossible for foreign service providers to gain market access. For example, foreign lawyers and doctors seeking to practise in Korea must have domestic licenses, which can be obtained only by passing the national examinations in Korean language. Effectively, foreign licenses are not recognized for providing these professional services. It should be noted, however, that most national governments do not recognize foreign licenses for these professional services.

## 3. RECENT TRENDS IN TRADE IN SERVICES

The service sector shows signs of growing importance in the Korean economy. Its share of GDP increased from 43.9 per cent to 52.7 per cent between 1980 and 1998 and its share of employment from 39.5 per cent to 59.8 per cent in this period. However, the share of the service sector in the domestic economy is still lower than it is in the US, Singapore and Japan, where the shares of the services sector in GDP were 74.1 per cent, 70.9 per cent, and 64.4 per cent respectively in 1996.[2]

Table 5.3 shows Korea's trade in services by modes of supply during the 1990s. The sum of exports and imports of cross-border supply, which is measured by commercial services in the balance of payments (BOP), except for tourism, increased from about $16 billion in 1991 to $39.6 billion in 1998. In 1998, the total amount of Korea's tráde in services, except commercial presence,[3] amounted to almost 20 per cent of the amount of trade in goods. Korea's share in the world's total trade in services, except commercial presence, also rose from 1.2 per cent in 1991 to 1.8 per cent in 1998.

*Table 5.3 Trade in Services by Modes of Supply, 1991, 1995, 1998*

(unit: $ million)

| | 1991 | | 1995 | | 1998 | |
|---|---|---|---|---|---|---|
| | Exports | Imports | Exports | Imports | Exports | Imports |
| Cross-border supply[a] | 7158 | 8953 | 17 677 | 19 465 | 18 647 | 21 053 |
| Transportation | 3873 | 4897 | 9272 | 9645 | 10 204 | 8983 |
| Communications | 353 | 204 | 561 | 642 | 656 | 1133 |
| Consumption abroad[b] | 2856 | 3214 | 5150 | 6341 | 5933 | 2898 |
| Commercial presence | n.a. | n.a. | n.a. | n.a. | n.a. | n.a. |
| Movement of natural persons[c] | 604 | 54 | 774 | 132 | 446 | 4.2 |
| Total | 10 618 | 12 221 | 23 601 | 25 938 | 25 026 | 23 993 |
| | (1.2) | (1.3) | (1.8) | (2.0) | (1.8) | (1.7) |

*Notes*:
[a] BOP commercial services minus travel.
[b] BOP travel.
[c] BOP compensation of employees.
( ) Indicate percentage shares in the world's trade in services.
'n.a.' denotes 'Not Available'.

*Source*: International Monetary Fund, *Balance of Payments Statistics Yearbook*, 1999.

The data in Table 5.4 indicate the significant increase in trade in services through commercial presence since the 1980s. FDI inflows in services increased from $1.6 billion dollars over the eight-year period 1982–90 to $6.3 billion over the two years 1998–99. They increased further to $4.4 billion in the single year 2000. Hotels were the largest recipients through the 1980s. However, in the 1990s, FDI increased remarkably in the services sector, particularly in distribution services (wholesale and retail), transportation services and financial services. FDI in distribution services increased from $20.1 million in 1982–90 to $956.7 million over the two years 1998–99 and further to $448 million in 2000. FDI in transportation services also increased by more than tenfold, from $9.6 million in 1982–90 to $150.2 million in 1996–97, although we see a dramatic decline to $9.4 million in 1998–99. FDI in financial services experienced a sharp increase after the 1997 financial crisis, from $480.8 million in 1996–97 to $2.3 billion in 1998–99 and further to $1.4 billion in 2000. Finally, the increase in FDI in other services was most remarkable after the financial crisis from $367.4 million over two years (1996–97) just before the crisis to $1.8 billion over the two-year period 1998–99 and further to $1.2 billion in 2000.

*Table 5.4 FDI Inflows in Service Sub-sectors, 1962–99*

(unit: $ million)

| Sub-sector | 1962–81 | 1982–90 | 1991–95 | 1996–97 | 1998–99 | 2000 |
|---|---|---|---|---|---|---|
| Total FDI in services | 412.2 | 1600.2 | 2078.7 | 2213.1 | 6330.9 | 4404.4 |
| Electricity and gas | 0 | 0 | 26.1 | 0 | 378.7 | 212.6 |
| Construction | 10.4 | 40.1 | 21.4 | 79.8 | 9.6 | 9.5 |
| Wholesale and retail | 0 | 20.1 | 103.4 | 586.6 | 956.7 | 448.2 |
| Trading | 0.4 | 55.5 | 394.7 | 306.5 | 336.1 | 238.6 |
| Restaurants | 0 | 4.2 | 60.2 | 7.1 | 9.4 | 20.8 |
| Hotels | 206.0 | 956.9 | 362.3 | 211.4 | 64.5 | 4.7 |
| Transportation | 28.7 | 9.6 | 9.9 | 150.2 | 9.4 | 18.4 |
| Financial | 109.7 | 384.9 | 710.3 | 480.8 | 2292.9 | 1379.8 |
| Insurance | 3.0 | 77.3 | 158.0 | 23.2 | 407.9 | 591.9 |
| Real Estate | 0 | 0 | 1.8 | 0.1 | 33.0 | 269.8 |
| Other | 53.9 | 51.4 | 230.5 | 367.4 | 1832.5 | 1210.3 |
| Total FDI into Korea | 1477.8 | 4385.1 | 5057.2 | 5394.2 | 15 489.7 | 10 182.3 |

*Note*: Based on actual investment.

*Source*: Ministry of Commerce, Industry, and Energy, 'Trends in Foreign Direct Investment', various years.

## 4. IMPACT OF THE LIBERALIZATION OF TRADE IN SERVICES ON PRODUCTIVITY IN KOREA

To evaluate the effect of the liberalization of the service sector on the national economy, we have tried to assess the effect of the sector's liberalization in the 1990s on productivity growth in both this sector and in the manufacturing sector that uses the service sector's liberalized services as input. Potential sources of gain in productivity in the service sector arising through liberalization are technology transfers from FDI, economies of scale and improved efficiency through increased competition. Various studies have provided positive evidence of the productivity spillovers of FDI (Caves 1974; Globerman 1979; Borensztein et al. 1998). Based on an analysis of approximately 670 British companies, Nickell (1996) shows that competition, as measured by increased numbers of competitors or by lower levels of rent, is associated with a significantly higher rate of total factor productivity growth.

Moreover, liberalization of trade in services may result in improved productivity in other sectors, including manufacturing, by providing other sectors access to a broader variety of better-quality and lower-cost services as input. Using a model of increasing returns due to specialization, Rivera-Batiz and Rivera-Batiz (1992) argue that FDI in the business service sector stimulates specialization and raises the productivity of the industries that use them.

To assess the impact of Korea's liberalization of trade in services on productivity, we first compare the level of labor productivity of the Korean service industry with those of some advanced countries. We then examine the growth rates of labor productivity and total factor productivity (TFP) in the service sector in these countries since 1970. Finally, we attempt to see whether or not productivity growth in the manufacturing sector is associated with the liberalization of trade in services.

### 4.1 Description of the Data

The sectors we chose for our study were selected on the basis of their availability for output and factor use and we used the sector classification of the International Standard Industrial Classification System. Output was measured as value added in constant prices, the data for which was obtained from the National Accounts of Korea collected by the Bank of Korea. We considered two inputs, capital and labor. Although it is desirable to adjust capital and labor inputs by their quality measures, data on the quality of inputs at the sectoral level are not available. We use gross fixed capital stock for capital inputs and total employment for labor inputs. We acknowledge that it is also desirable to have actually utilized input levels by using data for working hours and utilized capital. However, the data on hours worked, both for capital and labor, have limited use for our purposes. For working hours, the published data concern the hours paid rather than hours actually worked. Also, data on the capacity utilization rate at the sub-sector level are not available, particularly for the service sub-sectors. Due to the failure to allow for cyclical variations in hours worked and capacity utilization, there is a cyclical bias in our measurements of TFP growth in the short run. However, this problem is lessened in the long run by the booms being offset by recessions.

The labor input was measured as total employment. The *Annual Report on the Economically Active Population Survey* (AREAPS) provides data on total employment. However, the AREAPS reports do not classify most of the service sectors for periods before 1991.[4] Thus, we computed the ratio for each service sub-sector based on the data from *Yearbook of Labor Statistics* by the International Labor Organization and the *Employment Tables from Input-Output Tables* and estimated the total employment for each sector by applying the computed ratio to the data in AREAPS on the total employment of the service sectors.

Capital input is defined as gross fixed capital stock and was computed by applying the Perpetual Inventory Method (PIM) to the data on the gross fixed capital formation of each industry in constant prices obtained from the National Accounts. To use the PIM, we needed data on benchmark capital stock and depreciation rates. However, reliable data on these two variables are not available. Therefore, we extrapolated the gross fixed capital formation back to 1930 based on the time trend from 1953 to 1960 to avoid the problem of benchmark capital stock, and accumulated the investment from 1930.[5] For the depreciation rate for each industry, we used the average rates of the corresponding Japanese industries, calculated from the International Sectoral Database (ISDB) published by the OECD, on the assumption that the structure of the Korean economy is most similar to that of Japan among the developed countries covered by the ISDB.[6]

Finally, to compute the TFP, we needed data on the share of labor in value added. The labor share is calculated by dividing the compensation of labor by value added. Since the data from the National Accounts on the compensation of employees do not include the compensation of self-employed labor, we adjusted the compensation of employees on the assumption that compensation of the self-employed is comparable to that of the employed. That is:

The share of labor in value added = (compensation of employees +
[compensation of employees / total employees] x
[total employment – total employees]) / value added

Data on the compensation of employees and current value added were taken from the National Accounts. The number of total employees is taken from the *ILO Statistical Yearbook* and the *Employment Table of the Bank of Korea*. The shares of agriculture and fisheries, communities, social and personal services, retail and wholesale trade, and restaurants and hotels, computed as above, appear to be higher than we may expect. This indicates that employment in these industries include a large proportion of unpaid or underemployed family workers. Thus, when comparing the data for Korea with ISDB data for other countries, we assumed that the unpaid workers were compensated at half the rate of paid workers. After adjustment, the shares of labor in valued added that we calculated for these industries were comparable with the estimates of Kim and Park (1985). Finally, the data on other countries were taken from the International Sectoral Database of the OECD, which provides the sectoral output and input data of OECD countries from 1970 to 1990.

### 4.2 Sectoral Labor Productivity: An International Comparison

In Table 5.5, we have compared the levels of labor productivity in Korea with those of the G-5 developed countries in 1990. Labor productivity is calculated as the value added per worker. For the G-5 countries, the value added is converted, for comparison, by using 1985 purchasing power parity exchange rates. Since the purchasing power parity exchange rate for each sector is not available for Korea, we converted the labor productivity of Korea by using the average market exchange rate for the period from 1980 to 1990.

Data in Table 5.5 show that the labor productivity of the Korean service sector in 1990 was much lower than that of the US, the three European members of G-5 and Japan in all sub-sectors. The labor productivity of 'construction' and 'finance' in Korea was about 40 per cent of that in the US. Even worse was the Korean labor productivity in 'distribution' and 'social services' which were 18 per cent and 15 per cent of US levels, respectively.

### 4.3 Productivity Growth over Time in Korea

Table 5.6 tabulates the growth rates of labor productivity in the service sub-sectors since 1970. 'Finance', which had been practically closed to foreign suppliers until the late 1990s, experienced the worst performance with negative growth rates in labor productivity throughout the period, except for 1985–90, when the Korean economy was booming with a large trade surplus. 'Distribution', which was almost completely liberalized in 1996, shows increases in labor productivity from 0.41 per cent in the 1990–95 period to 1.54 per cent in the 1995–97 period. Similarly, 'transport and communication', which was partially liberalized in the 1990s, showed increases in labor productivity in the late 1990s from 5.09 per cent in the 1990–95 period to 7.17 per cent in the 1995–97 period.

*Table 5.5 Labor Productivity of Selected Countries Relative to the US, 1990*

(US=100)

| | Agri-culture | Mining | Manu-facturing | Util-ities | Const-ruction | Transport, commun-ication | Distri-bution | Finance | Social services | Total economy |
|---|---|---|---|---|---|---|---|---|---|---|
| France | 74 | 31 | 82 | 86 | 84 | 73 | 100 | 105 | 130 | 93 |
| Germany | 53 | 19 | 70 | 81 | 63 | 60 | 70 | 166[b] | 178 | 86 |
| UK | 53 | n.a. | 66 | 90 | 85 | 54 | 60 | 257[b] | 86 | 73 |
| US | 100 | 100 | 100 | 100 | 100 | 100 | 100 | 100 | 100 | 100 |
| Japan | 25 | 31 | 79 | 89 | 106 | 50 | 70[a] | 148 | 78 | 70 |
| Korea | 16 | 10 | 34 | 42 | 68 | 23 | 18 | 40 | 15 | 26 |

*Notes*:
a This figure is for comparison of retail and wholesale trade only, excluding restaurants and hotels.
b These figures are for comparison of finance and insurance only, excluding real estate.
'Utilities' includes electricity, water, and gas. 'Distribution' includes retail, wholesale, restaurants and hotels. 'Finance' includes finance, insurance, real estate and business services. 'Social services' includes community, social, and personal services.

*Source*: Estimated by the authors.

*Table 5.6 Annual Average Growth Rates of Labor Productivity in Service Sub-sectors, 1970–97*

(unit: %)

| Period | Manu-facturing | Construc-tion | Utilities | Transport, communic-ations | Distrib-ution | Finance | Social services | Total economy |
|---|---|---|---|---|---|---|---|---|
| 1970–75 | 5.62 | –4.60 | 10.62 | 11.20 | 5.13 | –2.45 | 7.64 | 5.26 |
| 1975–80 | 6.06 | 2.10 | 12.54 | 2.24 | –2.87 | –6.26 | 3.16 | 4.40 |
| 1980–85 | 6.39 | 6.16 | 15.95 | 4.26 | 3.39 | –1.70 | 7.65 | 6.96 |
| 1985–90 | 4.76 | 4.19 | 3.05 | 3.49 | 7.37 | 1.02 | 3.65 | 6.08 |
| 1990–95 | 8.63 | –0.14 | 9.43 | 5.09 | 0.41 | –1.06 | 6.46 | 5.34 |
| 1995–97 | 9.87 | 1.48 | 6.32 | 7.17 | 1.54 | –1.13 | 0.57 | 4.83 |
| 1970–80 | 5.84 | –1.25 | 11.58 | 6.72 | 1.13 | –4.36 | 5.40 | 4.83 |
| 1980–90 | 5.58 | 5.17 | 9.50 | 3.88 | 5.38 | –0.34 | 5.65 | 6.52 |
| 1990–97 | 8.98 | 0.32 | 8.54 | 5.68 | 0.74 | –1.08 | 4.78 | 5.20 |
| 1970–97 | 6.56 | 1.54 | 10.02 | 5.40 | 2.60 | –2.02 | 5.33 | 5.55 |

*Sources*: Estimated by the authors.

## 4.4 Total Factor Productivity in the Service Sector

Since labor productivity is influenced by the magnitude of capital, which in turn is affected by FDI inflows, we next compare changes in total factor productivity in the same period. Total factor productivity is defined as:

$$\text{TFP} = \frac{Y}{K^{\alpha}L^{1-\alpha}}$$

where Y, K and L are output, capital and labor inputs respectively, and $\alpha$ is the elasticity of the production of capital. Thus, total factor productivity (TFP) growth is calculated as the residual of output growth net of the weighted growth of factor inputs. The underlying assumption is to use the factor shares in total costs as factor weights under constant returns to scale, Hicks neutral technical progress and the profit maximization of firms in competitive markets.

In Table 5.7 we can see that similar patterns can be detected across the sub-sectors for changes in total factor productivity. As was the case for labor productivity, 'finance' recorded negative TFP growth rates throughout the period, except for 1985–90. 'Transport and communications' showed a gain in TFP growth in the late 1990s, from 2.2 per cent in 1990–95 to 4.12 per cent in 1995–97. TFP for 'distribution' also improved in the late 1990s, from –0.41 per cent in 1990–95 to –0.02 per cent in 1995–97.

*Table 5.7 Annual Average Growth Rates of Total Factor Productivity in Service Sub-sector, 1970–97*

(unit: %)

| Period | Manu-facturing | Construc-tion | Util-ities | Transport, communic-ations | Distrib-ution | Finance | Social services | Service total | Total economy |
|---|---|---|---|---|---|---|---|---|---|
| 1970–75 | 3.58 | –2.04 | 7.52 | 6.63 | 4.16 | –4.87 | 5.32 | 2.17 | 1.52 |
| 1975–80 | 5.23 | –0.64 | 3.29 | –0.58 | –3.93 | –5.60 | 2.54 | –2.35 | –1.13 |
| 1980–85 | 5.81 | 1.81 | 3.33 | –2.20 | 1.65 | –1.56 | 7.54 | 0.77 | 2.89 |
| 1985–90 | 2.99 | 3.39 | 6.56 | 1.69 | 3.95 | 1.27 | 2.65 | 3.20 | 2.65 |
| 1990–95 | 4.90 | –2.52 | 2.39 | 2.20 | –0.41 | 2.82 | 4.44 | –0.31 | 0.99 |
| 1995–97 | –0.54 | –0.01 | 2.71 | 4.12 | –0.02 | –2.72 | –1.04 | –0.15 | 0.71 |
| | | | | | | | | | |
| 1970–80 | 4.41 | –1.34 | 5.41 | 3.02 | 0.11 | –5.24 | 3.93 | –0.09 | 0.20 |
| 1980–90 | 4.40 | 2.60 | 4.94 | –0.25 | 2.80 | –0.15 | 5.10 | 1.98 | 2.77 |
| 1990–97 | 3.35 | –1.80 | 2.48 | 2.75 | –0.30 | –2.79 | 2.87 | –0.26 | 0.91 |
| | | | | | | | | | |
| 1970–97 | 4.13 | 0.00 | 4.47 | 1.74 | 1.00 | –2.72 | 4.09 | 0.63 | 1.34 |

*Source*: Estimated by the authors.

It is virtually impossible to prove absolutely the causality between the liberalization of trade in services and productivity changes in the service sub-sectors. Nevertheless, the improvement in the productivity of 'transport and communications' and 'distribution' in 1995–97, as well as the negative TFP growth in 'finance' throughout the periods, imply that liberalization may have positively contributed to the productivity of the liberalized service sub-sectors.

### 4.5 Contribution of the Liberalization of Trade in Services to Manufacturing

The hypothesis that liberalization of trade in services may increase the productivity of manufacturing sub-sectors that use liberalized services as inputs can be examined by comparing the growth rates of productivity by manufacturing sub-sectors (Table 5.8) and the input coefficients of services to those manufacturing sub-sectors (Table 5.9).

*Table 5.8 Annual Average Growth Rates of Total Factor Productivity in Manufacturing, 1970–97*

(unit: %)

| | Food | Textiles | Wood | Paper | Chemi-cals | Non-metals | Metals | Mach-ines | Other | Manu-facturing total |
|---|---|---|---|---|---|---|---|---|---|---|
| 1970–75 | 2.57 | 8.11 | 6.04 | –1.02 | –1.42 | 5.54 | 23.62 | 7.96 | 8.23 | 3.58 |
| 1975–80 | 9.15 | 4.67 | –3.63 | 5.43 | 6.31 | –0.09 | 16.09 | 2.00 | 7.52 | 5.23 |
| 1980–85 | 1.90 | 4.02 | 10.32 | 8.37 | 3.38 | 4.64 | 9.90 | 8.69 | 7.51 | 5.81 |
| 1985–90 | 2.59 | 1.00 | 6.39 | 1.16 | 3.04 | –2.00 | 6.74 | 2.97 | –5.61 | 2.99 |
| 1990–95 | 0.69 | 3.49 | 4.34 | 9.14 | 2.81 | 0.13 | 8.18 | 5.96 | –2.24 | 4.90 |
| 1995–97 | 0.04 | –1.02 | 2.66 | –1.47 | 0.65 | –0.55 | –0.13 | –1.47 | 1.71 | –0.54 |
| 1970–80 | 5.86 | 6.39 | 1.20 | 2.21 | 2.44 | 2.73 | 19.85 | 4.98 | 7.88 | 4.41 |
| 1980–90 | 2.24 | 2.51 | 8.36 | 4.77 | 3.21 | 1.32 | 8.32 | 5.83 | 0.95 | 4.40 |
| 1990–97 | 0.50 | 2.20 | 3.86 | 6.11 | 2.20 | –0.06 | 5.81 | 3.84 | –1.11 | 3.35 |
| 1970–97 | 3.13 | 3.87 | 4.54 | 4.17 | 2.66 | 1.48 | 11.94 | 5.00 | 2.98 | 4.13 |

*Source*: Estimated by the authors.

*Table 5.9 Input Coefficients for Selected Manufacturing Sub-sectors, 1995*

| **Output** / **Input** | Food | Textiles | Wood and paper | Chem-icals | Non-metal | Metal products | Mach-inery | Elect-ronics |
|---|---|---|---|---|---|---|---|---|
| Utilities | 0.008 | 0.013 | 0.023 | 0.023 | 0.034 | 0.015 | 0.007 | 0.007 |
| Construction | 0.000 | 0.001 | 0.000 | 0.001 | 0.001 | 0.001 | 0.001 | 0.000 |
| Distribution | 0.026 | 0.029 | 0.032 | 0.023 | 0.018 | 0.025 | 0.028 | 0.026 |
| Restaurants, etc. | 0.000 | 0.000 | 0.000 | 0.000 | 0.000 | 0.000 | 0.000 | 0.000 |
| Transportation | 0.013 | 0.011 | 0.019 | 0.014 | 0.038 | 0.013 | 0.013 | 0.010 |
| Communications | 0.001 | 0.002 | 0.003 | 0.002 | 0.005 | 0.002 | 0.002 | 0.003 |
| Financial services | 0.014 | 0.038 | 0.033 | 0.024 | 0.029 | 0.025 | 0.024 | 0.018 |
| Real estate, etc. | 0.028 | 0.024 | 0.018 | 0.032 | 0.023 | 0.020 | 0.022 | 0.025 |
| Public administration | 0.000 | 0.000 | 0.000 | 0.000 | 0.000 | 0.000 | 0.000 | 0.000 |
| Education, health | 0.003 | 0.003 | 0.002 | 0.014 | 0.006 | 0.004 | 0.014 | 0.030 |
| Social services | 0.000 | 0.001 | 0.001 | 0.001 | 0.001 | 0.001 | 0.001 | 0.001 |
| Other services | 0.013 | 0.024 | 0.014 | 0.017 | 0.017 | 0.022 | 0.016 | 0.011 |
| Total | 0.108 | 0.146 | 0.148 | 0.152 | 0.173 | 0.128 | 0.129 | 0.132 |

*Source*: Bank of Korea, 'Input-Output Tables', 1995.

However, it seems to be difficult to extract any consistent pattern from the growth rates of TFP in the manufacturing sub-sectors and the input coefficients of the service sub-sectors. In general, the sum of the input coefficients of services in the manufacturing sub-sectors is in the range of 0.1 and 0.17, which is not large enough to have a significant impact on the productivity of the manufacturing sector.

## 5. THE LIBERALIZATION OF DISTRIBUTION SERVICES IN KOREA

Distribution services was one of the least developed service sub-sectors in Korea, until the mid-1990s, along with financial services. The productivity of Korea's wholesale and retail service sector, in terms of sales per store or sales per employee, was far below that of Japan in 1994 (Table 5.10).

*Table 5.10 Comparison of Productivity in Distribution Services, Korea and Japan, 1994*

(unit: $1000)

| | Wholesale | | Retail | |
|---|---|---|---|---|
| | Korea | Japan | Korea | Japan |
| Sales per store | 693 | 11 724 | 117.8 | 935.2 |
| Sales per employee | 170 | 1099 | 57.8 | 190.0 |

*Note*: Applied exchange rates are $1 = 716.4 Korean won and $1 = 102.18 Japanese yen.

*Sources*: Korean National Statistical Office, 'Annual Report on the Survey of Wholesale and Retail Trade as of 1994'; and Ministry of Industry and Trade, Japan, 'Annual Statistical Report of Commerce in 1994'.

We may partly attribute the low productivity of the Korean distribution services to the regulations on zoning and land development. These regulations reduced the availability of land, hence limiting the scale of business operations.[7] However, a remarkable transformation has taken place in Korea's distribution services industry since the government lifted some of the restrictions that kept foreign service suppliers out of the country until 1996 (Table 5.11).[8]

In particular, the limitations on the store numbers and store spaces of retailing businesses were eliminated for both domestic and foreign retail firms. As a result, a number of large discount stores or supermarkets have been established by both domestic and foreign firms since 1996. The total number of supermarket stores reached 164 in 2000 with almost 30 per cent of them established by foreign firms (Table 5.12).

The increasing number of supermarkets is changing the manufacturer-dominated structure of the Korean retail industry, which hitherto deterred productivity improvements and price competition. The increased buying power of the supermarkets places price setting in the hands of retailers rather than manufacturers and thus leads to price competition. Foreign retail firms also transferred advanced management know-how in merchandising and inventory management, and introduced new technologies.

Figure 5.1 shows the growth of sales value in wholesale and retail trade per employee from 1979 to 1998. Sales value per employee, which is widely used as a measure of productivity and efficiency of the distribution system, shows that the productivity of the Korean distribution sector has continually increased over time. Sales value per employee increased notably in 1996, which may be a result of the market liberalization and resulting inflow of FDI. However, we must wait to see whether this trend continues in the longer term after the economy recovers from the deep recession of 1998.

*Table 5.11 Liberalization of Distribution Services, 1989–2000*

| Year | Liberalization measures |
|---|---|
| 1989 | • Allow FDI in wholesale of medicine<br>• Expand permissible imports by branches of foreign companies |
| 1991 | • Allow FDI in retailing, up to ten stores with floor space of 1000 square meters or less, for each foreign-invested company |
| 1993 | • Expand store and space-related limits to 20 stores with floor space of 3000 square meters or less for each company |
| 1996 | • Eliminate requirements on the number of stores and floor space<br>• Liberalize five business categories, including commodity chains, and the retailing of meat |
| 1997 | • Liberalize ten business categories, including general trading, and the retailing of grain |
| 1998 | • Abolish the economic needs tests on department stores and shopping centers<br>• Liberalize the operation of gas stations |
| 2000 | • Allow FDI in the wholesaling of meat |

*Source*: Unpublished internal reports prepared by the Department of Distribution, The Ministry of Commerce, Industry and Energy.

*Table 5.12 Trends in the Establishment of Supermarkets in Korea, 1997–2000*

| Name | Year of entry | Number of stores | | | |
|---|---|---|---|---|---|
| | | 1997 | 1998 | 1999(E) | 2000(E) |
| Carrefour | 1996 | 3 | 6 | 11 | 20 |
| Wal Mart | 1996 | 4 | 4 | 5 | 10 |
| Costco | 1998 (1994) | 2 | 3 | 3 | 5 |
| Promodes | 1999 | – | – | 2 | 5 |
| Tesco | 1999 (1997) | 1 | 1 | 2 | 7 |
| Total of foreign companies | | 10 (15%) | 14 (16%) | 23 (20%) | 47 (29%) |
| Total of Korean companies | | 55 (85%) | 74 (84%) | 92 (80%) | 117 (71%) |
| Total | – | 65 | 88 | 115 | 164 |

*Note*:
( ) around year indicates when foreign company acquired local company.
( ) around % indicates ownership share of the total number of stores.

*Source*: Korean Association of Retailing (1999).

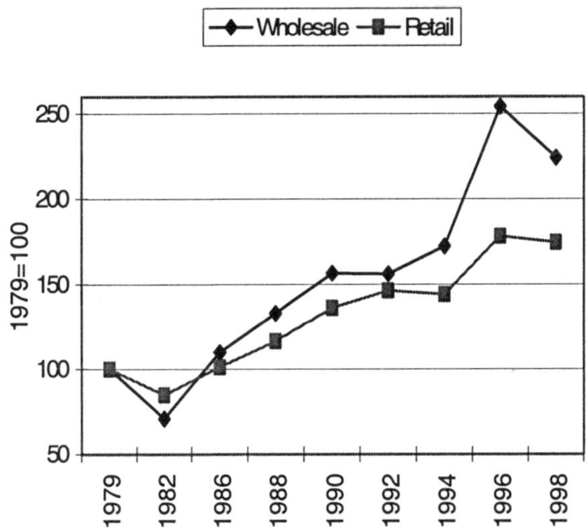


*Note*: The value amount of sales is deflated using the producer and consumer price index for wholesale and retail, respectively.

*Source*: Korea National Statistical Office, *Annual Report on the Survey of Wholesale and Retail Trade*, various years.

*Figure 5.1 Sales Value Per Employee in Distribution Services, 1979–98*

Figure 5.2 breaks down the sales per employee of retail stores depending on store size. We see here that sales per employee of large retail stores (with five or more employees), recorded a noticeable increase in 1998, while sales per employee of small retail stores (with fewer than five employees), have been stagnant since 1996. This may be because liberalization of the retail sector brought about enhanced competition in the large retail stores through the establishment of hypermarkets by foreign retailers. Enhanced competition may be ascertained by the lower price margins of supermarkets and department stores, falling from 17.8 per cent and 24.2 per cent in 1995 to 13.6 per cent and 21.7 per cent in 1998, respectively (Table 5.13).

In sum, a rough observation of the measures of efficiency points to enhanced productivity of the Korean distribution services with the liberalization of this sector in the 1990s, although we cannot provide definite evidence due to limited data. Particularly, the inflow of FDI with the opening of hypermarkets by foreign firms introduced best-practice management and challenged domestic retail stores. In addition, changing shopping patterns following the introduction of discount stores may have forced many small stores to specialize their services, and existing domestic retail firms to enlarge to take advantage of scale effects.

*Source*: Korea National Statistical Office, *Annual Report on the Survey of Wholesale and Retail Trade*, various years.

*Figure 5.2 Sales Value Per Employee in Small and Large Retail Stores, 1989–98*

*Table 5.13 Price Margin Trends for Supermarkets and Department Stores, 1995–98*

(unit: %)

| | 1995 | 1996 | 1997 | 1998 | Change in 1995–98 |
|---|---|---|---|---|---|
| Supermarkets | 17.8 | 16.1 | 15.0 | 13.6 | –4.2 |
| Department stores | 24.2 | 24.8 | 22.6 | 21.7 | –2.5 |

*Source*: Bank of Korea, 'Impact of Changes in Distribution Structure on Price Levels', 26 January 2000 (in Korean).

## 6. CONCLUDING REMARKS

With intensive industrialization at the expense of services during the 1970s and 1980s, the service sector in Korea was grossly underdeveloped prior to the early 1990s. Numerous regulations and restrictions on incoming FDI in the service sector prior to this time prevented competition and stifled efficiency, thereby impeding the development of higher-value services. Since the mid-1990s, the Uruguay Round negotiations and OECD accession have forced Korea to gradually open its service sector to foreign suppliers. The financial crisis of late 1997 accelerated the liberalization of the Korean service sector.

Liberalization of the service sector is expected to generate productivity gains not only within the sector but also in the manufacturing sector that uses liberalized services as inputs. In searching for some evidence of this in Korea, we examined the changes in productivity of the service and manufacturing sub-sectors in the period 1970–97 for a relatively short period of time. Since the liberalization process has been under way it is difficult to prove definitively that liberalization of trade in services has caused an increase in productivity in Korea. However, we found that the service sub-sectors of 'distribution' and 'transport and communications', which were liberalized in the 1990s, showed significant improvements in productivity in the late 1990s, whereas 'finance', which had been almost fully closed until the late 1990s, showed negative TFP growth rates throughout the period under study.

The experience of the distribution services provides some evidence of enhanced competition due to liberalization in the sense that the price margins of department stores and supermarkets fell significantly after the government allowed the establishment of supermarkets by foreign retailers. It seems to be only a matter of time before the enhanced competition brought about by liberalization ultimately leads to an increase in productivity.

Apart from the remaining sectoral restrictions in the areas of broadcasting, telecommunications and transportation services, some *de facto* discrimination still persists against foreign service providers operating in Korea. For example, to practice law or accounting legally in Korea, one must pass a national examination that is given in the Korean language.

In the ongoing WTO services negotiations, it is expected that Korea's major trading partners will request the removal of these remaining entry barriers. In particular, trade partners will demand that foreign lawyers be permitted to do business as foreign legal consultants, that foreign universities be allowed to establish local affiliates, and that the screen quota for Korean films be abolished or reduced.[9] To further liberalize the service sector, the Korean government needs to take these requests into positive consideration and to persuade the domestic stakeholders who continue to resist these moves fearing that further market opening will damage their interests.

Besides these entry barriers, other remaining obstacles are the internal barriers faced by both foreign and domestic suppliers. In particular, ambiguous tax laws as well as cumbersome regulations are regarded as the most serious impediment to foreign investors (KOTRA 1998). A common problem faced by foreign business people is that regulations are subject to various interpretations by different regulatory authorities. This implies that deregulation should focus not only on reducing the number of regulations but also on enhancing the transparency of enforcement.

In the process of deregulation, the government should also be careful to ensure that regulations are not excessive in relation to their intended objectives. In the case of the financial services sector, there are minimum investment requirements in terms of paid-in capital. These requirements are considered prudential regulations but foreign investors complain that the level is so high as to deter entry by smaller investors (Kim 1999).

Another important area that has not been adequately addressed is labor market inflexibility. Lay-offs are still difficult to execute on a large scale in Korea and are allowed only in cases of emergency. The limitations on lay-offs may discourage foreign service suppliers from establishing local subsidiaries, which otherwise can create employment. Also, onerous procedures for visa applications and overly restrictive limitations on the length of stay, both of which often are the subject of complaints by foreign service providers, need to be addressed in order to facilitate trade in services in the form of temporary movement of independent service providers.

## NOTES

1. The section on productivity growth rates of service sectors in Korea draws on 'Liberalization of Trade in Services and Productivity Growth in Korea', presented at the 11th NBER Annual East Asian Seminar on Economics held in Seoul, Korea on 22–24 June 2000, which will be included in the forthcoming NBER-EASE volume 11, *Trade in Services in the Asia-Pacific Region*, published by the University of Chicago Press.
2. From various issues of *National Accounts*, published by the Bank of Korea.
3. 'Commercial presence' is defined in the General Agreement on Trade in Services as any type of business or professional establishment, including through (1) the constitution, acquisition or maintenance of a juridical person, or (2) the creation or maintenance of a branch or a representative office, within the territory of a member for the purpose of supplying a service.
4. AREAPS currently classifies service sectors as electricity; gas and water; retail and wholesale trade; restaurants and hotels; transport; storage; communications; financial institutions; insurance; real estate and business services; and community, social and personal services,
5. We assumed the investment to be zero between 1950 and 1953 during the Korean War.
6. Other studies have used different estimates of Korea's capital, such as that by Professor Pyo Hakkil who used data from the National Wealth Survey. We chose our method for calculating estimates on the basis of the experiences in this field by one of the co-authors of this chapter.
7. In terms of deregulation of zoning, in 1993 the semi-agricultural and forest areas were redefined to allow retail stores occupying less than 30 000 square meters to be built in these areas. In 1996, large discount retailers under 10 000 square meters were allowed to do business in the so-called green areas, where development is regulated by law. The objective of the 1996 deregulation was to promote discount stores (McKinsey 1998).
8. In most of the service sub-sectors, the Korean government implemented domestic deregulation and external liberalization almost simultaneously. It used external commitments to liberalization to reduce any opposition or resistance to domestic deregulation and/or implemented domestic deregulation to help domestic firms establish their market position before foreign penetration. Hence, it is difficult to differentiate the impact of domestic deregulation from the impact of external liberalization.
9. One of the most controversial issues will be the screen quota issue for import films. Currently, Korean cinemas are required to screen Korean movies for a minimum of 146 days a year per screen.

## REFERENCES

Bank of Korea, 'Impact of changes in distribution structure on price levels', 26 January 2000 (in Korean), Seoul.

Bank of Korea, 'Input-Output Tables', various years, Seoul.

Bank of Korea, *National Accounts*, various years, Seoul.

Blomstrom, Magnus and Hakan Persson (1983), 'Foreign investment and spillover efficiency in an underdeveloped economy: evidence from the Mexican manufacturing industry', *World Development*, **11**, 493–501.

Borensztein, E., J. de Gregorio and J.W. Lee (1998), 'How does foreign direct investment affect economic growth?', *Journal of International Economics*, **45**, 115–35.

Caves, Richard E. (1974), 'Multinational firms, competition and productivity in host-country markets', *Economica*, **41**, 176–93.

Globerman, Steve (1979), 'Foreign direct investment and "spillover" efficiency benefits in Canadian manufacturing industries', *Canadian Journal of Economics*, **12**, 42–56.

International Labor Organization, *Yearbook of Labor Statistics*, various years, Paris.

International Monetary Fund (1999), *Balance of Payments Statistics Yearbook*.

Kim, Jong-Il and June-Dong Kim (2000), 'Liberalization of trade in services and productivity growth in Korea', KIEP Working Paper 00–10, Seoul: Korea Institute for International Economic Policy.

Kim, June-Dong (1999), 'Inward foreign direct investment regime and some evidences of spillover effects in Korea', KIEP Working Paper 99–09, Seoul: Korea Institute for International Economic Policy.

Kim, Kwang-Suk and Joon-Kyung Park (1985), *Sources of Economic Growth in Korea: 1963–1982*, Seoul: Korea Development Institute.

Korea National Statistical Office, *Annual Report on the Survey of Wholesale and Retail Trade*, various years.

Korean Association of Retailing (1999), *A Management Revolution in 21st Century Asian Retailing*, Seoul, 27 December (in Korean).

Korean National Statistical Office, 'Annual Report on the Survey of Wholesale and Retail Trade as of 1994', Seoul.

KOTRA (1998), *Survey on Business Obstacles Faced by Foreign Investors* (in Korean), Seoul: Korea Trade and Investment Promotion Agency.

McKinsey (1998), *Productivity-led Growth for Korea*, Seoul/Washington: McKinsey Seoul Office/McKinsey Global Institute.

Ministry of Commerce, Industry and Energy, 'Consolidated public notice for foreign investment', March 2001, Seoul.

Ministry of Commerce, Industry and Energy, 'Trends in Foreign Direct Investment', various years.

Ministry of Finance and Economy (2001), 'Five-Year Foreign Investment Liberalization Plan'.

Ministry of Finance and Economy, 'Five-Year Foreign Investment Liberalization Plan', various years.

Ministry of Industry and Trade, Japan, 'Annual Statistical Report of Commerce in 1994'.

National Statistical Office, *The Annual Report on the Economically Active Population Survey*, various years, Seoul.

Nickell, Stephen J. (1996), 'Competition and corporate performance', *Journal of Political Economy*, **104**, 724–46.

Organization for Economic Cooperation and Development, International Sectoral Database.

Rivera–Batiz, Francisco L. and Luis A. Rivera–Batiz (1992), 'Europe 1992 and the liberalization of direct investment flows: services versus manufacturing', *International Economic Journal*, **6**, 45–57.

*Appendix Table 5.1 Service Sub-sectors* in which FDI is Restricted, as of January 1990*

| Wholly restricted | Partially restricted |
|---|---|
| • Production, collection and distribution of electricity | • Wholesale of agricultural raw materials, live animals, food, beverages and tobacco |
| • Publishing (newspapers, periodicals and books) | • Wholesale of household goods (medical goods and cosmetics) |
| • Collection, purification and distribution of water | • Wholesale of non-agricultural intermediate products, waste and scrap (fertilizers) |
| • Drinking places | • Other wholesale (foreign trade brokers) |
| • Transport via railways | • Retail sale of food, beverages and tobacco in specialized stores |
| • Scheduled air transport | • Other retail trade of new goods in specialized stores |
| • Non-scheduled air transport | • Land transport |
| • Post and courier activities | • Sea and coastal water transport |
| • Telecommunications | • Inland water transport |
| • News agency activities | • Travel agencies |
| • Radio and television broadcasting | • General financial intermediation (banking) |
| • Gambling | • Other financial intermediation (investment, trusts, securities) |
| | • Insurance and pension funding |
| | • Real estate rental and development |
| | • Renting of other machinery and equipment (construction equipment) |
| | • Research and experimental development of social sciences and humanities |
| | • Legal, accounting, book-keeping and auditing activities; tax consultancy; market research and public opinion polling; business and management consultancy |
| | • Research and experimental development on social sciences and humanities |
| | • Advertising |
| | • Other business services (personnel supply services, investigation and security activities) |
| | • Adult and other education (vocational training schools, etc.) |
| | • Human health activities |
| | • Veterinary activities |
| | • Motion pictures, and other entertainment activities |
| | • Libraries, archives, museums and other cultural activities |
| | • Sporting and other recreational activities |
| | • Other service activities (barbers, beauty shops, wedding chapels, etc.) |
| | • Other recreational activities (parks, beaches, etc.) |
| | • Personal services (tutors, maids, etc.) |

*Note*: * in KSIC 3-digit level.

*Source*: Ministry of Finance and Economy, 'Five-Year Foreign Investment Liberalization Plan', various years.

*Appendix Table 5.2 Service Sub-sectors* in which FDI is Restricted, as of November 1997*

| Wholly restricted | Partially restricted |
|---|---|
| • Collection, purification and distribution of water | • Wholesale of agricultural raw materials, live animals, meat, food, beverages and tobacco |
| • News agency activities | • Production, collection and distribution of electricity |
| • Radio and television broadcasting | • Publishing (newspapers, periodicals and books) |
| • Gambling | • Other retail trade of new goods in specialized stores (gas stations) |
| | • Land transport |
| | • Sea and coastal water transport |
| | • Scheduled air transport |
| | • Non-scheduled air transport |
| | • Telecommunications |
| | • General financial intermediation (banking) |
| | • Other financial intermediation (investment, trust, securities) |
| | • Insurance and pension funding |
| | • Real estate rental and development |
| | • Credit information agencies |

*Note*: * in KSIC 3-digit level.

*Source*: Ministry of Finance and Economy, 'Five-Year Foreign Investment Liberalization Plan', various years.

# Part III

# Strategy for Business, Finance and Investment

# 6. A New Framework for Government–Business Relations in Korea[1]

**Sung-Hee Jwa**

## 1. INTRODUCTION

The 1997 Asian economic crisis drew widespread attention and criticism to Korea's large corporations, the *chaebols*. Much of the criticism was that the *chaebols'* business strategies focused on increasing market share and diversification rather than profitability and specialization. They were criticized for overinvestment, excessive borrowing of foreign capital, and poor management of debt, as well as having weak corporate-governance structures. The response to these criticisms was a flood of reform measures for corporate restructuring from the new Kim Dae-jung government under the recommendations of the international community, especially the IMF. Nevertheless, given Korea's remarkable economic recovery since the outbreak of the crisis, and that the Korean economy performed impressively long before any of these reform policies were implemented, it is questionable whether this heavy onslaught on the *chaebol* was in any way justifiable – especially, given that unfounded resentments about certain aspects of *chaebol* behavior have been common.

This chapter traces the impact of government policy towards the corporate sector in Korea. The analysis and discussion here are firmly grounded on the new-institutional economics (NEI). To illustrate the nature of the political economy on relations between the Korean government and business, I begin by discussing the formation, growth and characteristics of *chaebols*, and show how these are the outcome of Korea's earlier industrial policies. I then review the government's regulation and reform efforts in relation to the corporate sector, and argue that because reform efforts have hitherto been theoretically ill-informed and empirically weak, we cannot be surprised that these efforts have been ineffective at influencing corporate behavior. On the current reform agenda of the government–*chaebol* relationship, I argue the urgent need for a change of focus in government policy from direct control of the private sector to indirect management of the overall economic environment and its institutions. Specifically, I show how corporate governance is the key to understanding the role of government and public policy in influencing corporate behavior.

## 2. THE LEGACY OF KOREA'S INDUSTRIAL DEVELOPMENT STRATEGY AND GROWTH OF THE *CHAEBOLS*

In the mid-20$^{th}$ century Korea was seen as one of the world's poorest agrarian societies. The nation began on its path of remarkable economic growth with the launching of the first five-year economic development plan, 1962–66. In less than four decades, the Korean people achieved what has been described as the 'economic miracle on the Han River', Korea's GNP per capita recorded $10 610 in 1996, boosting the country's international ranking to 11$^{th}$ place in terms of economic scale, and in the same year Korea became the 29$^{th}$ nation to join the OECD. The government-led economic development strategy contributed greatly to the radical economic transformation of Korea. This strategy placed the government at the center of control over the private as well as the public sector, in major areas of finance, commerce, education, and other aspects of Korean society.

### 2.1 Formation of the *Chaebols*

In the 1970s the Korean government steered the focus of the economy from light industries to heavy and chemical industries. The government authorized entry into electronics, machinery, petrochemical, ship-building and automobile-manufacturing industries. Through this process, the government allocated resources and industries to specific firms that eventually grew into the industrial conglomerates known as *chaebols*. To ensure the growth of the targeted heavy and chemical industries, preferential treatment in terms of credit access, tariffs and tax benefits was usually extended to the selected firms. Since these industries were subject to huge economies of scale, the size of the corporations could only grow further. This practice set the stage for further government intervention in the course of national economic development. Subsequently, the larger corporations were given preferential entry into other targeted industries, which restricted entry to other private firms that could not easily meet the capital requirements. The *chaebols* thus benefited from further financial benefits, giving them every incentive to diversify their operations according to the government's industrial targeting policy. These large business groups were also reinforced by the government's policy of transferring the ownership of insolvent firms to the ever-growing *chaebols*.

### 2.2 The Rise of the *Chaebols*

The economic might of the *chaebols* soon became a burden to economic policy. Since they were accountable for a large share of the Korean economy's assets, sales and debts, the *chaebols* inevitably influenced the majority of the industrial policy measures to suit their own interests. In this coveted position, the *chaebols* initiated large-scale projects without fear; in fact, strategic concerns in oligopolistic markets forced them to expand their capacity. They grew larger and larger, generating the notorious 'too big to fail' mythology. Through this period Korea's financial system was skewed heavily towards indirect financing through banks, with relatively little financing directly through the stock market. The *chaebols* were never allowed to own banks, in order to avoid excessive lending concentration to the private sector. Rather, the banking system was firmly under government control, which constituted an important policy tool for controlling the flow of financial resources to the *chaebols*. However, contrary to what government originally intended, one result of this financial arrangement and targeted corporate expansion was that the *chaebols* became more and more leveraged with increasingly higher debt–equity ratios. The story does not end here. An important feature of the government–business relationship in Korea is that particularly in the 1990s, public policy went so far as to bail out some non-viable *chaebols*, so that the conglomerates had no real opportunity or need to restructure themselves according to market discipline.

## 2.3 The Industrial Policy Cycle

The government's industrial policies during much of this period can be depicted as a development cycle with three phases. First, the government selected industries and corporations to be supported (entry regulation). In the second phase, government laid out trade policies and mobilized tax and financial resources to support those selected industries (government support and protection). The third phase consisted of government-led restructuring of industries and corporations that were found to be in distress (exit regulation). The government intervened and featured heavily at every phase of this cycle, using entry and exit barriers, financial and tax supports, and setting up various institutions, laws and social policies as tools to carry out and support industrial policies. Entry and exit barriers, and financial and tax supports were the main tools of this type of industrial policy. Entry barriers basically allowing only the existing large corporations to enter targeted industries, and other policies designed to support these corporations, contributed to the rise of the huge and diversified *chaebol* complexes. Financial support included loans of scarce financial resources at preferential, subsidized rates with long maturity periods, to corporations chosen to operate in selected industries. Exit barriers erected as a result of active government intervention in industrial and corporate restructuring inhibited the natural flow of economic resources from non-viable firms to viable ones.

## 2.4 Structural Problems in the Corporate Sector

The government-led industrial policy generated various structural problems in the corporate sector. First, government policies targeting industries and certain firms greatly distorted resource allocation as these frequently substituted for the price mechanism. One result was overinvestment in the heavy and chemical industries (HCIs) and the subsequent government-initiated restructuring of these industries. Preferential industrial policies worsened economic concentrations, resulting in monopolistic economic structures and structural imbalances between large firms and the small and medium-sized enterprises. Second, persistent government intervention essentially took away the incentive for private firms to innovate and maximize efficiency, making the private sector dependent on government guidance and coordination. This generated the 'too big to fail' myth, a fallacy resulting in moral hazard. Third, the government's preferential industrial policy generated scope for rent-seeking. Together with the significant lobbying power of the large firms and the scope for corruption, this contributed to an increasingly prevalent anti-*chaebol* sentiment among many Koreans.

The legacy of interventionist industrial policies severely eroded the effectiveness of market discipline and encouraged moral hazard within the economy. With the economy lacking market flexibility and adaptability, it was not resilient enough to endure sudden external shocks, as the 1997 economic crisis clearly demonstrated. In the aftermath of the 1997 crisis, as we shall see, the government was forced to intervene again to clear up the mess brought about by its own interventionist policies. Old practices and habits usually die hard and one can only wonder whether an alternative development strategy to improve the corporate sector is actually possible in Korea. Before I present the alternative paradigm needed to secure Korea's future prosperity, I review in the following section some of the important past and current reform efforts that have aimed at restructuring the *chaebols*.

## 3. *CHAEBOL* POLICY: PAST AND PRESENT

The government has made numerous efforts to regulate *chaebol* behavior over the past 30 years, aiming to limit economic concentration of these large corporations. In fact, to carry out *chaebol* reform policy, the Korea Fair Trade Commission was set up in 1981. We can generally distinguish between three broad areas of *chaebol* policy: the loan management system, the antitrust laws and the recent reforms by the Kim Dae-jung regime that followed the 1997 economic crisis.

### 3.1 The Loan Management System

The government's loan management system, active mostly in the 1980s, was the first significant attempt at curbing the *chaebols'* economic power, mainly by limiting bank borrowing and inducing financial-structure improvements. Bank borrowing was restricted through major creditor banks on the basis of proportional guidelines for equity capital, while financial restructuring was encouraged through the imposition of a self-financing requirement in the case of capital investment and in the acquisition of real estate. Based on this system, the government directly intervened to promote the specialization of business lines and attempted to disperse the *chaebol* ownership structure. For example, in June 1991, to induce more specialization, a core-firm system was set up that excluded the more specialized firms, as well as other firms with widely diffused ownership structures, from the application of the loan management system. The core firm system was extended to a core business-area system in October 1993. In January 1997 this system was abolished with abandonment of the government-driven business specialization policy to encourage autonomous business specialization. From February 1992, and also based on the loan-management system, a policy regulating lending and temporary payment among affiliates was re-enforced, in particular prohibiting temporary payments to dominant stockholders and individuals with special links to a *chaebol*.[2]

### 3.2 Antitrust Laws

During the late 1980s and the 1990s, the government increasingly resorted to antitrust laws in its attempts to regulate the *chaebols'* management behavior and, particularly, to regulate what were considered to be unfair trade practices of the big business conglomerates. In July 1992, regulations were introduced to address intra-conglomerate trade that restrained competition through the abuse of one's dominant position. Six types of 'unfair trade practices' were specified and investigations were conducted on actual cases of intra-conglomerate trade, covering 574 firms affiliated to 30 largest *chaebols* (Korea Fair Trade Commission 1993). However, the implementation of regulations on 'unfair trade practices' has often been exercised in a hazardous manner, and largely remains the prerogative of the government.

Other measures include regulations on cross-ownership, equity investment of affiliate firms, and cross-debt guarantees. In April 1987, attempts were made to regulate cross-ownership between affiliate firms within certain limits and the dissolution of any excessive cross-ownership was pursued. Cross-debt guarantees were eventually banned and the *chaebols* were to be rid of this practice by March 2000. This ban seems reasonable on the grounds that it does not make good business sense for *chaebol* affiliates to guarantee debts on behalf of each other. Nevertheless, government interference in corporate business activities would be unnecessary if in the first place banks could practice their loan screening functions efficiently, according to the prudential regulations limiting excessive lending to a single borrower. Furthermore, the holding company system was banned, only to be reintroduced, albeit in a very restrictive form, in 1998. Regulation on equity investment in affiliated firms for the 30 largest *chaebols* was set to 25 per cent of net assets of the investing firm. In February 1998, this regulation on equity investment was abolished only to be reintroduced again in April 2000 (*Korea Herald* 29 March 2000). The constant erection and dismantling of various regulations only added to the public's disillusion with government policies, and demonstrated the absence of any concrete rationale for these policies.

### 3.3 Post-crisis Reform Efforts

With the onset of the 1997 economic crisis, a new set of *chaebol* policy measures was introduced immediately. These measures coupled the so-called DJ Reforms[3] with IMF recommendations on which the IMF bailout funding was conditional. The intention here was not only to limit economic concentration but also to directly improve the efficiency and competitiveness of the *chaebols*. These corporate reform policies have emphasized three broad areas. First, reforms aimed at improving the corporate-governance structure and management transparency. In February 1998 the compulsory establishment and appointment of outside directors became effective, and in May 1998, the voting rights of minority shareholders were strengthened. Limits on the voting rights of institutional investors were also lifted. Laws regarding legal liability of controlling owners have been strengthened to enhance accountability. In October 1998 firms were to adopt international accounting principles and standards and from 1999 consolidated financial statements were required to be produced. To strengthen accountability, firms have been asked to increase the legal liability of controlling owners by designating them as outside directors (June 1998) and to allow voting rights of institutional investors (September 1998).

A second area of emphasis in the post-crisis *chaebol* policy seeks to improve their financial conditions and the capital structure. This included the complete elimination of cross-debt guarantees among group affiliates and reduction in the debt–equity ratio to 200 per cent by the end of 1999. Most of the top five *chaebols*' cross-debt guarantees were dissolved by January 2000. The debt–equity ratios were also reduced considerably, to well below the target. Furthermore, a 'workout' program was introduced as a kind of private corporate reorganization process between credit banks and debtor firms that were in danger of defaulting. This aimed to restructure debtor firms under government guidance, with the process of financial restructuring closely monitored by the Financial Supervisory Committee before these firms became non-viable so that they and their banks could avoid the agony of corporate bankruptcy.

A third area of reform has aimed to improve business competitiveness primarily by streamlining business activity. To facilitate the exit or reorganization of insolvent firms, the bankruptcy and corporate reorganization laws were revised in February 1998. In the early phase of the crisis, 55 non-viable firms belonging to the 64 largest *chaebols* were forced to close down (*Korea Now* 18 November 2000). In particular, as part of the efforts to streamline business activity, the top five *chaebols* agreed to decrease the number of their affiliates and to concentrate on three to five core businesses to solve the problems of over-diversification and overinvestment. In May 1998, M&A activities were fully liberalized and as from June 1998, laws were made to allow for the adoption of a corporate-split system, improvement in the M&A procedures, and liberalization of foreign ownership of real estate. Moreover, the government continues to strongly encourage 'big deals', which are essentially a form of business swap among various firms with the aim of restricting the number of business lines of each *chaebol*, as part of government measures to vitalize the domestic M&A market. The 'big deals', or more precisely business-swap deals, have taken place in eight major industries including the semiconductor and automobile industries.[4]

### 3.4 Evaluation

Any economic entity, whether a single firm or corporation, may be viewed as adopting a system of optimal management behavior encouraged by its efforts to maximize profits, where this self-selected behavior is an economically determined endogenous variable. That is, the *chaebols* are themselves the product of economic circumstances, and consequently their managerial behavior is also a response to the demands of the economic environment to maximize the probability of their own survival in the competitive world. As such, behavioral changes forced upon the *chaebols* without the necessary creation of appropriate economic institutions would eventually destroy their survival capability, and will tend to be accompanied by resource misallocation as a result of economic distortions and uncertainty. Thus, irrespective of problems related to the *chaebols'* formation and behavior it is highly likely that direct regulation (interference in management decision variables) that does not address the fundamental causes of their business behavior will amount to nothing but unnecessary constraints that adversely affect the firms. Needless to say, firms may then have incentive to increase their lobbying efforts against such policies that only add to policy ineffectiveness and to transaction costs. It therefore follows that the government should create an appropriate economic environment backed by viable market institutions to discipline *chaebol* behavior so that it is consistent with government policy goals. Government should also avoid directly regulating management decision variables that are best left to the *chaebols* themselves.

In many ways, the post-crisis *chaebol* policies, especially those directed at improving corporate-governance structures, have shown marked improvement in the sense that they emphasize reforming the external economic environment rather than directly intervening in the corporate management variables. Nonetheless, there still remain practices and habits reminiscent of the past interventionist industrial restructuring attempts of the 1970s and 1980s.[5] For example, implementation of a uniform 200 per cent debt–equity ratio is detrimental to corporate management as it directly affects endogenous decision variables and so creates the possibility of distorting the decisions of corporate management. Even if there may be reasons to resort to such measures, it is still unreasonable to apply these debt–equity decisions across the board and uniformly, without taking into account inherent differences among individual corporate characteristics.

In the case of the 'big deals', the government forced M&As upon firms, provided deadlines by which they must be completed, and even determined the acquiring and acquired firms in advance. In doing so, the government underestimated both the transaction costs involved in M&A activity and the differences in production technologies and technological levels among the merging firms. This resulted in time-consuming and often uncertain negotiation processes. Furthermore, these measures infringe on the property rights of companies participating in the restructuring programs. The 'big deals' remain controversial and run counter to the liberalization trend in that they represent nothing more than government intervention, and may even lead to a significant increase in market concentration.

In a similar vein is the 'workout' program that the government initially put in place with good intention to assist weak corporations to recover from debt burdens. The program is far from satisfactory as the arrangement in fact encouraged moral hazard to prevail. Weak firms continued to participate in the market through dumping practices, which led to all sorts of market distortions.

In sum, 'old style' regulation seems to have given way to 'new style' reform, the latter putting more emphasis on factors concerning the economic environment rather than the direct control of managerial decision variables. This is a big improvement in the right direction. Nevertheless, I warn that certain instruments of the current reform process still pay too much attention to changing outward symptoms of economic difficulty rather than addressing the fundamental causes of the problems. Correct institutional and incentive structures need to be established. Broadly speaking, the government should focus on establishing a regime of fair competition in the economic and social systems by providing proper economic institutions – that is, the rules of the game – so that the discovery function of the market order may become effective. Government-led restructuring without providing an appropriate institutional foundation cannot have a lasting effect.

## 4. THE GENERAL FRAMEWORK FOR ANALYZING GOVERNMENT–BUSINESS RELATIONS

Here I present a framework for better understanding the role of government, and particularly the nature of government–business relations that should evolve to allow for the continued growth of private corporations. I then specifically apply this framework to analyze Korea's corporate disciplinary system. It soon becomes evident why a comprehensive understanding of the corporate-governance structures is important to reveal what kind of government–business relationships are appropriate to induce the better corporate performance that is needed for national economic growth.

### 4.1 The External Economic Environment and the Corporation: The Corporate-Governance System

New-institutional economics (NIE) is particularly useful for interpreting and sharpening our understanding of the nature and workings of corporate-governance systems. Let us begin by looking at the external institutional environment surrounding corporations.

Figure 6.1 shows the different levels of the external environment that constitutes the exogenous variables to a corporation. By exogenous variables, we mean those aspects of the wider economy that are beyond the immediate control of the corporation. Thus, the decisions of corporations are dependent on the external economic environment from the remote to the immediate, the cultural and social factors, the political system, the government's economic policies and the financial system. Culture and tradition act as the overall exogenous factor constraining all other actors in the economy from the political system to government economic policymaking, and to the type of financial system as well as the behavior of corporations. Political systems, in turn, constrain all other actors by building the legal institution (rules of the game). The government in the narrow sense affects the financial system as well as the corporate sector through economic policy. Finally, the financial system constrains corporate behavior by imposing a particular type of finance upon corporations. The government is pivotal; in a broad sense its role is to cultivate and enhance such an external or exogenous environment if it wishes to affect corporate behavior in a particular direction.

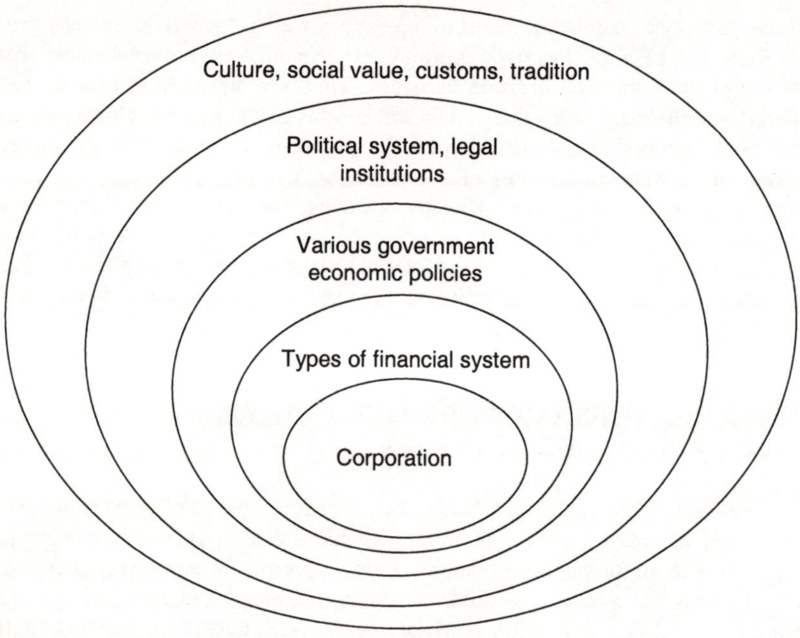


*Figure 6.1 The External Economic Environment and the Corporation*

## 4.2 Corporate Disciplinary Systems

Concerning corporate governance, Figure 6.2 shows the specific factors exogenous and endogenous to corporations, which are identified as constituting parts of the corporate disciplinary system.

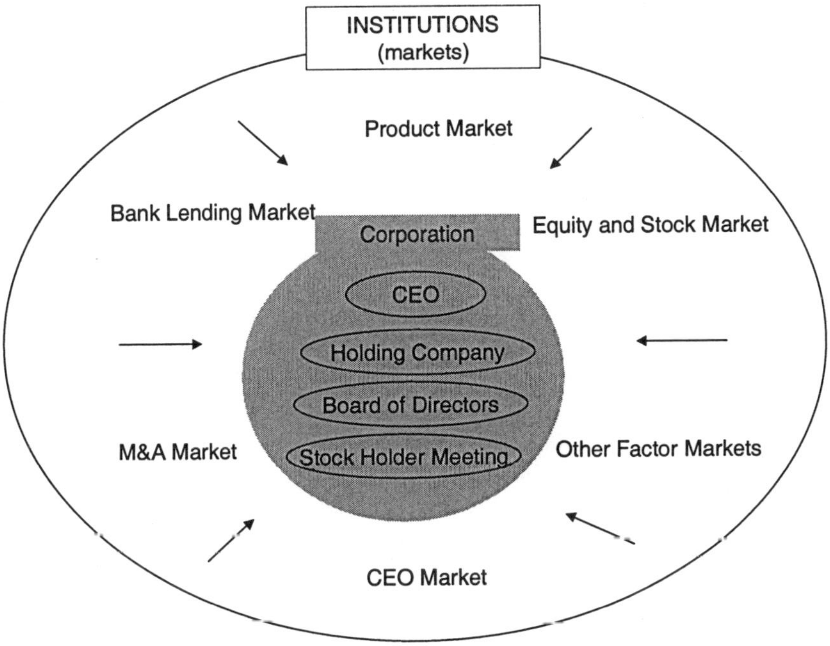


*Figure 6.2 Corporate Disciplinary System*

The figure summarizes the general institutional factors related to corporate governance, which act to monitor and check corporate behavior. These can be classified into two categories:

1. the market disciplinary system that essentially consists of the exogenous institutions of the external environment; and
2. the internal disciplinary system that constitutes the firm's endogenous decision variables.

The market disciplinary system can be subdivided into the product, M&A, financial and CEO-market disciplinary mechanisms. The product market plays the most important role in disciplining business activity by driving out inefficient and incompetent firms through consumers' evaluation and selection of products. The M&A market contributes to promoting the efficiency of business management by driving out inefficient management through hostile takeovers, mergers and acquisitions. As for the financial market, banks in the indirect financial market act as a check on business management decisions through credit screening and *ex post* monitoring for the smooth retrieval of loans. In the direct financial market, shareholders can monitor business activity through exercising their shareholder rights. The CEO market will help induce increased managerial efficiency by weeding out inefficient managers through fierce competition between them.

On the other hand, corporate discipline can be achieved partly through internal control mechanisms such as a holding company system, the CEO, stockholder meetings and the board of directors. Moreover, management control methods such as the selection of non-executive board members by institutional investors can be regarded as a disciplinary system, which lies somewhere between market and internal discipline measures.

### 4.3 Exogenous and Endogenous Factors

This shows that the market disciplinary system is worthier of attention than the internal control system when considering government policy measures. Here, the distinction between exogenous and endogenous economic variables is an important first step. That is, the market disciplinary system by definition determines the exterior environment of business management, and therefore constitutes the exogenous variables to the firms. On the other hand, a firm's management is responsible for setting up and deciding upon its internal strategic variables, which are endogenous by definition. The most important implication is that a firm's growth may be hindered or distorted if rigid constraints are placed on, or even worse if there is direct interference in, these internal decision variables by outsiders, such as government control of management decision variables. More specifically, the government must take into consideration that excessively rigid and detailed regulation of the internal governance structure could become an impediment to the evolution of firms by hindering the promotion of management efficiency. In this sense, it might be better to allow firms to choose internal control mechanisms suitable to their own needs.

What, then, is the main implication for corporate policy of the theory of corporate governance described above? The role of government is to promote the monitoring function of the various markets such as those depicted in Figure 6.2, by providing proper economic institutions for each market, that is to say, the rules of the game. These markets constitute the exogenous constraints to the firm, which should be distinguished from endogenous management decision variables that are to be independently decided upon by private corporations. Building an effective market disciplinary system, while allowing private firms to choose freely their business objectives and survival strategies, is an important government responsibility.

## 5. PARADIGM SWITCH: FROM GOVERNMENT CONTROL TO MARKET ECONOMY

### 5.1 Discrimination as a Mechanism of Economic Development

The factor most important to the success or failure of an economy is whether policy can allow for the effective discrimination of viable and non-viable firms through competition. Competition is nothing more than a discrimination process selecting viable entities from non-viable ones, whether these entities are individuals, firms or societies. In the spirit of this evolutionary perspective, competition is the mechanism behind the selection process, through which relatively better entities will survive while the weaker entities will be culled. This selection process is readily observable in the realm of economies. Here, competition guarantees the continued survival of efficient firms while inefficient firms will eventually exit the market when they fail to be competitive. Needless to say, a country with stronger and more efficient firms that survive competition will have a stronger economy than those countries where inefficiencies continue to be nurtured in their economies.

### 5.2 Development by 'Government-led Discrimination'

The argument above implies that a country with institutions that enhance competition should exhibit continued economic development as in the case of the Anglo-Saxon advanced capitalist economies. Advanced capitalist economies are characterized by strong market institutions that have allowed competition to act as a discovery procedure. Korea, too, has experienced tremendous growth during the past decades, although the development strategy here, unlike in the West, has been based on strong government intervention. So an interesting question comes to mind: how does one explain Korea's 'miracle' growth in the past four decades despite the problems typical of a government-controlled system? Basically, rapid growth was possible at that time precisely because the government acted effectively as the discriminating agent, substituting, though imperfectly, for the market. The government favored large Korean conglomerates that were high achievers in terms of sales volume and exports, and these firms in turn became the driving engine of economic progress. It may be appropriate to term this process 'government-led discrimination' for which industrial policies were designed as the chief instrument.

Effective discrimination is important for economic development as mentioned above, but also critical is the criterion of discrimination implicitly or explicitly pronounced by national policy. I do not deny that 'government-led discrimination', emphasizing sales volume and exports, did contribute to Korea's rapid economic development. However, a more critical and difficult assessment is whether such a strategy can continue delivering the goods indefinitely. Although it has contributed to Korea's rapid economic growth, a system of discrimination by the government comes with its own set of problems.

### 5.3 Development by 'Market-led Discrimination'

Government-driven economic policy has been based on the belief that the government has sufficient information about the changing economic environment and has the ability to anticipate fully the optimal industrial structure. However, the economic environment has been changing rapidly, particularly in the era of globalization, bringing more uncertainty than in earlier decades. Many now recognize that market participants have more incentive than the government to acquire relevant information about changes in the economic environment. In addition, as the economy grows in size and complexity, it becomes less and less possible for the government to absorb all information relevant to economic circumstances and to determine the optimal industrial structure, and how to achieve it on behalf of the private sector. In the era of globalization, it is increasingly difficult, if not impossible, to predetermine the optimal industrial organization. Therefore, instead of adopting an active interventionist industrial policy that requires a tremendous volume of information and analysis but does not necessarily guarantee an ideal outcome, an effective response is to let the market order prevail in discovering the optimal business and industrial structure. In the era of open society, there is only one viable way forward for sustaining a strong national economy: discrimination by the market, not the government. After all, the market is nothing else but the spontaneous institution that discriminates effectively between viable and non-viable entities through unfettered competition.

## 6. CONCLUSION

In this chapter I have argued that the private sector must be granted maximum freedom to make its own voluntary structural adjustments in response to market competition. Accordingly, the role of the Korean government should be confined to creating a suitable environment with proper institutions and incentive structures. This means that it should aim to preserve the spontaneity and endogeneity of the market order and to cultivate a better economic environment for the market to operate smoothly. For this reason, revamping competition promotion policy through establishing appropriate institutions to enhance the market's monitoring and discriminatory functions in all sectors of the economy is paramount – not only to improve corporate competitiveness in Korea but also to guarantee Korea's continued economic development. Here the role of government is to create economic institutions that reinforce the role of markets, so that market competition can play its role effectively in selecting viable firms above non-viable firms and encouraging the discovery of new business opportunities. As I have argued in this chapter, it is now critical that Korean government policies focus on streamlining exogenous variables – the rules of the game – while leaving endogenous decision variables to be decided by the internal management of market players.

The Korean 'economic miracle' was achieved during a period of history that was clearly conducive to the interventionist style of successive Korean governments. However, the policies that guided this national economic achievement depended heavily on international economic conditions that continue to disappear as the reach of globalization expands worldwide.

The Korean government has begun to respond to the dramatic changes in international market conditions. It must now continue to move the nation forward with economic policies that recognize the validity of new-institutional economics during the present era when markets rather than governments determine economic outcomes.

## NOTES

1. Many of the ideas here derive from my books Jwa, Sung-Hee (2001 and 2002).
2. See Appendix A1 to Chapter 4, Jwa (2002) for further details.
3. These reforms were given the initials of the Korean President Kim Dae-jung at the time of the crisis and who guided the post-crisis reform process.
4. For further details, see Appendix A2 to Chapter 4, Jwa (2002).
5. I argue in the next section that corporate-governance systems can only be improved by adopting wider measures that essentially encourage the functioning of market disciplinary systems to effectively monitor and check corporate behavior.

## REFERENCES

Jwa, Sung-Hee (2001), 'A new paradigm for Korea's economic development: From government control to market economy', London: Palgrave.
Jwa, Sung-Hee (2002), 'The evolution of large corporations in Korea: A new-institutional economics perspective of the *Chaebol*', London: Edward Elgar.
Korea Fair Trade Commission (1993), 'Fair Trade Commission Annual Report', Seoul: Policy Planning Division.
*Korea Herald*, 29 March 2000.
*Korea Now*, 18 November 2000.

# 7. Will East Asia Follow Korea's Lead in Liberalizing Foreign Direct Investment Policy?

**Bernie Bishop**

## 1. INTRODUCTION

In the early 1990s Korea's foreign investment policy evolved from a relatively restrictive regime towards a much more liberal and open stance. The Korean government has transformed previously complex approval processes in most industries into a mere formality. It has reduced the range of restricted industries to barely a handful and it has abolished almost all limitations on foreign equity for both Greenfield investment and investment by way of merger and acquisition.[1]

This chapter examines how Korea's foreign investment policies now compare to its East Asian neighbors and more interestingly whether other East Asian countries are likely to follow Korea's recent lead in investment liberalization. This is an important issue for international firms because restrictions on FDI limit opportunities for business expansion in the region. I argue that Korea's foreign investment policies are now among the most liberal in East Asia. Nevertheless, economic development considerations, political constraints and national security concerns all impede liberalization initiatives. As I explain in this chapter, Korea was able to liberalize its FDI regime only after constraints were overcome and then only as a result of a unique set of domestic and international circumstances. Therefore one needs to be cautious in predicting whether other economies in the region will soon follow Korea's lead.

To compare foreign investment policies, it is necessary first to be clear about what is meant by the term. Foreign investment policy can be defined as the specific requirements that foreign investors have to meet when making a direct investment as compared to the requirements confronting domestic investors making the same investment. In other words foreign investment policy is closely related to the extent to which governments give national treatment to foreign investors and abide by non-discrimination principles.

Thus foreign investment policy can be seen as the initial set of hurdles that a foreign investor must negotiate when making an investment in a particular country. These hurdles most often take the form of approval processes, sectoral restrictions and limitations on foreign equity. Foreign investment policy needs to be distinguished from the operational requirements that confront both foreign and domestic investors alike. Once an investor negotiates their way through the hurdles erected by a country's foreign investment policy, the investor will then be confronted with various regulations and procedures concerning, for example, trade, foreign exchange, the hiring of expatriate staff, taxation and obtaining the general business licenses applicable to their particular industry. Domestic investors engaged in international business activities also face these obstacles. Thus these operational requirements are not properly regarded as foreign investment policy.

The following discussion therefore compares foreign investment policies in East Asian countries in terms of approval processes, sectoral restrictions and limitations on foreign equity in certain industries. Because sectoral restrictions often include limitations on foreign equity these two are treated together.

## 2. APPROVAL PROCESSES

Table 7.1 summarizes the extent to which foreign investors are confronted by approval processes in ten East Asian countries. An attempt is made to rank countries from most-liberal through to least-liberal in this regard. The table has been compiled from countries' individual entries in the APEC Investment Guidebook.

*Table 7.1 Approval Processes*

| | |
|---|---|
| Singapore | No special approval processes for FDI without incentives |
| Philippines | No special approval processes for FDI without incentives |
| Japan | Notification after the event for all but restricted industries |
| Korea | Prior or post notification of all but restricted industries |
| Australia | Notification (approval) of all FDI over certain $A amounts |
| Taiwan | Approval needed if FIA* status is desired |
| Thailand | Approval needed if majority foreign equity in restricted industries is desired |
| Malaysia | All manufacturing FDI needs license and all FDI in other areas with greater than 30 per cent foreign equity needs approval |
| Indonesia | All FDI must be approved |
| China | All FDI must be approved |

*Notes*: * FIA: Foreign Investment Approved.

Table 7.1 shows Singapore as the most liberal in terms of approval processes because a foreign investor establishing a business in most industries or taking over an existing business is treated no differently to a domestic investor. The Philippines is surprisingly liberal when it comes to approval for investment without incentives. An investor needs to simply lodge the documents needed to establish a company with the Securities and Exchange Commission. While there is a separate form for foreign investment where the equity is greater than 40 per cent of the shares in the company being established, this step is only required to check if the investment is in one of the industries that have equity limits attached. As I note below, there are many of these industries, and accordingly while the Philippines rates well in terms of approval process its overall foreign investment policy is restrictive in many sectors.

Japan is listed next because in all but restricted industries, the foreign investor needs only to lodge a notification of their investment after the event. Korea has closely followed the Japanese model and also requires notification, but in many cases requires prior notification rather than notification after the event.

Australia still examines foreign investment proposals in Greenfield projects above a certain amount and mergers and acquisitions over a specified dollar amount. While most are approved, the government's policy still allows a considerable degree of screening and therefore discretion to reject if a proposal is considered to be contrary to the national interest.

Taiwan's system for approving foreign investment resembles the system used by some of its Southeast Asian neighbors in that while formal approval is not strictly required in many instances, there are incentives for obtaining approval. In the Taiwanese case, if the investment proposal is not approved, it will be subject to the onerous conditions of Taiwan's company law, which contains many provisions (including directors' domiciliary requirements) for investment that proceeds outside the approval system.

Thailand's system for investment approval is that for industries on its restricted list (as set out in the Foreign Business Act), foreign investors must obtain approval from the bodies specified on that list. The list consists of three categories of industries with different bodies required to approve foreign investments for each list. However, if an investment is in an area outside the list and the investor does not want incentives then, as in the Philippines, it is simply a matter of dealing with the company registration authorities.

Malaysia is slightly more restrictive. All foreign investment in the manufacturing sector requires a manufacturing license, thereby effectively allowing screening of all foreign and domestic investment proposals in that area. In the service sector, all foreign investment with more than 30 per cent foreign ownership also requires approval by Malaysia's foreign investment committee, thereby resulting in *de facto* screening of almost all foreign investment in services. In Indonesia and China all foreign investment must be approved.

## 3. SECTORAL AND EQUITY RESTRICTIONS

I now turn to an examination of sectoral restrictions. It is extremely difficult to draw a meaningful comparison between countries based on entry barriers alone. This is because while a particular sector may appear to be equally open to foreign and domestic investors alike, licensing requirements at the operational level can in fact be applied to favor domestic investors if there is a wide degree of government discretion in the granting of these licenses. Telecommunications and finance come to mind. It is for this reason that institutions such as the Korea Investment Ombudsman are so important to the overall liberalization process. Conversely, although a sector is shown as restricted, foreign investors may have no difficulty in investing in that industry if the industry is in need of capital at a particular time. Ideally, each industry needs to be dealt with individually, taking into account both entry barriers to foreign investors (foreign investment policy) and the licensing procedures that apply to both foreign and domestic investors alike (operational barriers).

With these limitations in mind, Table 7.2 attempts a very broadly based comparison by grouping industries in the general categories of land and agriculture, natural resources, manufacturing, general services and sensitive service sectors. Land and agriculture refer to both land ownership, whether urban or rural, and agricultural production itself. The category of natural resources covers mining, fishing and timber. Manufacturing includes all categories of the production of goods. Sensitive services include telecommunications, electricity production and distribution, finance, media and transport. General services are all other services including construction, tourism, professions, retail and wholesale activities, and trading. The information to compile Table 7.2 has been taken from individual countries' entries in the APEC investment guide. Not all countries provide detailed information on all sectors, resulting in absences that add to the complexity of the task. Table 7.2 attempts to rank countries by their degree of freedom on FDI, with more open countries appearing higher in the table.

Several observations can be made from Table 7.2. First, most countries welcome FDI in manufacturing industries. All of the developed countries in the sample have either no restrictions or very few. However, Japan restricts manufacturing investment in leather goods, aircraft and shipbuilding. Taiwan also has some restrictions in sensitive manufacturing industries including medicines, fertilizers and chemicals – the last two being considered to contribute to pollution problems. Among the developing countries the newly industrializing countries of Southeast Asia also have a liberal stance towards manufacturing investment, other than in traditional products and those that are produced by small-scale firms. Both Indonesia and Thailand restrict manufacturing investment in those sectors. This approach seems to acknowledge that the superior competitive advantages of MNCs may lead to crowding out of local industries. However, in the case of industries seen as priorities for development, Indonesia and Thailand not only have minimal restrictions but offer generous incentive packages particularly if the foreign investor is also an exporter. China has a slightly different approach. An examination of its encouraged, restricted and prohibited industry lists tends to suggest that foreign investment is restricted in industries where the government considers there is enough foreign investment (such as consumer electronics and basic chemicals), or where the government wishes to protect local producers for infant industry or for other reasons.

Second, the degree of openness of general service industries depends on the level of economic development. The more developed countries in the sample have relatively open policies for general services whereas developing countries tend to require majority local ownership. Thus industries such as construction, tourism, wholesale and retail activities and trading are not restricted in Japan, Korea, Australia and Singapore but are to some degree in Taiwan. However, a different picture emerges when looking at the developing economies. General service industries are restricted in some way in all of the developing countries in the sample. The most common form of restriction is a limit on the extent of foreign equity allowed. As I explain further below, both economic and political factors explain these restrictions. Some observers suggest that these restrictions tend to limit significantly the benefits that these countries could otherwise receive from foreign investment (Thomsen 1999; OECD 1998; Moran 1998). However, the contrary point of view is that without some form of sectoral restriction, foreign investment might crowd out local enterprises leading to severe economic and social dislocation.

Third, most countries are quite restrictive in the sensitive service sectors. The most common forms of restrictions in these sectors are either set limitations on the extent of

*Table 7.2 Sectoral Restrictions on FDI and Foreign Equity Limitations in East Asian Economies*

| | Land and agriculture | Natural resources | Manufacturing | General services | Sensitive services |
|---|---|---|---|---|---|
| Singapore | Residential apartments | No restrictions | Few restrictions | No restrictions | Media and telecoms limited |
| Australia | Residential land | Few restrictions | No restrictions | No restrictions | Finance, media, international air transport and national telecom carrier |
| Korea | Some restrictions in agriculture | No restrictions | No restrictions | Few restrictions | Some areas of media, transport, telecoms and power |
| Japan | Some restrictions in agriculture and land | Individual ministry approval for some sub sectors | Few restrictions | Few restrictions | Some areas of finance media telecoms and power |
| Taiwan | Agriculture off limits; land needs ministry approval | Special approval needed | Few restrictions | Some sectors restricted (construction) | Some areas of media, power, transport, finance and mainline telecoms |
| Malaysia | State government approval needed | 30 per cent foreign equity limit subject to negotiation | Few restrictions | 30 per cent foreign equity limit subject to negotiations | Various levels of foreign ownership permitted |
| Thailand | Predominantly minority foreign participation | Special approval for majority foreign ownership | Few limitations except in traditional industries | Special approval for majority foreign ownership in many sectors | Most are restricted to minority foreign participation – except finance |
| Philippines | Majority Philippine ownership required | Majority Philippine ownership required | Few restrictions | Most require majority Philippine ownership | Majority Philippine ownership in most sectors |
| Indonesia | Predominantly reserved for local small scale farmers foreign land ownership not permitted | Contracts with the state required | Many reserved for small and medium scale industries or require joint venture | Many reserved for small and medium scale industry or require joint venture | Media and transport closed. Power, telecoms and finance allow significant foreign ownership |

*Table 7.2 (continued)*

| | Land and agriculture | Natural resources | Manufacturing | General services | Sensitive services |
|---|---|---|---|---|---|
| China | Land and agriculture predominantly off limits | Case by case basis if permitted at all | Separate lists for encouraged, restricted and prohibited industries | Most are on the restricted list | Most are either restricted or prohibited |

foreign equity or a system of case-by-case approval. The developed countries appear to be more transparent than developing countries because in many sensitive services such as telecommunications, air transport and media, specific foreign equity limits are published. Thus, Australia, Japan and Korea all allow in the vicinity of 30 per cent foreign equity in major telecommunications carriers. Various limits apply in the three countries to investment in media and broadcasting and in airlines. In most cases foreign interests are limited to a minority share. Taiwan is also moving towards a similar approach to its telecommunications industries but is more restrictive in transport and media than the other three economies. The finance sector in all developed economies has varying degrees of openness depending on the type of financial institution being established. There are often detailed requirements for establishing a new business or taking over an existing financial service provider.

One explanation for the generally restrictive approach to foreign investment in sensitive service sectors is the fear that a completely liberalized approach might jeopardize national security given the political and economic importance of these industries. A further explanation is that these industries have traditionally been quasi monopolies often owned by the state and it is only in recent years that industries such as telecommunications have seen wider competition. In the finance sector, there is a concern to ensure that foreign institutions meet prudential requirements in their own countries and comply with international standards.

The Southeast Asian countries have been engaged in privatization of industries such as power generation, telecommunications and transport for the past decade or more. To make these industries competitive, governments have sought a percentage of foreign investment in them. This percentage varies by industry and by country and sometimes varies within the same industry in the same country. Not all countries publish foreign equity limits in these industries, making it difficult to draw meaningful comparisons. This is due partly to the nature of the privatization process, whereby differing levels of foreign participation are sought depending on government perceptions as to what is an acceptable level and what the market will bear. Somewhat surprisingly, Indonesia appears on paper to be quite liberal, often allowing up to 95 per cent foreign ownership in some transport infrastructure industries, power generation projects and the newer telecommunications industries. Thailand and the Philippines also have 'build operate–transfer' laws that allow the construction and operation of some infrastructure projects. Almost without exception, foreign investment in the broadcasting industries is prohibited in these countries.

All of the Southeast Asian countries were affected by the 1997 Asian crisis and external pressure has resulted in a change of approach to foreign investment in the finance sector. Thailand, for example, has now become considerably more open to foreign investment in the finance sector, as has Indonesia. Malaysia has always had varying degrees of foreign participation in its banking and insurance industry. In recent years the government has faced considerable external pressure to further open this sector. However, this has met with resistance, particularly from existing providers in the industry.

A fourth observation is that most countries are still highly protective of their agriculture and resource sectors. Again national security concerns and the traditionally strong lobbying power of agricultural groups provide explanations. In addition, developing countries are concerned about the social and economic impact of opening up the agricultural sector, which has traditionally been dominated by small-scale farmers and which still employs a very large percentage of the population.

The foregoing indicates that the Korean economy is relatively open to FDI, in terms of both approval processes and sectoral restrictions. If the two tables are considered together, it could be argued that Korea is surpassed only by Singapore in the openness of its economy.

## 4. WILL EAST ASIAN COUNTRIES FOLLOW KOREA'S LEAD?

We can now address the question of whether other countries in the region will follow Korea's lead in the significant liberalization that the Korean government has undertaken recently. I argue that there are both political and economic constraints to other East Asian nations following Korea's example in widely liberalizing FDI.

I turn first to economic constraints. Of the group discussed above, Malaysia, the Philippines, Indonesia, China and Thailand can still be categorized as developing countries. Governments in these countries are well aware that foreign investment can result in positive benefits such as increased exports, employment opportunities, technology transfer and overall economic growth, but it can also have negative consequences. These can include the elimination of local firms and jobs, an excess of imports over exports and the failure of foreign firms to pass on any product or process knowledge to their local suppliers or partners. Most significant to developing countries may be the need to ensure that foreign investment contributes positively to building a strong and competitive local industrial base. If foreign investment plays this role then all the other benefits mentioned previously will follow and the negative consequences will be avoided.

For this reason many developing countries insist on maintaining some control over foreign investment and have tended to steer it into sectors of industry where they see it making the most significant contribution to economic development. They use approval processes, sectoral and equity restrictions and technology transfer requirements for this purpose. Governments fear that without such policy tools, foreign investors will establish themselves simply as export platforms utilizing cheap labor and imported components. The investors will keep their technology to themselves, thereby contributing little to the development of local firms. In addition, foreign investors will enter service sectors where they will easily out-compete local service providers and may even, in the absence of effective competition laws, acquire monopoly or oligopoly status.

There is keen debate internationally as to the wisdom of maintaining controls over FDI. Those who favor continued monitoring of foreign investment tend to say that policy measures are necessary to ensure a positive contribution to development goals. The authors of the 1999 World Investment Report tend to lean in this direction, arguing that some policy measures may be needed to prevent the ill effects of crowding out, and to develop local industrial capabilities (UNCTAD 1999: 318–27) Those who argue that developing countries should follow Korea's lead and abandon most policy restrictions tend to suggest that unless developing countries do this then the foreign investment that does flow in will not embody the latest production, process management or marketing techniques. They also argue that insisting on joint venture requirements deters investors, thereby depriving developing countries of the most competitive international firms. Proponents of an open-door approach suggest that screening mechanisms also deter desirable foreign investment because of the bureaucratic hurdles involved in the process and because of the possibility of corruption (Moran 1998; Thomsen 1999).

Evidence is scarce to support either side in this debate. Case studies dealing with the role of foreign investment in building up local industry tend to produce contradictory findings. A number of case studies that I have reviewed elsewhere suggest that while foreign investment has played a role in developing a local industrial base in some countries and in some industries, there is as yet insufficient evidence to show that this is always the outcome (Bishop 2001: 91–7). The problem becomes even more difficult when trying to establish whether a liberalized investment environment would be better or worse in this regard. Commentators here can only speculate, as few countries, if any, have relied on a completely liberal approach in the past. As Wells (1998) notes, developing countries are left to rely on faith alone in order to accept the proposition that a completely open-door approach will produce desirable development outcomes. The end result is that those advocating an open approach argue that because government failure is more likely than market failure, developing countries should take this risk. Advocates say that the disappointing results in local industry development are due to restrictive government controls over the type of investment that is allowed in. On the other hand, those who believe in continued government intervention tend to believe that market failure is a bigger risk than government failure and point to those case studies that show successful examples of local industry development and attribute these to the policy measures adopted.

One would think that the earlier development experience of nations such as Japan, Korea, Taiwan and Singapore might assist in resolving this dilemma. However, in all of these cases, rather than a liberal approach to foreign investment, governments were quite discriminating about what investment projects should be allowed in, and which should be filtered out, to contribute to national economic development. The restrictive approach to foreign investment adopted by Japan, Korea and Taiwan during their earlier economic development is well known. It is less known that despite Singapore's welcoming stance towards foreign investment, the government took considerable pains to court investment (through incentives) only from companies that it felt would support the government's development goals at the time (Lim and Fong 1991).

The earlier East Asian developers were able to pursue a restrictive approach because they had ready access to alternative sources of finance to complement FDI in their development efforts. Today's developing countries do not seem to have the same capacity to access internal sources of finance and they bear greater risks in using external sources of finance for their economic development. They are therefore in a different position to that of Japan, Korea, Taiwan and Singapore in their earlier stages of development. Developing nations currently face the dilemma of removing restrictions on FDI and risking the negative consequences mentioned earlier, or leaving the restrictions in place and risking missing out on the best source of external finance available to assist in their development process.

The earlier East Asian developers also had the bureaucratic and political capacity to closely monitor the foreign investment that they allowed in to ensure that it contributed positively to the economy. I have argued elsewhere that the degree of bureaucratic and political capacity needed for such a state-led approach to development is not achieved easily (Bishop 1997). The combination of factors needed for a successful state-led development process is not present to the same degree in most of today's developing countries in the region, for two basic reasons. First, it is much more difficult to achieve successful state-led development in pluralistic and democratic societies. State-led development has tended to rely on a cohesive industry policy. In pluralistic and democratic societies it is difficult to gain the degree of consensus required to devise, and more importantly to implement, a cohesive industry policy because of the greater need for policy compromise to secure continued electoral support. Second, the world economic environment has changed, making it much more difficult to engage in the protectionist policies that the earlier developers adopted to build their own industrial base. Thus, even if today's developing countries wanted to follow the Japan model they would find it much more difficult and there is no guarantee that the results achieved in Japan, Korea and Taiwan would be replicated. Accordingly, these earlier developers do not provide a policy model for today's developing countries to follow in dealing with foreign investment. Thus, a more difficult domestic and international economic policy environment coupled with uncertainties about the benefits of an open door approach suggest that today's developing countries will adopt a cautious approach to liberalization of foreign investment policy.

I turn now to the political constraints on further investment liberalization. Political constraints affect the pace and nature of liberalization in both developed and developing countries. Thus these constraints not only help to explain whether the developing countries will follow Korea's lead in liberalizing their investment regimes but also provide some insight into whether the developed countries in the sample are likely to remove their existing restrictions. Political constraints on the liberalization process emanate from three sources. The first source is business interests that are threatened by opening their industry to foreign competition. The second source of opposition comes from bureaucracies in some countries. The third source is politicians themselves, who perceive electoral disadvantage in moving too fast towards liberalization. Let us look at each of these in more detail.

There will always be some businesses that win from liberalization decisions and some that lose. Those that fear foreign competition tend to lobby policymakers either to keep foreign investment out or devise measures that will disadvantage foreign competitors. A recent study of investment restrictions in the United States found that several industry groups had successfully lobbied for measures that disadvantaged foreign investors (Crystal 1998). While these measures were not strictly foreign investment policy measures, they had the effect of favoring local producers. Such measures included rules of origin, government procurement and limitations on subsidies to foreign firms. This illustrates well that although foreign investment policy may appear to be liberal, it is always necessary to look at the operational barriers within a particular industry to gain an accurate picture. This study also highlights the danger that even if entry barriers to foreign investment are removed, it is possible that new sets of restrictions will spring up at the operational level to replace them.

In the East Asian region, examples can be found to illustrate the influence of business on the liberalization process. I will refer briefly to three of these. The first is the case of attempts to open the retail sector in the Philippines to foreign investment. Both the Ramos and Estrada administrations sought to allow foreign investment into this sector. However, in both instances there was strong opposition from local retailers and it was impossible to find agreement on how far the proposed changes should go. Thus business interests have been able to stall liberalization in this sector (Macdonald 1999). The second example concerns the finance sector in Malaysia. Attempts by former deputy Prime Minister Anwar

Ibrahim to open this sector to greater foreign competition were strongly resisted by local banks on the grounds that these banks were not yet ready to compete with the stronger international financial institutions (Daneels 1997; Bell 1998). The banks' arguments found favor with many political figures because the banks are an essential plank in the implementation of Malaysia's industry policy. The third example concerns attempts to amend the Alien Business Law in Thailand. This was first proposed in 1995 and yet, due to opposition from local businesses that would be affected by liberalization, it was delayed until March 2000. Again a number of industries lobbied the government to restrict FDI in their sector because they were not ready to face international competition. On the other hand, sections of the international business community argued for much wider liberalization. In the end a list of industries was produced identifying sectors where the government felt that the firms concerned were not yet ready to face foreign competition. These three examples show how business interests can successfully lobby governments to resist the investment liberalization process.

Yet opposition to this liberalization also comes from within the state itself. While senior-level bureaucrats often appreciate the benefits for the nation from liberalization, those lower in the administration sometimes frustrate their efforts by failing to implement policy change. It has been suggested that this problem is particularly acute in the transition economies where bureaucrats are still operating in the mode of a command economy and insist on examining proposals in great detail (Rosen 1999). This not only serves their own interests by ensuring that they have a continued role in the investment process but also results from pressure placed on them to do this by their constituent base.

Some politicians also oppose various liberalization measures if they feel it is in their political interests to do so. It has been observed that the maintenance of policy measures such as joint-venture requirements are a useful political tool because they provide a means by which politicians can reward supporters (Conklin and Lecraw 1997). Joint venture and screening requirements also allow politicians to allay public fears about the impact of FDI by arguing that these policy measures show that politicians are serious about monitoring foreign investment to ensure that a net benefit results. Even in the developed countries we find that politicians may intervene in foreign investment proposals if they feel that there will be an adverse community reaction to those proposals. This is one reason why screening requirements continue to exist for larger investments in Australia, New Zealand and Canada. It can be argued that recent protest movements against globalization have the potential to slow the liberalization process considerably, with politicians increasingly concerned about the extent to which such views are widely held in the community.

Finally we need to consider national security as a ground for governments to restrict FDI in certain industry sectors. Countries often argue that national security concerns warrant restrictions particularly in agricultural and resource-based industries and in the sensitive service sectors. While there is some merit in these arguments, it is necessary to ask how national security is likely to be jeopardized if foreign investment is allowed in these areas. Academic opinion suggests that in many cases national security arguments are simply a smokescreen for other political factors. However, there may be instances where an industry has so few players that countries may be justified in using the national security reason for restrictions (Moran 1998).

When we add these political constraints to the economic development concerns of East Asia's developing economies, it seems clear that it will not be easy for developing countries to quickly follow Korea's lead.

## 5. HOW DID KOREA SURMOUNT THE CONSTRAINTS TO LIBERALIZATION?

At the beginning of the 1990s Korea had a restrictive approach to foreign investment. Attempts had been made to simplify the approval process and remove sectoral and equity limitations since the early 1980s. Yet progress occurred primarily in the manufacturing sector where there was a consensus that Korean companies were internationally competitive and therefore had little to fear from incoming foreign investment. Progress in other sectors was minimal, if at all. Evidence of this restrictive approach can be found in a Hong Kong Bank survey of the investment environment in various Asian countries in 1990. The survey was reported to have commented that Korea was not really interested in foreign investment, with the government pushing self-sufficiency harder than ever (*Korea Economic Daily* 4 September 1990). Further, in 1992, one foreign investor suggested that while some areas had been opened up due to US pressure, mid-level bureaucrats continued to decide 'what the fatherland should or should not have' (*Asian Business* April 1992: 47).

Serious attempts at liberalization began in 1993 with the publication of a five-year plan for opening up most industries to 100 per cent foreign ownership over the five-year period. A simplified notification system was introduced with the effect that once an industry was 'liberalized' foreign investors only had to notify their intention of making an investment in that industry. In 1998, Korea was engulfed in the Asian economic crisis, and greater opening to foreign investment was one of the conditions of the IMF rescue package. Laws restricting foreign investment by way of merger and acquisition were scrapped and a new Foreign Investment Act was introduced in September of that year to give legal effect to the policy changes of the previous five years. The new Act simplified the notification system and reduced still further the range of industries that would remain restricted.

Thus the liberalization of Korea's foreign investment policies did not occur overnight. It was the result of a protracted internal policy struggle lasting over almost two decades (Bishop 1997). What were the factors that explain Korea overcoming economic concerns and political constraints to liberalization? First, there was an increasing consensus within the Korean bureaucracy that the Korean economy needed foreign investment to provide a competitive spur to Korean industry. This consensus was built only gradually over the 1980s and 1990s. The strong leadership of Kim Young Sam in the early period of his presidency, and his insistence that a five-year plan for liberalization be introduced, tipped the balance in favor of those advocating liberalization. Kim's appeal to the public that the Korean economy needed to embrace globalization was successful in minimizing domestic political opposition to the liberalization initiatives. Big business offered little opposition to the changes. It wanted controls over outward investment relaxed so it would be seen as inconsistent if they advocated continued controls over inward investment. Disunity within the labor movement and its difficulty in accessing policymaking processes may have contributed to the lack of coordinated opposition by labor to liberalization policies.

However, internal forces for change may not have been sufficient of themselves to bring about the change. Since the mid-1980s the United States had pressured the Korean government to liberalize investment and other markets. These attempts had achieved results only on a case-by-case basis. What may have been more decisive was the Kim Young Sam government's objective of joining the OECD. To obtain OECD membership Korea had to liberalize its foreign investment policies to meet the criteria of the OECD's Committee on Capital Movements. This provided a major external impetus to Kim's attempts at reform. The liberalization task was completed under pressure from the IMF when Korea had little option but to comply with IMF conditions in order secure IMF financing.

In summary, Korea overcame the constraints to liberalization only after many years of internal policy debate and perhaps in the end mainly as a result of external pressure. Because of the unique combination of both domestic and external forces in the liberalization process in Korea, one is hesitant in predicting how those forces will play out in the other East Asian economies. Each case needs to be analyzed individually.

Throughout this chapter I have referred to the removal of entry barriers to foreign investment. However, this is only part of what is needed to achieve an entirely liberalized environment for foreign investment. As noted, the entire administrative and regulatory system within an economy can pose significant hurdles for foreign investors after they gain entry. While Korea has made entry relatively easy, one cannot say that the business environment confronting investors when operating within Korea is equally as easy or benign. It is difficult to assess this operating environment other than on an industry-by-industry basis. Further research in this area could prove useful. This research is important because if current attempts to have investment issues included within the auspices of the WTO are successful and countries are compelled to liberalize their foreign investment policies, then the issue of administrative or operational barriers will become more significant.

## 6. CONCLUSION

By reviewing the Korean experience, this chapter has considered whether East Asian countries will follow Korea's lead in liberalizing FDI policies. I have argued that Korea is now one of the most liberal of the East Asian countries in terms of formal entry barriers to foreign investment, a position I have supported by comparison of their approaches to approval of FDI and the sectors in which FDI is restricted.

I have argued that in the cases of the developing nations of East Asia, there are concerns that a completely open door approach will not lead to the development outcomes these nations desire from FDI. In particular, governments of these nations are concerned that without appropriate policy measures, FDI may have more negative than positive outcomes. They could well point to the success of the restrictive approach taken earlier in Korea, Japan and Taiwan to support their case. However, as I have argued, it is difficult for developing countries today to replicate the experience of the early industrializers since the domestic and international contexts – economic and political – have changed considerably.

On the other side, there are arguments that an open approach to FDI must be pursued if countries want to maximize the advantages that FDI can induce. The difficulty with this argument is that few countries have tried such an approach. Thus, developing countries are left to rely on faith in market forces and the automatic diffusion of the benefits of foreign investment if they adopt this approach. Unfortunately, neither side in this debate is able to produce clear incontrovertible evidence to support their argument. Much more research is needed before we can even begin to understand the impact of foreign investment in either a restricted or a liberalized policy environment.

Economic development concerns are not the only constraining factor to East Asian countries following Korea's lead. There are also political considerations. I have argued that some business interests, politicians and bureaucrats will oppose or thwart liberalization initiatives. This applies in both the developed and developing countries of the region. It therefore seems that given both the economic development concerns and political constraints, it is likely to be some time before all of the East Asian countries have as liberal an approach to FDI as does Korea.

Securing the domestic consensus needed for a more open approach took nearly two decades in Korea. Even then, the liberalized environment may only have been achieved as a result of external forces tipping the balance in favor of liberalization. The developing countries of East Asia may well follow suit but it is likely that, unless foreign investment is brought within the purview of the WTO, the extent to which liberalization is achieved in any economy will depend on a unique combination of domestic and external factors. As I have noted here, liberalization of entry barriers is not of itself sufficient to achieve a liberal policy environment for foreign investors. One also needs to consider industry-specific operating conditions. It is here that further research on the Korean liberalization experience could prove useful in determining the depth of liberalization that has been achieved in Korea.

## NOTES

1. Greenfield investment refers to the establishment of a new business. 'M&A', on the other hand, refers to the acquisition of an industry business.

## REFERENCES

*Asian Business*, April 1992, p. 47.

Bell, A. (1998), 'Malaysia delays foreign owner divestment', *National Underwriter*, **102** (24), 18 and 40.

Bishop, B. (1997), *Foreign Direct Investment in Korea: The Role of the State*, London: Ashgate Publishing.

Bishop, B. (2001), *Liberalising Foreign Direct Investment Policies in the APEC Region*, London: Ashgate Publishing.

Conklin, D. and D. Lecraw (1997), 'Restrictions on foreign ownership 1984–1994: Developments and alternative policies', *Transnational Corporations*, **6** (1), 1–30.

Crystal, J. (1998), 'A new kind of competition: How American producers respond to incoming Foreign Direct Investment', *International Studies Quarterly*, **42** (3), 513–44.

Daneels, J. (1997), 'KL in a quandary', *Asian Business*, **33** (11) 30–33.

*Korea Economic Daily*, 4 September 1990.

Lall, S. (1995), 'Employment and foreign investment: Policy options for developing countries', *International Labour Review*, **143** (4–5), 521–41.

Lim, L. and P. Fong (1991), *Foreign Direct Investment and Industrialisation in Malaysia, Singapore, Taiwan and Thailand*, Paris: OECD.

Macdonald, C. (1999), 'Odds on favourite', *Asian Business*, **35**, (1), 36–45.

Moran, T. (1998), *Foreign Direct Investment and Development*, Washington, DC: Institute for International Economics.

OECD (1998), *Foreign Direct Investment and Economic Development – Lessons from Six Emerging Economies*, Paris: OECD.

Rosen, D. (1999), *Behind the Open Door: Foreign Enterprises in the Chinese Marketplace*, Washington, DC: Institute for International Economics.

Thomsen, S. (1999), *Southeast Asia: The Role of Foreign Direct Investment Policies in Development*, working paper on international Investment, Directorate for Financial, Fiscal and Enterprise affairs, Paris: OECD.

United National Conference on Trade and Development (1999), *World Investment Report 1999: Foreign Direct Investment and the Challenge of Development*, New York and Geneva: United Nations.

Wells, L. (1998), 'Multinationals and developing countries', *Journal of International Business Studies*, **29** (1), 101–14.

# 8. Korea's Strategy for Financial Reform: A New-Institutional Economics Perspective

**Sung-Hee Jwa and Guangsug Hahn**

## 1. INTRODUCTION

Rapid deregulation and liberalization in the world's international and domestic financial markets, helped along by telecommunications and computer technology advances, has changed dramatically the financial environment in many parts of the world. In Korea, there has been a spurt of growth in the equities and bonds markets, as well as in the derivatives market, in part due to reform measures following the recent financial crisis. The recent developments notwithstanding, the financial system still needs further improvement if Korea is to survive the challenges of global competition. There has been widespread effort to put in place the features of the US 'securities market-based' financial system that emphasizes the role of the securities market *vis-à-vis* 'bank-based' finance on the one hand, and the Anglo-Saxon corporate governance system that champions individual investors over the entrepreneur on the other hand. US business and financial practices are often viewed as the standard model to be pursued by Korea, which explains partly the direction of recent changes in Korea's financial structures towards developing a stronger market-based financial system. Similarly, in the corporate sector Anglo-Saxon corporate governance structures have featured heavily in the government's reform agenda, which includes, for example, the call for increased management and accounting transparency, lowering corporate debt–equity ratios, and the introduction of an outside directors system. The rapid opening of Korea's financial markets, which has allowed not only foreign ownership but also entry of foreign business practices, has introduced competition on a global scale that requires all business organizations to grapple with 'global standards'. The results of this transition, however, remain varied, and Korean policymakers and others who are involved here continue to try to understand the far-reaching implications of having to strive towards 'global standards' in the financial as well as corporate sectors.

Making decisions for the future is a very difficult task, since so many important dimensions can be quite elusive. For example, there are questions about whether the 'global standards' in financial and management systems, which many people understand poorly but attempt to pursue nonetheless, are the ideal path for developing countries to strive towards. Questions also remain about whether the choice of 'global standards' or what can more appropriately be termed 'US standards' or the 'Anglo-Saxon economic system' will guarantee improved financial as well as corporate performance. In the context of financial systems, we broadly define 'global standards' as those features that complement and emphasize the economic role of the securities market over the bank-lending market. This is an important distinguishing feature that is better understood under the new-institutional economics framework, which suggests that the choices of a country's financial system and corporate structures are not to be separated. That a country's financial and corporate sector are intricately tied to each other, in a way we describe in greater detail later in this chapter, suggests that corporate decisions, whether about organizational strategies or financial strategies, are to a large extent determined endogenously. The private sector's endogenous decision variables should be carefully separated from the exogenous institutional constraints that include the financial market institutions, the country's political and legal systems, traditions, culture and so forth. In this chapter we also present from the new-institutional economics perspective a vision for the future of Korea's financial system, and discuss reform policies to realize this vision.

Specifically to the Korean case, we observe that from as early as the 1960s, Korea's interventionist industrial policy directly controlled and allocated bank loans to targeted industries. As a consequence, banks and other financial firms did not develop fully into autonomous profit-oriented business units. The role of these financial institutions in establishing a healthy financial sector diminished, while at the same time government complacency over the banking sector increased to the extent that even the prudential regulation became lax. On the other hand, with easy access to bank loans, corporations expanded their debt-dominant capital structure. Often the too-big-to-fail legacy was helped by this loan concentration, which allowed various corporate inefficiencies to creep in. Effectively the government protected the survival of banks, which essentially acted as industrial banks, as well as corporations that were the target of industrial policy, thereby nurturing widespread moral hazard behavior.

After an overview and evaluation of the current state of Korea's financial system, we argue that the banking sector's autonomy and monitoring roles should be restored. The country's major financial institutions should concurrently become more active players in the securities market. In Korea, banks have been the major source of corporate finance, and from the viewpoint of new-institutional economics, path dependence implies that these banks should become more active in the securities market. We argue in particular that a universal banking system should be fully encouraged so that banks can take advantage of economies of scope by providing a broader array of financial products and claims including equity investment, underwriting, securitization and insurance services. Needless to say, such a system should be backed by the necessary institutional arrangements including a corresponding set of deregulations, enhanced competition policy in the banking sector, and the proper execution of financial supervision. With a universal banking system in place, the financial system should then be allowed to evolve towards an endogenously efficient structure through an unhindered competition process. At the same time, specialized banking should not be ignored, and a universal banking system must be flexible enough to accommodate specialized banking particularly when this is appropriate to do so from business perspectives. The corporate sector as a result of such a system will have a wider and better set of alternative financial sources to choose from, which will increase efficiency within the sector. Whether a market-based or bank-based financial system eventually comes to dominate the economy is unimportant. More important is that a system evolves that allows corporations maximum freedom to adopt a management system that is consistent with the exogenous financial system, government policy, the legal framework and the broader institutional environment.

In sum, after having identified inherent weaknesses in Korea's financial system, and having applied the new-institutional economics framework to examine conceptually the evolution of a financial system, its relation to a country's institutional setting, and how these circumstances affect corporate behavior, we provide in this chapter a conceptual analysis for the basis of the vision presented here for Korea's financial sector and reform policies. The remainder of this chapter is organized as follows. In the next section, we explain the current status of Korea's financial system, explaining its evolution as a bank-based financial system and some of its weaknesses. We also consider the difficulties in nurturing a much-needed securities market within this financial system. In section 3 we present a theoretical framework for explaining the interaction between a country's financial system and its large corporations using the new-institutional economics perspective to show how culture, customs, traditions, the legal system and government policies act as exogenous constraints on endogenous firms (financial as well as non-financial). In section 4 we present our vision for the future of Korea's financial system and in section 5 we discuss specific policy measures and policy-related recommendations needed to realize this vision. Section 6 concludes this chapter.

## 2. WEAKNESSES OF KOREA'S FINANCIAL SYSTEM

Korea is not unique in having a bank-based as opposed to a market-based financial system. Many countries with a bank-based financial system, such as Germany and Japan, built strong economies after the Second World War and maintained these for the rest of the 20th century. Korea's financial system after the Korean War (1950–53) followed a path similar to that taken by Germany and Japan.[1] Indeed the genesis of Korea's bank-based financial system can be traced to the 1960s, when the Park Chung Hee government intervened extensively in national economic development. The Korean economy was then characterized by extremely low levels of capital accumulation, so the government took control over banks' financial-resource mobilization activities, and even created new banks to help further the accumulation of domestic capital that was desperately needed for economic reconstruction and industrial development. For almost four decades the Korean economy has maintained record growth rates under such a bank-based financial system, eventually joining the OECD in 1996. Numerous achievements notwithstanding, the financial meltdown in 1997 exposed many of the inherent weaknesses of the Korea-specific bank-based financial system.

A fundamental factor responsible for weakening Korea's financial system is the government's industrial policy, which has left a clear mark on the country's industrial organization. Encouraged by easy credit and backed by the government, firms were attracted to participate in the targeted industries that the government's heavy and chemical industry policy assigned as the most important for Korea's economic growth. This policy regime fostered growth of certain corporations in these industries. There were few alternative domestic funding sources beyond bank loans, and the government made bank funds even more attractive since it controlled interest rates and kept them artificially low. The gradually strengthened industry–bank nexus therefore encouraged the high leverage ratio characteristic of Korean corporations. This, together with the 'too-big-to-fail' legacy, accelerated loan concentration to big companies. It made the corporate capital structure debt-dominated, while helping firms to pursue their expansion strategies. This arrangement was brought to an abrupt halt with the outbreak of the 1997 economic crisis. Elsewhere, for example in Jwa (2001), we have identified the unsophisticated exchange-rate policy and inappropriate sequencing of financial liberalization measures as immediate causes of the 1997 financial crisis. Behind these were two other major considerations: the inherent weakness of the financial system, which was an outcome of almost four decades of active government interventionist policy, and the economy-wide prevalence of moral-hazard behavior in both the financial and corporate sectors, which has been responsible for various structural bottlenecks. To address these problems, the government once again called for financial and corporate restructuring, this time under IMF guidelines. This restructuring introduced more rigorously the pursuit of 'global standards' in both the financial and corporate sectors.

Initially, to rescue Korea's financial situation immediately after the outbreak of the crisis, a huge amount of public funds was injected into various financial firms to clear their balance sheets. The financial sector quickly recovered some stability and most financial institutions, with the exception of some non-bank financial firms, passed the capital-adequacy ratio required by government policy. More recently, Korea's financial sector has experienced profound change with the introduction of many new types of financial institutions and contracts, such as financial holding companies, mutual funds, asset-backed securities, and mergers and acquisitions between financial firms. Financial reform has helped to restore some of the stability needed for economic recovery. Nonetheless, there is still a high possibility that non-performing loans may re-emerge. This is partly because some of the debt problems of large corporations remain unresolved. Furthermore, of greater concern, moral hazard behavior on the part of banks seems likely to continue. For example, despite the good intentions of policy to help failing financial firms by injecting them with public funds, this may actually encourage moral hazard behavior, and is reminiscent of past government policy to guarantee these firms' survival.

The government has recently aimed at improving the efficiency of Korea's financial system, which is a prerequisite if Korea is to achieve sustained economic growth in the highly competitive financial world. The effort towards restructuring Korea's financial sector has nonetheless experienced various difficulties. First, improving competitiveness in the banking sector and restoring its autonomy remain as a difficult task. Given that the banking industry has a widespread impact on the economy, the government tends to prohibit a non-financial firm from owning banks. Moreover, with the imperative for financial restructuring, the government has increased its ownership of banks so that its influence over banking decisions is still far from being abated. For these reasons, autonomous bank management is yet to be realized. Banks are still regulated to the extent that their main activities are more or less confined to making loans to clients principally through their deposit-taking function. As a result, banks have limited profit opportunities, thereby adversely affecting their competitiveness compared to their counterparts in advanced countries. Regulations on entry into the banking industry are still highly prohibitive and most of the mergers and acquisitions activities among banks continue to be under government influence. These explain partly the lack of competitive pressure in the banking industry. Because competitive pressure is mild and banks enjoy government protection, there is a lack of strong motivation to increase profits or develop new financial technologies among banks. For example, although banks have increased their loans based on borrowers' credit ratings, they still continue to lend on the basis of criteria that depend mainly on borrowers' collateral. This reflects banks' inability to discriminate between viable and non-viable investments. Bank supervision is not only affected by political factors, but often supervision agencies fall short of expertise in monitoring banks' risks. Consequently, there is still much to be done before the banking sector's autonomy and competitiveness are restored.

Second, Korea's securities market still lags behind their international counterparts as a key financial institution. The securities market in Korea plays only a minor role as a source of corporate finance and a mechanism to monitor corporate behavior, despite government efforts to improve the securities market particularly since the early 1990s. This is partly because the major investors in Korea's securities market are individuals, rather than financial institutions. As is well known, the role of individual investors in Korea is somewhat weakened because they do not usually have good access to information on firms, their investments are widely dispersed, they have a myopic view of investments, and they shy away from long-term investments. Individual investors are also more vulnerable in accepting losses from high-risk investments. Individual equity investors in Korea do not yet enjoy protection comparable to that afforded to private corporations and financial institutions in Korea, and to individual investors in more advanced countries like the US. Moreover, the securities market is so thin that insider trading has been prevalent in Korea, making investment risks generally on the high side. Despite recent government efforts to increase transparency in corporate accounting and management, there is still much to be done. Korean government policies towards the securities market, and to a certain degree the banking markets, have often been inconsistent. Thus it follows that the securities market in general still remains behind bank loans as a source of corporate finance in Korea.

Another important dimension here is the deep conflicts within the country's institutions and contemporary culture. Low levels of trust prevail in Korean business and society, the rule of law is not yet a dominant feature, and deep-rooted cronyism continues. These features have acted as institutional bottlenecks that hinder the development of Korea's financial markets, particularly the securities market.

Given the various arguments above, the government should continue to foster the securities market by inducing institutional investors' participation. Banks and other economic agents participating in the securities market should serve as an important monitoring mechanism that disciplines corporate behavior. This will help to balance the bank-dominated financial system that led to the structure of excessive corporate debt that helped trigger the 1997 crisis. We shall continue this argument in detail in section 4, after developing a conceptual framework for this argument in section 3 below.

## 3. THE EVOLUTION OF FINANCIAL SYSTEMS AND CORPORATE STRUCTURES[2]

A large empirical and theoretical literature has compared the merits of bank-based and market-based financial systems.[3] In this section, by comparing the evolutionary process of the financial systems of Anglo-Saxon countries with those of other countries that have a bank-based financial system, we illustrate why the securities market and banks should be treated as complementarities rather than as substitutes. We also explain how a country's financial system affects individual and corporate behavior in that country. First, we argue that a country's financial system is intrinsically related to corporate structures, and both are subject to a broad array of institutional factors including the country's culture, tradition, legal system, and government policies. In this context, to better understand the evolution of a country's financial sector, we need to look more closely at the interplay between the choice of financial system and corporate structure and behavior.

New-institutional economics regards the firm as an organization that endlessly adapts itself to the surrounding institutional environment. The adaptation is a process through which firms adjust and undertake necessary restructuring to maximize their chance of survival given the economic and social environments. More specifically, a firm's behavior depends on the external or exogenous environment that consists of cultural and social factors, the political system, the government's economic policies and the financial system, which we have ordered here from the remote to the immediate. Culture and tradition act as the overall exogenous factors that constrain all other actors in the economy – from the political system and government economic policymaking, to the type of financial system and the behavior of firms. Political systems, in turn, constrain all other actors by building the legal institutions (the rules of the game). The government in a narrow sense affects the financial system and the corporate sector through economic policy. The financial system constrains corporate behavior by offering a selected type of finance for firms.

Table 8.1 lists the essential differences between the financial systems of advanced Anglo-Saxon countries that represent the 'global standard' and those of other economies in continental Europe, Japan, Korea, and other East Asian countries where the banking sector features heavily. Here we have in fact separated the essential features of countries where market-based finance is important from those of countries where bank-based finance is dominant.

The table shows that advanced Anglo-Saxon economies are characterized by respect for formal relationships and institutions, and the prevalence of the rule of law, which leads to strong respect for formal business contracts. All of these features are basically in line with the securities-market culture. Therefore, securities markets become a prominent source of corporate financing in such economies and the dominance of securities markets dictates that the corporate sector cannot but maintain accountability and transparency in management and must respect shareholder value.

On the other hand, in countries such as Korea that are heavily influenced by informal institutions and tend to be characterized by higher transaction costs, a different situation arises. Cronyism results from the need to nurture personal relationships in an environment where respect for formal relationships is relatively unimportant. Here the 'rule of person' becomes prevalent in contrast to the 'rule of law'. A culture of informal institutions where the written contract is not seen to be legally binding tends to necessitate direct business contacts and personal relationships, which are conducive to a financial system dominated by the bank-lending market. Since bank loans are usually made after processing background information about the borrower, and more often than not this information is far from enabling a true assessment, it is widely observed that informal and personal relationships become a prominent feature of banking activities. Further, individual investors in securities markets in countries where the rule of law and formal relationships are weak, tend to make relatively arbitrary decisions and have a short investment horizon. Corporate structure and behavior that evolve under the financial markets dominated by bank lending are usually characterized by a less transparent management system and usually demonstrate less respect for shareholders who are seen to be of secondary importance. In this case, banks tend to play a more important role than securities markets in determining the corporate structure and behavior.

*Table 8.1 Culture, Financial System and Corporate Structure*

| Variables | | US, UK | Continental Europe, Japan, Korea |
|---|---|---|---|
| Institutional constraints | Cultural background | Formal relationship | Informal relationship/ cronyism |
| | National governance tradition | Rule of law | Rule of person |
| | Legal tradition | Common law | Civil law |
| Evolution of financial system | Financial system | Market-based | Bank-based |
| Evolution of corporate structure and behavior | Corporate financing | Equity financing | Debt financing |
| | Ownership structure | Dispersed | Concentrated |
| | Corporate management and objectives | • High transparency<br>• Investor protection<br>• Strong outside BOD<br>• Low debt–equity ratio<br>• High respect for shareholder value | • Low transparency<br>• Entrepreneur protection<br>• Weak BOD<br>• High debt–equity ratio<br>• Low respect for shareholder value |

A nation's choice of financial system is also constrained by the level of capital accumulation. This links the choice of financial system, and hence the type of corporate structure and behavior, to the nation's level of economic development. Economies in continental Europe, as well as Japan and Korea, lacked a sufficient capital base for start-ups and growth, particularly during their catch-up stage, when compared to their Anglo-Saxon counterparts that were more advanced and with a stronger capital base during their post-war economic reconstructions. Thus, to generate sufficient capital to finance new business start-ups or to expand existing businesses, banking institutions were emphasized. The banks' deposit-taking function proved to be ideal in quickly gathering small savings into large pools of capital that were made available for large borrowings. In this way, given the path-dependent nature of these institutions, the consolidation of a bank-based financial system in countries such as Germany, Japan and Korea was locked in at the early stage of economic catch-up. These countries continue to have bank-based financial systems as their primary source of corporate finance.

The consequences of level of capital accumulation have obvious implications for the type of corporate structure and behavior that evolves. For example, like Germany and

Japan, Korea has a bank-based financial system. Corporate financial structure is characterized by high debt–equity ratios as corporations have to borrow heavily, and at times they borrow excessively from the loan market. On the other hand, Anglo-Saxon countries such as the UK and the US that were early movers in the industrial revolution have been able to build well-developed equity markets supported by their early capital accumulation. In these countries the debt–equity ratio is kept low, and management transparency and respect for shareholder rights are the norms of corporate behavior. Table 8.2 corroborates our argument. Corporations in the UK and the US rely on securities markets for more than two-thirds of corporate finance, whereas corporations in Germany, Japan and Korea acquire funds from banks to finance relatively large parts of their investment projects. Furthermore, the dependence of Korean companies on the equity market was a mere 17.3 per cent in 1999, which is the lowest among the countries studied and indicates that Korean equity markets are rather thin and shallow.

*Table 8.2 Pattern of Corporate Finance for Selected Countries, 1999*[a]

(%)

| Countries | Securities Markets | | | Loan Markets |
|---|---|---|---|---|
| | | Equities | Bonds[b] | |
| Germany | 56.6 | 54.3 | 1.3 | 33.3 |
| Japan | 43.1 | 33.8 | 9.3 | 38.8 |
| Korea[c] | 43.9 | 17.3 | 26.6 | 32.1 |
| UK | 76.4 | 70.0 | 6.4 | 18.6 |
| US | 74.8 | 66.6 | 8.2 | 12.1 |

*Notes*:
a Expressed as shares of the total liability of private non-financial corporations.
b Corporate bonds and non-equity securities.
c In Korea, large corporations issued massive amounts of corporate bonds in 1998 to avoid liquidity problems as soon as the interest rates were reduced to a single-digit figure.

*Sources*: Bank of Japan (2000) and Bank of Korea (2002).

## 4. VISION FOR FINANCIAL REFORM

A future vision for a country's financial system must consider the following two points. First, the path-dependence of the economic system should never be ignored. There is currently much pressure for financial institutions to adhere to 'global standards', that are often announced as prerequisite for achieving global competitiveness. Leaving aside the issue of which is better – market-based versus bank-based financial systems – it must be remembered that changing quickly from one system to another is never an easy task, precisely because the financial system is constrained by broader institutional factors as explained above. To switch to another system may incur huge transaction costs or even prove to be inefficient, particularly if the new system is incompatible with the country's culture, business conventions and other institutional factors.

Second, it must be assessed carefully whether differences in financial systems are a critical determinant of national economic performance. Controversy over the role of a financial system in strengthening economic performance has a long history.[4] Although the merits and demerits of the Anglo-Saxon market-based system versus the German and Japanese bank-based system have been discussed extensively in the economics literature, there is still no consensus on which is the better financial system.[5] Some authors, however, find that compared to individual investors, banks enjoy economies of scale in monitoring firms (Diamond 1984) and are important particularly when making loans requires costly information on the quality of investment projects. On the other hand, securities markets have the advantage of aggregating the diverse views of market participants (Allen 1993) and as such are ideal supporters of corporate investments on which there exist a variety of expectations. What this means is that each corporate investment may be systematically associated with a particular form of finance, and it is not appropriate to insist on a particular financial system as the 'correct' one guaranteeing better economic performance. In any case, as we have already seen in section 3, some successful countries have a market-based financial system, while others have a bank-based financial system. This implies that it is not necessarily the case that one system is a superior system that should be pursued by all countries.

We think it better that Korea adopt a financial system to encompass merits of both the market-based and bank-based systems, and we argue that this kind of accommodating system may be achieved by taking an open-ended policy which allows the two financial systems to coexist and complement each other. Corporations, as a result, will have added freedom to choose between the broad range of financing sources. In this context, considering Korea's historical heritage as well as the current status of financial markets and institutions, it is a good strategy to allow a universal banking system, where the commercial banks continue their vital function in the loan market, and at the same time become important players in the securities market as well, by extending their business realm to that of investment banks. This point will be elaborated in the next section. Furthermore, since the financial system is exogenous to the firm and critically affects corporate activities, as has been explained, it is necessary that an efficient financial system be allowed to evolve through an interactive process between financial markets and corporate strategies. Such a system should create a stable and sound corporate sector, as well as promote economic prosperity in line with the Korea-specific cultural, social, political and legal traditions.

Figure 8.1 summarizes our vision for Korea's financial system. Since individual investors in Korea's securities market play only a limited role due to their investment behavior marked by short-term outlook and often neglect investment risk, they are better off by engaging indirectly in the securities market through universal banks rather than investing directly. That is, universal banks should become major players in the securities market as well as in the loan market. In this way banks will add disciplinary market pressure to firms by monitoring their behavior on behalf of individual investors in financial markets. However, uncertainty about the prospects of the global financial regime makes it increasingly difficult, and undesirable, for policymakers to decide *ex ante* which financial systems and corporate forms are preferable, and hence we suggest a policy that is open-ended on the future financial system. On the corporate side, both the bank-based corporate form, which depends mainly on bank loans as in the case of German firms, and the market-based corporate form, which finances investment projects usually through the securities market as with the Anglo-American firms, should be free to evolve together, according to the characteristics of their management strategies as well as management environment including corporate cultures. We believe the best form of financial and corporate structures will evolve under the auspices of competition for survival.

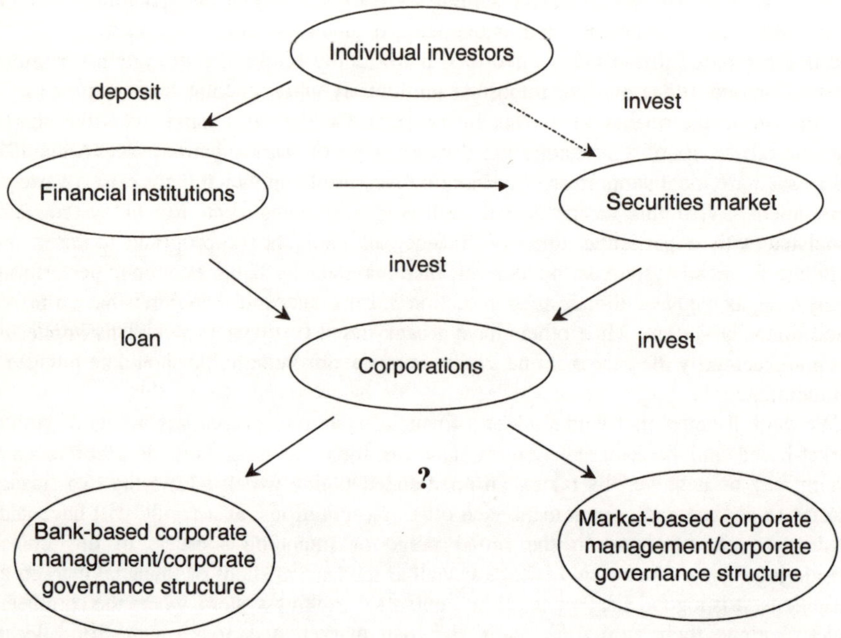


*Note*: ----▶ indicates that individual investors play a limited role in securities markets.

*Figure 8.1 Vision for Korean Financial System*

# 5. GUIDELINES FOR KOREA'S FINANCIAL REFORM

What specific policy innovations are needed to implement this vision for Korea's financial system given the Korea-specific institutional environment? Two areas need to be emphasized: the role of the securities market and the role of banks. Both institutions are important in supporting and monitoring corporate decisions. A prerequisite to any further reform, whether financial or corporate, is institutional reform. In this section, we will discuss the specialized versus universal banking systems, deregulation and promotion of competition, and prudential regulations.

## 5.1 Improving the Institutional Background for the Financial System

As mentioned in section 3, it is imperative that we fully understand Korea's specific economic environment, particularly those factors concerning financial markets and corporations. In devising appropriate policy measures towards this vision, we need to identify constraints as well as opportunities for the smooth transition to an optimal financial system. It is important to realize that institutional factors including Korea's cultural and legal traditions, which are deeply rooted in the government's past development strategy, have helped to shape the underdeveloped financial system. We have already mentioned that government intervention in the decision-making process of financial institutions and in the financial markets as a whole has hindered the growth of a market-oriented financial system. It is necessary, therefore, to upgrade financial market institutions by ensuring more protection for investors, requiring transparent accounting and management standards for corporations, reducing government intervention and stabilizing the government's financial policies. By enforcing global market rules upon investors, the government is indirectly correcting investors' attitude and behavior and corporations' management behavior. Investors should find that it is hopeless to rely on government intervention in the financial market so they should take full responsibility for their decisions and accept the consequences, whether favorable or otherwise. Similarly, corporations will learn that they cannot survive without conforming to global market rules. Through such reforms, Korea's financial system should come to closer synchronicity with 'global standards', although history teaches us that restructuring of this magnitude will require a long gestation period.

## 5.2 Universal Banking System as a Main Instrument towards the Vision

In section 4, we proposed a universal banking system as a main instrument to realize the vision we propose for Korea's future financial system. The main thrust of our vision is to create a system such that the merits of both the market-based and bank-based financial systems are accommodated. The universal banking system not only allows this but has many other advantages as well.

First, the universal banking system can help commercial banks to become major investors in the securities market. As mentioned above, many of the weaknesses in Korea's financial system derive from its heavy leaning towards bank loans and a lax prudential regulatory framework. This is why Korea is being urged to develop a stronger securities market as an important alternative source of corporate finance to complement bank loans. There is still much to be done in developing the securities market. It is still shallow so that insiders often manipulate stock prices. Since individual investors generally have a myopic view of investments, are less prepared to accept investment losses, and have widely dispersed investments, they do not constitute a solid demand base in securities markets. Thus, to establish a fully functioning securities market for the corporate sector, it will be appropriate to encourage the strong participation in the securities market of institutional investors such as commercial banks, together with individual investors.

Second, the profitability of banks can be improved by a universal banking system. With strong global competition, it is increasingly difficult for banks to maintain their competitive edge simply by operating on the margins of customer services for deposits and loans. Furthermore, regulations on assets and liability management more often than not worsen the profitability of the banking sector. A variety of investment opportunities gives depositors strong incentives to find better places for their investment than traditional deposits such as in the commercial paper market, finance companies and mutual funds.

However, a universal banking system impels banks to enhance their competitiveness against domestic and global competitors by providing a rich array of financial products and services and by holding a variety of claims such as demand deposits, subordinated debt, equity, securitization back-up, and swap counter-party positions. Financial services for off-balance sheet items, such as securitization and underwriting, will also help banks to expand their customer base.

The universal banking system has further merits and advantages. For example, a bank can enhance its risk position by diversifying its asset holdings through new activities. More importantly, there are strong economies of scope in combining financial products within a financial institution.[6] These economies of scope arise from savings on the costs of selling a range of financial products to a client. There are also economies of scale in information gathering and monitoring because a bank keeps track of a borrowing firm's performance when it extends a loan, with which it can easily evaluate the risk and potential of customers. As banks have far greater capacity than individual investors to monitor corporate activities and gather information about individual firms, they can make financial investment decisions and control investment risk in more sophisticated ways. Individual investors will increasingly depend on bank products to utilize their savings, while businesses will search for optimal financing not only from banks but also from the securities market. Consequently, banks will play a major role not only as lenders in the loan markets, but also as investors in the securities market.

The US and UK have expedited financial deregulation since the 1980s, and Korea has followed this trend in the 1990s by providing commercial banks with more opportunities to expand their business activities. Yet financial deregulation has not made commercial banks major institutions in the securities market. Commercial banks can make investment in the stock market in a very limited way and are usually prohibited from direct engagement in stock business such as the brokerage and underwriting of equities.[7] Instead of direct engagement a commercial bank is allowed to deal indirectly with securities through establishing a securities firm as a subsidiary. But it is almost impossible for banks to obtain economies of scope because, with the strict regulations on their involvement, there is hardly any interaction between the mother bank and its securities firm, even in areas such as information sharing, financial-product innovation, promotion and sales, and cross-over of directors. This means that in practice Korea's banking system is still no more than a specialized banking system.

On the other hand, strict regulations on the securities industry also prevent even the securities firms from performing many genuine functions of investment banks. For example, a securities firm can engage in dealing, brokerage and underwriting but cannot handle consulting business, trust funds, and most futures and options (the exception is the Kospi200 index futures and options), which are assigned to the subsidiaries of the securities firms. In particular, the debarring of trust funds from securities firms has diminished the firms' capability as institutional investors, and therefore hampered the development of Korea's securities markets.

We argue that putting into place a universal banking system should augment Korea's financial sector. This enables the smooth evolution towards an optimal financial system by allowing banks to play a more active role in the securities markets by participating as institutional investors to complement individual investors. In the major OECD countries a universal banking system has been adopted in various forms. Introduction of the universal banking system in Korea can be a major step to enhance not only the competitiveness of domestic banks but also the role of the securities market in the financial system. A fully fledged universal banking system can best be developed through in-house integration of commercial banks and investment banks, so that banks can participate directly in the securities market. Further deregulation of Korea's securities industry will also be required to help complete the establishment of this system.

While we have considered the strengths of the universal banking system, we must also take account of its weaknesses. Some observers criticize the universal banking system on the ground that involvement in securities services can increase the risk of banks' portfolios. However, this may not be a persuasive claim since buying equity in a firm is equivalent to buying a call option and selling a loan to a firm is equivalent to selling a put option with the firm's value as the underlying asset.

Simply implementing a universal banking system is not enough to ensure desired outcomes. The universal banking system needs to be supplemented by policies that improve its efficiency and stability. To achieve maximum efficiency, it will be important to deregulate banking ownership and relax legal entry requirements to generate competitive pressure within the industry. Stability, on the other hand, requires that sophisticated prudential regulation be upheld strictly, to avert moral hazard behavior. These two issues of efficiency and stability are discussed further as we examine the promotion of competition and prudential regulation in the following two sections.

## 5.3 Deregulation and Promotion of Competition in the Financial Sector

The autonomy of commercial banks should be established and maintained. There have been small steps in the past to increase the autonomy of banks, such as selling the government's shares in all major commercial banks and privatization of special government-owned banks. Since the outbreak of the financial crisis in 1997, however, the government has injected a huge amount of public funds into banks required for financial and corporate restructuring. As a result, the government's shares exceed 70 per cent of shareholding in many banks, and in effect put these banks on the verge of being nationalized. Under these circumstances we can expect moral hazard to continue unabated; when banks are in deep financial trouble, it is highly probable that the government will have little choice but to bail them out with public funds. This relapse into *de facto* nationalization of commercial banks should be corrected promptly to restore the autonomy of commercial banks by promptly selling off the government's shares in these banks.

It will also be necessary to relax bank ownership regulations so that non-financial firms can become major shareholders of commercial banks.[8] Deregulation of bank ownership may not only reduce moral hazard behavior caused by the currently dispersed ownership structure (except for government's shares), but may also ward off future government intervention in bank management. It is important, however, that the deregulation of bank ownership is accompanied by establishment of a well-defined and effective prudential regulatory system because the ownership of non-financial firms could induce unsound loan concentration. Thus, after deregulating ownership of financial institutions the government should gradually move away from intervening in bank management such as selection of CEOs, a typical case that is usually loaded with political incentives.

Privatizing government-owned banks should also be more rigorously pursued, such as the Korea Development Bank, which has played a major role in providing liquidity to insolvent companies in 2001 by buying their bonds in the form of collateralized bond obligation (CBO) and collateralized loan obligation (CLO). Such government intervention in financial markets can only increase moral hazard, which encourages borrowers to take greater risks than otherwise – particularly in the Korean case – rendering the market discipline of financial markets less meaningful, and thereby contributing to economic inefficiencies.

Increasing competition improves economic efficiency. The banking sector is no exception to this rule. Competition can be stimulated by lowering legal barriers on entry into the banking industry and by helping markets to provide reliable signals. In Korea, legal entry barriers imposed on the banking industry appear to be excessive. For example, a high level of capital is required to enter the banking industry, which makes the incumbent banks enjoy charter rent for almost nothing. Lowering the minimum capital requirement to the level of EU countries or of the US[9] should induce competitive pressure from potential entrants and force the established banks to make more efficient investments decisions than otherwise. To make this arrangement effective, the fit-and-proper test must be kept to a minimum so that market entry is not swayed by political incentives. Due to economic barriers such as investment in physical capital, branches, reputation and other intangible assets, the banking industry may not be highly competitive in the usual sense. However, provided that economic barriers can generate economic profits, the banking industry with a minimal legal entry barrier can be thought of as a contestable industry. In a contestable industry, mergers and acquisitions should not be regulated and competition should be the principal guide. In this respect, deregulation of bank ownership is also an important factor in maintaining competitiveness in the banking industry.

## 5.4 Prudential Regulation to Minimize Risks in a Universal Banking System

A universal banking system may aggravate the inherent instability of a commercial banking system by allowing banks to undertake riskier activities. Competition may also increase the instability of a financial system by encouraging banks to choose risky strategies to attract customers. It is therefore important to provide well-designed safety nets to keep the financial system stable. Deposit insurance that was introduced in 2001 is serving to help stabilize the banking sector. However, since banks are charged flat-rate insurance premiums regardless of their lending risks, they have no disincentive to taking on more risk. Therefore we propose a risk-based insurance premium for banks to handle moral-hazard problems arising from the flat-rate insurance premium. Several studies have considered the efficacy of deposit insurance pricing.[10] Nonetheless, it is important to note that a differentiated premium provides a necessary signal about the quality of a bank and helps to induce competition between banks, particularly when depositors are sensitive to these signals.

A flat-rate capital-adequacy ratio applied to all banks uniformly is another instrument commonly used to ensure the stability of the banking system. This requires that banks reduce leverage and reshuffle their portfolio of assets. Although this measure was introduced in Korea prior to the 1997 financial crisis, only after the crisis was it strictly enforced by the supervisory agency. Nonetheless, it turns out that the capital-adequacy ratio is ill-founded and seems to ignore benefits from diversification. The risk weights are too simple and do not reflect risk adequately, and banks have found ways through financial innovation to reduce capital-adequacy ratios without necessarily improving their soundness. The Bank for International Settlements (BIS) has recognized these shortcomings in 2001 and put forward a new version of the capital-adequacy program, which suggests that a supervisory agency attach to a bank a sophisticated risk-sensitive capital requirement based on a proper evaluation of risks. Korea plans to adopt this sophisticated risk-sensitive capital-adequacy program in the near future.

Finally, because prompt corrective action is important, the bank regulatory and supervisory agency needs to be sufficiently independent from the political process, which tends to hide problems and encourage regulatory forbearance.

## 6. CONCLUDING REMARKS

It is widely recognized that banks and other financial institutions perform useful functions not only in terms of lending, but also by providing filtering services that weed out unsound projects. As the major source of finance in Korea, banks have purportedly served to help promote industrialization. Because the government has featured heavily in the banks' managerial decisions, often deciding on loan allocations, staff appointments and the like, Korean banks have hardly exercised their vital monitoring function nor have they exerted disciplinary pressure on corporations.

In this chapter, we explained why different countries have different financial systems. In particular, we traced and contrasted the evolution of financial systems in Anglo-Saxon countries where securities markets feature heavily, with financial systems of the more bank-dominant economies like Germany, Japan and Korea. By adopting the new-institutional economics perspective, we have also shown the intricate relationship between financial systems, corporate behavior, and the less immediately observable institutional variables such as government policy, legal systems, culture, tradition and so on. In particular, we find that exogenous factors should not be ignored in the design of any reform plan, since these act as constraints on the extent to which reform can take place. The inherent weaknesses of Korea's financial system became clear with the outbreak of the financial crisis in 1997, after which the Korean government together with international institutions such as the IMF set up various reform programs. Securities markets, reminiscent of the Anglo-Saxon economies, are increasingly being emphasized as an alternative source of corporate finance. Imposing 'global standards', although welcome to a certain degree, is not the only solution to Korea's current financial problems. Instead we have proposed an open-ended policy.

Financial systems nonetheless should not be upgraded blindly. Maximizing the effectiveness of any reform effort requires proper understanding of the country-specific institutional environment, and the interactions between various financial-market players. Our model here suggests emphatically that the ultimate configuration of a country's financial structure will be determined by the country-specific institutional environment and market factors including the production technologies of financial firms, the size of financial markets, and the interactive process of financial markets and corporations.[11] Indeed, it cannot be overemphasized that the ultimate form of the financial system and corporate structure of any country will evolve through competition for survival in the global environment.

In the context of the Korea-specific institutional environment, we suggest that the universal banking system be introduced to complement the current specialized banking system. In this way banks will play a major role not only as lenders in the loan market but also as investors in the securities market. Autonomy in financial institutions must be restored and competition must be allowed to improve the overall efficiency of Korea's financial sector. Finally, an effective prudential regulatory system should be firmly put in place and upheld to enhance the stability of the financial market.

## NOTES

1. We will provide a comparative analysis of the bank-based versus market-based financial and corporate systems in the next section and argue in section 4 that one system is not necessarily superior to the other such that all countries should pursue it.
2. This section is adapted from Jwa (2001).
3. See, for example, Allen and Gale (2000).
4. An overview of the literature on the influence of financial, corporate and legal systems on economic performance can be found in Carlin and Mayer (2000).
5. Around the late 1980s, it was widely held that the Japanese bank-based financial system was superior to the Anglo-Saxon market-based financial system, given that at that time the Japanese economy had grown faster than the US or UK economies. Early in the 2000s, the situation is reversed after the long recession in Japan during the 1990s.
6. Using international data, Jwa and Lee (2001) find that a financial firm is more likely to choose business diversification as its firm size expands or the financial market is larger, and supports our vision that the universal banking system should be adopted.
7. Regulations on banks stipulate that a bank can invest up to 60 per cent of its capital in securities and can issue bonds worth up to three times its capital. A bank cannot acquire more than 15 per cent of a firm's total shares that have voting rights.
8. In Korea, an individual investor can acquire only up to 10 per cent of shares in a commercial bank and for a non-financial firm up to 4 per cent. Further acquisition is possible with the permission of the regulatory authority, although this is generally not given. We hold that Korea's financial system should adopt new ownership regulations, that correspond with the regulations of advanced OECD countries. These countries do not impose limits on bank ownership *ex ante*. For example, Germany requires only that a major shareholder report to the central bank when their share exceeds the thresholds of 20 per cent, 33 per cent and 50 per cent of the shareholding. The federal regulations of the US are somewhat stricter than those of Germany, but they are much more liberal than those of Korea.
9. For example, in the US and the UK, the minimum capital requirements are $1 million and £1 million respectively, while the Korean requirement is 100 billion won (about 80 times that of the US).
10. See, for example, Chan, et al. (1992) and Kupiec and O'Brien (1998).
11. For example, when market demand expands, financial production activities with economies of scale tend to be specialized through the advantage of mass production leading to establishment of the specialized banking system. However, when market demand is too low to realize the advantage of economies of scale, financial activities with economies of scale and economies of scope are likely to become integrated with other financial production activities. See Jwa (2001) for details.

## REFERENCES

Allen, F. (1993), 'Stock markets and resource allocation', in C. Mayer and X. Vives (eds), *Capital Markets and Financial Intermediation*, Cambridge University Press.

Allen, F. and D. Gale (2000), 'Comparing financial systems', MIT Press.

Bank of Japan (2000), *Comparative Economic and Financial Statistics, Japan and Other Major Countries.*

Bank of Korea (2002), *Monthly Bulletin* (in Korean), January.

Calomiris, C.W. (1988), 'Universal banking "American-style"', *Journal of Institutional Theoretical Economics*, **154**, 44–57.

Carlin, W. and C. Mayer (2000), 'How do financial systems affect economic performance?', in X. Vives (ed.), *Corporate Governance: Theoretical and Empirical Perspectives*, Cambridge University Press.

Chan, Y.S., S.I. Greenbaum and A.V. Thakor (1992), 'Is fairly priced deposit insurance possible?', *Journal of Finance*, **47**, 227–45.

Diamond, D. (1984), 'Financial intermediation as delegated monitoring', *Review of Economic Studies*, **51**, 393–414.

Jwa, S. (2001), *A New Paradigm for Korea's Economic Development: From Government Control to Market Economy*, London: Palgrave.

Jwa, S. (2002), *The Evolution of Large Corporations in Korea: A New-Institutional Economics Perspective of the Chaebol*, London: Edward Elgar Publishing.

Jwa, S. and I. Lee (2001), *International Comparison of Diversification in the Financial Sector and its Implication*, Korea Economic Research Institute (in Korean).

Jwa, S. and I.K. Lee (eds) (2000), *Korean Chaebol in Transition: Road Ahead and Agenda*, Korea Economic Research Institution.

Kupiec, P.H. and J.M. O'Brien (1998), 'Deposit Insurance, Bank Incentives, and the Design of Regulatory Policy', *Federal Reserve Board, Finance and Economics Discussion Series*, Working Paper No. 10.

Mishkin, F.S. (2000), 'Financial markets reform', in A.O. Krueger (ed.), *Economic Policy Reform*, Chicago: University of Chicago Press.

Santos, J.A.C. (2000), 'Bank capital regulation in contemporary banking theory: A review of the literature', *BIS Working Paper No. 90.*

Vives, X. (1991), 'Banking competition and European integration', in A. Giovannini and C. Mayer (eds), *European Financial Integration*, Cambridge University Press.

World Bank and IMF, Global Banking Law Database (http://www.gbld.org).

# Part IV

# Strategy for Primary Industries

# 9. Korea's Agricultural Strategy in the Globalization Era

**Chul Ho Yoo**

## 1. INTRODUCTION

The agricultural sector in Korea faces unprecedented challenges for survival. The sector has been shrinking in terms of its contribution to GDP since the 1970s with rapid industrialization of the economy, and from around the mid-1990s in particular, Korean agriculture has suffered from globalization. The influences of globalization upon domestic agriculture in Korea promote both liberalizing the domestic agricultural market and strengthening the international competitiveness of domestic agriculture. Both of these increase the difficulties of the Koreans whose livelihood depend on this sector.

In accordance with the mandate on market opening for all agricultural products under the Uruguay Round Agreement on Agriculture in 1994, the volume of Korea's agricultural imports continued to increase through the second half of the 1990s, which helped to arouse a sense of crisis among people in the rural sector about the potential for grave damage to the agricultural sector as a whole. Signs of the gravity of damage have become ever clearer as evident in the accelerated decrease in the number of farms and the more volatile price fluctuations of some agricultural products. Meanwhile the Korean government has strengthened efforts to restructure the sector to make it more competitive in the global market.

The ongoing World Trade Organization negotiations on agriculture are expected to deal further blows to Korea because many of the countries exporting agricultural products are powerful nations and they are expected to demand wider market access through phasing out both trade barriers and tariffs. There is also serious concern that China's accession to the WTO with the launch of the Doha Development Agenda in November 2001 will help to cripple the Korean agricultural sector by enabling the indiscriminate flow of Chinese agricultural products into the country. China, which is geographically next door to Korea, is known to be preparing to export rice, the Korean staple food grain and hence the nation's most sensitive product politically and economically. Because of this sensitivity, the Korean government continues to try to protect domestic rice production in particular, among all products in the agricultural trade negotiations. China also has recognized potential to export high value-added agricultural products such as fresh vegetables and fruits at low prices. China's exports to Korea will directly challenge Korea's main agricultural policy target of producing high value-added products as a way of increasing agricultural competitiveness in the era of globalization.

How will Korea meet the challenges arising from these drastic changes in the global and regional agricultural environment? This chapter begins with an overview of development in Korea's agricultural sector during the period 1990–2000, a decade of major and unforeseen change that has challenged the very survival of this sector. It then examines strategies for strengthening the competitiveness of the Korean agricultural sector to meet the demands that globalization has imposed. The chapter then turns to consider the implications for Korean agriculture of the negotiations for freer trade of agricultural products at the WTO round at Doha in 2001. This discussion not only provides an overview of Korean agriculture but will also shed some light on its future development.

## 2. AGRICULTURE IN TRANSITION (1990–2000)

The 1990s were a period of transition across virtually all aspects of Korean agriculture. The land available for agriculture has declined since the 1970s as the direct result of increasing demands for land for industrial–residential purposes in the course of rapid industrialization. Korea's total land area was 9.9 million hectares in 2000. Of the total land mass, the land utilized for agriculture was only 1.9 million hectares or 19 per cent in 2000, a 17.8 per cent reduction from the 2.3 million hectares in 1970 (MAF 2002). Wet land or paddy used mostly for the production of rice accounted for 60.8 per cent of the land under cultivation in 2000. The remaining cultivated land was used for dry-land cereal crops, fruits and vegetable.

Along with the reduction in land for agricultural use, the intensity of usage also declined remarkably from a labor shortage problem in rural areas as young workers migrated to urban and industrial areas. The total cultivated acreage decreased from 3.3 million hectares in 1970 to 2.1 million hectares in 2000, a decrease of 35.7 per cent (Table 9.1), while, as indicated above, land available for agriculture declined from 2.3 million hectares to 1.9 million hectares over the same period.

Despite the negative impacts of industrialization, the total value of agricultural products grew from the 1970s. Nevertheless, this growth rate was far behind the growth rate of the overall economy. As shown in Table 9.2, during the 1990s the value of agricultural products in current prices increased by 5.5 per cent per year from 17.7 trillion won in 1990 to 31.8 trillion won (or $28.1 billion) in 2000. During the same period, the value added in agriculture at current prices increased from 12.8 trillion won to 20.6 trillion won, or a 4.7 per cent average annual growth rate, while the GDP of the Korean economy grew at an annual rate of 11.2 per cent during this period. As a result, the contribution of agriculture to GDP has declined over time to 4 per cent in 2000 (NSO 2001). This relative decline in the contribution of agriculture to the national economy reflects the difficulty faced by the Korean agricultural sector.

The composition of agricultural products has also changed over time. Livestock's proportion of agricultural products by value increased at the expense of crops. The former increased from 22 per cent to 25.5 per cent over the 1990–2000 period, while the latter decreased from 78 per cent to 74.5 per cent. As for the composition of crops by value in 2000, rice took the lion's share of 33 per cent, followed by vegetables with 21.1 per cent, fruits with 8.1 per cent, and other crops including oil crops, Chinese herbs, and horticultural products with 12.4 per cent. Among the commodity groups of minor proportions in value, horticultural products showed a remarkable increase in value; it more than doubled during the 1990–2000 period, from 239 billion won to 539 billion won (MAF 2002).

*Table 9.1 Changes in the Acreage of Major Crops Produced, 1990–2000*

| | 1990 | 1991 | 1992 | 1993 | 1994 | 1995 | 1996 | 1997 | 1998 | 1999 | 2000 |
|---|---|---|---|---|---|---|---|---|---|---|---|
| Total cultivated area ('000 hectares) | 2409 | 2332 | 2260 | 2285 | 2205 | 2197 | 2142 | 2097 | 2118 | 2116 | 2098 |
| Food crops[a] (%) | 69.3 | 67.0 | 65.4 | 64.2 | 63.6 | 61.3 | 62.6 | 62.7 | 62.9 | 62.7 | 62.8 |
| rice | 51.6 | 51.8 | 51.2 | 49.7 | 50.0 | 48.1 | 49.0 | 50.2 | 50.0 | 50.4 | 51.1 |
| barley | 6.6 | 5.5 | 4.6 | 5.1 | 3.9 | 4.1 | 4.4 | 3.3 | 4.0 | 3.6 | 3.2 |
| others[b] | 11.0 | 9.7 | 9.7 | 9.4 | 9.8 | 9.2 | 9.1 | 9.2 | 8.9 | 8.7 | 8.5 |
| Fruits(%) | 5.5 | 5.9 | 6.5 | 6.7 | 7.4 | 7.9 | 8.0 | 8.4 | 8.3 | 8.2 | 8.2 |
| Vegetables(%) | 11.5 | 12.8 | 17.5 | 13.9 | 13.7 | 18.4 | 18.2 | 17.4 | 17.0 | 17.8 | 18.4 |
| Others[c](%) | 13.7 | 14.3 | 14.7 | 15.1 | 15.3 | 12.4 | 12.4 | 11.5 | 11.8 | 11.3 | 10.6 |

*Notes:*
a Due to rounding errors, sums of components are not equal to the totals for some years
b Pulses, potatoes and grains such as wheat and sorghum.
c Including horticultural plants, mulberry trees, oil crops, and Chinese herbs

*Source*: Ministry of Agriculture and Forestry, *Major Statistics of Agriculture and Forestry 2001 and 2002*, Seoul: Ministry of Agriculture and Forestry.

Another facet of the transition of Korean agriculture is the decrease in the number of farm households and in the farm population. As shown in Table 9.2, the number of farm households decreased by 21.7 per cent from 1.767 million in 1990 to 1.384 million in 2000, and farm population decreased by 39.5 per cent from 6.661 million to 4.032 million during this period. During the same period, the proportion of the number of farm households to the total household number decreased by 21.7 per cent to 9.7 per cent, and the proportion of farm population to total population by 39.5 per cent to 8.7 per cent, respectively.[1] This decline in the population reflects the decline in the agricultural sector as farmers have emigrated to urban and industrial areas in search of a different source of income. As a result of decreases in the number of farm households, the average size of arable land per farm increased to 1.4 hectares, even though the total cultivated land decreased substantially (Table 9.2).

The income of farm households consists of agricultural income, off-farm income and government subsidy payment. As shown in Table 9.2, the proportion of agricultural income declined from 56.8 per cent in 1990 to only 47.2 per cent in 2000. This indicates that farmers may not survive on agricultural activities alone. The situation represents a paradox, since to maximize agricultural productivity, it is better for full-time farmers to concentrate on agricultural production exclusively. However, agricultural production has become in effect a sideline job for farmers, a situation that works against achieving a high degree of productivity and competitiveness in agriculture.[2]

*Table 9.2 Changes in Major Indicators of Agricultural Production, 1990–2000*

| | 1990 | 1991 | 1992 | 1993 | 1994 | 1995 | 1996 | 1997 | 1998 | 1999 | 2000 |
|---|---|---|---|---|---|---|---|---|---|---|---|
| Value of agricultural products (trillion won in current price) | 17.7 | 19.2 | 20.4 | 20.7 | 23.4 | 25.9 | 28.1 | 29.3 | 29.6 | 31.9 | 31.8 |
| Cultivation[a] | 13.8 | 14.7 | 15.8 | 15.7 | 18.1 | 19.9 | 21.2 | 22.4 | 22.1 | 23.9 | 23.7 |
| Livestock[b] | 3.9 | 4.4 | 4.6 | 5.1 | 5.3 | 6.0 | 6.9 | 6.9 | 7.5 | 7.9 | 8.1 |
| GDP share of agriculture (%) | 7.2 | 6.4 | 6.3 | 5.6 | 6.1 | 5.2 | 4.9 | 4.5 | 4.2 | 4.3 | 4.0 |
| Growth rate of GDP (%) | 9.0 | 9.2 | 5.4 | 5.5 | 8.3 | 8.9 | 6.8 | 5.0 | -6.7 | 10.9 | 9.3 |
| Growth rate of value added in agriculture (%) | –6.7 | 3.3 | 10.4 | -3.9 | -0.1 | 9.4 | 4.2 | 4.3 | -6.5 | 6.6 | 3.2 |
| Number of farms ('000) | 1767 | 1702 | 1641 | 1592 | 1558 | 1501 | 1480 | 1440 | 1413 | 1382 | 1384 |
| Farm population ('000) | 6661 | 6068 | 5707 | 5407 | 5167 | 4851 | 4692 | 4468 | 4400 | 4210 | 4032 |
| Average farm income ('000 won) | 11.0 | 13.1 | 14.5 | 16.9 | 20.3 | 21.8 | 23.3 | 23.5 | 20.5 | 22.3 | 23.1 |
| Share of agricultural income in total farm income (%) | 56.8 | 53.7 | 50.7 | 49.8 | 50.8 | 48.0 | 46.5 | 43.4 | 43.7 | 47.3 | 47.2 |
| Average size of farm land (hectare) | 1.2 | 1.2 | 1.3 | 1.3 | 1.3 | 1.3 | 1.3 | 1.3 | 1.4 | 1.4 | 1.4 |
| Rice paddy (hectare) | 0.8 | 0.8 | 0.8 | 0.8 | 0.8 | 0.8 | 0.8 | 0.8 | 0.8 | 0.8 | 0.8 |
| Upland (hectare)[c] | 0.4 | 0.4 | 0.5 | 0.5 | 0.5 | 0.5 | 0.5 | 0.5 | 0.5 | 0.5 | 0.5 |

*Notes*:
a Including oil seeds, medical herbs, horticultural products, mushrooms.
b Including hog, broiler, milk, honey, small animals.
c Due to rounding errors, the sums of components are not equal to the totals for some years.

*Source*: Ministry of Agriculture and Forestry, *Major Statistics of Agriculture and Forestry 2001*.

Allocation of land acreage has also changed over time. As shown in Table 9.1, the acreage proportion for food crops decreased overall during the 1990–2000 period, while the acreage proportion for high-valued crops such as vegetables and fruits increased. The percentage distributions of acreage by crops in 2000 (based on the total cultivated land of 2098 thousand hectares) were: 62.8 per cent food crops (including 51.1 per cent for rice), 18.4 per cent for vegetables, 8.2 per cent for fruits and 10.6 per cent for others (Table 9.1). The change over time in crop mix indicates that Korean farmers have diverting their land and other resources from cereals where demand has decreased to high-priced crops such as fruits and vegetables, for which demand has increased with increased household income.

The pattern of food consumption has changed remarkably over time, forcing corresponding changes in the composition of agricultural products, as observed above. As shown in Table 9.3, expenditures on food by urban households slightly more than doubled from 220 800 won in 1990 to 447 000 won in 2000, while household income increased 2.5 times during the same period. Table 9.3 shows that the proportion of food expenditure on cereals decreased remarkably from 20.3 per cent in 1990 to only 12.7 per cent in 2000. Almost all of the losses discussed here have been taken up by a spectacular increase in one food expenditure category, eating out, which almost doubled from 20.3 per cent of total food consumption in 1990 to 39.4 per cent in 2000. These changes in food expenditure indicate shifts in family eating patterns in the recent past. Over this period the proportions for other foods (meats, dairy products, fish, vegetables and seaweed, fruit and condiments) decreased slightly, even though the absolute amounts of expenditure for these types of food increased remarkably. The trend under way in food expenditure is expected to continue in the foreseeable future with consumers spending less on cereals such as rice and more on foods such as meat and dairy products, fruits and vegetables.

Korea is poorly endowed with agricultural land resources and has to rely heavily on imported grains. Grain production has declined over time, while its consumption has increased, resulting in a declining self-sufficiency rate for grains (including rice, barley, wheat, soybean, corn, pulses and so on) and increased imports. As shown in Table 9.4, over the period from 1990 to 2000, total grain production fell from 7 million tons to 5.9 million tons, while consumption increased from 16.3 million tons to 20 million tons. This resulted in a decrease in the self-sufficiency rate for grains from 43.1 per cent in 1990 to 29.7 per cent 2000. Imports of agricultural products were regarded as inevitable even before settlement of the Uruguay Round Agreement on Agriculture in 1994.

Korea has maintained self-sufficiency in rice, the main staple grain, which has been regarded as the most sensitive food item, politically and economically. Annual production of rice declined substantially over the 1990s from 5.9 million tons in 1990 to 5.3 million tons in 2000 (Table 9.4). This may reflect an adjustment of rice production to its declining consumption. Per capita consumption of rice decreased from 119.6 kg per year in 1990 to 93.6 kg in 2000, a 21.7 per cent decrease over the ten-year period. During this period, overall rice consumption in Korea decreased by 6.1 per cent. Although Korea imported rice in some intervening years in the early 1980s, it has managed to maintain self-sufficiency for rice (Table 9.4).

As shown in Table 9.5, demand for meat, poultry and dairy products has increased with the increase in per capita income. For beef, total consumption increased 2.4 times over the ten-year period from 1990 to 2000. Likewise, per capita consumption of beef more than

*Table 9.3 Monthly Household Expenditure by Food Groups, 1990–2000*

| | 1990 | 1991 | 1992 | 1993 | 1994 | 1995 | 1996 | 1997 | 1998 | 1999 | 2000 |
|---|---|---|---|---|---|---|---|---|---|---|---|
| Household income (1000 won)[a] | 943.3 | 1158.6 | 1356.1 | 1477.8 | 1701.3 | 1911.1 | 2152.7 | 2287.3 | 2133.1 | 2224.7 | 2386.9 |
| Total expenditure (1000 won) | 685.7 | 818.3 | 941.9 | 1021.9 | 1140.4 | 1265.9 | 1426.9 | 1489.5 | 1316.2 | 1478.9 | 1632.3 |
| Expenditure for food (1000 won)[b] | 220.8 | 258.6 | 285.7 | 301.7 | 341.6 | 367.1 | 409.5 | 427.5 | 365.9 | 412.1 | 447.0 |
| (%) | (100.0) | (100.0) | (100.0) | (100.0) | (100.0) | (100.0) | (100.0) | (100.0) | (100.0) | (100.0) | (100.0) |
| Cereals and bread (%) | 20.3 | 18.1 | 16.1 | 15.0 | 13.6 | 12.7 | 13.3 | 12.5 | 13.2 | 13.7 | 12.7 |
| Meats (%) | 11.8 | 12.5 | 12.2 | 11.9 | 11.2 | 11.5 | 10.8 | 10.2 | 10.5 | 10.3 | 10.1 |
| Dairy products % | 5.4 | 5.0 | 5.2 | 5.1 | 4.8 | 4.7 | 4.3 | 4.2 | 5.2 | 4.7 | 4.3 |
| Fish and shellfish (%) | 9.5 | 9.7 | 9.8 | 9.4 | 8.9 | 9.1 | 8.8 | 8.2 | 8.0 | 7.6 | 7.2 |
| Vegetable and seaweed (%) | 11.2 | 11.2 | 10.8 | 10.2 | 10.7 | 9.7 | 9.2 | 9.1 | 9.6 | 9.0 | 8.0 |
| Fruits (%) | 7.1 | 8.0 | 8.0 | 7.4 | 8.2 | 7.8 | 7.4 | 7.2 | 6.1 | 6.2 | 6.1 |
| Condiments[c] (%) | 5.3 | 5.3 | 5.3 | 5.1 | 4.9 | 4.3 | 4.0 | 3.7 | 4.4 | 3.8 | 3.4 |
| Breads for snack and confectionery (%) | 3.7 | 3.8 | 3.9 | 3.7 | 3.7 | 3.7 | 3.6 | 3.6 | 4.3 | 4.2 | 3.9 |
| Tea and drinks including alcoholic beverage (%) | 3.7 | 3.8 | 3.9 | 3.7 | 3.9 | 3.7 | 3.6 | 3.6 | 3.9 | 3.8 | 3.7 |
| Other food items (%) | 1.2 | 1.2 | 1.5 | 1.7 | 1.5 | 1.3 | 1.4 | 1.2 | 1.2 | 1.1 | 1.2 |
| Meals away from home (%) | 20.3 | 21.4 | 23.4 | 26.4 | 28.6 | 31.5 | 33.3 | 36.3 | 33.6 | 35.5 | 39.4 |

*Notes:*

a Monthly household income (national average) in current prices.

b Expenditures for food groups and meals away from home are expressed as percentage of total expenditure for food. Due to rounding error, sums of components (per cent) are not equal to the totals (100 per cent) for some years.

c Including edible oils, red pepper, garlic, soy sauce, etc.

*Source*: National Statistics Office (2001).

*Table 9.4 Balance of Grains, 1990–2000*

| Crop year[a] | 1990 | 1991 | 1992 | 1993 | 1994 | 1995 | 1996 | 1997 | 1998 | 1999 | 2000 |
|---|---|---|---|---|---|---|---|---|---|---|---|
| Production | | | | | | | | | | | |
| (1000 tons) (A) | 7013 | 6563 | 6256 | 6205 | 5465 | 5816 | 5504 | 6031 | 6122 | 5831 | 5931 |
| Rice | 5898 | 5606 | 5384 | 5331 | 4750 | 5060 | 4695 | 5323 | 5450 | 5097 | 5263 |
| Imports (1000 tons) | 10 022 | 11 078 | 12 103 | 12 174 | 13 073 | 14 258 | 14 278 | 14 167 | 13 141 | 13 860 | 14 624 |
| Rice | – | – | – | – | – | – | 115 | – | 75 | 97 | 107 |
| Consumption | | | | | | | | | | | |
| (1000 tons) (B) | 16 282 | 17 467 | 18 322 | 18 336 | 19 530 | 19 974 | 20 867 | 19 814 | 19 469 | 19 858 | 19 961 |
| For food[b] | 9981 | 10 250 | 10 303 | 10 118 | 10 373 | 10 601 | 10 495 | 10 402 | 10 633 | 10 040 | 10 014 |
| rice | 5444 | 5478 | 5524 | 5509 | 5414 | 5557 | 5225 | 5070 | 5216 | 5278 | 5114 |
| For animal feed | 6301 | 7219 | 8019 | 8218 | 9157 | 9373 | 10 372 | 9412 | 8835 | 9106 | 9285 |
| Year-end stock | | | | | | | | | | | |
| (1000 tons) | 3657 | 3831 | 3868 | 4011 | 3019 | 3119 | 2034 | 2418 | 2198 | 2031 | 2625 |
| Rice | 2025 | 2141 | 1999 | 1820 | 1156 | 659 | 244 | 497 | 806 | 722 | 978 |
| (A)/ (B) x 100 (%) | 43.1 | 37.6 | 34.1 | 33.8 | 23.0 | 29.1 | 26.4 | 30.4 | 31.4 | 29.4 | 29.7 |
| Rice | 108.3 | 102.3 | 95.5 | 96.8 | 87.8 | 91.4 | 89.9 | 105.0 | 104.5 | 96.6 | 102.9 |
| Per capita consumption (kg) | 167.0 | 165.7 | 163.8 | 159.2 | 160.9 | 160.5 | 160.2 | 157.9 | 156.4 | 156.9 | 153.3 |
| Rice | 119.6 | 116.3 | 112.9 | 110.2 | 108.3 | 106.5 | 104.9 | 102.4 | 99.2 | 96.9 | 93.6 |

*Notes:*

a Crop year starts 1 November in the previous year and finishes at the end of October in current year.

b Figures along the row refer to all amounts of grains used for other than animal feeds, including for seeds and grain weight loss during storage. They are attained by subtracting the tonnages of grains used for animal feeds from the total consumption for each year.

*Source:* Ministry of Agriculture and Forestry, *Major Statistics of Agriculture and Forestry 2001*, Seoul: Ministry of Agriculture and Forestry.

*Table 9.5 Major Livestock Products, 1990–2000*

| | 1990 | 1991 | 1992 | 1993 | 1994 | 1995 | 1996 | 1997 | 1998 | 1999 | 2000 |
|---|---|---|---|---|---|---|---|---|---|---|---|
| **Beef** | | | | | | | | | | | |
| Total consumption (1000 tons) | 177.0 | 223.3 | 226.9 | 233.0 | 269.8 | 301.2 | 322.9 | 362.0 | 345.5 | 392.7 | 402.4 |
| Domestic production[a] (1000 tons) | 94.9 | 98.5 | 99.6 | 129.6 | 147.3 | 154.7 | 173.7 | 227.7 | 260.1 | 239.7 | 212.4 |
| import (1000 tons) | 82.1 | 124.7 | 127.3 | 103.4 | 122.5 | 146.5 | 149.2 | 134.2 | 85.4 | 153.0 | 190.0 |
| export (1000 tons) | 0.0 | 0.0 | 0.0 | 0.0 | 0.0 | 0.0 | 0.0 | 0.0 | 0.0 | 0.0 | 0.0 |
| Rate of self-sufficiency[b] (%) | 53.6 | 44.1 | 43.9 | 55.6 | 54.6 | 51.4 | 53.8 | 65.4 | 79.0 | 61.1 | 53.2 |
| Per capita consumption (kg) | 4.1 | 5.2 | 5.2 | 5.3 | 6.1 | 6.7 | 7.1 | 7.9 | 7.4 | 8.4 | 8.5 |
| **Pork** | | | | | | | | | | | |
| Total consumption (1000 tons) | 504.8 | 510.8 | 585.0 | 613.2 | 632.2 | 661.7 | 697.0 | 698.3 | 700.8 | 755.4 | 779.9 |
| Domestic production[a] (1000 tons) | 502.2 | 495.1 | 583.1 | 613.2 | 613.9 | 625.0 | 655.0 | 630.7 | 650.8 | 616.1 | 674.0 |
| import (1000 tons) | 2.6 | 15.8 | 1.9 | – | 18.3 | 36.7 | 42.0 | 67.6 | 49.9 | 139.3 | 105.9 |
| export (1000 tons) | 5.8 | 3.6 | 8.5 | 11.3 | 11.1 | 14.3 | 36.9 | 51.6 | 88.3 | 80.3 | 16.2 |
| Rate of self-sufficiency[b] (%) | 100.6 | 97.7 | 102.8 | 102.5 | 98.9 | 96.6 | 99.3 | 100.1 | 106.9 | 94.2 | 93.5 |
| Per capita consumption (kg) | 11.8 | 11.8 | 13.4 | 13.9 | 14.2 | 14.8 | 15.4 | 15.3 | 15.1 | 16.1 | 16.5 |
| **Broiler** | | | | | | | | | | | |
| Total consumption (1000 tons) | 171.7 | 206.5 | 231.5 | 240.8 | 244.6 | 268.1 | 283.3 | 279.0 | 260.4 | 283.0 | 327.3 |
| Domestic production[a] (1000 tons) | 126.2 | 206.5 | 231.5 | 240.8 | 244.6 | 262.3 | 273.5 | 261.0 | 247.4 | 237.0 | 259.8 |
| import (1000 tons) | 0.0 | 0.0 | 0.0 | 0.0 | 0.0 | 5.8 | 9.8 | 18.0 | 11.7 | 46.0 | 67.5 |
| export (1000 tons) | 0.0 | 0.0 | 0.0 | 0.0 | 0.1 | 0.2 | 0.2 | 0.4 | 0.8 | 1.0 | 1.7 |
| Rate of self-sufficiency[b] (%) | 100.0 | 100.0 | 102.3 | 101.6 | 100.7 | 98.7 | 98.4 | 95.0 | 95.3 | 84.1 | 79.9 |
| Per capita consumption (kg) | 4.0 | 4.8 | 5.3 | 5.5 | 5.5 | 6.0 | 6.3 | 6.1 | 5.6 | 6.0 | 6.9 |

*Table 9.5 (continued)*

| | 1990 | 1991 | 1992 | 1993 | 1994 | 1995 | 1996 | 1997 | 1998 | 1999 | 2000 |
|---|---|---|---|---|---|---|---|---|---|---|---|
| **Eggs** | | | | | | | | | | | |
| Total consumption (A) (100 million) | 71.5 | 76.7 | 77.1 | 81.3 | 80.1 | 82.6 | 85.4 | 86.9 | 82.9 | 84.0 | 87.1 |
| Domestic productiona (B) (1000 tons) | 71.5 | 76.7 | 77.1 | 81.3 | 80.1 | 82.6 | 85.4 | 86.9 | 82.9 | 84.0 | 87.1 |
| import (100 million) | 0.0 | 0.0 | 0.0 | 0.0 | 0.0 | 0.0 | 0.0 | 0.0 | 0.0 | 0.0 | 0.0 |
| export (1000 tons) | 0.0 | 0.0 | 0.0 | 0.0 | 0.0 | 0.0 | 0.0 | 0.0 | 0.0 | 0.0 | 0.0 |
| Rate of self-sufficiencyb (%) | 100.0 | 100.0 | 100.0 | 100.0 | 100.0 | 100.0 | 100.0 | 100.0 | 100.0 | 100.0 | 100.0 |
| Per capita consumption (number) | 167 | 178 | 177 | 184 | 181 | 184 | 189 | 189 | 178 | 180 | 187 |
| **Milk and Dairy Products** | | | | | | | | | | | |
| Total consumption (1000 tons) | 1879.0 | 1869.2 | 1920.4 | 1983.7 | 2078.3 | 2143.8 | 2465.4 | 2439.9 | 2286.3 | 2747.4 | 2798.3 |
| Domestic productiona (1000 tons) | 1879.0 | 1698.2 | 1850.7 | 1947.3 | 1917 | 1948.0 | 1990.7 | 1995.4 | 2004.7 | 2291.5 | 2158.7 |
| import (1000 tons) | 0.0 | 171.0 | 69.7 | 139.7 | 131.0 | 195.9 | 474.6 | 444.5 | 281.7 | 455.9 | 639.6 |
| export (1000 tons) | 0.0 | 0.0 | 0.0 | 0.0 | 0.0 | 0.0 | 0.0 | 11.3 | 12.6 | 4.7 | 8.3 |
| Rate of self-sufficiencyb (%) | 101.2 | 94.3 | 98.0 | 95.3 | 94.4 | 93.9 | 85.2 | 85.8 | 92.4 | 85.2 | 82.1 |
| Per capita consumption (kg) | 43.3 | 43.2 | 44.0 | 45.1 | 46.8 | 47.8 | 54.5 | 53.3 | 49.2 | 58.6 | 59.2 |
| Per capita GNP (US$) | 5886 | 6810 | 7183 | 7811 | 8998 | 10 823 | 11 380 | 10 307 | 6742 | 8581 | 9628 |
| Population (10 000) | 4287 | 4330 | 4375 | 4420 | 4464 | 4509 | 4555 | 4599 | 4643 | 4686 | 4728 |

*Notes:*

a The amount consumed from domestic production and from imports during each calendar year. The amounts of imports and exports below the unit are also expressed as 0.0.

b Rate of self-sufficiency (%): (calendar-year consumption from domestic production + exports + year-end stock)/ (calendar-year total consumption) x 100.

*Sources*: Ministry of Agriculture and Forestry, *Major Statistics of Agriculture and Forestry 2001*, Seoul and National Agricultural Cooperative Federation, *Materials on Price, Supply & Demand of Livestock Products 2001*, Seoul.

doubled over the same period. Domestic beef production, although it increased substantially over time, met only about half of domestic consumption. For pork, Korea was self-sufficient over the 1990s, with some exports and imports at times, as domestic consumption and domestic production increased to roughly the same extent. Total consumption of broiler meat also almost doubled over the 1990s. Domestic supply satisfied consumption until the mid-1990s. Since then, however, the self-sufficiency rate declined to 79.9 per cent in 2000. Similarly, total consumption of dairy products increased 1.5 times over the ten-year period and the self-sufficiency rate declined over time to be 82.1 per cent in 2000.

The increased demand for livestock products (meats, dairy products and poultry products) has been met with increased domestic supply of those products using imported feed grains that Korea can not supply domestically. The vast bulk of feed grains has been imported. In 2000, for instance, 8.2 million metric tons, or 97 per cent of total feed grains used (corn, wheat, rye and others) were imported. Imports of feed grains increased with greater demand for meats and dairy products which in turn increased with per capita income. However, as liberalization of the domestic market for all meats and dairy products proceeds, imports of meats and dairy products have increased at the expense of supply from domestic sources. The number of livestock farms and cattle are projected to decrease further with liberalization of the beef market in 2001 (Yoo 2000a: 25). This will decrease the demand for imported feed grains.

As indicated by the low and declining self-sufficiency rates for a number of agricultural products, Korea has to import agricultural and food products to a large extent. Given the limited land resources for agriculture, increases in national income and changes in dietary preferences have forced Korea to rely increasingly on imported agricultural products to meet the rising and diversifying demand for food. As shown in Table 9.6, the value of imported agricultural products increased from $3.8 billion in 1990 to around $6.8 billion in 2000, a 6 per cent annual growth over the period. There were remarkable increments in agricultural imports from 1994 to 1997, mainly due to the opening of the Korean market in the wake of the Uruguay Round of the GATT in 1994. Agricultural imports slumped in 1998 following the financial crisis but recovered substantially in 2000. Major import source countries are the United States, China, Australia, England, Thailand and Canada, and their Korean agricultural market shares in 2000 were, respectively, 34.1 per cent, 16.4 per cent, 11 per cent, 3.1 per cent, 3 per cent and 2.9 per cent (Korea Trade Association 2001). The proportion of livestock imports to total imports increased over time at the expense of that of grains imports. As of 2000, the former was 24.8 per cent with the latter being 75.3 per cent (Table 9.6). Major import items of grains and others include wheat, corn, soybean, pulses, oil seeds, tobacco, fruits and vegetables. Of these, imports of feed grains accounted for a substantial value share of the total agricultural imports.

Imports of livestock products increased rapidly through the 1990s, amounting to $1.7 billion in 2000 (Table 9.6). The major beef-exporting countries to Korea in 2000 were the US, Australia, Canada and New Zealand with market shares of, respectively, 55.3 per cent, 29.6 per cent, 7.8 per cent and 4.7 per cent (Korea Meat Trade Association 2001). Since quantitative restrictions on imports of beef and wholesale and retail of foreign beef were eliminated as of January 2001, it is expected that imports of livestock products will increase further in the future.

*Table 9.6 Trade of Agricultural Products, 1990–2000*

| | 1990 | 1991 | 1992 | 1993 | 1994 | 1995 | 1996 | 1997 | 1998 | 1999 | 2000 |
|---|---|---|---|---|---|---|---|---|---|---|---|
| Imports (US$ million) | 3751 | 4420 | 4767 | 4571 | 5425.7 | 6899.0 | 8152.0 | 7609.1 | 5419.9 | 5926.5 | 6783.3 |
| Grains and others (%) | 88.1 | 84.4 | 85.3 | 88.0 | 82.8 | 82.3 | 84.8 | 82.6 | 86.1 | 79.0 | 75.3 |
| Livestock products (%) | 11.9 | 15.6 | 14.7 | 12.0 | 17.2 | 17.8 | 15.2 | 17.4 | 14.0 | 21.0 | 24.8 |
| Exports (US$ million) | 795 | 756 | 800 | 810 | 951.8 | 1242.2 | 1424.1 | 1507.8 | 1390.7 | 1411.2 | 1277.2 |
| Fruits, vegetables and processed items (%) | 91.4 | 92.2 | 89.5 | 87.5 | 87.8 | 87.5 | 81.7 | 78.8 | 72.1 | 71.1 | 88.7 |
| Livestock products (%) | 8.6 | 7.8 | 10.5 | 12.5 | 12.2 | 12.5 | 18.3 | 21.2 | 27.9 | 28.9 | 11.3 |
| Trade balance (US$ million) | –2956 | –3664 | –3967 | –3761 | –4473.9 | –5656.8 | –6727.9 | –6101.3 | –4029.2 | –4515.3 | –5511.1 |

*Source*: Ministry of Agriculture and Forestry, *Major Statistics of Agriculture and Forestry 2001*, Seoul: Ministry of Agriculture and Forestry.

Korean agricultural exports are largely limited to processed foods and beverages such as confectionery, alcoholic beverages, noodles and coffee. Most of the crude materials for food processing are imported, which restricts the growth of Korea's agricultural exports. Hence, agricultural exports annually have fallen far behind agricultural imports, resulting in a trade deficit in agricultural products. As shown in Table 9.6, the value of agricultural exports was about one-fifth the value of agricultural imports throughout the 1990s. Agricultural exports increased over the 1990s, but at an average rate of 4.8 per cent per year. This was lower than the average growth rate of 6 per cent annually for agricultural imports. As a result, the deficit in agricultural trade increased from just under $3 billion in 1990 to just over $5.5 billion in 2000. This persistent and rising agricultural trade deficit has remained the major concern of Korean agricultural policy.[3]

## 3. CHALLENGES AND STRATEGIES

The Korean agricultural market has been liberalized incrementally under the WTO Agreement on Agriculture. In 2000 the market was liberalized 99.8 per cent in the sense that of the 11 036 types of agricultural products in the market, 11 012 had been made automatic-approval products (MAF 2002). Nonetheless, the countries that export agricultural products still view the Korean agricultural sector as highly protected (Fisher et al. 2001), implying that there is still external pressure on Korea to further open its agricultural market.

Korean agriculture faces a number of challenges. For the nation to meet a growing demand for food, it has to rely increasingly on agricultural imports. Further liberalization of the domestic agricultural market will yield adverse impact on the domestic agricultural sector and the already debilitating rural communities. To minimize the deleterious impact of increasing agricultural imports, Korea will need to undertake structural readjustments in the agricultural sector, painful as they will be. Structural reform can be used to transform the now severely weakened traditional sector into a competitive and viable sector of the economy. In meeting these challenges, a set of specific strategies should be put forward and implemented. Some strategies that have been identified and are being implemented include the following (KREI 1999a: 6).

### 3.1 Improving the Competitiveness of Agricultural Products

Efforts to improve the competitiveness of agricultural products have been under way particularly since the early 1990s. The rising production costs of major agricultural products have been contained in the past few years, and for some products the production costs have fallen. For example, the production cost of rice increased much less over the 1990s than the 1980s, and the production cost of beef cattle actually decreased during the late 1990s (MAF 2000). This may be attributable to the effects of massive government investment for structural improvement of agricultural production, which was begun in the early 1990s in the face of the forced market opening for agricultural products with the then impending settlement of the Uruguay Round Agreement on Agriculture. However, farms are too small to realize the economies of scale in production. This is particularly so for rice production, even though the number of farms has declined and government has continued to support programs to enlarge farms and increased the scale of rice production (Kwon and Kang 2000). For other categories of animal products, such as beef and dairy cattle, swine and broiler, the number of farms decreased significantly during the 1990s and some were developed into large-scale farm enterprises. In this process, production costs were decreased significantly, although they could not be made low enough to compete on price with imported products in the market. Nevertheless, some of the domestically produced products have been able to fetch higher prices for their quality, appealing to some consumers more than imported generic products.

Enhancing the quality of agricultural products as a way to offset the disadvantage in price competition has become a strategy for 'surviving' since the early 1990s. The strategy clearly shows some signs of success, with some agricultural producers being able to develop niches at the high end of the market for their products. The trend suggests that further efforts to focus on quality products will be able to further develop high-end market niches. The quality competitiveness in large part derives from the attributes of the product, such as freshness, flavor and safety considerations. As a realistic approach to differentiating products in the markets and cultivating niches for higher-priced quality products, the government has encouraged domestic producers to attach a name to their brand name product to differentiate it from other products of the same generic name. Brand names have been taken from various sources including the name of the producer, the producing region, or other attributes that signify high quality to attract consumers. Other brand names derive from some ingredients supposedly contained in the product, which are known to be conducive to human health, or have 'functionally' good for alleviating some health problems. A case in point is high-priced quality beef produced by a differentiated feed mix of various dried herbal plants or other materials supplemented to commercial feeds.

The government's system of quality certificates since 1998 facilitated the development of markets for 'quality' products. Some producers obtained patents for their products through the Office of Patents. As of 2000 there were 4082 brands for agricultural products. Of these, 868 brands were for food crops such as rice and potatoes, 426 brands were for vegetables, 768 brands were for fruits and 380 brands were for livestock products (MAF 2001a: 14). More than half of these brand products had not completed the process of registering a patent. Livestock products had the highest rate of registration with 61 per cent and food crops had the minimum with a registration rate of 27 per cent. Other government measures to reinforce product differentiation include enforcing the labeling of country of origin on agricultural products, and crackdowns on the false labeling of imported agricultural products as domestic products. These measures, to encourage and reinforce product differentiation can also be seen as part of the campaign to promote consumption of domestic products at the expense of foreign counterparts.

### 3.2 Revamping Regulations Restricting Efficient Use of Agricultural Land

The agricultural sector has maintained numerous regulations protective of the sector. Among them, regulations regarding diversion of agricultural land for crops other than food crops had long been restrictive in spite of a growing demand for the land for residential and industrial uses. Prohibition of ownership of agricultural land over 3 hectares per farm also had long been in place. These overly restrictive regulations were successively revamped in the last decade with recognition of an urgent need for enhancing competitiveness of the sector. The cap on the ownership of agricultural land was also abolished in the 1990s to encourage enlargement of farming operations to reap the benefits from economies of scale.

Since the settlements of Uruguay Round Agreement on Agriculture in 1994, the Korean government has continued to review existing domestic laws and rules including those in the use of agricultural land, and repealed or relaxed numerous regulations which posed as restricting competitiveness of the sector (Lee 2000). However, there still remain more regulations to be repealed in order to realize the potential for enhancing agricultural competitiveness. One typical example restricting alternative use of agricultural land is the prohibition both of growing crops other than rice in some designated rice paddy areas and switching of the paddy land to other agricultural purposes such as building barns for crops storage or building facilities for raising animals.

### 3.3 Enforcing Product Standards and Enhancing the Compatibility of Domestic Product Standards with those among Major Trade Partners

Standardization for domestically produced agricultural products should be promoted and implemented further. The standardization of agricultural products contributes to enhancing their competitiveness; it reduces the costs associated with marketing of farm products from producers to consumers. Proper representation of the quality grade, weight and volume consistent with labeling on the package also contributes to increasing the welfare of consumers; it helps them make right choices in purchasing.

According to the Agricultural Products Quality Management Act of 1999, standards for marketing of agricultural products in Korea have been established for quality grades, packaging, labeling and so on. However, confusion occurred as a result of slow implementation of standardization for overall agricultural products, causing inefficiency in the trade of the goods even in domestic markets. Trade units even for a single commodity from farms to retail outlets are different from one marketing stage to another for major fruits and vegetables, requiring repackaging and reweighing (Jeon 1996). Slow progress in the implementation of quality grades for some agricultural products is blamed on consumers; they tend not to trust the current standards on quality grades and packaging, due to lack of recognition of them (KFRI 2002). With the Agricultural Products Quality Management Act in place, the situation has been improving, although the pace has been slow (MAF 2001b: 15).

In order to promote the exports of agricultural products, efforts for the standardization should be extended beyond national boundaries. A case in point is the export of tangerine oranges to Canada, which started in the early 1990. Despite meeting domestic standards, the exporter is required to repack the product to comply with the Canadian trade standard for items such as package unit and labeling As the export outlets for the product have increased, so too has the necessity for enhancing the compatibility of domestic product standards with trade partners.

### 3.4 Enhancing the Level of Food Safety

The issue of enhancing the level of food safety for agricultural products produced domestically has emerged as one of the important areas to tackle for continued growth of the agricultural sector. The consumers' concerns for food safety have also been growing in recent years; they are willing to pay higher prices for safety-guaranteed products, regardless of the country of origin of the products.

In order to enhance the level of food safety, the government has actively participated in the process of preparing for the Codex Alimentarius Commission's guidelines (http://www.codex.org) in setting the maximum residue levels (MRL) of pesticides, veterinary drugs, and so on in agricultural products since the 1990s. The guidelines have contributed to upgrading the level of food safety for agricultural products including meats and dairy products. With enactment of the Act for the Promotion of Environment-Friendly Agriculture in 1997 and the Act for the Quality Management of Agro-Fisheries Products in 1999, various policies have been in place to enhance the level of safety for agricultural products produced domestically. They include the introduction of differentiated labeling for the products grown, by and large under different levels of chemical pesticides and fertilizers applied. By this labeling system, the products of the same generic items are to be differentiated from the 'ordinary' products and imported products. This labeling system has been increasingly adopted by farmers producing fresh goods such as lettuces and tomatoes. As for the safety of meats and dairy products, the Hazard Analysis Critical Control Point (HACCP) system is to apply (Article 9 of the Act for Livestock Products Processing of 1997).

However, some reported incidences of agricultural products in excess of the MRLs of pesticides, detected at such places as the wholesale markets by the inspection authorities, indicate that the producers do not follow the guidelines set for food safety. And the slaughter houses that adopted the HACCP system as of late 2001 numbered only 26 out of 174, according to a survey report on the HACCP adoption (http://www.maf.go.kr). In order to promote the adoption of the system in slaughter houses, the government plans that adoption be compulsory by 2003 (MAF 2001b). The slow adoption of food safety measures indicates that further action such as farmer and process worker education is required.

### 3.5 Increased Investment in Research and Development

To ensure continued development of Korea's agricultural sector and, indeed, its very survival, investment should be directed towards development of cost-saving technology and production technology for yielding high value-added agricultural products. It is highly likely that as the effects of globalization reach further into the domestic agricultural market, the source of strengthened competitiveness in agricultural production will be the national level of agricultural technology rather than the size of conventional factors of production such as land. In order to enhance the level of agricultural technology, funds for research and development (R&D) for the sector should be increased.

The need for an increased fund for investment in R&D for the sector was acknowledged during and after the settlement of the Uruguay Round Agreement on Agriculture in 1994. The R&D fund for the sector started to increase in the early 1990s with an inflow of special tax, collected to finance the restructuring of the sector (MAF 1999). The fund for R&D for the sector increased from 0.49 per cent of GDP in 1993 to 1.12 per cent in 1997 (KREI 1999a: 6). However, the R&D fund for the sector in Korea still falls far behind other advanced countries such as the US, the EU countries and Japan. The proportions of the funds to GDP were 4.4 per cent in Australia and 3.9 per cent in Japan in 1994, and 4 per cent in the Netherlands in 1995 (KREI 1999a: 6).

Recent developments in bio-technology augur well for application in numerous fields to increase agricultural productivity, including development of a high-yielding crop variety. Concerted efforts will be required to mobilize more R&D funds for developing bio-technology to realize this potential in the agricultural sector.

### 3.6 Intensified Efforts to Increase Agricultural Exports

Efforts to increase exports of agricultural products should continue, including continued development of new export items. Korea's imports and exports of agricultural products continued to increase up to the mid-1990s in dollar value and peaked in 1996 (Table 9.6). In response to the 1997 financial crisis, Korean imports of agricultural products started to increase after a one-year dip while Korean exports of agricultural products have stagnated.

Many problems have been identified in expanding the exports of Korea's agricultural products. One much-mentioned problem is the wide and unpredictable fluctuations in the domestic price of the products, which impairs the ability of exporters to maintain reliable export outlets. Some products have problems of packaging, labeling and standardization, which are typical problems at the initial stages of exporting. Another problem which has been of an increasing importance is to improve the level of food safety of export food products. Clearly, overcoming these problems will be a major move forward in increasing agricultural exports. To this end, the government has implemented a number of policies such as enforcing labeling standards for agricultural products and the HACCP system that applies in meat processing.

Another issue concerning agricultural exports is national food security. The cause should not be abused or disguised as a pretext for restricting agricultural trade among trade participants. Given these sensitivities, the rationale for food security should be articulated clearly so that it is properly understood, based on mutual acknowledgment of the importance of the product(s) among the trading countries with an objective mode of assessing the extent of the restricted trade. The criteria for assessing the importance of the food commodity for the purpose could include:

1. the availability of the product (not in a generic sense) in the world market at all times at a predictable and stable price;
2. the product's proportion in the average diet on a calorie intake or other basis;
3. the frequency and extent of socio-economic turmoil caused by imbalances in supply and demand for the product in a given period of time.

Another way of promoting agricultural exports is through establishing free trade agreements (FTAs) with other countries. FTAs are regarded as an effective approach for expanding intra-regional trade by removing trade barriers between countries that are party to the agreement. In 2002, negotiations with Chile for a free trade agreement continue. Progress has been slow here mainly because of strong opposition from Korea's agricultural sector that fears a possible influx of low-priced fruits and livestock products from Chile. The issue of free trade agreements not only with Chile but also with other countries including a three-way free trade agreement with Japan and China must be dealt with more seriously as a way of expanding Korean exports including agricultural products. Considering the potential damage as the agricultural lobby group argues against FTAs, a reliable mechanism to compensate the loss to be incurred by the sector needs to be established to facilitate the FTA negotiations.

### 3.7 Maintenance of Viable Rural Communities

Rural communities are still home to many Koreans. These communities have a high intrinsic value in Korean society and help to alleviate social and pollution problems in urban areas. Hence, enhancing the viability of rural communities should be an important part of Korea's social development policy as well as its agricultural policy. To this end, the government has attempted a number of innovative campaigns, including the Saemaul (New Community) Movement at the beginning of the 1970s.[4]

Undoubtedly the Saemaul Movement contributed to the development of the national economy as well as rural communities. It helped to reduce the income disparity between the urban and farm sectors by boosting farm income. Over time, however, its efficacy diminished. Despite its basic principle of the voluntary participation of villagers, the Movement became centralized and authoritarian, which discouraged villagers' participation and cooperation. The Movement transformed into a centralized bureaucracy that acted like a branch of government, exercising its influence not only on many of the government agencies but also on leading business circles. It became a source of corruption, and virtually self-disintegrated by the mid-1980s.

Since the disintegration of the Saemaul Movement, there has been no serious campaign to improve the viability of rural communities. As market liberalization has proceeded since the early 1990s, various symptoms have appeared that indicate deterioration of the conditions for people in rural communities. They include decreases in income from agricultural sources with deteriorating terms of trade, an increasing number of dilapidated houses in rural areas, and the increased acreage of non-cultivated land. These problems pose serious concerns about the viability of rural communities and the future prospects of agriculture. Since agriculture has long been regarded as the backbone industry of the nation and the most reliable provider of national food security, taken together with the high intrinsic value attached to rural communities in Korean society, the deterioration of rural communities will have serious implications for social stability if unchecked. To enhance the viability of rural communities, improving infrastructure and social amenities in rural areas up to the level comparable with those of urban areas will be critically important. Only through improving infrastructure and social amenities, will dynamic entrepreneurial farmers be attracted to stay in or return to rural communities. To this end, one urgent agricultural policy task in Korea is to increase financial support for rural communities (Yoo 2001). The government has been implementing various income safety-net programs and increasing funds for social amenities for the people living in rural areas. They include introduction of insurance arrangements for various agricultural disasters, direct payment for rice farming, and establishment of health management facilities in rural areas (MAF 2001b).

## 4. AGRICULTURAL ISSUES ON THE WTO DOHA DEVELOPMENT AGENDA AND THE KOREAN GOVERNMENT'S PROPOSAL

After initially slow progress in negotiations on freer trade in agricultural products, moves that were in keeping with Article 20 of the Uruguay Round Agreement on Agriculture in 1994, the launch of the new WTO round at Doha, Qatar in November 2001 is expected to bring momentum to these negotiations.[5] The agricultural section of the Doha Development Agenda states that the WTO will consider tariff cuts, reduction of export subsidies with a view to eventually phasing them out, and substantial reductions in trade-distorting domestic subsidies. Initial requests from all WTO members will be collected by 30 June 2003 to meet the December 2004 deadline for negotiations.

Agricultural negotiations are Korea's biggest concerns in the new round of negotiations. A report prepared by the Korea Institute for International Economic Policy (KIEP) anticipates that if Korea is forced to reduce taxes by 30 per cent on in-bound products, Korea's agricultural production will contract by 2.9 per cent and agricultural imports will grow by 19.4 per cent (KIEP 2001).

The positions of WTO members in the Doha Round of agricultural negotiations are inevitably diverse and most members have much at stake in the outcome of these negotiations (McNiel 2001; KIEP 2001). Documented positions revealed by major players such as the US, the Cairns Group and the EU indicate that reaching a settlement on most of the 'contentious' issues will involve arduous give-and-take among the players in this round of agricultural negotiations (MAF 2001c: 16).

Two key areas of the Doha negotiations on agriculture that particularly concern Korea are market access and domestic support. Korea's position on these issues is presented in the Proposal for WTO Negotiations on Agriculture Submitted by the Republic of Korea (WTO 2001). Let us consider these two areas in turn.

### 4.1 Market Access

Three issues are of particular concern in this category: tariffication, non-trade concerns and safeguard measures.

First, Korea holds that it is important to maintain the framework of tariffication adopted at the Uruguay Round to facilitate a consistent reform process. The Korean government has eliminated most import restrictions since the Uruguay Round and has substantially lowered the level of tariffs. This leaves the remaining tariffs as the nation's main border-protection measure. While Korea is in this position, substantial tariff reduction even further is likely to cause tremendous disruptions in the agricultural sector. For this reason, the Korean position is that gradual, minimal tariff reduction is appropriate and should be based on the final bound rates of the Uruguay Round commitments, with various types of tariffs to ensure flexibility. The tariff rate quota (TRQ) also needs to be administered in a flexible way since the main purpose of the TRQ administration is to cope with the risks of market disturbances that may occur in a two-tiered tariff system.

Second, it is important for Korea that negotiations take into account non-trade concerns. One particularly significant non-trade concern for Korea is food security, as I have discussed earlier in this chapter. For the food-security reason, special consideration should be given to a nation's key staple crops – rice in Korea's case – in determining market-access commitments.

A third important concern for Korea is relaxing the criteria and procedures for invoking safeguards and special safeguards (SSG).[6] Because Korea was not allowed to invoke SSG for some products such as meats and dairy products at the Uruguay Round on Agriculture in 1994, for reasons not fully accounted for (Park 2000; Yoo 2000b: 24), the dairy industry in particular has faced a continued problem of a high accumulated stock of dairy products due to an influx of lowed priced products from abroad with the market liberalization for dairy products in 1996. Korea therefore maintains that the current strict criteria need to be relaxed in a transparent way to enhance the efficacy of the measure for enabling viable safeguards. Korea sees that ongoing negotiations are particularly important in this regard for the steady growth of subsectors of perishable or seasonal products as well as meats and dairy products. This will also help in enabling WTO members like Korea to cope effectively and promptly with extreme market disturbances that result from a sharp increase in imports.

### 4.2 Domestic Support

Here, too, a number of considerations have particular importance for Korea. First, on the matter of agricultural reform, Korea recognizes the need to keep the current framework of 'Amber Box' (subsidy to be reduced), 'Blue Box' (direct payment on the condition of production control) and the 'Green Box' (subsidy permitted) to ensure that agricultural reform is carried out consistently. For 'Green Box' issues where subsidies are permitted, the level of subsidy actually used in Korea has been lower than the level allowed under the Uruguay Round (KREI 2001), indicating that the Korean government can allocate more funds to increase the subsidy level. The low level of government funds actually expended in other categories of subsidies as well indicates the lack of government funds (KREI 1999b: 7). The Korean position is that the scope and criteria of the 'Green Box' need to be made more flexible to accommodate the various positive functions of agriculture that are embodied in the phrase 'multifunctionality of agriculture'. The notion represents that agriculture has various positive roles, in addition to helping to ensure domestic food security. That is, agriculture contributes to shaping the landscape and providing environmental benefits such as land conservation, sustainable management of renewable natural resources and biodiversity, and strengthening socio-economic viability in rural areas (MAF 1998). The notion of multifunctionality of agriculture has been espoused, by and large, by the net food importing countries to moderate the speed of phasing-out of agricultural subsidies so as to minimize the adverse effects on their agricultural sector.

Second, Korea accepts a reduction of the level of domestic support for the agricultural sector on a gradual and aggregative basis according to the reduction commitment. However, a possible change in the existing measures which have been exempt from the reduction commitment under the Uruguay Round Agreement on Agriculture need to be thoroughly reviewed. They include support for the various projects under the category of 'Green Box': food security, natural disasters, crop insurance, environmental protection, farmland conservation and so on.

Third, Korea holds that it is important to extend the scope of income safety-net programs as a form of domestic support. Extension of these programs would apply especially to enhancing the productivity of small-scale family farms, which are the basis of agricultural production in rural communities. Increasing the flexibility of the criteria for these safety-net programs will therefore be important, particularly so with recognition of the need to help reduce income risks that are heightened by market liberalization, weather anomalies and price fluctuations.

Fourth, Korea will argue for increased flexibility in the administration of domestic support. The essential elements of Korea's position are to maintain the status quo under the current framework of tariffication, which is the basis on which Korea supports 'gradual' tariff cuts and strongly opposes further 'substantial' tariff cuts. This position is certain to face opposition from the countries that export agricultural products because for these countries the main purpose of the current round of negotiations is to expand trade in agricultural products by securing both further cuts in tariff levels and 'substantial reductions' in trade-distorting domestic support. Korea's position, arguing for more flexible administration of domestic support, acknowledges the need to change existing arrangements for domestic support but without substantially reducing it.

Fifth, Korea seeks to maintain its status of *de minimis* level, the cap on the financial subsidy permitted on a commodity basis, which amounts to 10 per cent of the commodity value of production in current price allowed for developing countries, according to the Uruguay Round Agreement on Agriculture in 1994. Agricultural exporting countries will almost surely express strong opposition to the Korean position on the ground that, as a member of the OECD, Korea cannot be seen as a developing country. Korea will argue that its status be given *de minimis* level on the grounds that the structure of Korea's agricultural sector is weak and at a level comparable to that of developing countries.

A final concern in these negotiations relates not to the Korean position but rather to how the Korean government presents this position. Some observers point to past problems in the Korean government's preparedness for negotiations. In earlier WTO negotiations Korea was criticized harshly on several grounds including frequently changing government bureaucrats who were in charge of the negotiations, a lack of technical expertise in conducting negotiations, and failure to draw together a concerted opinion from those with a direct interest in the outcomes, such as farmers and people in both the agribusiness sector and agricultural organizations (Park 2000).

## 5. CONCLUSION

The Korean agricultural sector faces continued challenges for survival as globalization inflicts further damage on this sector of the national economy, already weakened by the consequences of swift and intensive industrialization from the 1970s. Korea is not alone in experiencing mounting difficulties in trying to sustain a viable agricultural sector. Enforced liberalization of markets for agricultural products worldwide is forcing governments of individual countries to devise agricultural policies that move into a new, more liberal phase in unison. This is in pursuit of the ideal of a global standard in agriculture, a concept that is embedded in the philosophy driving international agricultural negotiations in both the Uruguay Round of GATT early in the 1990s and the Doha Round of the WTO that is currently under way.

At this juncture, the survival of the domestic agricultural sector in any country depends on how effectively national policies to revamp the hitherto protected agricultural sectors can promote competitiveness so that the domestic agricultural sector can survive competition from agriculturally strong countries that are able to penetrate their domestic markets ever further. Policy regimes that are out of kilter with this trend of globalization in agriculture fear stagnation or destruction of the sector. Yet restructuring the sector in line with the philosophy driving the globalization of agriculture provides a promising opportunity for developing the sector as a viable and prosperous part of the national economy.

Restructuring along these lines requires creative policies that effectively weave the requirements and capacities of the agricultural sector with those of other sectors in a liberalizing economy. It also requires people engaged in the agricultural sector to intensify their efforts to increase the sector's competitiveness. Furthermore, it also requires a nationwide acceptance of the socio-economic damage to be incurred from restructuring, as an unavoidable sacrifice to be borne not just by those in the agricultural sector who suffer directly but to be shouldered through redistributive policy measures that spread the costs and the benefits from the globalization across all sectors of the economy. To this end, the several regimes that have been outlined in this chapter would serve as useful strategies for the future of Korean agriculture in a fiercely competitive global market. They should thus be pursued strenuously.

## NOTES

1. During the 1990–2000 period, the population of Korea increased by 10.3 per cent to 47.3 million, and the number of households increased by 26.1 per cent to 14.3 million (MAF 2002).
2. Although it is difficult to directly compare the level of farm income with that of urban income, farm household income has been in general lower than urban household income. During the 1990s until 1998, the former was about 80 per cent of the latter. See Kwon and Kang (2000).
3. Agricultural trade deficits accounted for the major portion of Korea's overall trade deficit, ranging from 35 per cent to more than 100 per cent during the 1990–98 period. See Kwon and Kang (2000).
4. For a detailed examination of the Saemaul Movement, see Moon and Sul (1997), Park (1996).
5. From early in 2000, member countries submitted their proposals on the objectives of negotiations, and subsequently agreed on a work program and technical details.
6. The SSG was intended to encourage participants in the Uruguay Round to undertake tariffication, especially to reduce the risks of converting non-tariff barriers to tariff equivalents. However some countries have raised the question of its continuation after the Uruguay Round on the ground that it has limited use, even though the Agreement on Agriculture clearly provides for its continuation throughout the reform process (McNiel 2001).

## REFERENCES

Fisher, B.S., J. Penn, T. Greeson, and S. Turner (2001), 'Prospects of Australian agricultural exports to Korea', a paper presented at the Conference on Australia–Korea Economic Cooperation in the 21st Century, Griffith University, Brisbane, Australia.

Jeon, Chang-Gon (1996), *A Study on the Marketing System Analysis and Its Change of the Vegetables and Fruits,* p. 139, Table 4-8, Unpublished Ph.D. Dissertation, Seoul: Korea University (in Korean).

KFRI (Korea Food Research Institute) (2002), *Studies on Standards of Agricultural Fresh Produces,* Research Report Series GA 0288-0201, Seoul (in Korean).

KIEP (Korea Institute for International Economic Policy) (2001), 'Prospects of new round after WTO Doha meeting', a mimeograph, Seoul, Korea (in Korean).

Korea Meat Trade Association (2001), *Meat Trade Information,* February, no. 65, Korea Meat Trade Association, Seoul, Korea (in Korean).

KREI (Korea Rural Economic Institute) (1999a), *21st Century Agricultural Vision and Policy Tasks*, Research Report Series C99–31, Seoul, Korea (in Korean).

KREI (1999b), *Study on the Prospects and Countermeasures for the Next Round WTO Agricultural Negotiations,* Research Report Series C99-36, Seoul, Korea (in Korean).

KREI (2001), *Study on the Strategy for WTO By-Agricultural-Commodity-Basis Negotiations*, Research Report Series C2001-8 (in Korean).

KTA (Korea Trade Association) (2001), *International Trade Yearbook 2001*, KTA, Seoul, Korea (in Korean).

Kwon, Oh Yul and Chang Yong Kang (2000), *Recent Developments in Korean Agriculture: Implications for Australia*, Brisbane, Australia: Griffith University.

Lee, Dong-Phil (2000), 'Evaluation of performance in the efforts for reform in the agro-fishery sector and tasks', a paper presented at KREI (in Korean).

MAF (Ministry of Agriculture and Forestry) (1998), 'Non-trade concerns in net food importing countries,' a paper submitted to the 16th WTO Committee on Agriculture on 22 September, MAF, Seoul, Korea.

MAF (1999), *A History of Korean Agricultural Policies in 50 Years,* Chapter 12: *Agricultural Tax Policy*, pp. 946–9, Seoul, Korea: MAF (in Korean).

MAF (2000), *Livestock Production Cost*, Seoul, Korea.

MAF (2001a), *Annual Report of Agricultural Policy for 2001*, Seoul, Korea: MAF (in Korean).

MAF (2001b), *Brand Labelings for Agricultural and Livestock Products*, MAF Bureau of Agricultural Marketing Data Series 2001–24, Seoul, Korea: MAF (in Korean).

MAF (2001c), *WTO Negotiating Proposals by Countries,* MAF Bureau of International Agricultural Cooperation Data Series 2001–15, Seoul, Korea: MAF.

MAF (2002), *Major Statistics of Agriculture and Forestry 2001*, Seoul, Korea: MAF.

McNiel, D.E. (2001), 'Further reform of agricultural policies in the WTO negotiations', a paper presented at KREI.

Moon, Pal Yong and Sul, Kwang-Eon (1997), 'Agricultural policies and development', in Dong-Se Cha, Kwang Suk Kim and Dwight H. Perkins (eds), *The Korean Economy 1945–1995: Performance and Vision for the 21st Century,* Seoul: Korea Development Institute.

NACF (National Agricultural Cooperatives Federation) (2001), *Materials on Price, Supply and Demand for Livestock Products 2001*, Seoul: NACF.

NSO (National Statistical Office) (2001), *Major Statistics of Korean Economy*, Korea: NSO.

Park, Jin-Hwan (1996), *The Saemaul Movement: Korea's Approach to Rural Modernization in the 1970s*, Research Series S22, KREI.

Park, Jin Do (2000), 'Prospects for the next round of the WTO agricultural negotiations and our response', a paper presented at the Training Center of the National Livestock Cooperatives Federation, Anseong, Korea, January (in Korean).

Song, Yoo-Cheul, Ji-Hyun. Park, Tae-Gon. Kim, Song-Soo. Lim and Jeong-Bin. Im (2001), *Agricultural Policy Changes in Major Countries and their Implications for the WTO Negotiations,* Joint-Research Series on WTO Issues, no. 01–02, KIEP (in Korean).

WTO (World Trade Organization) (2001), 'Proposal for WTO Negotiations on Agriculture', Submitted by the Republic of Korea', G/AG/NG/W/98, Seoul, Korea: MAF.

Yoo, Chul Ho (2000a), 'Liberalization of the beef market and prospects of the Korean beef cattle sector', *Journal of Rural Development*, **23** (2), December, pp. 183–208, KREI.

Yoo, Chul Ho (2000b), 'The new round and a development strategy for the Korean livestock industry', a paper presented at the Symposium Commemorating the Launching of a New Academic Association for Korean Animal Scientists, Seoul, Korea (in Korean).

Yoo, Chul Ho (2001), 'Preparing for a change in the paradigm of agricultural policy', *The Korea Agricultural Policy Weekly News*, 1 November, Seoul, Korea (in Korean).

# 10. Energy and Resources Procurement Strategy in Korea

**Ki-Yual Bang and Woo-Jin Chung**

## 1. INTRODUCTION

Korea is relatively poorly endowed with natural sources of energy. Thus, from Korea's three decades of intense industrialization from the 1960s to the 1980s and through to the present, Korea has relied almost completely on imports for its energy supplies. Consequently, the Korean government has maintained active involvement in the energy sector, seeking to secure a stable supply of energy to fuel an energy-hungry industrial economy. Another imperative, involving macroeconomic management, has underscored heavy government involvement in the nation's energy supplies: an aspect curbing inflation. The government continued to control energy prices tightly as one way to help manage inflation, recognizing the strong inflationary pull of rising energy prices. For this reason the government used energy prices as a socioeconomic tool for the greater welfare of society, scrutinizing carefully any request for a price increase to avoid disrupting economic growth or fueling inflation.

The strategic importance of energy remains as great as ever. However, in a globalizing international environment ever more influenced by pressures to liberalize markets of all kinds, government policy has shifted to recognize that security of energy supply can be best delivered via competitive market forces. The shift involves recognition of the undesirable effects that the lack of competition within the energy sector fosters, and has precipitated calls for structural reform of the energy sector within broader reform of the Korean economy. The Korean energy sector is thus readying for major structural reform aimed at improving economic efficiency through greater reliance on market forces.

This chapter explores structural changes in the Korean energy industry as international policy shifts this industry toward a deregulated and competitive market. We consider generally what these changes involve and why they are being undertaken. We begin with a review of the energy situation in Korea that has been shaped profoundly by very high dependence on overseas energy suppliers. We then consider changes already under way that are moving the energy industry toward a market-oriented structure, followed by a review of the reform plans that the Korean government has announced. We then turn to the energy procurement strategies of Korean companies and consider how these evolving circumstances are impacting upon the implications for overseas suppliers of energy to Korea in this era of market deregulation.

## 2. THE ENERGY SITUATION IN KOREA

### 2.1 Heavy Dependence on Overseas Suppliers

The Korean economy continued to grow rapidly from the 1970s, with an average annual growth rate of 7.2 per cent during the years from 1985 to 2000. Energy consumption has grown even more rapidly than this high economic growth. The average annual growth in national energy consumption during this period is 8.6 per cent, which is among the world's highest for this period (Table 10.1). The high growth rate of energy consumption was mainly due to heavy investments in energy-intensive industries such as petrochemicals, steel and shipbuilding. A substantial reduction of the energy demand growth relative to the past is expected, because of a steep drop of investments in energy-intensive industries and anticipated slower economic growth.

*Table 10.1 Major Energy and Economic Indicators in Korea*

| | 1985 | 1990 | 1995 | 1997 | 1998 | 1999 | 2000 |
|---|---|---|---|---|---|---|---|
| Energy consumption (million toe) | 56.3 | 93.2 | 150.4 | 180.6 | 165.9 | 181.4 | 192.9 |
| Growth of energy consumption (%) | 5.2 | 14.1 | 9.6 | 9.3 | –8.1 | 9.3 | 6.4 |
| Economic growth rate (%) | 6.5 | 9.6 | 8.9 | 5.0 | –6.7 | 10.7 | 8.8 |
| Per capita energy consumption (toe/1000$) | 1.38 | 2.17 | 3.34 | 3.93 | 3.57 | 3.87 | 3.31 |
| Primary energy sources (%) | | | | | | | |
| Petroleum | 48.2 | 53.8 | 62.5 | 60.4 | 54.6 | 53.6 | 52.0 |
| Coal | 39.1 | 26.2 | 18.7 | 19.3 | 21.7 | 21.0 | 22.3 |
| LNG | – | 3.2 | 6.1 | 8.2 | 8.4 | 9.3 | 9.8 |
| Hydro | 1.6 | 1.7 | 0.9 | 0.7 | 0.9 | 0.9 | 0.7 |
| Nuclear | 7.4 | 14.2 | 11.1 | 10.7 | 13.5 | 14.2 | 14.2 |
| Others | 3.6 | 0.9 | 0.7 | 0.7 | 0.9 | 1.0 | 1.0 |

*Note*: toe refers to Ton of Oil Equivalent.

*Source*: KEEI, *2001 Yearbook of Energy Statistics*, 2001.

Among energy sources, petroleum is Korea's most important fuel. As we see in Table 10.1 since 1990 petroleum has accounted for more than half the total energy consumed. Next is coal, which is mostly the bituminous type that is not produced domestically. This is followed by nuclear fuel and natural gas, with a tiny proportion (about 1 per cent) from hydroelectricity.

Korea is poorly endowed with natural resources. Production and consumption of anthracite, the only fossil fuel produced in Korea, have decreased sharply since 1990 due to higher production costs and inconvenience when compared to imported fuels. Thus Korea must meet almost all its energy needs from foreign sources, resulting in heavy dependence upon overseas suppliers. This high overseas dependence for resources that are essential to Korea's economic strength has at times constrained the economy and has kept energy as one of the most important factors in this nations' international trade balance. Inevitably, the vulnerability that this dependence on foreign suppliers creates ensures that energy supply is also a particularly important factor in national security. Energy imports account for about 13–21 per cent of Korea's total import costs, depending on the amounts purchased and international energy prices. The marked increases in energy imports since 1990 would be attributable to the sharp decrease in consumption of anthracite, the only fossil fuel produced in Korea.

In Table 10.2 we see that the Korean economy is almost completely dependent on overseas energy suppliers, with a dependency rate above 97 per cent from 1996. It is interesting to note that in 1985 when Korea imported just over three-quarters of its energy supplies, energy accounted for more than a quarter of the country's total imports. Yet as the overseas dependency rate and the value of imported energy increased, energy's share of total imports decreased. This happened because the value of total import has more rapidly increased than that of energy import due to the decline of energy prices.

*Table 10.2 Korea's Dependence on Overseas Energy Sources*

| | Dependence on overseas energy (%) | Amount of energy imported | |
|---|---|---|---|
| | | Suppliers value (million $) | % of total imports |
| 1985 | 76.2 | 7144 | 26.8 |
| 1990 | 87.9 | 10 759 | 16.9 |
| 1995 | 96.8 | 18 445 | 14.8 |
| 1996 | 97.3 | 24 018 | 18.5 |
| 1997 | 97.6 | 26 747 | 19.3 |
| 1998 | 97.1 | 17 836 | 13.5 |
| 1999 | 97.2 | 22 286 | 15.2 |
| 2000 | 97.2 | 37 099 | 21.1 |

*Source*: KEEI, *2001 Yearbook of Energy Statistics*, 2001.

## 2.2 Overseas Energy Suppliers

### 2.2.1 Oil

At the time of the second oil price shock in the late 1970s, Korea imported almost all of its crude oil requirements from three nations in the Middle East: Saudi Arabia, Kuwait and Iran. The Korean response to the 1970s oil shocks was to diversify not only overseas suppliers but also the types of energy it imported. This strategy led to a reduction in oil imports overall, and particularly from the Middle East, from 97 per cent of total oil imports in 1980 to 55 per cent in 1985 (Table 10.3).

*Table 10.3 Korea's Crude Oil Imports by Supplier Nations*

(Unit: %, million barrels)

| Year | Saudi Arabia | Kuwait | Iran | UAE | Other Middle East | Indo-nesia | Australia | Others | Total crude oil import |
|---|---|---|---|---|---|---|---|---|---|
| 1970 | 31.7 | 36.2 | 32.1 | | | | | | 100 (69.2) |
| 1980 | 61.2 | 27.1 | 8.5 | | | 0.1 | | 3.2 | 100(182.9) |
| 1985 | 6.9 | 8.8 | 17.2 | 10.1 | 11.9 | 10.2 | | 34.9 | 100(198.3) |
| 1990 | 12.8 | 5.5 | 11.1 | 16.2 | 22.8 | 6.2 | 0.2 | 25.1 | 100(308.4) |
| 1995 | 36.3 | 4.0 | 10.9 | 11.3 | 14.7 | 5.0 | 0.8 | 16.9 | 100(624.9) |
| 1999 | 27.7 | 6.1 | 9.4 | 13.4 | 12.7 | 4.8 | 1.8 | 24.2 | 100(874.1) |
| 2000 | 29.6 | 7.5 | 9.1 | 14.3 | 12.5 | 4.1 | 3.9 | 18.9 | 100(893.9) |

*Note*: Figures in parenthesis are total imports values of crude oil.

*Source*: Korea National Oil Co. (2001).

Nevertheless Korea's oil consumption rose from the mid-1980s, as international oil prices fell and demand for oil in the transport sector grew rapidly. Korea's reliance on Middle Eastern crude oil consequently increased steadily to reach 73 per cent of total crude oil imports in 2000 (Table 10.3). Saudi Arabia has been the largest source of crude oil imports to Korea, with a share of around 30 per cent. A variety of policies including diversification of oil-import sources have been planned to reduce Korea's high dependency on Middle Eastern oil, but these have been largely unsuccessful because the import cost from the Middle East was lower than those from other sources.

**2.2.2 Natural gas**

Natural gas was introduced into Korea in the form of LNG to the Pyongtaek power plant in October 1986. LNG is in general supplied on the basis of long-term contracts (usually 20–25 years). LNG export facilities and transport ships take four or five years to build and thus LNG producers start to build export facilities after concluding contract terms with buyers. Therefore LNG is supplied on the basis of projects between exporters and importers. However, for exceptional cases when existing exporters have surplus LNG or buyers are in an emergent situation due to unexpected increases in demand, there are short or spot contracts. Thus, from 1983 until the end of the 1990s, the Korean government has signed long-term contracts to secure supplies with natural gas producing countries mainly in Southeast Asia, including Indonesia, Malaysia and Brunei. However, the export capacities for natural gas in the Southeast Asian region decreased due to fast growth of demand exceeding the slower growth of supply in the region. The Korean government has therefore sought alternative suppliers from the Middle East such as Qatar and Oman. Korea has also signed short-term contracts with Indonesia and Malaysia, and has made several spot purchases of LNG from Australia, Indonesia and Brunei. As we see in Table 10.4 demand for natural gas in Korea is forecast to surpass the contracted supply amounts after 2005. Korea Gas Corporation is looking for a new LNG supplier to fill the gap between the anticipated demand and contracted supply.

*Table 10.4 LNG Supply Contracts in Korea by Sources*

(Unit: 1000 tons)

| | 2000 | 2001 | 2002 | 2003 | 2005 | 2008 | 2010 |
|---|---|---|---|---|---|---|---|
| Demand (A) | 13 806 | 15 986 | 16 650 | 16 818 | 18 300 | 21 064 | 20 971 |
| Contracted LNG (B) | 16 220 | 16 712 | 16 980 | 16 980 | 16 980 | 14 680 | 14 680 |
| Indonesia | 6308 | 5300 | 5300 | 5300 | 5300 | 3000 | 3000 |
| Malaysia | 2168 | 2000 | 2000 | 2000 | 2000 | 2000 | 2000 |
| Brunei | 700 | 700 | 700 | 700 | 700 | 700 | 700 |
| Qatar | 3420 | 4320 | 4920 | 4920 | 4920 | 4920 | 4920 |
| Oman | 2000 | 4000 | 4060 | 4060 | 4060 | 4060 | 4060 |
| A – B (unmet demand over supply) | +1238 | +726 | +330 | +162 | –1320 | –6384 | –6291 |

*Source*: Unpublished internal data of Korea Gas Co., 2001.

### 2.2.3 Coal

Korea has greatly expanded its use of coal after the oil shocks in the 1970s, and primary coal consumption has since grown more than sevenfold. Most of this increase has come from industries and power generation, while gas and electricity have largely replaced coal use in the residential sector. Coal demand for electricity generation is expected to continue to grow, and by 2010, coal is expected to generate about 35 per cent of the electricity produced.

The Korean government has continued to import bituminous coal such as steaming coal for power and coking coal for power generation, steel production and for other industries. The main sources of coal are Australia and China. Australia, as the largest supplier of coal to Korea, accounted for more than 40 per cent of total Korean coal imports in 2000. In the case of coking coal, more than half is imported from Australia. Imports from China have outgrown those from Australia since 1995. Australia, China, Canada and South Africa account for around 90 per cent of Korea's total coal imports (Table 10.5).

## 3. CHANGES IN ENERGY POLICIES AND INDUSTRIAL STRUCTURES

### 3.1 The Influence of Energy Policies on Energy Procurement and Distribution

The government has intervened in almost all energy procurements from abroad. It has also continued to regulate and subsidize the distribution of energy through public energy companies and other forms of regulation. The government has justified its extensive intervention in this sector on the grounds that its stable procurement and tightly regulated distribution of energy are important for energy security, which is important for national security. The government has also maintained that its heavy intervention is to protect consumers from abuse of market power by monopolized or oligopolized energy companies.

*Table 10.5 Coal Imports by Source Nations and Usage in Korea, 2000*

(Unit: 1000 tons)

| | Steel | Power | Industry | Total | Ratio (%) |
|---|---|---|---|---|---|
| South Africa | | 2151 | 352 | 2503 | 4.2 |
| USA | 1419 | | | 1419 | 2.4 |
| Russia | 395 | 1973 | 198 | 2565 | 4.3 |
| Thailand | | | 60 | 60 | 0.1 |
| Indonesia | 209 | 3372 | 12 | 3593 | 6.0 |
| China | 2781 | 13 466 | 5195 | 21 442 | 36.0 |
| Canada | 4097 | 1647 | | 5744 | 9.6 |
| Australia | 10 641 | 9715 | 1882 | 22 238 | 37.3 |
| Japan | | | 3 | 3 | |
| Others | 33 | | | 33 | 0.1 |
| Total | 19 575 | 32 324 | 7702 | 59 600 | 100.0 |

*Source*: KEEI, *Internal data of Korea Coal Association*, 2001.

However, the currently dominant economic orthodoxy of market liberalization in a globalizing international economy today compels governments to privatize public utilities and to invite competition wherever possible so that forces of the market determine distribution. The Korean government is no exception, as economic reform policies attest. Thus the government is now entrusting the role of securing energy supply to market forces, departing from its long tradition of central intervention.

Among various government strategies that influence the energy industry, the push to strengthen the market mechanism will have the most profound impact on energy procurements. It is now seen that over time, heavily regulated prices and supplies have distorted both the market and the allocation of resources. To correct these distortions and misallocations, the government is taking measures to allow the market mechanism to operate through facilitating competition in the energy market, hence pushing the energy industry towards privatization and competitive practice. Plans for restructuring the electric power and natural gas industries were announced in 1999, and the restructuring process has already begun in the electricity industry (Ministry of Commerce, Industry and Energy 1999).

Another measure with which the Korean government is strengthening the market mechanism is by removing price controls. This means no government intervention in price setting by energy companies. Many energy prices have been set for social and other purposes, such as the protection of poor people and the promotion of export industry, rather than on a cost basis. However, as price control or price subsidy is employed to attain certain social objectives, it is bound to have adverse impacts on efficient resource allocation.

Another measure is to reform the energy tax system. The current energy tax system lacks consistency. Many types of energy taxes have been imposed for social, economic or political considerations. Such taxes distort the market, and without tax reform, price deregulation will not achieve efficient energy resource allocation. In other words, even if prices are set competitively, it would not constitute fair competition without a non-distortionary tax system in the market.

The government is currently considering a tax system that levies tax on energy sources according to their heat content. Another plan is to introduce a new tax system according to the carbon content emitted from energy use. This new system of taxing according to heat and carbon content, is being investigated at the government think tank, the Korea Energy Economic Institute, with the aim of achieving fair competition in the free market and reducing the use of pollutant energy. This new tax system will significantly affect energy industries and consumer behavior, as it is expected to change the structure of price differentials among different sources of energy.

While the market mechanism is strengthened across the national economy, the stable supply of energy will remain a policy priority. Energy security through ensuring continuous supply from abroad will remain a permanent government policy objective, so long as no new energy source is found in Korea. Even though this policy objective of continuous energy supply continues unchanged, the method used to achieve this objective is forced to change by pressures within the globalizing economy that are obliging governments to open markets. Under a free decentralized market environment, stability of energy supply will be achieved through market forces rather than through direct intervention of government in the energy market. Hence, the challenge that Korea faces in the coming years is to secure the stability of energy supply through the market mechanism as the government retreats from intervention in supply, demand and price of energy. Let us consider the circumstances in key energy industries.

## 3.2 Structural Changes in Specific Energy Industries

### 3.2.1 Oil industry

A number of regulations and government controls on the domestic market have been removed in the oil industry. Only a few years ago, oil imports and new refinery construction and expansion of existing refineries had to be approved by the government, even though these were the actions of private companies. As mentioned earlier, there were also price controls. The prices for almost all petroleum products had to be approved by the government authority. The government also regulated the profits of importers and refineries, including the margin generated at every step of distribution. Deregulation of the oil industry that was started in 1995 gradually abolished many of these regulations. As of 2002, there remain just a few regulations such as responsibility for oil stockpiling and reporting sales and purchases to the government for emergency preparedness, and industry controls for public safety. Private companies can now freely import oil, construct refineries and set their own prices for the petroleum products they sell. Even foreigners can import oil and construct and manage refineries inside Korea and can do business in retailing without tight government regulations on their operations.

### 3.2.2 Gas industry

KOGAS, which is a state-owned entity, is the only importer and wholesaler of natural gas. It owns the LNG receiving terminals and the main pipeline network. Where possible, the government wants to introduce competition in the gas industry, as it has done in the electricity industry. The restructuring plan announced in November 1999 indicates the direction in which the government will steer the gas industry, privatizing much of the public sector involvement, including KOGAS, to stimulate competition. The main contents of the plan are as follows (Ministry of Commerce, Industry and Energy 1999):

- The import and wholesale businesses of KOGAS will be separated from pipeline and storage facility operations in 2002.
- Three subsidiaries for import and wholesale businesses will be formed within KOGAS, and existing long-term LNG purchasing contracts will be apportioned to them.
- Two of these subsidiaries will be sold off to private investors, while the other subsidiary will remain under KOGAS control until it is sold off later.
- Most of the government's stake in KOGAS will be sold off, but the government will hold a portion of the shares in consideration of the public nature of the company.
- LNG import for private use will be allowed from 2001, and access to the import terminals and transmission network will be open on a non-discriminatory basis.
- An independent regulatory body will be established to redefine the current regulatory structure.

When these measures are enforced, the government-controlled gas market is expected to change into a competitive market as the wholesale business and transport facilities of LNG such as import terminals and pipelines are all open to the private companies and the control over gas prices and supply are highly diminished. Under a competitive market, the key issue would be how fairly the market operates. Therefore, the role of government would shift from a controller of the gas market to the supervisor for fair competition.

Competition in retail services will be introduced in phases after successfully launching competition in the wholesale business. The first phase will permit competitive supply to large customers by retailers and wholesalers. The second phase will split retail gas services into the operation of facilities and sales which are bundled. In the third phase, full-blown competition will be introduced, allowing competition for supply to smaller customers. The government will soon reveal a detailed implementation plan and schedules for the natural gas industry restructuring after working out the finer details.

### 3.3.3 Electricity industry

The Korean Ministry of Commerce, Industry and Energy is committed to the overall restructuring of the electric power industry. The objectives of this restructuring are to deliver more efficient and sustainable use of both capital infrastructure and energy resources. The restructuring pursues an open electricity market as a way to minimize energy consumption and achieve energy security and environmental objectives. It promotes implementation of pricing practices that reflect the true cost of supply. It also promotes capital flows through the progressive removal of impediments to funding for infrastructure.

Consistent with these principles, the government is moving the electric power industry towards deregulation and privatization. The Ministry of Commerce, Industry and Energy (MOCIE) announced in January 1999 the Electric Power Industry Restructuring Plan, which is a blueprint for privatizing the electricity market. The plan is divided into four phases as we see in Table 10.6. It includes unbundling the vertically integrated electric power industry to promote efficiency, customer choice and energy security particularly through reliability of supply.

*Table 10.6 Phases in the Plan for Electric Power Restructuring*

| Phase | Plan |
|---|---|
| Phase I:<br>Preparation<br>(December 1998 – December 1999) | • Preparation, including legislation, valuation and separation of KEPCO's assets (generation, transmission and distribution)<br>• Formation of generation subsidiaries (Gencos)<br>• Beginning of development of a wholesale electricity pool |
| Phase II:<br>Introducing competition in electricity generation<br>(October 1999 – December 2002) | • Privatize or divest KEPCO's generation subsidiaries<br>• Generate competition between Gencos in a wholesale electricity pool (one-way bidding)<br>• Form new distribution companies<br>• By the end of this phase, commence privatization of distribution companies and introduce two-way bidding |
| Phase III:<br>Wholesale Competition<br>(2003–2009) | • In preparation for retail competition |
| Phase IV:<br>Retail Competition (after 2009): | • Gradually eliminate supply franchises |

*Source*: Ministry of Commerce and Industry, Energy (MOCIE), *Restructuring Plan of Electric Power Industry in Korea*, 1999.

As shown in Table 10.6, the plan envisages a gradual transition to wholesale competition over four years (1998–2002) with the introduction of retail competition following wholesale competition after 2009. The key feature of this plan, phase I, involved splitting KEPCO into three categories: generation, transmission and distribution. This was implemented as planned. As a result, electricity generation will be opened to Independent Power Producers (IPPs), excluding nuclear plants. This is a response to the need for competition, efficiency improvement and reduction of the capital burden in the electric power industry.

According to this restructuring plan, power generation was separated from KEPCO in April 2001. Six subsidiary generating companies (gencos) were formed after considering the size of the generation equipment. Five of these companies will be privatized, the sixth, the nuclear and hydropower generation subsidiary, will remain in KEPCO's hands. The Korea Power Exchange (KPX), the semi-government body which controls the electricity transactions between the six subsidiaries and KEPCO, was inaugurated in April 2001 as the footing institute for free market electricity transactions in the retail and wholesale market after privatization is completed. An independent regulatory body will be established for fair competition in a privatized electricity market.

# 4. PROSPECTIVE STRATEGIES FOR ENERGY PROCUREMENTS

## 4.1 The Prospective Changes of Energy Procurement Strategies

As discussed in the previous sections, the energy industry in Korea is in transition from a government-directed central planning system into a decentralized market-oriented system. State-owned public utilities are being privatized, the vertically integrated monopoly structure is being dismantled, and industry is being deregulated to introduce competition where possible. In short, the government has loosened its tight grip on the energy sector and has encouraged market forces.

In a competitive market, minimizing cost is a decisive factor for the survival of companies. Thus the new private energy companies in Korea will try to reduce costs. Before privatization, the procurement costs of energy from overseas usually accounted for 60 to 80 per cent of total energy supply costs. This means that reducing procurement costs will be a high-priority task in the management strategies of the energy companies. In a monopolized or highly regulated market that prevailed for many years, the energy procurers could pass on to consumers the prices they contract with overseas energy suppliers, even if these prices were higher than the procurement prices of other companies operating outside the closed Korean market. Since deregulation, however, companies that procure energy at higher costs than those of rival companies will be forced out of the competitive market.

Private energy companies in Korea will also try to reduce or avoid risks in procuring energy. As with costs in the earlier regulated or government-directed market, the risks incurred in supplying energy to the domestic market could be passed on to Korean consumers. For example, state-owned energy companies included as procurement cost, most of the loss from the exchange rate fluctuation between the points of contracting with suppliers and selling to the domestic market while the state regulated consumer price. Most energy companies, whether private corporations or public utilities, preferred to purchase energy under long-term contracts with suppliers rather than purchase on the spot markets. Long-term contracts presented a more stable way to supply energy to the domestic market and could reflect the domestic energy companies' contract prices in the consumer price even when spot market prices were significantly lower than the contracted prices.

In a deregulated competitive market, however, the risk in energy procurements will belong to the energy supply companies. There will not be an intervening body such as government to protect these companies, and the losses they incur from energy procurements in the international market can be transferred to the consumers only if other suppliers do likewise, given new competition in the domestic market. This will greatly change the future procurement strategies of the energy companies in Korea. The purchasing decisions of these companies will favor low price and risk avoidance, over stable supply in energy procurements. These companies will be more eager to find lowest-price suppliers and will require flexible conditions in contracting with the suppliers. The companies will also prefer short-term contracts or the spot markets for purchasing energy in the international market. This will force overseas suppliers to make the systems of market supply more flexible.

It is expected that Korean energy companies will more positively employ advanced financial methods such as futures trading and hedging in their energy procurements in order to disperse price risks. These moves will diversify energy markets and advanced energy trading such as brokerage, auctions and internet-based trading will develop in the domestic energy market as the financial market develops.

### 4.2 Inter-regional Cooperation for Energy Procurements

As described in the previous section, lower prices and avoiding risk will be top management tasks for Korean companies in procuring energy. Under the old regime of vertically integrated monopoly public utilities, it was clear where the responsibility for security of the national energy supply lay. With the decentralized competitive energy industry, however, such responsibility is dispersed and obscure. This could create additional concerns about the stability of Korea's energy supply, which can be affected adversely by the possibility of strong fluctuation in energy prices in the short term. Hence, a challenge facing Korea in this transitional phase is to efficiently secure a stable energy supply within the market-dominated framework.

Under these circumstances, the solution to secure a stable and efficient national energy supply may lie in regional cooperation. It is expected that energy cooperation among countries within Northeast Asia will lessen heavy import dependence on the Middle East, and provide benefits from the complementary effects of interconnecting energy supply systems. The Northeast Asian region has great potential for resource development and trade that can mutually benefit the countries within the region. The eastern part of Russia is endowed with abundant resources that remain unexplored. Heavy energy-consuming countries such as Japan, China and Korea are situated in this region. Moreover, Japan and Korea have few indigenous energy resources.

The much discussed energy transport network encompassing the countries within the region is difficult to implement because the region does not have sufficient market-economy bases. In addition, the harsh weather conditions of East Russia, long-distance transport to end-use sites, lack of infrastructure and high investment risks, cast doubts on the economic feasibility of resource development projects in East Russia.

Nonetheless, the possible benefits from cooperative energy projects by the Northeast Asian countries are tremendous. The construction of energy transport networks will enable these countries to derive complementarity from the differences in their energy consumption patterns and energy industry structures, leading to improvement in energy consumption efficiency and better utilization of expensive supply facilities. Stable institutional systems for developing and transporting energy will also enhance efficiency in investment and trade. Moreover, with mounting pressure for environmental conservation such as that brought on by the UN Framework Convention on Climate Change, the merits of energy supply development in East Russia increase. Of particular merit are projects for natural gas development and for electricity transport, which uses the hydroelectric resources of East Russia to supplies countries within the Northeast Asian region.

### 4.3 The Implications of Restructuring for Overseas Energy Suppliers to Korea

Changes in the Korean energy procurement system will force overseas energy suppliers to reconsider their export strategy to Korea. There is potential for mutual benefit to suppliers inside and outside Korea who are preparing to explore the Korean market for new commercial opportunities. Market restructuring of the oil, gas and electricity industries has forced energy companies in Korea to compete in a deregulated market where fluctuations from volatile international energy prices are no longer absorbed by the state so the level of uncertainty, and hence the risk factor, are much greater than in the regulated market. Strategies for managing risk and creatively securing a competitive edge will therefore be central to the success of energy suppliers to Korea.

In the natural gas sector, privatized companies that import natural gas and power generators that are potential importers of natural gas will give priority to cost reduction and risk management when deciding on procurements. Flexibility of the LNG supply is an important consideration since it presents opportunities to the gas supply companies to reduce their costs and risks. Without supply flexibility from gas producers, the supply companies in Korea will need to build storage tanks so that they can adjust their supply of LNG to meet high seasonal fluctuation in demand while importing evenly throughout the year. This means that natural gas producers can appeal to Koreans that have demand fluctuations for LNG. By offering the irregular, demand-driven gas supplies rather than a fixed, regular annual supply, suppliers in Korea will save the cost of building and maintaining storage tanks. Korean gas companies will also favor short- or mid-term rather than long-term contracts in purchasing LNG, since the domestic gas market is expected to change significantly and so holds many uncertainties in the longer term.

It should be noted that Korea would have significantly influential power in the Asian LNG market. There are a small number of LNG importers in Asia. The existing buyers in the Asian LNG market are Japan, Korea and Taiwan. Only China is a potential buyer within 2006. Korea has been the second-largest buyer after Japan, and the future additional demand for natural gas (potential volume of new LNG contracts with exporters) of Korea is forecast to surpass the additional demand of Japan. Taiwan's LNG market is relatively small. For the exporters who hope to sell natural gas to Asian markets like Australia, it is not easy to sell natural gas to non-Asian markets due to the long distance.

A strategic alliance between overseas suppliers and Korean importers and/or distributors and consumers is also expected to enhance LNG tradability. In the highly regulated Korean gas market, the roles of importer, distributor and consumer have been distinctive and exclusive as circumscribed by the state. However, in the deregulated, competitive market after restructuring, market players can have more than one role: for example an importer can also be a distributor, and a consumer can directly procure natural gas from overseas. Under these deregulated conditions, Korean procurers of LNG will diversify their operations in pursuit of profit, extending operations beyond natural gas importing to other businesses involved in supplying LNG to the domestic market. Some large consumers will therefore procure natural gas for two purposes: consuming it themselves, for example in industrial production, and selling it to other consumers whether small or large. To the LNG producers, therefore, strategic alliances with Korean gas companies will provide good opportunities for sales of natural gas and for participating in other gas businesses besides LNG exports such as natural gas sales at wholesale and retail markets in Korea. On the

Korean side, an alliance with LNG producers will secure a more stable gas supply for Korean consumers and create opportunities for Korean suppliers to reduce procurement costs and enhance their competitiveness *vis-à-vis* other companies in the domestic gas business.

Korean interests are trying to procure natural gas from East Russia by building pipelines through multinational cooperation in the Northeast Asian region as discussed earlier in this chapter. The venture will enhance the competitive stakes among LNG producers. But it also presents an opportunity for Korean suppliers to team up with the LNG producers in strategic alliances in the Northeast Asian PNG (Pipeline Natural Gas) projects. The LNG producers usually have considerable experience and technology for exploration and development of natural gas as well as for building gas pipelines. They are also providing the vast amount of capital required for this investment. Korea presents itself as a large market and stable purchaser of natural gas and as an investor in these projects, so Korean companies are expected to play an important role in the Northeast Asian gas projects. Participation in the Northeast Asian PNG projects by the LNG suppliers with experience, technology and capital, through alliance with Korean supplier companies, presents opportunities for great benefits for both sides in the alliance and could make the projects more viable.

Coal procurement is also expected to change noticeably in response to deregulation in this market. The government has loosened its grip on two major coal importers, KEPCO and Pohang Steel Company (POSCO). It has already sold much of its equity in POSCO (a coking coal importer) so that the state's share was only 4 per cent (through the state-owned Industry Bank of Korea) and the share of foreigners was almost half (49 per cent as of the end of 2000).[1] Generating companies that import steam coal will be soon privatized according to the reform plan for the power industry. The more competitive market will force privatized coal importers to change their strategies for coal procurement, favoring cost reduction and flexibility of purchase over stability of supply.

Coal costs account for around 30–50 per cent of the total generating costs of power-generating companies in Korea (Kepco 2000)[2]. Since this is a significant proportion of costs, lowering coal costs and price risks in coal procurement will be a priority objective for management of the generating companies.

One major change in Korean companies' procurement of coal has already begun. This involves a shift away from long-term contracts with overseas coal suppliers to shorter contracts or the spot market. Until market reforms began in the late 1990s KEPCO imported most of its coal on long-term contracts with overseas suppliers. Since 1998, KEPCO has shifted from long-term to short-term contracts with the introduction of restructuring in the electricity industry. Until 1998, KEPCO's total coal imports through long-term contracts were around 80 to 97 per cent. However, that share has reduced greatly while the share of short-term purchases through one-year contracts and the spot market has increased to more than 50 per cent (Table 10.7). Short-term purchases of coal in the privatized generating companies are expected to expand more in the future.

It is desirable for coal exporters to carefully observe the changing trends of the electricity market after the restructuring of the power industry in Korea. They also need to prepare to respond promptly to these changes, with various strategies like the flexible terms of supply to the importers, and the direct alliance with Korean coal consumers or importers to meet the requirements of the changing coal market.

Another strategy for overseas suppliers to expand energy exports to Korea would be for them to participate directly in the Korean domestic energy market. The Korean government opened the nation's energy industry to foreign companies in 1998. Most of the earlier restrictions on equity shares of foreigners and on the business of foreign companies in the energy industry have been abolished. The government has encouraged direct foreign investment in Korean industries and a number of foreign companies have invested in sectors of the energy market like refinery, city gas and district heating. Some of these foreign companies are preparing to invest in power generation and the wholesale sale of natural gas after the energy market has been restructured and privatized.

## 5. CONCLUSION

The energy industry has been a mainstay of economic growth in Korea for the last three decades, quenching the nation's energy-thirsty heavy industries. In 2001 more than 97 per cent of total energy used in Korea was imported from abroad. The importance of securing foreign energy can therefore not be overemphasized. Several traditional measures have been used to secure stable energy procurement in Korea. Among the most notable is direct government intervention in energy import and in domestic supply. In preparation for unexpected regional energy problems such as insufficient import supplies or energy price hikes, diversifying import sources and encouraging Korean companies to invest directly in overseas energy development have also been pursued. For energy sources that can be stored, such as oil, the government imposed a compulsory stockpile program on the energy companies in Korea, which is another effort to heighten energy security.

*Table 10.7 Changes in KEPCO's Manner of Coal Procurement*

(Unit: 1000 tons)

| | 1996 | 1997 | 1998 | 1999 | 2000 |
|---|---|---|---|---|---|
| Long-term contract | 19 011 | 20 587 | 19 848 | 14 634 | 14 090 |
| | (97%) | (93%) | (80%) | (55%) | (43%) |
| Year-term contract | 616 | 625 | 113 | 5420 | 8110 |
| | (3%) | (3%) | (1%) | (20%) | (25%) |
| Spot | – | 40 | 4824 | 6663 | 10 240 |
| | – | (4%) | (19%) | (25%) | (32%) |
| Total | 19 627 | 22 052 | 24 780 | 26 717 | 32 440 |

*Source*: Korea South-East Generation Co., *The direction of coal procurement in new generation company*, April 2001.

These days, however, the Korean government is loosening its grip on the energy sectors and is taking measures to introduce the market mechanism by facilitating competition among sellers and buyers where possible. With these measures, the Korean government is entrusting the role of securing energy supply to market forces. This is a departure from central intervention, as can be seen from the electricity and gas industry restructuring plans and deregulation of the oil industry that has already taken place. Korean energy importers will take low cost and risk avoidance as top priorities in their procurement strategies, in order to survive in a competitive market. In a rapidly changing market they will prefer short-term and flexible supply contracts to long-term contracts for stable energy supply. This will require overseas exporters to make the contract terms of energy supply more flexible and to consider strategic alliances with Korean importers in energy trading.

Major energy consumption countries in Northeast Asia are considering inter-regional cooperation for their energy procurement. They seek to establish an Asian common market for energy to enhance the security of energy supply and transportation, and to raise their bargaining power against energy suppliers. Also, to tap abundant natural gas in East Russia, Northeast Asian countries including China, Japan and Korea are exploring the development of natural gas in certain regions of that country.

To penetrate the restructuring Korean energy market, overseas suppliers may have to prepare to provide short-term flexible contracts instead of long-term secured contracts. They should seriously consider strategic alliances with Korean energy users and direct investment in the Korean energy industry in order to increase their energy exports to Korea.

## NOTES

1. POSCO after Privatization, 18th Korea/Australia Joint Committee on Energy and Mineral Resources, April 2001.
2. Generating costs, KEPCO, 2000. The ratio of coal cost to total generating cost depends on the operating rate of coal power.

## REFERENCES

ABARE & Korea Energy Economics Institute (1996), Energy Trade and Investment Between Australia and Republic of Korea, August, Seoul.

Chang, Hyun-Joon (1999), *Korea Energy Market in Transition*, Prepared for 20th Annual Conference of the USAEE/IAEE, Washington, DC.

Chang, Hyun-Joon (2001), *Energy and Environment*, Korea Energy Economics Institute, Seoul.

Chung, Woo Jin (1999), *Economic Cooperation in Northeast Asia: A Study on Regional Energy-resource Cooperation*, Seoul: Korea Energy Economics Institute.

Chung, Woo Jin (2000), *National Energy Futures Analysis and Energy Security Perspectives in the Republic of Korea*, Seoul: Korea Energy Economics Institute.

Doh, Hyun Jae (2000), *Introducing Competition and Natural Gas Pricing Practice in Korea*, Prepared for APERC mid-year workshop on research themes, Japan.

KEEI (Korea Energy Economics Institute) (2001), *2001 Yearbook of Energy Statistics*, Seoul.

Korea Gas Corporation (1997), *Feasibility of Northeast Asian Natural Gas Pipelines and Cooperation among Regional Nations: Study on Efficient Strategy for Northeast Asian PNG Projects*, Seoul: Korea Gas Corporation.

Korea South-East Generation Co. (2002), *The Direction of Coal Procurement in New Generation Company*, Seoul.

Korea National Oil Corporation (2001), *Korea Petroleum E & P Activities*, prepared for 18th Korea–Australia Joint Committee on Energy and Mineral Resources Consultation and Cooperation, Seoul.

Ministry of Commerce, Industry and Energy (1999), *Restructuring Plan of Natural Gas Industry and Privatization of KOGAS*, Seoul.

Ministry of Commerce, Industry and Energy (1999), *Restructuring Plan of Electric Power Industry in Korea*, Seoul.

Seung-Jin Kang (2001), 'Long-Term Energy Demand Forecast in Korea', *Korea Energy Review Monthly,* Seoul: Korea Energy Economics Institute.

Soga, Masayoshi and Dae-Hee Lee (1998), 'Future Developments on the Asian Oil Market and Japan-Korea Tie-up Option', *Energy in Japan*, Japan: Institute of Energy Economics.

# Part V

# Strategy for Labor Relations and Social Welfare

# 11. Industrial Relations and Labor Standards in Korea

**Won-Duck Lee and Byoung-Hoon Lee**

## 1. INTRODUCTION

From the mid-1990s, the industrial relations system in Korea has undergone dynamic transformation. During this period, democratization, globalization and the 1997 economic crisis have brought about profound changes in the country's industrial relations and labor standards. Advances towards democracy since 1987 dismantled the authoritarian regime that had pushed economic growth and stifled political development. These led to explosive growth of the labor movement in the late 1980s. Organized labor strengthened its leverage in industrial relations at both the firm and national levels. Workers pressured employers and government to improve working conditions, wages and labor standards through collective bargaining and institutional reforms.

From the early 1990s, globalization forces also exerted substantial influence over industrial relations and government labor policy. Faced with growing global competition, government and employers sought to control wage increases and maintain flexibility in the labor market. Trade unions demanded that labor rights be strengthened to comply with international standards. In 1996 the government initiated a nationwide tripartite dialogue with employers and workers in an effort to reform existing labor laws. After severe confrontations across the nation, a wide-ranging revision of labor-related laws was completed in early 1997.

The outbreak of the economic crisis in December 1997 had a profound impact on industrial relations in Korea. In January 1998, the government convened the Tripartite Commission to deal with a range of pressing issues including mass unemployment, economic restructuring, and reforming labor standards. The Commission produced the historic 'Social Pact' in February 1998, comprising agreements on legislative reforms to provide greater flexibility in the labor market as well as to improve labor rights. The government soon launched major programs to overhaul the economy. This caused intense conflict with trade unions that opposed large-scale dismissals in the private and public sectors. Concurrently, the government instituted legislation and social programs to protect the unemployed and women workers.

This chapter reviews the historical development of Korea's industrial relations and labor standards since 1987. It also outlines the current industrial relations system, including its three major players – workers, employers and government – as well as the institutional structures of interest, representation and conflict resolution. In conclusion, outstanding issues in social dialogue and labor standards facing Korea today are addressed.

## 2. INDUSTRIAL RELATIONS IN KOREA

### 2.1 Recent Developments

Until 1987, industrial relations were dominated by the government as part of national economic growth policies. During this period, the government's interventionist labor policy tightly controlled workers' collective actions to form trade unions or to strike. At the corporate level, while the government's labor-exclusionist policies restricted union activities, employers were free to exercise their managerial prerogatives in determining wages and work rules. Until 1987, because tightly controlled labor unions were too weak to voice their members' discontent and demands, industrial relations were by and large stable and static under the condition that state authority and employers' interests prevailed.

In June 1987, the growing power of the civil movement pressured the ex-military ruling group to proclaim the 'Declaration of Democratization', which provided critical momentum for political liberalization. The 'Great Labor Struggle' that closely followed the announcement of the Declaration forced the dismantling of the existing industrial relations system dominated by management and authoritarian government.

After 1987, as summarized in Table 11.1, industrial relations in Korea underwent four phases characterized by (1) expansion of organized labor; (2) neo-interventionist government policy; (3) a tripartite approach to labor reforms; and (4) economic and labor market restructuring.

#### 2.1.1 Expansion of organized labor (1987–89)

This phase began with a dramatic surge in labor disputes starting from the second half of 1987. As illustrated in Table 11.2, the number of recorded labor disputes skyrocketed from 276 in 1986 to 3749 in 1987, and more than 1600 were recorded in the following two years (1988–89). As shown in Table 11.3, the number of trade unions increased almost three-fold (from 2742 to 7883) between 1986 and 1989. During this period union membership nearly doubled from 1.050 million to 1.931 million, and the unionization rate also soared from 11.7 per cent to 18.6 per cent (Table 11.3).

Facing a now organized offensive labor, and succumbing to intense social pressures for democratization, the government abandoned its interventionist labor policy and officially recognized the autonomy of labor unions and management in dealing with firm-level labor issues.

The explosive growth of the labor movement in this period also transformed firm-level industrial relations towards a balance of power between labor and management. In the process, management's tight control over workers was substantially eroded, and labor unions in many large firms took control of the shop floor. Management was pressured to accept wage increases, improve working conditions and establish corporate welfare programs. Between 1987 and 1989, average nominal wage increases per year exceeded 12 per cent in all industries. In the manufacturing sector, average nominal wages increased 18 per cent year-on-year during the same period (Lee and Choi 1998).

*Table 11.1 Development of Industrial Relations in Korea since 1987*

| | 1st Phase (1987–89) Expansion of organized labor | 2nd Phase (1990–92) Return to government intervention | 3rd Phase (1993–97) Tripartite approach towards labor reforms | 4th Phase (1998–) Economic and labor market restructuring |
|---|---|---|---|---|
| Economic environment | • boom | • slump | • globalization | • crisis |
| Union activities | • explosive growth | • decline | • steady decrease | • stagnation |
| Labor disputes | • drastic increase | • sharp decrease | • overall stabilization | • steady increase |
| Labor policy | • recognition of labor and management autonomy from government | • intervention for social stability and wage control | • participatory dialogue for labor reforms | • tripartite commission and promotion of labor market flexibility |

*Table 11.2 Changes in Major Indexes of Recorded Labor Disputes*

| Year | No. of disputes | No. of participating workers (1000 persons) | Lost work days (1000 days) |
|---|---|---|---|
| 1986 | 276 | 47 | 72 |
| 1987 | 3749 | 1262 | 6947 |
| 1988 | 1873 | 293 | 5401 |
| 1989 | 1616 | 409 | 6351 |
| 1990 | 322 | 134 | 4487 |
| 1991 | 234 | 175 | 3271 |
| 1992 | 235 | 105 | 1528 |
| 1993 | 144 | 109 | 1308 |
| 1994 | 121 | 104 | 1484 |
| 1995 | 88 | 50 | 393 |
| 1996 | 85 | 79 | 893 |
| 1997 | 78 | 44 | 445 |
| 1998 | 129 | 146 | 1452 |
| 1999 | 198 | 92 | 1366 |
| 2000 | 250 | 178 | 1890 |
| 2001 | 234 | 89 | 1083 |

*Source*: Korea Labor Institute (2001).

*Table 11.3 Changes in Major Indexes of Trade Unions by Year*

| End of year | End of year (E/A) | Union Membership (1000 persons) | Union Density* (%) |
|---|---|---|---|
| June 1987 | 2742 | 1050 | 11.7 |
| 1987 | 4103 | 1267 | 13.8 |
| 1988 | 6164 | 1707 | 17.8 |
| 1989 | 7883 | 1932 | 18.6 |
| 1990 | 7698 | 1887 | 17.2 |
| 1991 | 7656 | 1803 | 15.9 |
| 1992 | 7527 | 1735 | 15.0 |
| 1993 | 7147 | 1667 | 14.2 |
| 1994 | 7025 | 1659 | 13.5 |
| 1995 | 6606 | 1615 | 12.7 |
| 1996 | 6424 | 1559 | 12.2 |
| 1997 | 5733 | 1484 | 11.2 |
| 1998 | 5560 | 1402 | 11.5 |
| 1999 | 5637 | 1481 | 11.8 |
| 2000 | 5698 | 1527 | 11.6 |

*Note*: * Union density = (number of union members/total number of employed workers) × 100.

*Source*: Korea Labor Institute (2001).

Remarkable changes took place in the composition of labor unions during this period. First, the most unionized industrial sector changed from the textile sector, whose workforce was mainly female, to the metal and chemical industries with an overwhelmingly male workforce. This shift reflects the change in Korea's economic structure taking place during the 1980s. Since 1987, male-dominated labor unions representing heavy industries have led the labor movement at the national level. Membership of white-collar labor unions in service industries such as banking, mass media and health care also grew sharply during this period.

Second, many of the newly organized trade unions were critical of the submissive stance of the Federation of Korean Trade Union (FKTU) toward the government's arbitrary labor policies and hence rejected affiliation with the FKTU. The so-called 'democratic unions' formed their own independent federations, which have since espoused militant unionism.

**2.1.2 Return to government intervention (1990–92)**

During the second post-1987 phase, the Korean economy entered recession. The government responded by resuming intervention in labor relations at the firm level, aiming to stimulate economic recovery. In 1991 and 1992 the government enforced a wage-control policy to hold rising labor costs in check and enhance corporate competitiveness. The government also took a hard-line stance on militant union activism and imposed heavy penalties on illegal union activities. During this period, the government urged management to apply a 'no work, no pay' policy to deter workers from engaging in strikes.

Unionization and the number of labor disputes began to drop during this period, as shown in Tables 11.2 and 11.3. The stall in union activism is attributable to (1) the economic slump; (2) the government's neo-interventionist labor policies; (3) significant improvements in working conditions, including wages, during the previous few years; and (4) waning public sympathy towards militant unionism after the collapse of the communist bloc in the late 1980s and early 1990s. In the meantime, two groups of independent unions established themselves as national-level organizations: the National Council of Trade Unions (NCTU) representing the manufacturing sector, and the Council of Occupational Trade Unions (COTU) representing the service sector.

During the second phase, employers began to implement new personnel policies such as flexible wage plans (for example merit-based remunerations) and performance appraisal for individual workers, to regain management control of shop-floor operations. However, these new personnel policies failed to take root in many firms due to strong opposition from unions. In response to the rising interest in reforming the institutional framework of industrial relations, in April 1992 the government formed the Labor Laws Review Committee (LLRC), composed of academic experts and workers' and employers' representatives as an advisory body to the Labor Minister. The committee conducted extensive studies on labor law reforms. President Kim Young-Sam, who took office in February 1993, established the PCIRR to launch a full-scale revision of labor laws in 1996. His regime viewed labor reform as the final task in national reforms and a prerequisite to the country's entry to the OECD.

### 2.1.3 A tripartite approach to labor reforms (1993–97)

By this time the complex forces of globalization had registered palpably in Korea, increasing the imperative to improve Korea's economic competitiveness internationally. The government took a new approach in its attempt to settle labor–management confrontations. Integral to the new government policy was the introduction of a 'social dialogue' model involving tripartite consultation at the national level among the three major parties – unions, employers and the government.[1]

Facilitated by the government, the two major labor federations – the FKTU and the Korea Employers Federation (KEF) – reached national-level agreements on wage increases and employment policy in 1993 and 1994. The FKTU–KEF agreements were used as a guideline for wage negotiations at the enterprise level. However, in 1995 workers halted these consultations as the FKTU was increasingly discredited for upholding the government's wage-control policy.

The Presidential Commission on Industrial Relations Reform (PCIRR), established in May 1996, further advanced tripartism. The Commission was formed as an advisory body to the President and comprised representatives from trade unions, employers' associations, public interest groups and academics. The PCIRR provided an open forum for social dialogue among various stakeholders with regard to labor law reform. The PCIRR included representatives of the KCTU (Korean Confederation of Trade Unions), the second national assembly of democratic labor unions. Born of a merger between the NCTU and the COTU in November 1995, the KCTU had yet to gain legal recognition at that time. Although the government did not participate directly in the PCIRR, it was heavily involved in the discussions and negotiations between the two core participating groups of workers and employers.

Following a number of public hearings, subcommittee workshops and plenary sessions, the PCIRR submitted to President Kim Young-Sam a consolidated set of recommendations on reforming labor legislation.[2] On 26 December 1996, however, the government and the ruling party passed their own bill revising existing labor laws while opposition lawmakers were absent from the parliament. The government's unilateral revision of labor legislation, which placed more emphasis on labor-market flexibility than on labor rights and unionization, triggered nationwide strikes and anti-government protests at the end of 1996 and early in 1997. Under heightened pressure from unions and the international community, the government conceded its contentious revision of labor laws and eventually revised these laws further through consultations with opposition parties in March 1997.[3]

Not only was there a noticeable decline in labor disputes during this period, but the agenda on the table also changed. As we see in Table 11.4, until 1994 the most important source of conflict between labor and management concerned workers' demands for increased wages. Since then, however, wage issues were overtaken by collective agreements as the major source of labor conflicts. More trade unions followed legal procedures in resolving disputes, providing prior notice and allowing a 'cooling-off period' before initiating a strike. The percentage of lawful practices rose from 20–30 per cent in the late 1980s to 70–80 per cent in the mid-1990s.

*Table 11.4 Major Causes of Labor Disputes*

(unit: %)

| Year | Demand for wage increase | Collective agreement | Overdue payment of wages | Worker dismissals | Others* |
|---|---|---|---|---|---|
| 1988 | 50.5 | 24.8 | 3.2 | 5.9 | 15.6 |
| 1989 | 45.9 | 27.7 | 3.7 | 5.0 | 17.7 |
| 1990 | 51.9 | 15.8 | 3.1 | 5.6 | 23.6 |
| 1991 | 56.4 | 24.8 | 2.1 | 3.0 | 13.7 |
| 1992 | 54.7 | 20.0 | 11.5 | 1.7 | 12.1 |
| 1993 | 45.8 | 36.1 | 7.6 | 0.7 | 9.8 |
| 1994 | 42.1 | 34.7 | 5.0 | 2.5 | 15.7 |
| 1995 | 37.5 | 55.7 | 0.0 | 1.1 | 5.7 |
| 1996 | 22.4 | 72.9 | 1.2 | 0.0 | 3.5 |
| 1997 | 23.1 | 65.4 | 3.8 | 0.0 | 7.7 |
| 1998 | 21.7 | 44.2 | 17.8 | 2.3 | 7.8 |
| 1999 | 20.2 | 44.9 | 11.1 | 0.0 | 23.7 |
| 2000 | 18.8 | 66.8 | 2.8 | 0.8 | 10.8 |

*Note*: * These include plant closings/lock-outs, unfair labor practices, and business restructuring.

*Source*: Korea Labor Institute (2001a).

### 2.1.4 Economic restructuring (1998–present)

The foreign exchange crisis in November 1997 had a profound impact on industrial relations. President-elect Kim Dae-jung established the Tripartite Commission in January 1998 to promote cooperation among the three key parties – government, labor unions and employers – in overcoming the economic crisis. On 9 February 1998, the Commission concluded a historic social pact covering an extensive agenda of 90 articles (Table 11.5). The social pact made an important contribution to coping with the economic crisis by improving the country's credibility as assessed by foreign financial institutions.

*Table 11.5 Key Contents of the Social Pact*

(1) Promotion of management transparency and corporate restructuring
(2) Stabilization of consumer prices
(3) Employment stabilization and policies to alleviate unemployment
- Improvement in the employment insurance system and expansion of its coverage
- Support for unemployed workers
- Enlargement of job placement service
- Expansion of vocational training
- Job creation

(4) Expansion and consolidation of the social security system
- Integration of the health insurance system and expansion of its coverage
- Enactment of Worker's Wage Claims Act

(5) Wage stabilization and the promotion of labor–management cooperation
- Securing the effectiveness of collective agreements

(6) Enhancement of basic labor rights
- Legalizing teachers' unions
- Securing trade unions' right to engage in political activities
- Establishment of works councils for government officials from January 1999
- Recognition of unemployed workers' rights to join sectoral trade unions

(7) Enhancement of labor market flexibility
- Introduction of a worker dispatch scheme
- Deregulation of restrictions on dismissals for managerial reasons

*Source*: KILF (1998).

Immediately after signing the social pact, however, the KCTU leadership faced strong criticism from its members for agreeing to the passage of legislation enabling dismissal of redundant workers. As a result, the KCTU withdrew its participation from the Commission, bringing to a halt the Commission's first round of consultations. The second round of Tripartite Commission consultations began in June 1998. The main objectives here were to monitor the implementation of agreements made by the first Commission, and to promote tripartite consultations over economic restructuring, particularly with regard to the banking, finance and public sectors. The second-round Commission made substantial progress by reaching tripartite agreements on detailed policy proposals, including legalization of teachers' unions and integration of the two-tiered health insurance system. This was despite facing obstacles such as mutual distrust among the parties and opposition to government-led economic restructuring from trade unions, the latter as demonstrated potently by KTCU-led general strikes. The Commission eventually reached a dead end when the KCTU withdrew its participation from the Commission for the second time in early 1999. Although the third round of the Commission started in September 1999, its role in promoting tripartite dialogue was weakened to a large extent by continued confrontations between the KCTU and the government.

In 1998, as shown in Table 11.2, the number of recorded labor disputes began to rise again – almost doubling from 129 in 1998 to 250 in 2000. This was a reversal in the trend of the previous three years (1995–97), when the average number of disputes was less than 100. A large number of conflicts during this period concerned overdue wage payments and business downsizing and restructuring (categorized as 'others' in Table 11.4). In particular, several large-scale confrontations took place at large firms, such as the Hyundai Motor Company, the Daewoo Motor Company, Korea Telecom, and commercial banks, since trade unions opposed both government policies to restructure the public sector and the banking industry, and management-led employment adjustment plans.

Trade unions made unprecedented concessions during the period of economic crisis. In particular, they agreed to wage freezes and reduced bonuses and welfare programs. As illustrated in Table 11.6, the overall wage increase in 1998 was –2.7 per cent. On the whole, the priority of labor unions shifted from members' benefits and working conditions to job security after experiencing massive employment adjustments and reduced demand for labor between 1998 and 1999. As the Korean economy showed some signs of recovery from the crisis in the second half of 1999, workers demanded renegotiations of earlier agreements, obtaining wage increases of more than 7 per cent in 2000.

*Table 11.6 Changes in Wage Contracts, 1998–2000**

(Unit: %)

| | 1998 | | 1999 | | 2000 | |
|---|---|---|---|---|---|---|
| | Gross wages | Base salary | Gross wages | Base salary | Gross wages | Base salary |
| All sectors | –2.7 | 0.0 | 2.1 | 2.1 | 7.6 | 7.2 |
| Private sector | –2.6 | 0.1 | 2.3 | 2.2 | 7.7 | 7.2 |
| Public sector | –3.1 | –0.7 | –0.5 | 0.0 | 7.2 | 6.9 |

*Note*: * These data are for establishments with more than 100 employees.

*Source*: Korea Labor Institute, *Quarterly Analysis of Labor Trends*, 1998–2000.

Widespread downsizing at unionized firms caused union membership to decline in 1997 and 1998. However, the total number of unions and members increased slightly in 1999 as new groups of workers such as teachers who were hitherto denied rights to unionize and non-standard employees formed labor unions. This period also witnessed mergers of industrial federations, most of them affiliated with the KCTU. Several industrial federations, including the Medical and Health Industrial Union (1998), the Banking Workers Industrial Union (2000) and the Metal Workers Industrial Union (2001) underwent structural changes to adopt the industrial union model.

## 2.2 Overview of Current Industrial Relations

### 2.2.1 Main actors

Trade unions in Korea are predominantly enterprise-based, although industrial unions have appeared in recent years. Such enterprise unionism has contributed to decentralized collective bargaining practices. Enterprise-level branches of industrial unions also exercise substantial autonomy in union administration and collective bargaining.

The labor movement in Korea is currently divided between two national federations: the FKTU and the KCTU. As of the end of 2000, the FKTU had 28 affiliates (industrial federations or industrial unions) made up of 3754 individual unions and 872 100 members, while the KCTU had 15 affiliates comprising 1362 unions and 615 000 members (Ministry of Labor 2000). The KCTU, which gained legal recognition in November 1999, tends toward militant activism, whereas the FKTU shows a more cooperative stance toward the government and employers. The average size of KCTU-affiliated unions (452 members) is almost twice that of FKTU-affiliated unions (232 members) (Ministry of Labor 2000). Many labor unions at large firms that organized after 1987 are affiliated with the KCTU.

Two national-level organizations represent the interests of employers: the Korea Employers Federation (KEF) and the Federation of Korean Industries (FKI). While the FKI consists mainly of *chaebol* (conglomerate) groups and deals with issues of economic policies, the KEF includes small firms as well as *chaebol* companies and focuses on industrial relations issues. The KEF, founded in 1970, is a nationwide umbrella organization encompassing 13 regional employers' associations, 20 economic and trade associations, and approximately 4000 enterprises in the manufacturing, construction, transportation, banking and insurance, and service industries (KEF 2000).

The KEF has been the official voice of Korean employers in national-level negotiations and consultations regarding industrial relations issues, as demonstrated by its representative roles in the PCIRR and the Tripartite Commission. In fact, KEF's growing role as a major player in industrial relations is attributable to growth in the labor movement in the late 1980s and government-initiated tripartite efforts in the 1990s.

The Ministry of Labor is the government body that administers labor policies. Within the Ministry, the Labor Policy Bureau and the Labor–Management Cooperation Office are in charge of policymaking and administration regarding industrial relations issues. The Labor Policy Bureau consists of three divisions: the Labor Policy Division, the Trade Unions Division and the Labor–Management Consultation Division.

The Ministry of Labor operates 46 local offices including six Regional Administration Offices located in major cities – Seoul, Pusan, Incheon, Daegu, Daejun and Kwangju – as well as 40 Regional Offices. Labor inspectors in each Regional Office are charged with supervising working conditions in accordance with the Labor Standards Act. These inspectors are also responsible for taking actions to address unfair practices and to resolve labor disputes at firms located in their regional area.

### 2.2.2 Systems of collective bargaining and consultation

Collective bargaining at most unionized firms is conducted primarily at the firm level in accordance with the enterprise-based union structure. There are a few exceptions, notably the transportation (for example taxi and bus) and textiles sectors, which conduct regional or industry-level bargaining. The Trade Union and Labor Relations Adjustment Act of 1997 stipulates that no collective agreement will remain valid after two years. In general, collective bargaining for wages is conducted yearly, while negotiations covering other working conditions take place every two years.

Although Korea's collective bargaining structure is decentralized, the influence of national federations over company-level bargaining is far from negligible. As illustrated in Table 11.7, the FKTU and KCTU make nationwide bargaining demands for wage increases and other contractual changes (for example in recent years, the reduction of working hours and improving employment security) at the beginning of every year, which serve as an influential guideline to enterprise-level collective bargaining. In response to these proposals by national union houses, the KEF offers its own negotiation guidelines to member companies.

*Table 11.7 Proposals for Wage Negotiations by Workers and Employers*

(unit: %)

| | Final Wage Contracts | KEF's Proposals | FKTU's Demands | KCTU's Demands |
|---|---|---|---|---|
| 1988 | 13.5 | 7.5–8.5 | 29.3 | – |
| 1989 | 17.5 | 10.9 (8.9–12.9) | 26.8 | 37.3 |
| 1990 | 9.0 | 7.0 | 17.3–20.5 | 23.3 |
| 1991 | 10.5 | 7.0 | 17.5 | 22.2 |
| 1992 | 6.5 | 5.7 (4.7–6.7) | 15.0 | 25.4 |
| 1993 | 5.2 | 4.7–8.9 | FKTU–KEF | 18.0 |
| 1994 | 7.2 | 5.0–8.7 | national agreement | 16.4 |
| 1995 | 7.7 | 4.4–6.4 | 12.4 | 14.8 |
| 1996 | 7.8 | 4.8 | 12.2 | 14.8 |
| 1997 | 4.2 | wage freeze | 11.2 | 10.6±3 |
| 1998 | 0.0 | 20% labor cost reduction | 4.7 | 5.1–9.2 |
| 1999 | 2.1 | wage freeze | 5.5 | 7.7 |
| 2000 | 7.6 | 5.4 | 13.2 | 15.2 |
| 2001 | – | 3.5 | 12.0 | 12.7 |

*Source: Korea Labor Institute* (2001a).

Labor–management councils are another channel that promotes communication and cooperation between employees and management. The legal base for labor–management councils is the Act on Promotion of Worker Participation and Cooperation (APWPC),[4] which stipulates that all companies with more than 30 workers should form a council and hold regular meetings every quarter. As shown in Table 11.8, the number of firms that formed a council under the APWPC grew by 72 per cent between 1996 and 1999.

The labor–management council is composed of the same number of representatives from employees and management, usually totaling three to ten persons from each side. The APWPC mandates that trade union leaders will represent employees in labor–management councils in companies where a majority of the workforce is organized. In addition, the Act requires certain issues such as workers' training and welfare plans to be endorsed by the council before they are implemented. Labor–management councils have become an effective vehicle of extended collective bargaining for many trade unions in organized firms.

*Table 11.8 Firms Covered by Labor–Management Councils*

| | 1993 | 1994 | 1995 | 1996 | 1997 | 1998 | 1999 |
|---|---|---|---|---|---|---|---|
| Eligible firms | 14 583 | 14 661 | 14 961 | 15 243 | 28 735 | 27 453 | 27 643 |
| LMCs | 14 490 | 14 606 | 14 782 | 15 197 | 24 411 | 26 249 | 26 172 |
| % of firms | 99.3 | 99.6 | 98.8 | 99.6 | 85.0 | 95.6 | 94.7 |

*Source*: Ministry of Labor, *Yearbook of Labor Statistics*, various years.

The Labor Relations Commission (LRC) is the official mediator of labor disputes in Korea. Membership is tripartite and consists of representatives of trade unions, management and the public interest. Members of the Commission representing the public interest are elected by representatives of labor and management. The LRC has local offices in 13 major cities. Its headquarters, the Central Labor Relations Commission, is charged with mediating disputes of significant magnitude involving two or more cities or provinces.

Arbitration for labor disputes in the public services sector is governed by the Trade Union and Labor Relations Adjustment Act (TULRA) of 1997. Conditions for arbitration in the public services sector are relatively stricter than those for private sector industries. TULRA divides the public services sector into 'general' and 'essential' services. State and private companies administering water, electricity, gas supply, oil refinery and supply services, telecommunications, railways and hospitals are classified as providing essential services. All disputes in these industries must be arbitrated by the LRC upon recommendation by a Special Mediation Committee, which is composed of three members representing the public interest.

## 3. LABOR STANDARDS IN KOREA

### 3.1 Historical Development of Labor Standards

The Labor Standards Act (LSA) outlines the basic framework for labor standards in Korea. The LSA was promulgated in 1953 during the Korean War. This Act contained many of the elements of worker protection in Japanese labor law and was considered fairly advanced given Korea's economic situation at the time. The LSA has since gone through several revisions. Amendments followed major political upheavals such as the military coup of 1961, the declaration of national emergency in 1974 and the democratic movement of 1987. The current LSA was revised comprehensively in 1997 as a result of tripartite consultations under the PCIRR. The Act was partially amended again in 1998 amidst the economic crisis, based on the social pact reached by the Tripartite Commission.

Following the enactment of the LSA, various labor laws have been passed during the 1980s and 1990s, further defining workers' rights and labor standards. Table 11.9 groups these laws into the following three categories in terms of their main objectives:

- Category A: protecting and promoting employment for target groups including women, the elderly, people with disabilities, temporary help agency (or dispatched) workers and the unemployed.
- Category B: improving wages, working conditions and benefits.
- Category C: promoting industrial safety and occupational health.

*Table 11.9 Historical Development of Labor Standards Legislation in Korea*

| Name of legislation (Category) | Time of enactment | Major amendments from 1997 |
|---|---|---|
| Labor Standards Act | May 1953 | March 1997; February 1998 |
| Act on the Prevention of Pneumoconiosis and Protection of Pneumoconiosis Workers (C) | December 1984 | December 1999 |
| Minimum Wage Act (B) | December 1986 | October 2000 |
| Equal Employment Act (A) | December 1987 | February 1999 |
| Industrial Safety and Health Act (C) | January 1990 | January 2000 |
| Act on Employment Promotion and Vocational Rehabilitation for the Disabled (A) | January 1990 | January 2000 |
| Employee Welfare Fund Act (B) | August 1991 | March 2001 |
| The Elderly Workers Employment Promotion Act (A) | December 1991 | December 1997 |
| Employment Insurance Act (A) | December 1993 | December 2000 |
| Act on Promotion of Welfare of Workers in Small and Medium Enterprises (B) | December 1993 | February 1998 |
| Industrial Accident Compensation Insurance Act (C) | December 1994 | December 1999 |
| Act on the Employment, etc., of Construction Workers (A) | December 1996 | |
| Assistance to Workers' Life Improvement and Employment Security Act (A) | August 1997 | February 1998 |
| Act relating to Protection, etc., for Dispatched Workers (A) | February 1998 | |
| Wage Claims Act (B) | February 1998 | December 2000 |
| Prevention of Gender Discrimination Act (A) | February 1999 | January 2001 |

*Source*: Ministry of Labor, *Labor White Paper*, various years.

### 3.2 Labor Standards Framework in Korea

The constitution of the Republic of Korea stipulates in Article 32 (3) that 'standards relating to working conditions shall be determined by law to guarantee human dignity'. The LSA, made effective by constitutional provision, sets forth the minimum level of working conditions required to guarantee workers' dignity and governs basic labor standards covering all aspects of employee–employer relations. The LSA has 12 chapters: (1) General Provisions, (2) Labor Contracts, (3) Wages, (4) Working Hours and Recess, (5) Women and Minors, (6) Safety and Health, (7) Apprenticeship, (8) Accident Compensation, (9) Rules of Employment, (10) Dormitories, (11) Labor Inspectors, and (12) Penal Provisions. This Act applies to all establishments where work is performed, with certain provisions for companies with less than five employees.[5] Here we delineate the key contents of labor standards prescribed by the LSA, focusing on basic labor rights, dismissal, compensation and working hours. We also discuss related labor laws.

#### 3.2.1 Employees' basic rights

The Labor Standards Act states explicitly that the conditions it sets out are an absolute minimum and no party is to undermine working conditions on the pretext of complying with this Act (Article 2). Labor contracts that do not meet the standards set by the LSA are declared void (Article 22). The Act prohibits discriminatory treatment (Article 5), forced labor (Article 6), violence (Article 7) and exploitation of workers by traffickers and intermediaries not recognized by the law (Article 8). Workers are guaranteed the right to exercise their civil rights (Article 9). In addition to the LSA, the Equal Employment Act and the Prevention of Gender Discrimination Act provide legal protection to women at work.

The LSA also states that working conditions for part-time workers are determined in proportion to the working hours of full-time employees engaged in the same kind of economic activity (Article 25). In early 1998, the Protection of Dispatched Workers Act was enacted to facilitate the employment of dispatched workers while protecting their rights.

#### 3.2.2 Dismissal for managerial reasons

In accordance with Article 30 of the LSA, employers are prohibited from dismissing a worker without justifiable reason. An additional article, Article 31, was adopted in the 1998 amendment of the LSA to provide for dismissals under urgent managerial needs that include the merger and acquisition of firms. To legitimately dismiss workers for managerial reasons, employers must first: (1) make every effort to avoid dismissal; (2) establish rational and fair criteria for selecting employees to be dismissed; (3) not discriminate on the ground of gender; (4) notify trade union and employee representatives of plans for dismissal 60 days in advance; and (5) report to the Minister of Labor when dismissing more than the number of workers specified by Presidential Decree. Article 31/2 requires an employer who has dismissed workers to make an effort to rehire those employees when recruiting new staff within the next two years. Under Article 32, dismissed workers must be given a 30-day advance notice or be paid full wages for the work days in that period in lieu of prior notice.

Although the provision on dismissals was born out of social accord among the tripartite partners, in practice employers relied more on early retirement packages and economic incentives for voluntary separation than on dismissals when restructuring their businesses. This was largely due to strong resistance from unions and workers. Trade unions argued for employment security and sought to abolish Article 31. On the other hand, employers, particularly multinational employers operating in Korea, demanded more flexibility so that dismissals could be at the discretion of employers as is the case in the United States.

### 3.2.3 Compensation

The LSA states that wages must be paid in cash on a fixed day more than once per month (Article 42). If a business is suspended for reasons attributable to the employer, the employer is to pay workers more than 70 per cent of their average remuneration during the period of business suspension (Article 45). In the event of bankruptcy, the LSA guarantees preferential reimbursement of workers' wages over taxes, public levies or other financial claims against the business (Article 37). A second recourse for workers seeking compensation is the Wage Claim Fund, which was created through the Wage Claims Act. This Act obliges the government to pay a share of overdue wages to employees of bankrupt companies. Article 34 of the LSA requires employers to set up a severance pay system that pays a retiring or dismissed worker an average wage of more than 30 days pay for each consecutive year of their employment with that employer's firm.

Article 55 designates that employees be paid additional remuneration in excess of 50 per cent of their normal hourly wage for extended work, night work, and work performed on holidays. Night work is defined as work carried out from 10 p.m. to 6 a.m.

Under Chapter 8 of the LSA, an employer must compensate employees for any job-related injuries, illness or death with compensation amounts that are set by law. The LSA mandates the establishment of various compensation plans related to industrial accidents, such as compensation for medical treatment, payment towards suspended work, disability insurance, and compensation for surviving family members in the case of worker's death. All workers must take out industrial accident compensation insurance as called for by the Industrial Accident Compensation Insurance Act. This protects workers against liabilities induced by occupational injuries in accordance with the LSA.[6]

The Minimum Wage Act (MWA), which came into effect in 1988, serves as the statutory basis for guaranteeing workers' basic needs. In accordance with this Act, the Minimum Wage Council (MWC) was established to determine annually the level of minimum wages. The Council comprises 27 members, with equal representation from trade unions, employers and public interest groups. From the 1990s minimum wages have continued to increase for some workers as we see in Table 11.10. During this period the rate of increase in minimum wages surpassed the rate of increase in consumer prices for all years recorded except at the time of the economic crisis (September 1997 to August 1998). However, the share of workers benefiting from the Minimum Wage Act has on the whole shown a decreasing trend since 1992, falling precipitously to a low of 0.4 per cent at the peak of the economic crisis. This decrease reflects that the increase in overall wage levels at all firms, including small firms, has been higher than the increase in minimum wages set by the MWC during this period. It must also be noted that statistics concerning worker beneficiaries of the minimum wage system are for regular workers only and it is estimated that the level of beneficiaries of this system be around 4 to 5 per cent of the workforce if non-standard workers are also taken into account. More workers benefited from a rise in minimum wages between 2000 and 2001 as a result of the government expansion of the coverage of the Minimum Wage Act from November 2000 to include all businesses.

*Table 11.10 Trends in Minimum Wages*[a]

| | Minimum wage per hour (won) | Increase in minimum wage (%) | Increase in consumer prices (%) | Extent of workers who benefited[b] |
|---|---|---|---|---|
| 1990 | 690 | 15.0 | 8.5 | 4.3 |
| 1991 | 820 | 18.8 | 9.3 | 8.6 |
| 1992 | 925 | 12.8 | 6.3 | 8.5 |
| 1993 | 1005 | 8.6 | 4.8 | 4.5 |
| Jan 1994 – Aug 1994 | 1085 | 8.0 | 6.2 (1994) | 2.1 |
| Sep 1994 – Aug 1995 | 1170 | 7.8 | 4.5 (1995) | 2.1 |
| Sep 1995 – Aug 1996 | 1275 | 9.0 | 4.9 (1996) | 1.9 |
| Sep 1996 – Aug 1997 | 1400 | 9.8 | 4.5 (1997) | 2.4 |
| Sep 1997 – Aug 1998 | 1485 | 6.1 | 7.5 (1998) | 2.3 |
| Sep 1998 – Aug 1999 | 1525 | 2.7 | 0.8 (1999) | 0.4 |
| Sep 1999 – Aug 2000 | 1600 | 4.9 | 2.3 (2000) | 1.1 |
| Sep 2000 – Aug 2001 | 1865 | 16.6 | 4.3 (2001) | 2.1 |

*Notes:*
a Throughout most of this period minimum wage guidelines applied to work establishments with 10 or more employees. Coverage was expanded in November 2000 to include all work establishments and this change is therefore recorded in data for the final year in this table.
b (Number of workers earning less than minimum wage/number of workers covered by Minimum Wage Act) x 100.

*Source*: Korea Labor Institute (2001b); Minimum Wage Council, *Handbook of Minimum Wages*, various issues.

### 3.2.4 Work hours

The LSA establishes 44 hours as the maximum work time per week (Article 49). The 1997 amendment of the LSA introduced flexible and selective systems for when work is performed. Flexible work hours are characterized according to time periods, usually of two weeks or one month. The two-week flexible work hour system permits work in excess of the weekly maximum in one week provided that during two weeks the number of hours worked does not exceed 88 hours, and in any one week the hours worked do not exceed 48 hours (Article 50). The one-month flexible working hour system is based on a written agreement between the employer and the workers' representative. Under the one-month system, workers may work in excess of statutory hours per week provided that average hours worked per week across the month do not exceed 44 and average hours worked per day do not exceed eight hours. However, the number of hours worked during any one week and on any one day must not exceed 56 and 12 respectively. The selective work hour system entrusts a worker to decide the starting and finishing times (Article 51). Implementation of this system requires a written agreement with the workers' representative. Employers must also provide workers with a recess of at least 30 minutes for every four hours worked, or at least one hour for every eight hours worked.

Articles 57 and 59 of the LSA refer respectively to workers' entitlements to paid leave annually and monthly. Employers must grant ten days of annual paid leave to workers after their first year of employment without absenteeism. The number of days of paid annual leave increases by one for each consecutive year of service. Employers must grant eight days of paid annual leave to workers with an attendance rate higher than 90 per cent during their first year. Under the LSA, an employer must allow every female worker one day off paid menstruation leave per month (Article 71) and offer pregnant female workers 60 days paid maternity leave (Article 72).[7] A female worker with an infant aged under 12 months is allowed to take at least 30 minutes of nursing time twice a day.

Although statutory holidays and leave days to which a regular Korean worker, whether male or female, is entitled amount to a total of 91 days plus an additional number of days according to years of service (as shown in Table 11.11), workers' use of their statutory holidays and leave is noticeably low in comparison with circumstances in other countries. Korean workers took an average of 78.8 days off work for holiday and other leave in 1998.

*Table 11.11 Workers' Use of Holiday Entitlement and Other Leave in Selected Countries*

(Unit: days)

| Entitlements | Korea[a] | US | Japan | UK | Germany | France | Taiwan | Singapore |
|---|---|---|---|---|---|---|---|---|
| Weekly holidays | 52 | 104 | 104 | 104 | 104 | 104 | 78 | 52 |
| Official holidays | 17 | 10 | 15 | 8 | 12 | 11 | 22 | 11 |
| Monthly leave[b] | 12 | – | – | – | – | – | – | – |
| Annual leave | 10+ | 4 wks by collective bargain | 10–20 | 20–25 by collective bargain | 24 | 30 | 7–30 | 7–14 |
| Total | 91+ | 142 | 129–139 | 132–137 | 140 | 145 | 107–130 | 70–77 |
| Actual usage | 78.8 ('98) | 126 ('95) | 132 ('97) | 136 ('96) | 144 ('96) | 139 ('92) | N/A | N/A |

*Notes:*
a Menstruation leave for women is not included in the Korean case.
b According to the LSA, every Korean worker is entitled to a day leave per month

*Sources*: Japan Institute of Labor (1999); Ministry of Labor, *Facts on Hours of Work, Holidays and Leave*, 1999.

The average number of hours worked per week such as by the Korean paid worker (47.9) is greater than that of paid workers in other industrialized countries such as the United States (34.6), Japan (42.3) and Singapore (46.8) (Table 11.12). Hence labor and government both maintain that the official number of weekly work hours should be reduced to improve the quality of life of Korean workers. However, employers in Korea maintain that Korean labor laws already provide for a relatively large number of paid leave days, making employers in Korea face higher labor costs than their counterparts in other developed countries.

*Table 11.12 Paid Hours Worked Weekly in Selected Countries, 1999*

(Unit: hours)

| | Korea | Spain | France | Japan | US | Singapore |
|---|---|---|---|---|---|---|
| All industries | 47.9 | 36.2 | 40.3 | 42.3 | 34.6 ('98) | 46.8 |
| Manufacturing industries | 50.0 | 36.3 | 39.6 | 42.7 | 41.7 | 49.2 |

*Source*: International Labour Organisation, *Yearbook of Labor Statistics*, 2000.

## 4. CONCLUSION: OUTSTANDING ISSUES IN KOREA'S INDUSTRIAL RELATIONS AND LABOR STANDARDS

Korea's industrial relations system is still transforming from the pre-1987 authoritarian model of industrial relations to a new model of negotiated partnership. The years of economic crisis in the late 1990s have presented challenges to this transformation; relationships between the three parties have often been confrontational at both the national and company levels as businesses were forced to restructure. Nevertheless, on the whole, Korea's labor standards have taken significant steps towards international norms since 1987 in particular, as evidenced by the large body of legislation passed in this period legally guaranteeing improved conditions for workers (Table 11.9).

We conclude this chapter by addressing several key issues that are at the heart of the heated social dialogue today. Perhaps the most contentious is the proposed reduction in the number of hours worked, as designated by law. Trade unions believe that reducing this from 44 to 40 hours per week will improve the quality of workers' lives and help bring down the unemployment rate. They propose making Saturday a non-work day for all (currently practices differ among enterprises). Employers stand equally firm in their position that a five-day working week will inevitably raise labor costs. They also argue that the current provisions for paid leave including annual and monthly leave and menstruation leave for women should be reduced. The Korean government has sought a compromise between the two widely differing views through the consultation process of the Tripartite Commission.

A second contentious issue is growth of the non-standard labor force. Official reports reveal that the share of men and women engaged in atypical work (that is temporary and daily workers) within the total labor force increased from 45.9 per cent in 1997 to 52.4 per cent in 2000. Trade unions and civil action groups call attention to the poor working conditions and unstable employment status of irregular workers. They are rallying support for legislation to protect and improve benefits and employment conditions for these workers. While the national labor centers – the FKTU and the KCTU – have launched campaigns for irregular workers to join them, atypical workers in some enterprises have organized their own trade unions to engage in collective action. Such separate moves have become an issue on their own. Employers are reluctant to extend social protection to irregular workers. Employers insist that the rigidity of existing regulations in employing full-time organized workers leaves them with no other choice than to recruit part-time workers. It can be foreseen that the changing composition of the labor market, resulting in the rapid growth of irregular jobs, will call for continued reform of current labor standards.

Third, in recent years there has been a shift in the organizational structure of trade unions in Korea, from the enterprise union model to the industrial union model. Powerful industrial unions such as the Metal Workers' Federation, the Medical and Health Care Workers' Union (both affiliates of the KCTU) and the Banking Workers' Union (an affiliate of the FKTU) demand that collective bargaining be centralized at the industry level. Employers have rejected this view thus far; hence discord over the bargaining mechanism is likely to persist in the foreseeable future.

Finally, there remain issues surrounding unionization itself. In recent years civil servants have been permitted to form workplace councils, but they are still prohibited from organizing in a union. Workplace council members and union leaders have petitioned the government to grant civil servants the right to organize. Other matters at hand are participation of unemployed workers in trade unions; abolition of legal restrictions and penalties on forming multiple unions within one establishment; and observation of the current policy requiring employers to pay full-time union officials. Of these matters, the issues of multiple unionism and payment of wages to union officials were suspended until 2007 upon agreement in the Tripartite Commission in 2001. This was viewed as a compromise between the KEF and the FKTU, which pursued the prohibition of multiple unionism and the continuation of wage payments to union officials respectively.

## NOTES

1. See Lee (1999) for a detailed chronological analysis of social dialogue in Korea.
2. Among the amendments recommended by the PCIRR, 107 of 148 cases were agreed upon, while 41 issues, including multiple labor unions, dismissal of redundant workers, teachers' right to organize, and replacement of striking workers, remained unresolved.
3. The PCIRR continued to perform its policy advisory function from March 1997 until February 1998. However, its recommendations failed to draw support from organized labor and the media after intensified labor–state confrontations in early 1997.
4. The Labor–Management Council (LMC) was introduced by the Labor–Management Council Act (LMCA) in 1980. Until 1987, LMCs numbered around 6700. The LMCA was replaced by the APWPC in 1997.
5. The LSA did not apply to establishments with less than five employees until amended in February 1998. Today, nine of the 12 chapters of the LSA apply to enterprises with less than five employees.
6. The Industrial Safety and Health Act seeks to ensure the maintenance of work and workplace conditions to prevent industrial accidents and guarantee occupational safety at the workplace. In accordance with this Act, every workplace is required to have a safety and health committee comprising managers and worker representatives to monitor and supervise safety conditions in the workplace.
7. Amendment of Article 72 of the LSA in July 2001 extended paid maternity leave for female workers from 60 to 90 days from November 2001.

## REFERENCES

Choi, Young-Ki (1998), *Labor Relations in the Restructuring Process: Prospects and Challenges (in Korean)*, presented in the KLI workshop on 14 April.

Choi, Young-Ki, Kwang-Suk Chun, Chul-Soo Lee and Bum-Sang You (2000), *Revision of Labor Laws and Labor Relations in Korea: History of Labor Law Reforms since 1987 (in Korean)*, Seoul: Korea Labor Institute.

Federation of Korean Trade Unions (2000), *Report on Activities* (in Korean).

Hyun, Chun-Wook (1999), 'The labor standards act system', in Korea International Labour Foundation (ed.), *Labor Relations in Korea*.

International Labour Organization (2000), *Yearbook of Labor Statistics.*
Japan Institute of Labor (1999), *Databook of Comparative International Labor.*
Korea Employers Federation (2000), *Report on Activities (in Korean).*
Korea International Labour Foundation (1998a), *Current Labor Situation in Korea*, Seoul.
Korea International Labour Foundation (1998b), *Labor Reforms in Korea toward the 21st Century*, Seoul.
Korea International Labour Foundation (1998c), *Handbook of the Social Agreement and New Labor Laws of Korea*, Seoul.
Korea International Labour Foundation (ed.) (1999a), *Labor Relations in Korea*, Seoul.
Korea International Labour Foundation (1999b), *Handbook of Korea's Labor Standards Act*, Seoul.
Korea Labor Institute (2001a), *2001 KLI Labor Statistics (in Korean).*
Korea Labor Institute (2001b), *The Profile of Korean Human Assets: Labor Statistics 2001.*
Korea Labor Institute, *Quarterly Analysis of Labor Trends (in Korean).*
Korea Labor Policy and Information Center (1998), *Labor Laws*, Seoul (in Korean).
Korean Confederation of Trade Unions (2000), *Reports and Data on Activities (in Korean).*
Lee, Byoung-Hoon (1999), 'Social dialogue and labor union's involvement', Presented at *the ILO-KLI regional meeting on 'Organized Labor in the 21st Century*, 7–8 December.
Lee, Byoung-Hoon and Bum-Sang Yoo (1999), 'New experiments of Labor politics in Korea: A comparative study of the PCIRR and the Tripartite Commission' (in Korean), *Korean Journal of Labor Studies*, **4** (1), 83–116.
Lee, Won-Duck (1997), *Industrial Relations Reform: Choice for the Future (in Korean)*, Seoul: Korea Labor Institute.
Lee, Won-Duck and Kang-Shik Choi (1998), *Labor Market and Industrial Relations in Korea: Retrospect on the Past Decade and Policy Directions for the 21st Century*, Seoul: Korea Labor Institute.
Minimum Wage Council, *Handbook of Minimum Wages* (in Korean).
Ministry of Labor (1998), *Labor Administration.*
Ministry of Labor (1999), *Facts on Hours of Work, Holidays and Leave.*
Ministry of Labor (2000), *Current Organizational Status of Trade Unions.*
Ministry of Labor, *Labor White Paper* (for the years 1987–97, in Korean).
Ministry of Labor, *Yearbook of Labor Statistics* (for the years 1990–2000, in Korean).
Park, Jong-Ilcc, Chun-Wook Hyun, Scott Balfour, Gyeong-Joon Yoo and Ha-Nam Phang (1998), *Korean Labor and Employment Laws: an Ongoing Evolution*, Seoul: Korea Labor Institute and Kim and Chang Law Offices.

# 12. Welfare Policy in Korea: Issues and Strategy

**Chong-Bum An and Kwang Choi**

## 1. INTRODUCTION

The importance of social welfare in Korean society and economy will continue in the 21st century. In Korea, as in many nations, rapid development in IT in the late 20th century has served to increase inequality through producing a so-called digital divide between high- and low-income earners, with more from the middle-income group slipping into the low-income group. This development, compounded by a rapidly aging society, is set to result in crises in the national pension and health programs. For these reasons the Korean government is pursuing a new paradigm for social welfare, a move resembling that of other national governments facing similar problems.

From the 1960s, the emphasis of national policy was firmly upon national economic growth, which disabled social welfare as a public means to support the vulnerable and elderly members of society. This policy approach was maintained until the late 1980s. During two decades of high economic growth, the welfare of some of the nation's citizens was therefore neglected in favor of rigorously promoting economic growth. However, with the swift development of political and social democratization in the late 1980s, quality of life suddenly became a major concern of many citizens, who were now freer to demand that their government provide adequate welfare. These new, vigorous demands for welfare forced the government to enhance existing welfare programs and create new ones. The advent of the financial crisis in 1997, however, fundamentally altered this direction. Problems of unemployment, poverty and inequality that Koreans had suffered before the 1960s resurfaced. Both public demand for, and government response to, the nation's welfare needs precipitated a shift in the nature of welfare programs.

Since 1997, two types of demand for welfare have coexisted in Korea. One is the short-run increase in demand for welfare that is typical of developing countries; the other is an increase in the long-run demand for welfare of the type usually provided in developed countries. The former type of welfare, demanded in response to the financial crisis, requires policies for reducing unemployment, poverty and inequality. The latter type of welfare, which is more of an ongoing concern, aims at enhancing quality of life. If these two types are not distinguished in considering appropriate measures for welfare policy, the result may be merely an increased welfare budget without capacity to enhance the people's welfare. Such an approach increases social risk and decreases the productivity of the nation as a whole. Thus, we argue in this chapter that there is clearly the need to introduce a new paradigm for informing welfare policy in order to distinguish between these two different types of welfare demand, and to find an efficient means of raising funds to finance welfare expenditures.

In the next section we briefly review the development of social welfare policy in Korea. In section 3 we discuss social and economic circumstances that have determined the types of welfare demand over time. In section 4 we first discuss the level of the Korean welfare budget through international comparison. Then we consider how the welfare budget is allocated by welfare category, before discussing the role of welfare policy in income distribution. We also consider the appropriateness of the welfare programs produced under this new paradigm under the Kim Dae-jung regime in terms of their ability to meet the current broad range of demands for welfare. In section 5 we turn to the new welfare paradigm in Korea – Productive Welfare – and explore strategies for enhancing welfare funding. In section 6 we discuss possible policy measures for reform of the welfare system to improve current welfare programs. We close this chapter with some concluding remarks.

## 2. HISTORICAL DEVELOPMENT OF WELFARE POLICY

The meaning of 'welfare' is construed broadly in discussions of national policy. Welfare can be linked closely to all basic economic aspirations such as growth, stability, equity and quality of life. Social security policy is at the heart of welfare policies, but many other policies such as those that concern stabilization of the economy, distribution of income, housing, education, environment, small and medium-sized business, and agriculture, can all be included in approaches to providing welfare. Since all policy areas have distinctive characteristics, social policies and welfare can be considered either in connection with, or separate from, problems concerning the distribution of income and wealth.

For our inquiry here into welfare policies in Korea, we need first to examine the changes that have shaped Korean society through the nation's years of high economic growth. Overall we find that welfare and national development policies were dominated by economic concerns – to achieve rapid industrialization, high economic growth and international competitiveness – while the social underlay for this policy strategy was a traditional family-oriented Confucian culture with its explicit understandings about family responsibility for welfare and care.

Korean society has experienced unprecedented change across the last half of the 20th century. These changes stretch well beyond economic activity into population expansion and mobility, education, family and social structures, housing and advancement in international status. After rapid economic growth began in the 1960s, the number of poverty-stricken citizens decreased rapidly, but as the relative gap in incomes expanded, new conflict began between generations, regions, labor and management, and the sexes.

Over the past 50 years government has transformed its social welfare policy approach from remedial to proactive. This is in response to political, economic and social change, and results from ongoing efforts to satisfy the social needs that these changes inspired. Developments can be recognized in four stages: the 1950s, 1960s to mid-1970s, mid-1970s to late 1980s, and late 1980s to the present. In the 1950s welfare policy centered on relief work; in the 1960s on social service; in the 1970s on public assistance; and in the 1980s on social insurance. Here we see that government priorities have differed significantly at each of these stages, but over time the government has increased its support for state-funded welfare. Indeed, with all the experimentation and shift, it can generally be said that the basic structure of the present welfare system was completed by the mid-1980s.

### 2.1 National Rebuilding and Reconstruction: 1945–59

Korean society was poverty-stricken in the late 1940s and 1950s. With Japan's World War II surrender in 1945, Korea regained independence from its colonizer and entered a period under military government by the United States. The 1950s began with the internal struggle of the Korean War. Social welfare at this time was the concern of a small group of humanitarians who emphasized sharing even in times of absolute poverty. Here the concern was to help Korean War refugees, yet this welfare work was considered to be charity provided by private citizens – just as was the philanthropic work of Western Christians, millionaires and the local enlightened cultural movements of nationalists involved in the independence movement. Welfare problems were not yet recognized as social problems caused by changes in capitalist distribution principles or family structure. Poverty and the collapse of family life were seen to be the result of colonial plundering and division of the peninsula through war, problems then thought to be incapable of resolution through government policy.

Demands for public relief became greater than ever during these years of national calamity and low-level industrial productivity. The bulk of the population was poor, abject poverty was common, and the nation was among the world's largest recipients of foreign aid. The parameters of Korea's social welfare system were set largely by private charity groups, especially foreign relief groups.

This was a period shaped by the historical landmarks of independence, war and division of national sovereignty. From establishment in 1948 of the government of the newly independent nation, through the division of the country, the war, and the military coup in the South in May 1961, Korean society experienced continued upheaval. War orphans, widows and widowers, and many others needed support or protection. Although the generally high level of poverty persisted, and calls mounted for government intervention in providing social welfare, the government was in chaos and unable to respond. The public social welfare system failed to function effectively under a weak and incompetent administration. Thus, until the 1960s, publicly provided welfare was limited to facilities for the very needy, and was supported heavily by foreign aid groups and charity work at the private level.

### 2.2 The High-Growth Period: the 1960s

The government of the Third Republic in the 1960s established economic growth and the construction of a welfare state as its major goals for the nation. However, this was to be a certain type of welfare state since the government believed that instead of providing public welfare, it could enable all Koreans to meet their own needs by favoring rapid national economic growth to increase their income themselves. Thus, through the 1960s government concentrated its attention foremost on rapid economic expansion. It showed no interest in raising worker productivity or securing workers' political loyalty through providing welfare programs. Under the national policy ethos of this time, welfare expenditures were seen as an unproductive prodigal outflow. The life protection plan that the government advocated had no relationship to the constitutionally guaranteed right to live decently and was instead a program of relief for the poor.

However, given the dominance of the welfare philosophy mentioned above that effectively delivered the welfare task to the family and the operations of the market rather than to the state, much of the official welfare action involved passing legislation rather than government funding and implementation of welfare programs. Amendments to the national constitution during this period state clearly that the people have the right to live decently (Clause 1, Article 30) and the state is obliged to provide welfare to the needy (Article 2). Because considerable legislation for social welfare was enacted during this period, it is sometimes referred to as the 'mass formation period' in discussion of social welfare legislation.

However, much of this legislation was no more than propaganda promises as the military regime struggled to obtain the legitimacy that it needed. Of the many laws passed, those that were actually carried out included provision of pensions for civil servants and military personnel. This was a system of social insurance involving selected occupational pensions. An insurance plan for industrial calamity compensation was introduced as a modification of the basic social insurance. Yet instead of operating as social insurance through which government could intervene to protect workers in regular industrial relations, this legislation emphasized the benevolence and obligations of the employer instead of the responsibility of the state.

Thus, as the government's welfare administration was consolidated and related laws were enacted, a system of social welfare was formed in Korea, at least in appearance. Government actions, especially through legislation, helped to embed the philosophy of locating responsibility for welfare outside the hands of government. These moves profoundly shaped the subsequent development of welfare in Korea through the years of high economic growth, to some extent both enabling and validating this approach to national economic and social management.

### 2.3 A Decade of Structural Change and Intensive Economic Growth: the 1970s

As results of the high-growth economic development plan became evident from the late 1960s with more people on higher incomes and fewer in poverty, in the following decade the government felt that it could deviate from the 'relief' or 'protection' approach to social welfare policy. Now it paid some attention to programs for the socially weak and outcast sectors of Korean society, aiming to help these people support themselves through voluntary self-rehabilitation. The Social Welfare Business Law was enacted in January 1970, outlining the basic business of social welfare along these lines.

One of the most profound welfare measures enacted during the 1970s was legislation for the national pension plan. The National Welfare Pension was enacted in February 1973, specifying how the national welfare pension plan and its funding scheme would operate. This was the precursor for the National Welfare Pension Insurance Law enacted in December that year. The pension laws were to help ensure stability in the lives of the Korean people, and to promote public welfare through a pension scheme for people in need including the aged, those with incurable diseases and the financial dependents of the deceased.

The national pension plan was not part of planning for the third five-year economic development plan under way when the pension plan was passed in 1973. The Social Security Deliberation Committee had pushed for a social security plan involving pensions since the early 1960s, but this type of plan was never considered in the national development planning process. However, once key policymakers recognized its usefulness for mobilizing internal resources to develop the heavy and chemical industries – then a crucial focus of national economic policy – the national welfare plan was legislated within a year.

The new pension plan was originally scheduled to be put into operation from 1974, but an amendment was passed deferring implementation for a year in response to sudden economic instability in the wake of the Middle East oil crisis. A series of subsequent actions including further legislative amendment, a Presidential Emergency Measure and a presidential order enabled the government to stall enactment of the plan until 1986, and it was not until 1988 that the National Pension Plan was finally put into effect.

The Health Insurance Law was also amended substantially in December 1976. This was to enhance social security by improving the health of the Korean people through national medical insurance, covering not only workers injured at the workplace but all people in sickness, injury or childbirth, as well as providing death insurance. A national health insurance plan enacted in 1963 was introduced on a trial basis. A 1970 amendment could not shift the program from trial to firm policy and it took a second amendment in December 1976, passing the health insurance law into statute, to secure a firm place for this national health insurance scheme.

### 2.4 The Period of Consolidation and Structural Change: 1980–Present Day

The 20 years of rapid national economic development through four five-year plans from 1962 not only increased income and employment levels but provided the foundation for Korea's expanding economic power as a nation. Yet this was a national development strategy focused firmly on economic growth; concerns such as social well-being were sidelined. Providing equal opportunities for Korean people was not part of the strategy and the government expanded its role to accelerate economic development. Two decades on, the negative consequences of this approach to development were evident: a dual economic structure, distortion of income distribution, a shortfall in facilities required to meet basic human needs and the deterioration of trust within Korean society. This approach to economic development was unsustainable for Korean society in the long term. Thus the government recognized that it must change its economic-growth approach to development in order to achieve a better balance between economic and social development. In the early 1980s the government set out new national goals emphasizing construction of a welfare state, pursuit of an equitable society, innovation in education and the promotion of culture. Policy direction was changed accordingly to meet these new objectives.

The constitution of the Fifth Republic, enacted in October 1980, incorporated the welfare state ideology by expanding the people's rights to include the pursuit of happiness, make appropriate wage demands, have access to social welfare and live in a stable environment. The economic articles and clauses of this constitution in particular included regulations to protect the socially weak.

The fifth five-year plan (1982–86) indicated this shift toward balance in the plan's new title: the economic and social development plan. Including social with economic development indicated a shift in philosophy about how to achieve national development, moving from a quantity-centered growth strategy to a quality-centered growth strategy. The 1982–86 fifth plan also shifted from previous plans by not setting an annual investment target and instead claiming to be merely indicative. This plan focused on institutional reform to solve structural problems in the Korean economy and society.

By the second half of 1986 the government was confident that the economy could continue to grow without such extensive government intervention. It held faith in prospects that GNP per capita would reach $4000 by the early 1990s, and on this basis established a social welfare plan to be pursued in the late 1980s. This involved the national welfare promotion policy and a basic plan to improve income distribution through a wider spread of wealth across Korean society. As part of the plan, in 1988 the government introduced measures such as the national pension plan that it had stalled since the 1970s, health insurance for farming and fishing families, and the minimum-wage plan. The minimum-wage plan sought to help create equality by increasing the growth rate of income for low-income earners above the growth rate of the national average income. Other moves aimed specifically at the poor included welfare measures to support those who were alienated from the benefits of national economic growth, including indigent people in the cities and the physically and intellectually handicapped.

From 1987, three ground-breaking changes altered the structure of the social welfare system. These were the introduction of a nationwide health insurance system, a national pension plan, and the Minimum Wage Law, which together constituted a major step forward for social welfare in Korea. The government also employed specialized social welfare workers to improve the provision of social welfare services.

A civilian government was finally established in 1993. This government replaced the seventh five-year economic and social development plan (1992–96) with the five-year New Economy Plan in June 1993, but the content of social welfare policy changed only slightly. The main characteristic of the new regime's welfare policy was not the introduction of a new system, but promoting the existing system and integrating welfare promotion with economic development by improving the efficiency of welfare policies and their management.

One clear example of the few changes the civilian government introduced in the welfare system is the Employment Insurance Law. Employment insurance could usually be cast more accurately as 'unemployment insurance' since it guarantees workers income security for a fixed period while they are unemployed if they are dismissed from their job. However, employment insurance in this instance was not only to provide income security through a period of unemployment but also to improve conditions for retaining employment, through unemployment prevention, employment promotion and training for the unskilled. The new employment insurance system became effective for all industrial firms in June 1995, and specific targets were set for firms with more than 30 full-time workers. Introduction of the employment insurance system meant that Korea had finally developed all the core elements that are usual in a national social-security system, except for child allowance. It is useful to note here the very short period of time during which the various components of this social security system were introduced, faster than in any country in the world.

## 3. CHANGES IN THE DEMAND FOR SOCIAL WELFARE

From the late 1990s, economic difficulty resulting from the financial crisis in 1997 has variously contributed to increases in the demand for social welfare in Korea. Demographic changes are also under way that will inevitably increase these demands further. In this section we will consider three factors that have served to increase welfare demand in recent years and are likely to continue expanding this demand. These three are (1) unemployment, poverty, and inequality since the 1997 financial crisis; (2) aging society; and (3) increases in both the budget deficit and public debt.

### 3.1 Unemployment, Poverty and Inequality since the 1997 Financial Crisis

The financial contagion that began in Southeast Asia a few months earlier struck Korea late in 1997. The economy contracted by 5.8 per cent in 1998, an 11 per cent downswing from the 5.5 per cent growth of 1997. The economic crisis and its consequences dealt a truly devastating blow to the Korean economy and Korean society, saddling many Koreans with severe hardship. Inevitably this produced a dramatic upsurge in demand for social welfare, while reduced employment cut the incomes of many who had, till this time, enjoyed financial independence and had no need for social welfare.

Table 12.1 summarizes the major employment indicators since the financial crisis. With the crisis, the unemployment rate soared from 2.6 per cent in 1997 to 8.6 per cent in February 1999. By September 2000 this rate declined to 3.6 per cent as part of a swift economic recovery. Yet despite the positive signs from this figure, the employment structure was damaged; the labor market was still unstable and employment uncertainties increased the shares in the labor market of temporary workers, long-term unemployed and young workers. The proportion of regular workers fell from 54.1 per cent in 1997 to 48.7 per cent in 2001. Most firms struggled to cope with economic uncertainty by increasing the flexibility of their demand for labor through employing temporary or day workers instead of full-time employees. The proportion of the long-term unemployed (for more than one year) increased from 10.6 per cent in 1997 to 15.1 per cent in 2001. The unemployment rate of workers aged between 15 and 24 became around twice that of the total unemployment rate.

*Table 12.1 Employment Trends, 1997–2001*

(Units: 1000 people; %)

| | 1997 | 1998 | 1999 | 2000 | 2001 |
|---|---|---|---|---|---|
| Economically active people | 21 662 (2.0) | 21 456 (–1.0) | 21 634 (0.8) | 21 950 (1.5) | 22 181 (1.1) |
| Participation in labor market | 62.2 | 60.7 | 60.5 | 60.7 | 60.8 |
| Employed | 21 106 (1.4) | 19 994 (–5.3) | 20 282 (1.4) | 21 061 (3.8) | 21 362 (1.4) |
| Unemployed | 556 | 1461 | 1353 | 889 | 819 |
| Unemployment rate | 2.6 | 6.8 | 6.3 | 4.1 | 3.7 |

*Note*: Figures in parentheses represent the percentage rate of change.

*Source*: Bureau of Statistics (2001c).

Trends in the poverty rate are similar to those in the unemployment rate, as shown in Table 12.2. By the third quarter of 1998 the poverty rate peaked at 7.5 per cent, which was 2.5 times the rate before the crisis. The poverty rate fell to 5.1 per cent in the fourth quarter of 1999, but this is still much higher than it was prior to the crisis.

*Table 12.2 Trends in the Absolute Poverty Rate*

(Unit: 1000 worker households)

| | 1997 | | 1998 | | | | 1999 | | |
|---|---|---|---|---|---|---|---|---|---|
| | | | 1/4 | 2/4 | 3/4 | 4/4 | 1/4 | 2/4 | 3/4 |
| Households in poverty | 183.2 | 391.2 | 374.9 | 410.1 | 426.1 | 381.0 | 380.3 | 379.1 | 308.6 |
| Total households | 6110.4 | 5741.0 | 5824.5 | 5775.4 | 5673.8 | 5690.4 | 5490.0 | 5562.8 | 5573.6 |
| Rate (%) | 3.0 | 6.8 | 6.4 | 7.1 | 7.5 | 6.2 | 6.9 | 6.8 | 5.5 |

*Source*: H. Moon (2000).

Trends in unemployment and in poverty form an inverted-U shape in graph form. Both rose suddenly from the crisis, peaked around mid-1998 and have fallen since. Unlike unemployment and poverty, however, income inequality has reached levels worse than before the financial crisis, as shown in Table 12.3. In 2000, the highest-income group had almost 5.3 times the income share of the lowest-income group. Those already on high incomes were able to increase their wealth easily through higher interest rates – almost double digit since the crisis – and lower taxation on income earned from this interest.[1]

*Table 12.3 Income Distribution, 1990–2000*

| | Incomes shares by classes (%) | | | | | Ratio of class I to class V | Gini co-efficient |
|---|---|---|---|---|---|---|---|
| | Income class I | Income class II | Income class III | Income class IV | Income class V | | |
| 1990 | 8.4 | 13.2 | 17.2 | 22.5 | 38.8 | 4.64 | 0.295 |
| 1995 | 8.5 | 13.5 | 17.5 | 23.0 | 37.5 | 4.42 | 0.284 |
| 1996 | 8.2 | 13.3 | 17.5 | 23.1 | 37.9 | 4.63 | 0.291 |
| 1997 | 8.3 | 13.6 | 17.7 | 23.2 | 37.2 | 4.49 | 0.283 |
| 1998 | 7.4 | 12.8 | 17.1 | 22.9 | 39.8 | 5.41 | 0.316 |
| 1999 | 7.3 | 12.6 | 16.9 | 22.9 | 40.2 | 5.49 | 0.320 |
| 2000 | 7.5 | 12.7 | 17.0 | 22.7 | 40.1 | 5.32 | 0.317 |

*Source*: Bureau of Statistics (2001a).

### 3.2 Aging Society

Problems associated with an aging society have not yet really begun to hit Korea seriously. The share of the population aged 65 and over was still relatively low at 7.6 per cent in 2001 when compared with most developed countries whose share exceeded 10 per cent.

However, the Korean share is expected to rise above 14 per cent by 2019, which could represent the fastest rate of aging in the world (Table 12.4). If forecasts are fulfilled, the time span during which the share of the aged increased from 7 per cent to 14 per cent of Korean society will be only 19 years, while this development spanned 45 years in the UK, 85 years in Sweden, and 115 years in France (Table 12.5). The rapidly aging population together with the current formula for the public pension system for the aged, which some find excessively generous, cannot but generate a severe crisis for the welfare system over the next 30 years.

*Table 12.4 Proportion of the Aged in the Korean Population**

(Units: million; %)

| | 1960 | 1970 | 1980 | 1990 | 1999 | 2000 | 2001 | 2002 | 2005 | 2010 | 2019 | 2026 |
|---|---|---|---|---|---|---|---|---|---|---|---|---|
| Total population | 25.0 | 32.2 | 38.2 | 42.9 | 46.9 | 47.0 | 47.3 | 47.6 | 48.5 | 49.6 | 50.6 | 50.6 |
| Population aged 65 and over | 0.1 | 1.0 | 1.5 | 2.2 | 3.2 | 3.4 | 3.6 | 3.8 | 4.4 | 5.3 | 7.3 | 10.1 |
| Ratio of those aged 65 and over | 2.9 | 3.1 | 3.8 | 5.1 | 6.8 | 7.2 | 7.6 | 7.9 | 9.0 | 10.7 | 14.4 | 20.0 |

*Notes*: * Aged is taken as 65 years and over.

*Source*: Bureau of Statistics (2001b).

*Table 12.5 International Comparison of Aging Societies*

| | Japan | USA | UK | France | Germany | Italy | Korea |
|---|---|---|---|---|---|---|---|
| | Year when specified aged ratios reached (actual and projected) | | | | | | |
| 7% | 1970 | 1942 | 1929 | 1864 | 1932 | 1927 | 2000 |
| 14% | 1994 | 2013 | 1976 | 1979 | 1972 | 1988 | 2019 |
| 20% | 2006 | 2028 | 2021 | 2020 | 2012 | 2007 | 2026 |
| | Time span for the share of the aged | | | | | | |
| (7% – 14%) | 24 | 71 | 47 | 115 | 40 | 61 | 19 |
| (14% – 20%) | 12 | 15 | 45 | 41 | 40 | 19 | 7 |

*Source*: Bureau of Statistics (2001b).

### 3.3 Increases in the Budget Deficit and Public Debt

The financial crisis of 1997 also changed significantly the conditions of the national budget. Until 1997, the Korean government had maintained balance in the national budget for 50 years, working on the principle of 'expenditures within revenue'. The balanced budget principle kept public debt to a minimum. The central government's gross debt was less than 10 per cent of GDP and its net debt was negative. This long period of balanced budget meant that there was revenue in the financial reconstruction and anti-unemployment accounts that the government could use to help rescue the economy from the 1997 financial crisis.

Following the crisis, however, the budget deficit and public debt both increased sharply to become a major concern for those interested in the nation's economic well-being. The consolidated budget deficit increased to 4 per cent of GDP from the balanced budget prior to the crisis. Public debt also increased dramatically, more than doubling from 12 per cent of GDP in 1996 to more than 20 per cent by 1999 (Table 12.6). Moreover, the recent rise in oil prices and the expected slowdown of the economy in coming years might lead to an even larger increase in the budget deficit and public debt in the years ahead. Such budgetary conditions can have a negative effect on the welfare budget, which in 2002 is already small by comparison with other areas of the national budget.

*Table 12.6 Consolidated Budget and Government Debt*

(Units: billion won; %)

| | 1996 | 1997 | 1998 | 1999 | 2000 | 2001 |
|---|---|---|---|---|---|---|
| Total budget | 84 429 | 100 327 | 115 430 | 120 960 | 128 007 | 142 487 |
| Budget balance | 1099 | –6959 | –18 757 | –13 120 | 6527 | 7268 |
| (% of GDP) | (0.3) | (–1.5) | (–4.2) | (–2.7) | (1.3) | (1.3) |
| General account | 13 998 | 13 984 | 7139 | 14 621 | 24 299 | 18 341 |
| Special account | –12 020 | –14 265 | –18 697 | –22 574 | –19 820 | –16 651 |
| Public fund | –436 | 871 | –1043 | –3615 | 3081 | 8546 |
| Others | –443 | –7549 | –6157 | –1552 | –297 | –269 |
| Government debt | | | | | | |
| (trillion won) | 49.7 | 65.6 | 87.6 | 98.6 | 111.3 | 122.1 |
| (% of GDP) | (11.9) | (14.5) | (19.7) | (20.4) | (21.3) | (22.4) |

*Source*: Ministry of Planning and Budget (2002).

## 4. WELFARE BUDGET AND WELFARE PROGRAMS

### 4.1 Korea's Welfare Budget by International Comparison

Compared with the welfare budget of OECD countries, Korea's welfare budget has been held continuously low through the second half of the 20th century. Public assistance and public health in particular appear to have the lowest support of the welfare areas. The small size of the welfare budget can be attributed to the tight focus of national policy on economic growth since the 1960s, which neglected other concerns such as social welfare.

As shown in Table 12.7, in 1998 the ratios of social welfare expenditure to GDP in some developed countries were more than three times higher than that of Korea. This comparison justifies the need to strongly increase the social welfare budget in Korea. Yet this international comparison needs to be used cautiously in determining the extent of welfare budget increases. We need to take into account at least two important considerations that influence the international comparability of Korea's social welfare budget.

First, when we compare welfare expenditures internationally, we need to take into account the tax burden rate together with the ratio of welfare budget to GDP. Most countries with a high ratio of welfare budget to GDP have high tax burden rates, implying that citizens' willingness to pay higher taxes is required when governments maintain a relatively high ratio for welfare budget to GDP. Korea's lower ratio for welfare budget along with lower tax burden rates implies that Koreans are willing to pay lower tax and receive less welfare benefits relative to developed countries. When we take into account Korea's low tax burden rate of 21.1 per cent (Table 12.7), this reduces the apparent poverty of the Korean welfare budget share *vis-à-vis* those of other countries.

*Table 12.7 Social Welfare Budget and Tax Burden Rate in OECD Countries, 1998*

*(Units: % of GDP)*

| | Korea | Japan | USA | UK | Germany | Sweden | France |
|---|---|---|---|---|---|---|---|
| Social welfare expenditure (A) | 5.94 | 14.66 | 14.59 | 24.70 | 27.29 | 30.98 | 28.82 |
| Pension benefits (old age, disabled, survivors) (B) | 2.22 | 7.07 | 6.90 | 13.42 | 12.00 | 10.25 | 13.05 |
| C (A-B) | 3.72 | 7.59 | 7.69 | 11.28 | 15.29 | 20.73 | 15.77 |
| Tax burden rate (D)* | 21.1 | 28.4 | 28.9 | 37.2 | 37.0 | 52.0 | 45.2 |
| A/D | 28.15 | 51.62 | 50.48 | 66.40 | 73.76 | 59.58 | 63.76 |
| C/D | 17.63 | 26.73 | 26.61 | 30.32 | 41.32 | 39.87 | 34.89 |

*Note*: * Social security contribution is included.

*Source:* OECD (1980–98).

Second, we must also take into consideration unpaid pension benefits in assessing the appropriateness of the Korean welfare budget. Although Korea's national pension system was begun in 1988, pension benefits will not be paid to normal retirees until 2008 and until then pension funds will be accumulated. Thus, we need to exclude pension benefit expenditures from the welfare budget since they are not yet being distributed. The Korean welfare budget share without pension benefits appears to be higher than it appears if pension benefits are included. The last row in Table 12.7 below shows a more appropriate way to compare the Korean welfare budget with those of other countries. As we see in Table 12.7, the Korean welfare budget share is still much lower than that of other countries, although the gap reduces when adjustments are made for pension benefits and tax burden rates.

The discussion above points to the low level of the Korean welfare budget by comparison with OECD countries, but we must note here that in recent years under different national policy direction, the government of Kim Dae-jung has increased the welfare budget dramatically. Table 12.8 summarizes recent trends in the welfare budget. The ratio of social security budget to general account almost doubled from 5.64 per cent in 1995 to 10.84 per cent in 2001, while the ratio of the budget of the Ministry of Health and Welfare to general account also almost doubled from 3.82 per cent in 1995 to 7.52 per cent in 2001.

## 4.2 Welfare Budget by Category of Welfare

Another significant factor also needs to be considered in assessing the Korean welfare budget: how it is allocated. The welfare budget can be divided into six categories: relief for livelihood and social welfare; social insurance; patriots and veterans affairs; welfare for laborers, job training and employment policy; public health and medical care; and general expenses for health and welfare. In 2001 relief for livelihood and social welfare took more than 35 per cent of the total welfare budget and social insurance took 33.68 per cent. The share of welfare for laborers, job training and employment policy was much smaller at only 7.28 per cent, and the share of public health and medical care including general expenses was even smaller at only 5.16 per cent.

*Table 12.8 General Account and Social Welfare Budget*

(Units: 100 million won; %)

| | Relief for livelihood (A) | Ministry of Health and Welfare (B) | Social security (C) | General account (D) | A/D | B/D | C/D |
|---|---|---|---|---|---|---|---|
| 1995 | 273 | 1984 | 2925 | 51 881 | 0.5 | 3.82 | 5.64 |
| 1996 | 361 | 2371 | 3528 | 58 823 | 0.6 | 4.03 | 6.00 |
| 1997 | 436 | 2851 | 4207 | 67 579 | 0.6 | 4.22 | 6.23 |
| 1998 | 575 | 2113 | 5576 | 75 583 | 0.8 | 4.12 | 6.05 |
| 1999 | 1135 | 4161 | 6150 | 83 685 | 1.4 | 4.97 | 7.30 |
| 2000 | 1377 | 5310 | 8074 | 88 736 | 1.6 | 5.98 | 9.10 |
| 2001 | 1680 | 7458 | 10 746 | 99 118 | 1.7 | 7.52 | 10.84 |

*Source*: Ministry of Health and Welfare (2001).

### 4.3 Role of Welfare Policy in Income Distribution

Using data from the 1991 and 1996 National Survey of Family Income and Expenditure conducted by the Korea National Statistical Office, Kim and Lim (2000) showed that tax policy played a more important role in income redistribution than did public transfer. Public transfer as a proportion of total national income was only 0.6 per cent in 1991 and 0.92 per cent in 1996. These data indicate an increase over time but they also suggest that with public transfer at such a minuscule proportion of national income, public transfer is unlikely to play a significant role in income distribution. We find a different story with taxation. Tax liability in proportion to total income was 9.07 per cent in 1991 and 7.81 per cent in 1996, indicating a slight decrease. This is because income tax policy has tended to decrease tax liability by raising deduction and exemption thresholds over time.

*Table 12.9 Welfare Budget by Category*

(Unit: %)

| | 2000 | 2001 |
|---|---|---|
| Relief for livelihood and social welfare | 35.71 | 38.89 |
| Social insurance | 32.14 | 33.68 |
| Patriots and veterans affairs | 16.67 | 15.00 |
| Welfare for laborers, job training and employment policy | 9.52 | 7.28 |
| Public health and medical care, and general expenses for health and welfare | 4.76 | 5.16 |
| Total | 100.00 | 100.00 |

*Source*: Ministry of Health and Welfare, *Health and Welfare Statistics Yearbook*, 2001.

Government policy on income redistribution also provides interesting indicators of the role of welfare in income distribution. Kim and Lim (2000) showed that public transfer made a relative contribution to income redistribution of 1.2 in 1991, and 0.61 in 1996. This suggests that while the absolute amount of public transfer is extremely low, its relative impact on reducing the level of income inequality is nevertheless moderate. Even so, public transfer's relative contribution almost halved over the five-year period.

Tax policy exhibits a rather different pattern. According to Kim and Lim (2000) the relative contribution of tax policy to reducing the level of income inequality was 2.2 in 1991, and 2.66 in 1996. The result of Kim and Lim (2000) indicates that during the period 1991–96, tax policy had a very strong impact on reducing income inequality in Korea and unlike the impact of public transfer which almost halved, tax policy impact increased by about one-fifth.

### 4.4 Public Assistance

The Minimum Living Standards Security Act (MLSSA) was legislated in August 1999. This was a government response to pleas by Koreans from all walks of life to reform the Living Protection Act that was widely seen to be inadequate in providing welfare for the needy. Under the Act, from October 2000 the government is to ensure that basic human needs including food, clothing, housing, education and health care are met for all citizens subsisting below the minimum living standard. Recognizing the minimum cost of living at 930 000 won for a four-person household, cash benefits are paid to the poor, regardless of their ability to work, to meet the gap between minimum living cost and their household income. The MLSSA was a step towards improving welfare for the needy. However, it has two core problems.

First, it is a disincentive to low-income earners to perform paid work. It can be seen as simply a negative income tax through which some low-wage earners receive less after-tax income by working more hours than by not working at all. Second, the system is prey to dishonesty since it depends on low-income earners reporting their household income honestly. If some welfare beneficiaries under-report their actual income, this discourages other welfare beneficiaries who receive less government benefit because they report honestly, and so eventually most people report smaller income amounts. Since the benefit is to meet the gap between low income and minimum cost of living, downward reporting of income inevitably increases the welfare budget expenditure.

### 4.5 Social Insurance

All four of Korea's public occupational pension schemes suffer serious financial problems. As shown in Table 12.10 the Military Pension exhausted its reserve fund in 1977 and its deficits have since been met by budget subsidies. The remaining three schemes have all been projected to exhaust their reserves; in 2001 for the Civil Service Pension, 2030 for the Private School Teachers Pension and 2040 for the National Pension Scheme.

The other social insurance programs also face financial problems. The National Health Insurance (NHI) program suffers from deficits that might expand further, although unifying the programs for workers and self-employed since July 2000 may help to overcome or at least rein in some of this deficit increase. The coverage of the Unemployment Insurance program was expanded rapidly since the program was launched in 1995, and since October 1998 this program covers all workers (see Table 12.11). Rapid expansion of coverage along with higher unemployment rates since the financial crisis have inevitably helped to intensify the financial problems of this program. The coverage of the Workers' Compensation Insurance was also expanded progressively, to include all workers by July 2000. Currently the Workers' Compensation Insurance scheme classifies industries into 67 categories for determining insurance premiums, so companies do not have incentives to lower their premiums by investing further in the safety of workplace facilities to reduce accident rates.

*Table 12.10 Overview of Current Pension System*

| | National | Civil servants | Private school teachers | Military |
|---|---|---|---|---|
| Year started | 1988 | 1960 | 1975 | 1960 |
| Pension benefit | 60% of lifetime income, payable at age 60[a] | 76% of last salary before retirement (for retiree with 33 year's service), payable at retirement[b] | | |
| Contribution rate | 9% | 15% | | |
| Year fund depletion is expected | 2040 | 2001 | 2030 | 1977 |
| Contribution rate needed | 17% | 30–35% | | |
| Budget support | 2200 won per month for fishermen | Retirement allowance, compensation pension for injury | | |
| Tax concessions | Pension income exempted | Pension income exempted | | |
| Policy issues | Financial instability, self-employment, generational equity | Financial unsustainability, inter-generation conflict, special treatment for military personnel | | |

*Notes*:
[a] to be extended to 65 years by 2033.
[b] 60 years for those who participate after 1996.

*Source*: Pension Reform Task Force (2000).

*Table 12.11 Expansion of Coverage of the Unemployment Insurance Program*

(Unit: 1000)

| | July 1995 | January 1998 | March 1998 | October 1998 |
|---|---|---|---|---|
| Coverage | 30 and more | 10 and more | 5 and more | all |
| No. of companies | 43 | 118 | 199 | 664 |
| No. of workers | 4280 | 5190 | 5710 | 8342 |

*Source*: Ministry of Labor (2000).

# 5. A NEW WELFARE PARADIGM AND PRINCIPLES OF WELFARE FUNDING

## 5.1 Productive Welfare Policy as a New Welfare Paradigm

In 2000, the Kim Dae-jung government announced a new welfare paradigm of Productive Welfare.[2] Productive welfare was introduced in a deliberate bid to strengthen Korea's weak welfare system. It seeks to help prevent erosion of basic human rights as occurred under the quantitative economic-growth policies of the past, while developing a system that nurtures equity as well as growth. Productive Welfare advocates distribution through an equitable market system, fair redistribution of wealth by government so that all are at least able to meet basic human needs, social investment for self-support, and expansion of investment to enhance the quality of life for all members of Korean society.

The philosophical foundations of productive welfare are sound, but by 2002 policy measures to achieve productive welfare are still immature. Some of the difficulty in implementing Productive Welfare as national policy arises from the potential tension between its two core goals of sustained economic growth and broad-based democracy; it is hard to develop appropriate policy measures that harmonize these two goals. Thus, we need to consider more carefully the present environment for welfare policy, marked by increases in both short-term and long-term demands for welfare as mentioned above in discussing tight budgetary conditions in section 2. It is one thing to have strong philosophical foundations but there is now a demonstrated need to produce and implement effectively the specific policy measures needed to meet these increasing demands for welfare on very limited funding.

One response is the concept of 'target efficiency'. This measures the cost-effectiveness of different types of welfare programs by assessing how these programs compensate welfare recipients for their losses, experienced through poverty, unemployment, injury, advanced age, and so forth. Hitherto, evaluation in welfare programs has proceeded from the program provider's perspective rather than that of welfare recipients. An individual finally becomes a welfare recipient after passing through various stages of assessment between experiencing the loss and receiving the final decision on whether they qualify for any of the available welfare programs. Thus, we can measure the target efficiency of welfare programs in terms of the welfare changes for individuals as they follow various paths between when they apply for welfare in response to loss and when they actually begin to receive welfare. In more detail, the target efficiency of multiple programs can be measured as 'post-program welfare (income) divided by expected pre-loss welfare (income)' where expected pre-loss welfare is the welfare that the individual would have earned had the loss not occurred.[3]

Given that target efficiency appears to be particularly useful for maximizing the outcome of limited welfare budgets, from here we will attempt to incorporate the target efficiency concept within the Productive Welfare paradigm. Re-evaluating the present welfare programs in terms of target efficiency can indicate how to improve not only the cost-effectiveness of various types but also the recipients' welfare level.

### 5.2 Welfare Policy to Meet Different Types of Welfare Demand

We discussed above two types of demand for welfare – short term and long term – and emphasized that policy measures to effectively meet those demand types differ. Let us consider here the different measures best suited to each demand type. Short-term demands for welfare caused by the financial crisis can be satisfied by recovering the potential for economic growth through effective restructuring of the economy to bring about more employment and higher income levels. The short-term increases in unemployment should be handled by anti-poverty policy rather than provision of unemployment allowance. This means that those who become unemployed may need support, but this support should be restricted to those whose income level drops below the poverty line because they have become unemployed. Anti-poverty policy has a different focus and should begin with reconstructing the infrastructure for a welfare program that guarantees delivery of benefits to those who need them.

Satisfying long-term welfare demand, which is concerned with quality of life rather than immediate basic needs, requires reassignment of the roles of central government, local government and the private sector. Local government should take a major role in social welfare services since this level of government is better informed about the needs of welfare services best suited to the particular characteristics of each region. The private sector can also participate in welfare funding, with government developing incentive schemes to stimulate the private sector's voluntary participation. Finally, long-term demands for welfare can also be met by social insurance reforms that strengthen the insurance function relatively more than the redistribution function of this form of welfare and provide room for greater private sector participation.

### 5.3 The Principles of Social Welfare Funding

Fund raising for social welfare programs is an important and urgent task in Korea. Here we will discuss four steps that need to be considered when thinking about raising and fairly distributing social welfare funds.

#### 5.3.1 Evaluating the efficiency of current welfare programs

Evaluating current welfare programs in terms of their target efficiency enables us to identify which programs spent more than was actually needed to achieve their goals. On the basis of results from target efficiency assessment, it is then possible to allocate the welfare budget more effectively among various welfare programs, to correct loopholes or drawbacks in each program, and eventually to save on the welfare budget as a whole. Efforts to evaluate the current system in terms of target efficiency can lead to more effective spending but they will not increase the overall budget so these efforts need to be accompanied by additional means to raise welfare funds.

#### 5.3.2 Improving the structure of government expenditure

As discussed earlier, welfare expenditure occupies a very small share of government expenditure, and the need to expand the welfare budget is implicit in this recognition. But following through with this recognition of shares of government expenditures, a useful early step is to identify expenditure areas that occupy a higher share of total expenditure than they really should, given both the prevailing economic and social environment and the size of citizens' demand for corresponding public goods. For example, it is possible to argue plausibly that the share of national defence expenditure can be reduced since we have reason to expect that peaceful relations between South and North Korea will continue. Reduction in national defense expenditures could be legitimately transferred to the welfare budget.

### 5.3.3 Obtaining support from related policies

Unequal distribution of income and wealth is a key factor precipitating the demand for welfare. The more unequal the distribution of income or wealth in a society, the greater will be the demand for welfare benefits by the poor and other welfare recipients, since relative poverty becomes more important than absolute poverty when there is high wealth inequality. The extent of demand for welfare can be lessened by forming closer alignment between welfare and other policies such as education policy and tax policy so that benefits allocated through these policies help to reduce welfare demand. Education subsidies or job-training coupons for low-income earners help to reduce the demand for welfare. Here, funding from education and labor budgets serves to replace eventual funding from the welfare budget. Tax policies can also contribute here. Global taxation of financial income, tax on capital gains from stock transactions, and heavier taxation of inheritance and gifts can partially meet the demand for welfare. The crowding-out effects of the tax measures end up producing a significant saving in the welfare budget.

### 5.3.4 Synchronizing welfare policy with other policies

Welfare policy can operate more powerfully when it is synchronized effectively with some other policies. As far as the welfare infrastructure is concerned, it is more effective to synchronize welfare administration with labor-policy administration and tax administration. Recently, the exact incomes of the self-employed have come under scrutiny since the national pension system was expanded to cover them, and the self-employed on low incomes are covered in the Minimum Living Standards Security System. The task of investigating true income can be conducted more effectively by tax administration. Therefore, tax administration should guide both labor and welfare policy administrations in investigating the income of the self-employed. This is an important step in constructing efficient welfare infrastructure and can save administrative costs of welfare programs.

## 6. REFORM OF SOCIAL WELFARE SYSTEMS

### 6.1 Harmonization of Welfare Policy with Tax Policy

Earlier in this chapter we discussed the two critical problems of the Minimum Living Standards Security System implemented in October 2000: more work yield with less after-transfer income, and the self-employed can under-report income resulting in a significant expansion of welfare budget expenditures. In this regard, the MLSSS violates the idea of productive welfare. Currently, there are calls to replace the MLSSS with another policy. One possibility that splices welfare and tax policy is the Earned Income Tax Credit (EITC), which had been introduced in the US. EITC is a refundable tax credit for earned income and provides assistance through the tax system to low-earning households. If the credit exceeds the tax-payment-before-credit, then these households can receive the difference as assistance. As a result, EITC can partially replace MLSSS by covering low-income earners who have the ability to work. Low-income earners without the ability to work would still be covered by the MLSSS.

Introduction of an EITC system can connect government expenditure to government revenue so that unnecessary expenditure can be minimized, making welfare expenditure more efficient. EITC also minimizes administrative costs by having tax administration guide all other institutions needing to conduct income scrutiny.

The tax system on income from labor also has some problems concerning income maintenance. Its exemption level is so high that the rate of taxpayers among labor force participants is very low by comparison with this rate in many developed countries. We propose alongside introducing an EITC, reducing the exemption level to almost half its current level. In introducing an EITC, it will be necessary to lower both the basic income guarantee level in the MLSSS and the exemption level in the current labor income tax system. These new schemes require overall reform of both the welfare and the taxation systems.

## 6.2 Pension Reform

A two-pillar pension system had been recommended by both the Commission on National Pension System Reform in 1997 and the World Bank.[4] However, the 1998 amendment to the National Pension System Act (NPSA) did not introduce the two-pillar pension recommendation and instead made two major changes to the Act. The amendment reduced the income replacement rate from 70 per cent to 60 per cent based on 40 years of participation in the paid workforce and increased the age for pension eligibility from 60 to 65. This amendment was not enough to stall the exhaustion of the pension fund, so there is still a need to further amend the NPSA.

We hold that the next amendment should adopt the earlier recommendation of implementing a two-pillar system. The two-pillar system divides the current system into a basic pension and an earnings-related pension. The system for a basic pension will need to be established anew and the earnings-related portion of NPS can be reorganized as part of the National Pension scheme. The basic pension is a universal basic pension scheme that, by covering all nationals aged over 18 years, truly provides 'one pension for everybody'. Those who currently participate in the public occupational pension schemes would join the basic pension scheme. The national pension scheme reorganized to operate as an earnings-related pension would cover only those participants with assessed income.

In Korea, the Retirement Allowance System (RAS) has functioned as both a corporate pension and an unemployment payments scheme since the allowance can be paid to workers leaving a job regardless of their age. Since there is now a system for unemployment insurance, the RAS should be converted to a corporate-pension system. Corporate pensions can be operated through a fully funded scheme with outside deposits. It will be important to encourage employees and employers to adopt the new scheme and two measures are appropriate for this task: tax incentives for corporate-pension contributions and tax incentives for the earnings-related portion in the new NPS system within the two-pillar system.

A new corporate pension licensed by the state could be designed to provide income protection for the self-employed and farmers who are excluded from the corporate pension. Tax concessions for this new corporate pension would be same as those for the existing corporate pension.

## 7. CONCLUDING REMARKS

The financial crisis in 1997 significantly changed social and economic conditions in Korea. The old-fashioned style of demand for welfare emerged while poverty, unemployment and unequal income distribution became major social issues. Currently, two types of demand for welfare coexist in Korea: an increased short-run demand that is typical of less-developed countries, and the long-run demand that is typical of developed countries. The former type of demand caused by the financial crisis requires policy measures for reducing unemployment, poverty and inequality, while the latter type requires measures aimed at enhancing the quality of life. If these two types of demand, which are very different in nature, are not distinguished in considering welfare policy measures, welfare monies will not be well spent. The budget for social welfare will continue to increase without curtailing the demand for welfare. Furthermore, we may observe an increase in social risk-taking and a decline in productivity as a whole. The Kim Dae-jung government introduced a new welfare paradigm, but as we have argued in this chapter, this new paradigm needs to be reconsidered so that it distinguishes between the two different types of welfare demands and is then better placed to devise efficient means for raising welfare funds and addressing real welfare needs.

We have suggested four steps that should be taken before raising the social welfare budget:

1. evaluate current welfare programs in terms of target efficiency;
2. increase the share of the welfare budget within the national budget through fine-tuning the structure of government expenditure;
3. secure support from other welfare-related policies such as education, labor and tax policies; and
4. harmonize welfare policy with other policies.

Finally, it remains important to design policy measures to reform and improve current welfare programs in line with the philosophy distinguishing the two types of welfare demands. In particular, the MLSSS anti-poverty policy and social insurance programs should be reconsidered and replaced by better policy measures that guarantee cost-effectiveness and target efficiency.

Korea has certainly made considerable progress in developing welfare policy since the 1990s, after several decades of national policies that directed extremely high economic growth while effectively sidelining welfare. However, the financial crisis was a loud wake-up call that much is still to be done so that welfare policy is best able to address short-term and long-term welfare demands as Korean society begins to age swiftly and the conditions for economic growth are far from certain.

# NOTES

1. Since 1998 income from interest and dividends is subject to a taxation rate of 20 per cent, which has been considerably lower than the rate applied to income from wages and salaries. Until 1998, income from interest and dividends was subject to the global taxation rate, which for the highest income levels was 40 per cent.
2. Full details can be found in Presidential Committee for Quality of Life, Office of the President, *DJ Welfarism: A New Paradigm for Productive Welfare in Korea*, January 2000. The Kim Young Sam government that preceded Kim Dae-jung's administration also attempted to establish a new welfare paradigm appropriate for the era of globalization. Both administrations recognized the need for a new welfare paradigm to achieve long-term balanced development. A new paradigm was also important symbolically, to signify a break from the previous welfare conception that created a dichotomy between growth and welfare.
3. Chong-Bum An, one of the authors of this chapter, attempted to measure the target efficiency of four major US welfare programs – the AFDC (Aid to Families with Dependent Children), Unemployment Insurance, Worker's Compensation and Food Stamp – using the PSID (Panel Study of Income Dynamics). In the paper, he found that welfare programs may result in overcompensation for the poor who are single parents with children. Such an excessive compensation of multiple welfare programs might provide welfare recipients with disincentive effects on their labor supply. See Chong-Bum An, 'Target Efficiency of Multiple Welfare Programs', a paper presented at the 56th Congress of the International Institute of Public Finance, Seville, Spain, 28–31 August 2000.
4. Refer to the Commission on National Pension System Reform (1997) and the World Bank (1994).

# REFERENCES

An, Chong-Bum (2000), 'Target efficiency of multiple welfare programs', presented at the 56th Congress of the International Institute of Public Finance, Seville, Spain, 28–31 August.

An, Chong-Bum, Suk Hoon Kang, Chong-Hoon Rhee and Keonbeom Lee (2001), 'Globalization and income inequality in Korea', presented at the Technical Meeting on FDI, Human Capital and Education in Developing Countries, OECD Development Centre, 13–14 December 2001.

Bureau of Statistics (2000), *Household Budget Trends of the Urban Worker Household*, March.

Bureau of Statistics (2001a), Annual Report on the Household Income and Expenditure Survey.

Bureau of Statistics (2001b), *Future Population Projection*, Seoul.

Bureau of Statistics (2001c), *Labor Force Survey*, December.

Choi, Kwang (2001), 'The Korean financial crisis and fiscal policy', O. Yul Kwon and William Shepherd (eds), *Korean's Economic Prospects from Financial Crisis to Prosperity*, Cheltenham: Edward Elgar.

Commission on National Pension System Reform (1997), *The Improvement of the Korean National Pension System Confronting the Expansion to the Entire Population*, Seoul.

Haveman, R. and B. Wolfe (2000), 'Welfare to work in the US: A model for other developed nations?', *International Tax and Public Finance*, **7** (1), January.

Hoffman, S. and L. Seidman (1990), *The Earned Income Tax Credit: Antipoverty Effectiveness and Labor Market Effects*, Upjohn Institute for Employment Research.

Holzmann, R. (2000), 'The World Bank approach to pension reform', *International Social Security Review,* **53** (1), 11–34.

Holzmann, R. and S. Jorgensen (1999), *Social Protection as Social Risk Management: Conceptual Underpinnings for the Social Protection Sector Strategy*, Social Protection Discussion Paper No. 9904, The World Bank.

Keane, M. and R. Moffitt (1996), *A Structural Model of Multiple Welfare Program Participation and Labor Supply*, Discussion Paper No. 1080–96, Institute for Research on Poverty, University of Wisconsin-Madison.

Kim, J. and B. Lim (2000), 'Tax equality and after-tax income inequality in Korea', *The Korean Journal of Public Economics*, **5** (1), 3–31 (in Korean).

Ministry of Health and Welfare (2001), *Health and Welfare Statistics Yearbook*.

Ministry of Labor (2000), *Improving Unemployment Insurance and Workers' Compensation Insurance*.
Ministry of Planning and Budget (2002), 'The Present Status of Public Credit and Debt', April.
Moon, Hyungpo (1998), *Growth with Equity: Experience of the Republic of Korea*, Korea Development Institute, October.
Moon, Hyungpo (2000), *Policy Measures for Improving Income Distribution*, Mimeo, Korea Development Institute, April (in Korean).
National Pension Corporation (1998), *Actuarial Estimates of the National Pension Scheme*, Seoul.
National Pension Corporation (1999a), *Guide to the New National Pension Scheme*, Seoul, January.
National Pension Corporation (1999b), *National Pension Scheme in Korea*, (Annual Report), Seoul.
OECD, (1980–98), *Public Social Expenditure by main category as a percentage of GDP*, (http://www.oecd.org).
OECD (1996), *Ageing in OECD Countries: A Critical Policy Challenge*, Social Policy Studies No. 20, Paris.
Palacios, Robert and M. Pallares (2000), *International Patterns of Pension Provision*, World Bank.
Pension Reform Task Force (2000), *Basic Plan for Pension System Reform*, September.
Scholz, J.K. (1994), 'The earned income tax credit: Participation, compliance and anti-poverty effectiveness', *National Tax Journal*, **47** (1), 59–81.
US Government Accounting Office (1993), *Earned Income Tax Credit: Design and Administration Could Be Improved*, Washington DC: GAO.
Ventry, D.J. Jr, 'The NIT: An intellectual history', (http://www.taxhistory.org).
World Bank (1994), *Averting the Old Age Crisis*, Oxford University Press.
World Bank (2000a), *The Korean Pension System at a Crossroads*, Report No. 20404–KO, May.
World Bank (2000b), *World Report 2000/01 – Attacking Poverty*.
Yun, Sukmyung (2000), *Generational Accounting for Korea: With Special Reference to Public Pension Schemes*, Korea Institute of Health and Social Affairs, September.

# Part VI

# Strategy for an Information- and Knowledge-based Economy

# 13. Korea's Drive for a Knowledge-based Economy

**Kwang Sun Pai, Ki-Hong Park and Suk-In Chang**

## 1. INTRODUCTION

Across the three decades from 1966 to 1996, Korea achieved one of the fastest rates of economic development of any country in the world, averaging 6.8 per cent annual per capita income growth during this period. The process culminated in the nation becoming an OECD member in 1996. Towards the end of 1997, however, Korea experienced its worst economic crisis since the Korean War of the early 1950s. The Korean economy recovered quickly from the 1997 crisis and subsequent 1998 recession, with output increasing almost 11 per cent in 1999 and 9 per cent in 2000, although the quick rebound came to an end in the fourth quarter of 2000.

Despite the rapid recovery, there is concern over the prospects for sustained future growth. The developments of 1997 and 1998 revealed fundamental structural weaknesses in the Korean economy. The country's input-driven growth strategy had already led to declining total factor productivity growth from the beginning of the 1990s (Kim 1999; World Bank 1999a). Concern also stems from an increasing awareness that competition in the global marketplace is intensifying rapidly and that radical changes are taking place in the use of goods and services, driven by what can be described as a knowledge revolution.

Accordingly, Korea is under strong pressure to shift its development strategy. Even prior to the crisis, some analysts predicted that the growth of the Korean economy, and indeed of other East Asian economies, was not sustainable (Krugman 1994). Recognizing the structural weaknesses of the Korean economy and the increasing importance of knowledge-based industries, the Korean government unveiled a proposal for a three-year master plan to serve as a blueprint for Korea's transformation into a knowledge-based economy from January 2000 (NEAC 2000). As identified by the OECD the knowledge-intensive sector includes finance, insurance and other business services; community, social and personal services; and communication services (OECD 1998b), in addition to medium- and high-technology manufacturing.

The three-year plan focused on five key themes:

1. developing a nationwide information infrastructure;
2. fostering a human resources system responsive to the knowledge-based economy;
3. improving national science and technology innovation capabilities;
4. developing new knowledge-based industries and digitizing older industries; and

5. addressing the digital and knowledge divide (NEAC 2000).

In this chapter we assess Korea's drive towards a knowledge-based economy and identify the key issues involved in the transition. In section 2, we consider the conceptual and policy framework required for a knowledge-based economy. We use this to take stock of where Korea stands just inside the 21st century, and to suggest further measures to facilitate Korea's transition to an advanced knowledge-based economy over the years ahead. In section 3, Korea's position is examined critically in the light of the needs of a knowledge-based economy. Finally, concluding remarks are presented in the last section.

## 2. THE FRAMEWORK OF THE KNOWLEDGE-BASED ECONOMY[1]

Knowledge is becoming more central than ever to economic and social development due to rapid technical progress, globalization and the development of information and communication technologies (ICTs). In this context, the so-called knowledge-based economy can be defined as one that 'is directly based on the production, distribution and use of knowledge and information' (OECD 1996). By this definition, all economies are knowledge-based. The difference at this time in history, however, is that rapidly growing economies are becoming increasingly dependent on the effective use of knowledge in a process that is enabled largely by rapid advances in science and the ICT revolution.

Yet knowledge is not a product that can be bought off the shelf to become immediately productive. For developed and developing countries alike, the ability to create and sustain a knowledge-based economy depends on the capacity to tap the global system that generates and transmits knowledge (for example through the Internet). Fundamental to developing this capacity are four preconditions:

1. a dynamic information infrastructure to facilitate the effective communication and processing of information;
2. an educated and skilled population who can create and use knowledge productively;
3. a system of research centers, universities, think tanks, firms and other organizations that tap into the stock of global knowledge, adapt it to local needs and create new knowledge; and
4. an economic and institutional regime that provides incentives for using existing knowledge efficiently, creating new knowledge and promoting entrepreneurship.

Properly met, these preconditions increase the efficiency and resilience of the economy and its ability to respond to new challenges, to stimulate the emergence of new firms and ensure that the benefits of economic growth are shared across the members of society. The rationale for these four factors is important for discussing the Korean example so we will consider different aspects of this rationale in turn.

### 2.1 A Dynamic Information Infrastructure

Rapid advances in ICTs are dramatically affecting economic and social activities, as well as the acquisition, creation, dissemination and use of knowledge. These advances affect how manufacturers, service providers and governments are organized, and how they function. Increased access to ICTs affects how people work, learn and communicate. Therefore an adequate information infrastructure to accommodate these new technologies is essential for economic growth as it reduces transaction costs and improves the efficiency of markets. It also enables and in some ways facilitates development of new products and services.

Information infrastructure consists of telecommunications networks, strategic information systems, related policy and legal frameworks, and skilled human resources needed to develop and use this infrastructure. Developing a powerful information infrastructure therefore requires mobilizing the many stakeholders involved in its deployment and use – government, business, individual users, telecommunications and information service providers, among others. They must collaborate on devising an information infrastructure strategy that involves identifying the opportunities and needs for information and communication in the economy. This also involves assessing existing information systems to identify common constraints and difficulties, and formulating goals and visions for the information infrastructure. The latter is the subject of government policy through which the resources of society are rallied effectively. The government therefore has a particularly important role in articulating its vision to the people, and this can be done most efficiently in a consultative process with other immediate stakeholders.

## 2.2 Skilled and Creative Human Resources

Skilled and adaptable people play a crucial role in taking advantage of the potential offered by the explosion of new knowledge and accelerating technical change. Researchers and technicians are necessary across a spectrum of information technologies, as are a workforce that can adopt and adapt the new technologies, and a general population who can efficiently use electronic products and information services. Addressing these needs requires developing and implementing education and training policies to prepare the appropriate human resources. In this regard, ensuring that expenditures on education are allocated efficiently, and that the general populace has the basic knowledge and skills to participate in the knowledge-based economy, demands particular attention.

In particular, opportunities for lifelong learning are essential. Creating a culture of continuous learning and receptiveness to new ideas is critical for the development of a knowledge-based economy. It should not be limited to the workplace, but must be expanded to other environments, such as the home and school. Methods may include structured continuing education courses, self-learning through the Internet, and computer-assisted instruction. To use new technologies, and in particular the fast-evolving ICTs, workers need new, specialized skills. Many firms in Korea complain that they have to invest heavily in retraining college graduates entering the workforce. This is an indication that despite producing high levels of educational attainment, the educational system is failing to meet the requirements of the knowledge-based economy. Continuing education programs can help satisfy this need.

## 2.3 An Effective Innovation System

The bulk of technical knowledge is produced in economically advanced countries. Estimates show that roughly 88 per cent of total R&D expenditures are undertaken by these countries, which account for roughly the same per cent in both patenting and production of scientific and technical papers (OECD–World Bank Institute 2000). On a per capita basis, the disparity in the production of technical knowledge is greater than the disparity in income between economically developed and economically developing countries. Fortunately, developing countries do not have to reinvent the wheel; there are many ways in which they can tap into and use the knowledge created in developed countries. But to do this requires an efficient national innovation system, consisting of the networks of institutions, rules and procedures that affect how a country acquires, creates, disseminates and uses knowledge.[2]

Key components in this creative process include universities, research centers and policy think tanks. Non-government organizations, private firms and the government are also part of the innovation system, to the extent that they produce new knowledge. Agricultural and industrial extension services, engineering firms and management consulting firms are also central to the dissemination of knowledge. However, the mere existence of these organizations is not sufficient. What matters is the extent to which they are effective in creating, adapting and disseminating knowledge to the firms, government, organizations and other people who put it to use. Therefore, networking and interactions between the different organizations, firms and individuals are critically important. The intensity of these networks, as well as the incentives for acquiring, creating and sharing knowledge, are influenced by the economic incentive regime in general. They are particularly affected by specific policies relating to, for example, imports of foreign technology through licensing, direct foreign investment, foreign collaboration and the protection of intellectual property.

## 2.4 An Effective Institutional Infrastructure[3]

Whether or not a country uses efficiently the vast and rapidly growing stock of global knowledge depends largely on its economic incentive regime and institutional set-up. A competitive institutional infrastructure induces firms and individuals to seek out knowledge in order to produce goods or services more efficiently or to produce new goods and services. In other words, competition and the resulting pressures for more efficient firms to expand and for less efficient firms to shrink or disappear, has a direct bearing on the diffusion of knowledge in an economy.

The creation of such an environment mandates good macroeconomic competition and regulatory policies, as well as the existence of financial systems to both allocate resources (including venture capital) to promising new opportunities and redeploy assets from failed enterprises to more productive uses. It also requires conditions that are conducive to entrepreneurship and risk-taking, the expansion of small enterprises, an adequate exchange of information between science and industry, and sufficiently flexible labor markets to ease the redeployment of labor. Flexibility in the labor market requires in turn the development of appropriate social safety nets, to facilitate the constant relocation and retraining of people for new jobs, and to assist those people who are adversely affected by such restructuring.

Less obvious but equally important for an effective institutional infrastructure are the norms that govern the rules and procedures in a society, which in turn determine how decisions are made and actions are taken. These include the relationships between legal rules and procedures, social conventions, firms, government, non-governmental organizations and markets. A key feature is the quality of government, as its integrity and effectiveness determine the basic rules of a society. Another important element is the extent to which the legal system supports property rights. The creation and dissemination of knowledge, for instance, is strongly affected by the degree to which intellectual property is valued and the rights to it are protected and enforced.

In light of the general preconditions for a knowledge-based economy, as examined above, we will turn to consider Korea's progress in fulfilling these preconditions and highlight the areas that still require attention. We will also present some key issues regarding the further promotion of knowledge-based activities that will have a positive impact on the Korean economy.

## 3. AN ASSESSMENT OF KOREA'S TRANSITION TO THE KNOWLEDGE-BASED ECONOMY AND KEY ISSUES[4]

### 3.1 Developing a Dynamic Information Infrastructure

Korea has been quick to recognize the importance of the global information and knowledge revolution, and in formulating a strategy to ensure that the country gains all possible benefits from the advances. Indeed, Korea has performed impressively in the information infrastructure sector in many areas – especially in mobile telecommunications and Internet access.

The cross-country comparison in Table 13.1 highlights the nation's focus on information technologies. Here we see how Korea invested heavily in information infrastructure through the 1990s. Korean investment averaged 0.8 per cent of GDP in the first half of the decade and more than doubled to 1.85 per cent of GDP in the second half. Compared with almost all other countries in the table, this performance is extremely impressive. In per cent of GDP terms, in the second half of the 1990s, Korea's investment rate was almost twice that of Hong Kong, and was more than five times that of Japan.

As a percentage of GDP, public investment in information infrastructure in Korea rose across the 1990s, and was higher than the total investment in information infrastructure in Japan and the United Kingdom. This trend is likely to continue as the three-year plan announced in 2000 has ambitious targets to upgrade the nation's information infrastructure to a level that would rank in the top ten globally. As part of the plan, the number of Internet users, which jumped from 3 million in 1997 to more than 20 million in 2001, is targeted for 30 million by 2002, almost two-thirds of the population (MOCIE 2002a).

Spectacular rises in ownership rates for increasingly popular hi-tech products is testament to this recent heavy investment in information infrastructure. One example is the number of mobile-phone subscribers, which grew from less than one million to 14 million (30.2 per cent of the population) between 1994 and 1998. This was higher than the OECD average of 25 per cent (OECD 2000b). In December 2001, the number of mobile-phone subscribers in Korea reached 29 million, or more than 60 per cent of the population. Another example is the number of Internet users. Estimates suggest there were nearly 24 million Internet users in Korea at the end of 2001. This was almost eight times the number in 1998 (3.1 million) which itself was almost double the 1997 figure of 1.6 million. A third example is code division multiple access (CDMA) technology where Korea is currently one of the world leaders, with SK Telecom as the world's largest CDMA operator and with numerous local vendors exporting CDMA equipment, especially handsets. In 2001 these companies exported $4 billion of CDMA-based phone sets, and the trade surplus in the ICT sector constituted 61 per cent of the nation's trade surplus ($84.2 billion) during the past four years (1998–2001) (MIC 2002).

*Table 13.1 Investment in Information Infrastructure*

| | Investment/GDP (%) | | Public investment (% of total) | |
|---|---|---|---|---|
| | Average 1991–95 | Average 1996–99 | Average 1991–95 | Average 1996–99 |
| Hong Kong | 0.58 | 0.98 | 0 | 0 |
| Japan | 0.14 | 0.34 | 0 | 0 |
| Korea | 0.80 | 1.85 | 48 | 25 |
| Malaysia | 1.12 | 1.04 | 6 | 5 |
| Singapore | 0.35 | 0.57 | 38 | 4 |
| UK | 0.23 | 0.35 | 2 | 2 |
| US | 0.58 | 0.52 | 0 | 0 |

*Source*: OECD–World Bank Institute (2000: 82).

New Internet businesses and e-commerce are also emerging in this environment and expanding their markets rapidly in Korea. For example, in 2001 almost 70 per cent of stock transactions were carried out on-line, and there were more than 1800 Internet shopping malls (MOCIE 2002). Internet banking services, auctions, Internet games and cyber education have also become major Internet businesses. The most important factor behind these remarkable developments has been the continual upgrading of telecommunication networks and services. This has led to the connection of most major Korean cities to the fiber optic backbone network, and to the introduction of high-speed Internet services for the access network through a mixture of Asymmetric Digital Subscriber Line (ADSL) and Cable TV (CATV) technologies.[5] As a result, the number of households connected by broadband lines increased exponentially, with more than 10 per cent of the population connected to broadband lines at the end of 2001, in comparison with the roughly 4 per cent marked in most developed countries. Well-established wireless telephone networks also contributed to the emerging mobile commerce (m-commerce) and mobile Internet services.

To preserve this strong record Korea will need to move toward a more efficient model of ICT provision and services. Clearly, continued advances in the quality of both fixed and wireless networks are central to further expansion of Internet use inside Korea, especially as consumers and businesses begin to demand an 'always on' Internet environment (the ability to stay on-line for extended periods).

In the absence of such advances, the picture is mixed on the prospect of maintaining a high level of investment in the sector. How, then, can better performance be ensured, especially in providing next-generation ICTs? Given the revolutionary nature of the sector, there is a vital role for government – especially in making services available for the disadvantaged – involving more open competition and investment policies. For instance, commerce laws that unnecessarily restrict e-commerce need to be amended in order to achieve the government's goal of expanding e-commerce up to 50 per cent of the total transactions by 2010 (MOCIE 2002b). It is also important to develop regulations that are consistent with rapidly evolving international agreements in this dynamic area, especially in the area of taxation. Finally, the framework for such transactions needs to be developed further, in areas involving electronic signatures and payment systems.

### 3.2 Developing Creative Human Resources through Education Reform

Korea has attained remarkable achievements in education over the past three decades, and with the quality of basic education internationally acclaimed. Since 1970 Korea has maintained full enrollment in primary education (Figure 13.1). From 1970 to 1997 illiteracy declined from over 10 per cent to virtually nil. Gross enrollment in secondary education increased from 40 per cent to become almost universal (World Bank 1999a). At the tertiary level, Korea ranks third among OECD countries in educational attainment, with 84 per cent of high school graduates entering university or college in 1998 (MOE 1998).

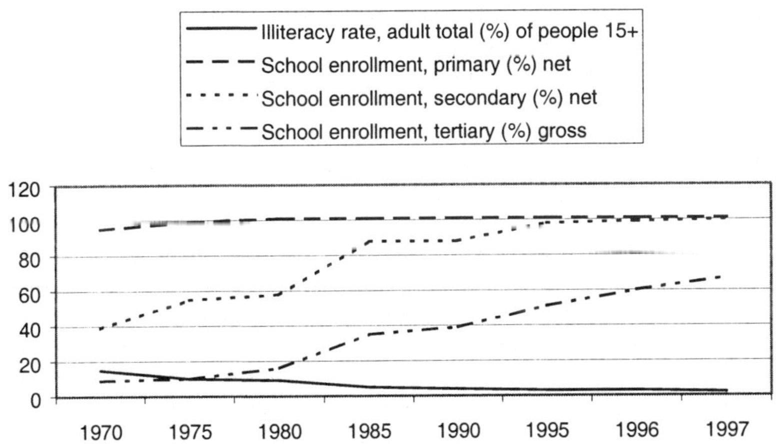


*Source*: World Bank (1999a).

*Figure 13.1 Education Indicators: Korea*

Korea has a unique education system characterized by large private-sector representation and a relatively small publicly financed sector. While total education expenditures increased from 8.8 per cent of GDP in 1966 to 13.3 per cent in 1998 (KEDI 1998), which was the highest share for any country at a similar level of development in 1998, only 4.4 per cent was from public financing. This is lower than the OECD average of 4.9 per cent recorded in 1995 (Table 13.2).

*Table 13.2 Public Expenditure on Education as a Percentage of GDP, 1995*

| | |
|---|---|
| Australia | 4.5 |
| Greece | 3.7 |
| Finland | 6.6 |
| Korea | 3.6 |
| Norway | 6.8 |
| Sweden | 6.6 |
| Turkey | 2.2 |
| US | 5.0 |
| OECD average | 4.9 |

*Sources*: OECD (2000a); World Bank (1999a).

The relatively low public investment in education has forced more of this expenditure onto parents and has continued to keep the Korean public education system weak. In 1998, parents spent 2.3 per cent of GDP on tuition and associated fees for formal education from the primary to the tertiary level. Korean households contributed almost 84 per cent of the costs of tertiary education, significantly more than in any other OECD country. The lack of choice and large class size in the public education sector, combined with a very strict national university admission system, led private individuals, usually parents, to invest another 3.2 per cent of GDP on private tutoring for their children. The remaining 3.4 per cent spent consists of general expenses for education, including the cost of study materials, uniforms, transportation fees, lodging, food and other costs (KEDI 1998).

These heavy investments in education should, in theory, lead to a satisfactory national education system, that provides a high quality education and meets the demands of the labor market. But in reality, students are less and less content with what they are taught at school and parents are not satisfied with the education their children receive, as evidenced in the amounts they spend on extra tutoring. Companies also complain about the lack of specialization and skills on the part of their newly recruited workers. Across the country there is serious concern about the ability of the education system to improve its performance in a global economy increasingly driven by knowledge. Why have the heavy investments in education not produced the results expected by Korean society? Why do Korean parents feel they need to spend so much money on private tutoring? The answers are clear to many Koreans: too much government intervention, a lack of diversification and insufficient public funding, combined with strong pressures that Korean parents place upon their children to enter elite universities in Seoul.

On the one hand, strong government intervention has played a major role in making basic education universal and providing skilled labor for the country's industrialization drive. On the other hand, government intervention has generated a range of regulations on the provision of educational services. The central government regulates matters such as type of schools, student admission, curriculum, textbooks and hiring of teachers for all educational institutions, whether public or private.

Without deregulation it will be hard to carry out the educational reforms needed for Korea's transition to an advanced knowledge-based economy. The government has recognized this problem and has embarked on a number of deregulatory efforts since the early 1990s. Some examples of the reform agenda include: greater autonomy for universities in admission and academic affairs, nurturing leading regional universities to meet the needs of local industry; establishing education and research networks with leading world universities to stimulate research at Korean universities; and realizing the vision of an open educational system through a new Education Credit Bank system. These efforts will need to be focused on developing a flexible education market with healthy competition. Granting greater autonomy to education providers, especially private institutions, will certainly increase their responsiveness to the needs of the labor market. It will also encourage them to diversify their education services, while maintaining common core standards set by the Ministry of Education. For various reasons, especially the lack of consensus-building in this process, these reforms have not been fully implemented as envisaged.

Some diversification has already begun, as exemplified by the government's Seventh Curriculum Reform and the Brain Korea 21 initiative that aims to establish a few centers of excellence in higher education through substantial public investment. However, investing in centers of excellence alone will not satisfy the demand for appropriate skilled human resources; some structural adjustments are also needed. For instance, the number of two-year junior colleges is currently only about half the number of four-year colleges and universities, even though junior colleges produce the middle-level technicians who are in growing demand in the new economy. Also, at both the college and school levels, very few programs are challenging enough for gifted students whose talents are important assets for the development of a knowledge-based economy in Korea. Thus, the kind of diversification in education and training needed in Korea is not limited to a particular education level or institution; rather it calls for a systematic effort to identify and implement necessary changes across the education system.

Here it is particularly important to facilitate opportunities for lifelong learning, which are not widely available in Korea at present. Lifelong learning as a 'cradle-to-grave' concept, that is not limited to adult learning, needs to be emphasized. Lessons can be drawn from economically advanced countries, as they usually have a proliferation of institutions and mechanisms that focus on lifelong learning through new learning methods and new media such as the Internet, increased use of television, distance learning and virtual universities.

Recognizing the importance of making learning opportunities available to the public, the government has begun to expand the high-speed Internet network to offer free public access to computers, to provide training in informatics and to promote English proficiency. It has also set up a special program to teach Internet and basic personal-computer skills to nearly half a million students from poor families to help address the issue of the digital divide in modern society (NEAC 2000).

### 3.3 Improving the Innovation System

Korea's innovation system (KIS) remains largely based on a catch-up model. In the past, this model was used effectively to achieve development goals in a short period of time and enabled Korean people to quickly master a wide range of industrial and technological activities. However, the model has its limitations. Private sector R&D, the lion's share of gross R&D spending, remains mainly oriented toward short-term technological development, while the majority of public sector R&D programs are highly mission-oriented but weak in terms of diffusion (STEPI 1998). Consequently, the capacity to generate codified knowledge (for example in the form of patents and publications) is relatively low compared to that of knowledge embodied in traded goods (Table 13.3). This is despite the fact that the nation's total R&D budget, in terms of current PPP US dollars, ranked seventh in the OECD in 1998, and that its ratio of researchers to the general population is near the EU average of 50 per 10 000 workers (OECD 2000b).

Other patent-related 'output' indicators shown in Table 13.3, such as technological strength and technological intensity, confirm that Korean R&D efforts contribute less to the generation of codified knowledge. The absence of a strong, basic foundation in the sciences is likely to have negative consequences in the future. Furthermore, because Korea's development strategy in science and technology strongly favored the rapid exploitation of mature and advanced technologies to expand markets in selected sectors, the KIS has had relatively weak global linkages. In other words, there has been little effective use of technology acquisition through foreign direct investment (FDI), strategic alliances or joint research programs. For instance, until the financial crisis FDI played a very minor role and joint ventures were not popular. Consequently, Korea did not take advantage of knowledge and technology inflows from multinational activities. The few exceptions include arm's-length methods used to acquire foreign knowledge such as formal technology licensing contracts. Today, Korea has come up against the limits of this strategy. In a world where trade, investment and production are increasingly globalized, the capacity to continuously develop, acquire, diffuse and commercialize knowledge requires a complementary relationship between 'partners' at international levels.

The same lack of interaction is also apparent in the Korean innovation system on the domestic level, which is overly compartmentalized. The private sector, for example, spent 97 per cent of its R&D outlays on its own research activities and only 3 per cent on contracts with universities in 1997 (STEPI 1998). Further, these private efforts are conducted mainly by large companies, with small firms (defined as firms with less than 500 workers) accounting for only 12 per cent of total business R&D in Korea, the lowest share among OECD countries (OECD 2000b). The most noticeable downside of these circumstances is that the effectiveness of the research efforts by large companies, particularly the *chaebols*, is limited to the extent that they often suffer from poor corporate governance and investment decisions. It is also still unclear if such large-scale R&D efforts are flexible enough to fully support the development of a knowledge-based economy in Korea.

Part of the underlying problem is that the government plays a fairly small role in Korea's overall innovation effort, accounting for only a fifth of total R&D spending, which, as with the sphere of small-business investment, is the lowest proportion among

*Table 13.3 Income and Technological Performance, 1998*[a]

| | Income level, 1996 GDP per capita as % of OECD average | Indicators of scientific and technological activities | | | | | | | |
|---|---|---|---|---|---|---|---|---|---|
| | | Gross domestic expenditure on R&D as a % of GDP, 1998[a] | Researchers per 10 000 labor force 1997[a] | Government-financed R&D as a % of GDP, 1998[a] | Government financing on R&D as a % of total R&D, 1998[a] | Business expenditure on R&D as a % of business GDP, 1998 | Scientific & technical articles per unit of GDP[b] | Technological strength per USD of R&D[c] | Technological intensity[d] |
| US | 140 | 2.8 | 74 | 0.8 | 30.6 | 2.3 | 20 | 410 | 10.4 |
| Norway | 128 | 1.7 | 76 | 0.7 | 42.9 | 1.3 | 21 | – | – |
| Switzerland | 126 | 2.7 | 55 | 0.7 | 26.9 | 2.3 | 37 | – | – |
| Japan | 121 | 2.9 | 92 | 0.5 | 18.1 | 2.3 | 15 | 354 | 10.6 |
| Iceland | 118 | 2.0 | 91 | 1.1 | 55.9 | 1.2 | 23 | – | – |
| Denmark | 117 | 1.0 | 61 | 0.7 | 35.7 | 1.9 | 31 | 87 | 1.6 |
| Canada | 114 | 1.6 | 54 | 0.5 | 31.9 | 1.3 | 25 | 203 | 3.3 |
| Belgium | 112 | 1.6 | 53 | 0.4 | 26.4 | 1.4 | 20 | 111 | 1.8 |
| Austria | 111 | 1.6 | 34 | 0.7 | 44.6 | 1.1 | 18 | 125 | 1.9 |
| Australia | 107 | 1.7 | 67 | 0.8 | 46.0 | 0.8 | 24 | – | – |
| Germany | 107 | 2.3 | 59 | 0.8 | 35.6 | 2.0 | 21 | 215 | 5 |
| Netherlands | 106 | 2.1 | 50 | 0.8 | 39.1 | 1.4 | 31 | 170 | 3.5 |
| France | 103 | 2.2 | 60 | 0.9 | 40.2 | 1.8 | 20 | 115 | 2.7 |
| Italy | 102 | 1.0 | 32 | 0.5 | 51.1 | 0.7 | 13 | 101 | 1 |
| Sweden | 100 | 3.9 | 86 | 1.0 | 25.2 | 4.4 | 41 | 147 | 5.3 |
| UK | 98 | 1.0 | 51 | 0.6 | 30.8 | 1.6 | 29 | 160 | 3.2 |
| Finland | 96 | 2.9 | 83 | 0.9 | 30.9 | 2.9 | 35 | 114 | 2.7 |
| Ireland | 92 | 1.4 | 51 | 0.3 | 22.2 | 1.3 | 16 | 69 | 1 |
| New Zealand | 88 | 1.1 | 45 | 0.6 | 52.3 | 0.4 | 29 | – | – |
| Spain | 77 | 0.9 | 33 | 0.4 | 43.6 | 0.5 | 16 | 21 | 0.2 |
| **Korea** | **72** | **2.9** | **48** | **0.7** | **22.9** | **2.5** | **5** | **25** | **0.7** |
| Portugal | 70 | 0.7 | 27 | 0.4 | 68.2 | 0.2 | 7 | 8 | 0 |
| Greece | 67 | 0.5 | 20 | 0.2 | 46.9 | 0.2 | 16 | – | – |
| Czech Republic | 64 | 1.3 | 24 | 0.5 | 36.8 | 1.0 | 15 | – | – |
| Hungary | 47 | 0.7 | 28 | 0.4 | 56.2 | 0.3 | 20 | 115 | 0.7 |
| Mexico | 36 | 0.3 | 6 | 0.2 | 71.1 | 0.1 | 2 | 15 | 0 |

*Table 13.3 (continued)*

| | Income level, 1996 GDP per capita as % of OECD average | Indicators of scientific and technological activities | | | | | | | |
|---|---|---|---|---|---|---|---|---|---|
| | | Gross domestic expenditure on R&D as a % of GDP, 1998[a] | Researchers per 10 000 labor force 1997[a] | Government-financed R&D as a % of GDP, 1998[a] | Government financing on R&D as a % of total R&D, 1998[a] | Business expenditure on R&D as a % of business GDP, 1998 | Scientific & technical articles per unit of GDP[b] | Technological strength per USD of R&D[c] | Technological intensity[d] |
| Poland | 35 | 0.8 | 32 | 0.5 | 59.0 | 0.4 | 17 | – | – |
| Turkey | 30 | 0.5 | 8 | 0.3 | 53.7 | 0.2 | 4 | – | – |

*Notes*:

a Or latest available year.

b Scientific and technological articles per billion USD of GDP. See National Science Foundation (1998).

c Technological strength is determined by multiplying the number of patents by an index of their impact. This index measures how frequently a country's recent patents are cited by all of a current year's patents. The patents refer to those granted at the US Patent and Trademark Office.

d Technology intensity compares the technological strength of a country with its GDP expressed in PPP USD. See OECD (1998a) for details.

*Source: OECD-World Bank Institute (2000).*

OECD countries, (although government outlays for R&D are substantial in absolute terms, reaching 0.7 per cent of GDP, the seventh-highest in the OECD). Consequently, government ability to coordinate the interactions of domestic players involved in research is weak. This may change, however, as the government's goal is to increase R&D spending, which rose from 3.7 to 4.1 per cent of its total budget in 2000, to 5 per cent by 2003 (NEAC 2000).

Compounding the situation, existing government support is focused on the nine government research institutes (GRIs), which tend to pursue the interests of their sponsoring ministry. It should also be noted, however, that the government has implemented policies, including tax incentives and direct financial support, to encourage private sector R&D by small and medium-sized enterprises (SMEs). While the effectiveness of the measures is difficult to assess, the government now accounts for about a quarter of SMEs' R&D outlays. In stark contrast, the government provides little funding for domestic universities. Reflecting the weak support and lack of research incentives for faculty members, universities perform only 10 per cent of the nation's R&D activities. Given that universities employ three-quarters of Korea's doctorate holders, university PhDs appear to be underutilized in the nation's R&D efforts (STEPI 1998).

Despite the gloomy outlook, there have been signs of change in the wake of the 1997 crisis, such as the downsizing of large research labs, the establishment of inter-company information networks, the encouragement of spin-offs and the introduction of performance-based pay for researchers. Additionally, SMEs' share of R&D increased significantly from 9 per cent to 15 per cent between 1997 and 1999 (OECD 2000b). Strengthening the protection of intellectual property rights (IPRs) is important to further these positive developments. Korea has already begun to upgrade its IPR-related laws and strengthened enforcement during the last few years. For instance, the Intellectual Property Rights (IPRs) law was strengthened in 1998, although its enforcement is still weak.

The government will also need to take other steps to raise the nation's base of science and technology to the level of a G-7 country. First, gradually increasing basic research will help lay the foundation for future technological advances in Korea. The universities and GRIs are logical places for such research, and this move would limit overlap with the private sector. Second, the government needs to promote greater linkages between the different players in the innovation system. Encouraging the mobility of researchers between universities, GRIs and the private sector would be one way to reduce the degree of segmentation. Third, the surge in FDI and the restructuring of the *chaebols*, which is now under way, offers an opportunity to internationalize the Korean innovation system and strengthen its links with global networks. Fourth, the government should encourage small companies to pursue R&D activities by involving them more closely in the work of the GRIs. Lastly, further protection of IPRs is essential to provide incentives for knowledge creation.

### 3.4 Reforming the Institutional Infrastructure

The 1997 crisis demonstrated vividly the need to re-examine the institutional regime in Korea, and emphasized that the main challenge facing Korea is to move away from past interventionist policies to foster a flexible, market-based and networked economy and society. The central elements of the changed role for government in this context are promoting competition and entrepreneurship, especially 'technopreneurship' which involves the use and development of ICTs, through deregulation of the market. This also requires a change in cultural attitudes towards failure. One reason for the high level of innovativeness and dynamism in the United States is that honest failure is socially acceptable. For Korea to achieve such a change in mindset and foster a more entrepreneurial culture, collective action will be necessary on the part of the government, the education system, the media and society at large (World Bank 1999a).

Other new, critical functions of the government include securing the rule of law and the accountability of market players by building a modern legal and institutional infrastructure applicable to the knowledge-based economy in areas such as IPRs, intangible assets and various Internet-related issues. The government must also provide public goods such as technology research and basic education, to address issues of equity and access. In addition, the government should try to nurture missing or underdeveloped markets by promoting new technologies and networking (for example between universities and firms), while being careful to foster market-led mechanisms.[6]

More generally, the Korean government needs to modernize and restructure itself to capture efficiency gains. Since the Asian crisis, it has made an impressive start in this direction through improved public sector management, with more transparency in expenditure, budget processes and human resource management, and more outsourcing to the private sector. Issues requiring future attention include the creation of appropriate salaries in the civil service; setting new modalities for policymaking in the context of greater globalization; building government information networks and better methods of knowledge sharing; and defining the role of government in knowledge-based activities. The privatization of state-owned enterprises to provide efficient and low-cost services, especially in the information infrastructure sector, should also be explored greater in depth.

## 4. CONCLUDING REMARKS

Korea has made rapid progress in developing a knowledge-based economy. To ensure continued progress, the government has an important role to play in areas such as providing information infrastructure, upgrading the education system, improving the innovation system and implementing institutional reforms.

With information infrastructure Korea has made impressive strides in rolling out and updating in such a fast-moving field. However, more is required, since the sector is changing and expanding by leaps and bounds worldwide. Some of the government's goals, such as creating new jobs and production, increasing the bandwidth of universal service, nurturing venture enterprises and increasing the number of Internet users, are admirable. But the sector's progress is constrained by an unwieldy and outdated regulatory and legal structure that needs to be streamlined. Without reform, the goals of the government will be unachievable – or will be achieved only at great cost. Moving toward independently regulated competition will allow for the more efficient upgrading of technology and provision of services.

Similar broad reforms are required to make the national educational system compatible with a knowledge-based economy. There is no instant solution guaranteeing quick results. These reforms will involve profound changes in all aspects of the education system, that is, not only in the inputs and their content and composition, but also in the institutional and governance infrastructures that deliver these changes. The largest changes will unavoidably entail deregulation and diversification of the existing education system, since without them the system will remain inflexible and uncompetitive.

Like the nation's education system, Korea's research capability compares well on the surface with those of other OECD countries. High R&D spending and relatively well-educated human resources are among its assets. However, Korea's innovation system is weak in terms of systemic linkages and interfaces among innovation actors. Korea's transition to a knowledge-based economy will therefore require reorientation of its innovation system.

Lastly, Korea will need to update its institutional regime. This move is critical for enabling Korea to position itself on a new and sustainable economic growth path, since such reforms are central to the overall functioning of, and flexibility required by, a knowledge-based economy.

As Korea entered the 21$^{st}$ century, its national economy was already preparing solidly to meet the requirements for a knowledge-based economic growth plan. Systemic change is already under way in many of the institutions that need to be reformed. With government, private sector and citizens contributing towards this goal, the chances of success are strong. Indeed, the entire population are stakeholders in Korea's drive for a knowledge-based economy.

## NOTES

1. This section draws heavily on the OECD–World Bank Institute (2000), OECD (2001b) and APEC (2000).
2. Innovation and technical progress are the result of a complex set of relationships between actors producing, disseminating, acquiring and applying various kinds of knowledge. So the concept of a national innovation system rests on the premise that understanding the linkages among the actors involved in innovation is the key to improving a country's technological performance. Linkages can take the form of joint research, personnel exchanges, cross-patenting, licensing of technology, purchase of equipment and a variety of other channels (OECD 1997).
3. A 2001 OECD report described an effective institutional infrastructure as a collection of 'sound fundamentals' in the sense that policies on ICT, human resources and innovation require fundamental economic and social stability for their success (OECD 2001b).
4. This section also draws on reports on Korea's transition to a new economic system published by the OECD and the World Bank, and other institutions. For more details concerning ongoing reform issues that still need to be addressed, see OECD–World Bank Institute (2000), APEC (2000) and the OECD's annual economic surveys on Korea.
5. The Korean government has plans to construct an Information Superhighway by the year 2005 (NEAC 2000).
6. For more details on recommendations for reforms in these areas, see the OECD's annual economic surveys on Korea. On financial sector reform, corporate restructuring and the labor market, see, especially, the surveys for 1998, 1999 and 2000.

## REFERENCES

APEC (2000), *Towards Knowledge-based Economies in APEC*, Singapore: APEC.

KEDI (Korea Education Development Institute) (1998), *Study on Education Expenditures in Korea* (in Korean), December, Seoul: KEDI.

Kim, Won-Kyu (1999), 'Total factor productivity and competitiveness in Korea', *APO Productivity Journal*, Summer.

Krugman, Paul (1994), 'The myth of Asia's miracle', *Foreign Affairs*, **73** (November/December), 62–78.

MIC (2002), *Performance of Information Promotion Policies* (in Korean), (http://www.mic.go.kr), Seoul: Ministry of Information and Communication.

MOCIE (Ministry of Commerce, Industry and Energy) (2002a), *E-Commerce in Korea* (in Korean), Seoul: Ministry of Commerce, Industry and Energy.

MOCIE (2002b), *Vision of Korea's Industrial Development toward 2010* (in Korean), Seoul: Ministry of Commerce, Industry and Energy.

MOE (Ministry of Education) (1998), *Educational Yearbook of 1998* (in Korean), Seoul: Ministry of Education.

National Science Foundation (1998), *Science and Engineering Indicators*, Arlington: National Science Foundation.

NEAC (National Economic Advisory Council) (2000), *Three Year Plan for Korea's Transformation into a Knowledge-based Economy* (in Korean), Seoul: National Economic Advisory Council.

OECD (1996), 'Special theme: The knowledge-based economy', in OECD (ed.), *Science, Technology and Industrial Outlook, 1996*, Paris: OECD.

OECD (1997), 'National innovation systems', free brochure, Paris: OECD.

OECD (1998a), *OECD Economic Survey: KOREA, 1998*, Paris: OECD.

OECD (1998b), *Technology, productivity and Job Creation: Best Policy Practices*, Paris: OECD.

OECD (1999), *OECD Economic Survey: KOREA, 1999*, Paris: OECD.

OECD (2000a), *Investing in Education: Analysis of the 1999 World Education Indicators*, Paris: OECD.

OECD (2000b), *OECD Economic Survey: KOREA, 2000*, Paris: OECD.

OECD (2001a), *OECD Economic Survey: KOREA, 2001*, Paris: OECD.

OECD (2001b), *The New Economy: Beyond the Hype*, Paris: OECD.

OECD–World Bank Institute (2000), *Korea and the Knowledge-based Economy: Making the Transition*, Paris: OECD.

STEPI (Science and Technology Policy Institute) (1998), *National Innovation System in Korea*, Seoul: Science and Technology Policy Institute (in Korean), Seoul: STEPI.

World Bank (1998), *World Development Report: Knowledge for Development*, Washington, DC: World Bank and Oxford University Press.

World Bank (1999a), *Republic of Korea: Establishing a New Foundation for Sustained Growth*, Washington, DC: World Bank.

World Bank (1999b), *EdStats* (Education Statistics Database), Washington, DC: World Bank.

# 14. A Development Strategy for Korea's Information Society

**Chang-Bun Yoon and Sang-Young Sonn**

## 1. INTRODUCTION

Korea has drawn international attention for its success in constructing a national information infrastructure. Policy researchers in various countries have begun to analyze Korean policies on informatization, promoting the use of information technologies to enhance work efficiency and quality of life. These policies form part of CYBER KOREA 21 which was put forward by the Korean government in 1999 as the blueprint for Korea's development of an information society in the 21st century.[1]

This chapter examines the major informatization policies and strategies that have been adopted and implemented in Korea since the establishment of CYBER KOREA 21. We also assess the effects of past policies on current conditions and consider their implications for the continuing evolution of informatization policies.

This chapter is organized as follows. In the next section we explain development of the CYBER KOREA 21 concept. Section 3 examines the major policies for advancing Korea's information infrastructure, and assesses their effects on the current information infrastructure and Internet usage. In section 4 we examine the informatization policies for enhancing national productivity, and analyze their successes and failures. Section 5 overviews various policies for creating new job opportunities in and through the Internet-based industries and the IT industry, and assesses the accomplishments of these policies. Section 6 reviews the R&D strategy of the IT industry. Section 7 is the closing section where we take stock of the effects of past policies on current conditions, and consider their implications for the direction of future informatization policies.

## 2. DEVELOPMENT OF THE CYBER KOREA 21 CONCEPT

In 1996, the Korean government established the Basic Informatization Promotion Plan as a national strategy to prepare for the development of an information society in Korea. One year after establishing the operational plans for the Basic Informatization Promotion Plan, Korea was hit by the Asian economic crisis at the end of 1997. As a direct consequence, the environment sustaining informatization efforts was affected profoundly. Major economic restructuring became an immediate national concern. A sharp rise in unemployment demanded immediate remedial attention, while responding to the opportunities as well as the upheaval arising from globalization. This response included searching for new ways to develop nascent business ventures and given the creative potential of electronic communication, the Internet was seen as an especially useful instrument for developing these ventures.

With the changes wrought by the economic crisis, revisions to the original informatization promotion plan were inevitable. Hence, at the end of 1998 the Ministry of Information and Communication established a new national strategy for building an information society. In March the following year, the Ministry presented CYBER KOREA 21 as the blueprint for the new information society for Korea in the 21$^{st}$ century, to replace the Basic Informatization Promotion Plan (MIC 1999b: 28).

The key concept behind CYBER KOREA 21 was to emphasize the need to transform the Korean economy into a knowledge-based economy and to stress the importance of informatization for this type of economy. This plan set out the importance of a national informatization strategy for resolving the critical problems facing Korea such as economic restructuring and job creation to help overcome the financial crisis and encourage growth in the emerging IT (Information Technology) industry.

CYBER KOREA 21 has four key objectives:

1. advancing information infrastructure to create an information society;
2. enhancing the productivity and transparency of all economic agents by using as effectively as possible high-speed telecommunications networks and other advanced technologies;
3. creating new businesses by using the information infrastructure and creating new jobs by developing the IT industry; and
4. focusing support for technology development by strategically selecting information technology items that can have a competitive edge in global markets.

## 3. ADVANCEMENT OF THE NATIONAL INFORMATION INFRASTRUCTURE

To advance the information infrastructure of Korea, the government's first task involved upgrading the nation's telecommunications networks. The main contents of the government's plan for the first task were set out in *The 1999 White Paper* prepared by the Ministry of Information and Communication where it set out the concept of CYBER KOREA 21:

> Subscriber networks will be established by leveraging all the national resources such as fiber optic cables, ADSL (Asymmetric Digital Subscriber Line) over existing copper-pair, cable-television networks, N-ISDN (Narrow-band Integrated Services Digital Network), wireless and satellite networks. As a result, the general public will be able to enjoy 1.5 to 2 Mbps level of high-speed services at affordable rates by 2002 (MIC 1999a: 17).

*The 1999 White Paper* indicates that the government will provide some support for investments required by telecommunications providers to construct a high-speed subscriber network and will take steps necessary to stimulate competition in the telecommunications market so that there will be fair competition in this market. The Ministry is to encourage private investment to rapidly establish information infrastructure, by creating a competitive environment among telecommunication service providers and introducing a new local telephone service provider (MIC 1999a: 17).

After change was made to the competition structure in the local telephone service, it was in the broadband Internet service sector, rather than in the local telephone service sector, where the market competition became intense. To gain a larger slice of the market, the broadband Internet access providers, such as Korea Telecom, Hanaro Telecom and Thrunet, strengthened investments, offered reasonable service rates of approximately $30 per month and implemented diverse marketing strategies to attract new subscribers.

As a result, high-speed subscriber networks were quickly being constructed from the second half of 1999 as rapid progress was made in the broadband Internet project using ADSL or cable modem technologies and the 'cyber apartment' project using LAN (Local Area Network) technologies. With intensive investments in the telecommunications networks, there was explosive growth in the number of Internet users and multimedia-related information quickly became widespread. As of the end of 2001, the number of Internet users in Korea totaled 24.38 million, and 7.81 million households had high-speed access to the broadband Internet services. This was a spectacular increase from three years earlier when there were 3.1 million Internet users and 14 000 households had access to the broadband Internet services (MIC 2002: 10). Korea's penetration rate of the broadband Internet per household had become the highest in the world by the end of 2001, as we see in Table 14.1.

*Table 14.1 Comparison of Penetration Rates of Broadband Internet per Household, end of 2001*

| Country | Korea | UK | US | Japan |
|---|---|---|---|---|
| Penetration rate (%) | 54.3 | 0.8 | 13.1 | 6.3 |

*Source*: MIC (2002).

From here the focus of the government shifted to establishing Korea as the world's leading computer-literate country. For this, the government set a plan for nationwide informatization education with a computer literacy certification system. To bridge the digital divide, informatization education would be expanded by offering training in computer literacy to housewives, the disabled and the unemployed. The goal of one personal computer per person would also be pursued to create an environment where computers can be accessed with relative ease at any time. Finally, to facilitate the use of the Internet, the plan included establishments of public Internet plazas to provide an environment with convenient access to the Internet (MIC 1999a: 25).

In the second half of 1999, the Ministry of Information and Communication began a program called 'Internet PC' to provide personal computers at 50 to 70 per cent of their market price. As a result of this effort, the penetration rate for PCs was 66 per cent at the end of 2000, with two out of every three households owning at least one computer (MIC 2000: 36).

To bridge the digital divide, the government has wired all elementary, middle and high schools in Korea to broadband Internet services and has provided e-literacy programs for the general public with special arrangements as required for the economically or physically disadvantaged. As a result, the number of disadvantaged Internet users grew swiftly as shown in Table 14.2.

*Table 14.2 Growth of Disadvantaged Internet Users*

(unit: %)

| | 1998 | 1999 | 2000 | 2001 |
|---|---|---|---|---|
| Over the age of 50 | 1.2 | 1.0 | 4.9 | 20.7 |
| Without college education | 1.7 | 2.8 | 11.9 | 48.9 |
| Income of 1 million won or less per month | 5.0 | 8.3 | 24.5 | 36.0 |

*Source*: MIC (2002).

The government has also made efforts to improve laws and regulations to facilitate the transition to an information society. Approximately 180 laws relating to e-government, e-commerce, distance learning and so forth were either enacted or amended by 2001. The purpose of these measures was to boost rapid transformation of the legal system in preparation for the information society. Improvements were also implemented in the laws and regulations that hindered the development of information society. However, there still appears to be a lack of in-depth legal research on the basic principles governing an information society. Thus, the government needs to examine the necessity of amending the relevant general laws, which include constitutional law, civil law, commercial law and criminal law for the purpose of general rules governing the information society. (MIC 2002: 51).

Another important task for advancing the information infrastructure involved creating a safe system for using information, and a sound ethics in relation to telecommunications. The main contents of the government's plan for this task are in *The 1999 White Paper* (MIC 1999a).

To ensure the safety and reliability of the nation's information system, a protection policy would be developed to examine the status of information concerning critical areas such as government administration, economy, national defense, aviation and transportation within the information infrastructure. Developing technology to ensure information security would be a new focus area, with the safety and reliability of information circulating in the Internet secured by overhauling laws and regulations concerning the promotion and development of encryption systems and by developing appropriate security technologies. In addition, a digital signature certification system will be implemented to secure the safety and reliability of on-line transactions. Information security was also recognized as essential in creating the foundations to facilitate e-commerce. And in an attempt to regulate information available through the Internet, the government would seek to prevent the distribution of indecent information, including obscene and violent materials, by establishing a sound telecommunications ethic (MIC 1999a: 28–9).

The legal and institutional foundations for information security were put in place with the enactment of the Digital Signature Act and the Act on Protection of Information Infrastructure, and revision of the Act on Promotion of Utilization of the Information and Communications Network. Despite the legislative arrangements, there has been rapid dissemination on the Internet of what the government recognizes as indecent information concerning pornography and violence. On-line acts of fraud, spamming, hacking and computer viruses have also become a more severe problem, and efforts by the government, Internet businesses and civic organizations to control and monitor these acts have been unable to stem the rise of these pervasive problems around Internet abuse and misuse.

## 4. INFORMATIZATION FOR ENHANCING THE OVERALL NATIONAL PRODUCTIVITY

The second key objective of CYBER KOREA 21 was to use the information infrastructure to increase the overall national productivity. This strategy involves two key tasks. One is to build a small but efficient digital government and *The 1999 White Paper* sets out a number of steps to achieve this.

To maximize the efficiency that information technology can generate, administrative procedures are to be re-engineered, thereby meeting the needs of a knowledge-based society. The government plans to quickly establish its own knowledge management system by moving from a paper documentation system to a paperless digital documentation system, with digital authorization and distribution of digital documents. To coordinate and improve access to civil administrative services, web-sites of all public institutions, government ministries and departments will be integrated within a multi-purpose single portal to make the complete range of government services easily accessible through sequenced paths from one website. A comprehensive administrative information system will also be established to enable provision of certificates and other services to the general public, wherever their location, through interactive on-line services (MIC 1999a: 32–6).

Informatization of the overall administrative processes in government has not only increased administrative efficiency but has also established a solid foundation for e-government. For example, informatization of customs services has shortened the processing time for exports from more than one day to less than two minutes; for imports from more than two days to less than two and a half hours; and has reduced logistics costs by at least 500 billion won a year. Informatization of public procurement services through the introduction of on-line services has enhanced productivity and transparency by reducing the time to process documents from more than two days to less than 30 minutes (MIC 2002: 11).

However, informatization in the public sector has not been fully realized as a result of the lack of information-sharing and system networking between government departments, organizations and agencies. In addition, government officials have been slow to disclose to the general public information about the new system of on-line administration. These shortcomings highlight the areas that will require remedial attention as the government moves to maximize the efficiency and effectiveness of administrative procedures and services to the public through judicious application of information technology.

The second task for increasing national productivity through information infrastructure is to improve the productivity of existing manufacturing and service industries by creating knowledge-management systems. Again *The 1999 White Paper* has detailed how this task is to be achieved. Among other steps, networks based on CALS (computer aided logistic support) are to link large companies and small and medium-sized parts vendors in the automobile, electronics and six other major industries by 2002, to reduce procurement and inventory costs. Industry, universities and research institutes are all to join in developing and promoting the Korean ERP (Enterprise Resource Planning) standards, which government will support with the necessary funds, technology and expert guidance (MIC 1999a: 40).

The application of information technologies has spread to major manufacturing industries such as steel, electronics, ship building, automobiles and textiles as moves are made to reduce costs and enhance corporate and national performance. POSCO, which has a 70 per cent share of the domestic steel market, has reduced costs by as much as 230 billion won a year through applying information technology such as the implementation of an e-commerce system. Financial institutions have utilized information and communications technologies to provide 24-hour electronic banking services. Currently, with 11.31 million customers subscribed to Internet-based banking services, the popularity of on-line financial transactions has risen dramatically. In 2001, 66.6 per cent of the total monetary value of stock trading was handled on the Internet as of December 2001 (MIC 2002: 11).

However, with many companies in Korea being SMEs (small and medium-sized enterprises), the utilization and application of information technologies have been low. This appears to be largely attributable to a weak infrastructure for e-business, which will need to include standardization, logistical support, legal structure and other features that enable coordination and development. Low transparency in accounting systems and unrecorded transactions are additional obstacles to the widespread usage of information and communication technologies in the SME sector and will need to be addressed so that the large number of small companies can take full advantage of e-commerce.[2]

## 5. CREATION OF BUSINESS AND EMPLOYMENT

The third key objective of CYBER KOREA 21 is to create new job opportunities by using the information infrastructure and developing the IT industry. *The 1999 White Paper* sets out the main contents of the government's plan to achieve this objective. Recognizing that growth in the Internet-based industries will lead to the creation of many new employment opportunities and stimulate the use of on-line transactions, the stability and reliability of the Internet should be secured so as to protect private information. The government plans to foster ISP (internet service provider) business at an industry level and will encourage joint lease of international transmission networks as a way of expanding Internet backbone networks for joint utilization of ISPs. To promote IPs (information providers), the government will give information providers a share of access charges generated for information provision. The Ministry of Information and Communication will build a system to support IP companies from company start-up to the development and marketing of their products. To promote IT venture companies, greater government support is to be provided for venture incubators in universities and the processes involved in establishing a venture company are to be simplified. To foster cultural industries, the government will increase venture capital funds available to video game and animation start-ups (MIC 1999a: 44–9).

The product groups that support or use the Internet continue to grow rapidly, along with businesses that support the business applications of the Internet. In 2001, 252 865 people were employed in the Internet sector, and the total revenue generated by this sector amounted to approximately $60 billion (Jo et al. 2002: 40, 45).

Clearly the IT industry enables other industries to increase their competitiveness and contributes hugely to the growth of the Korean economy. With an annual average growth rate of 18.8 per cent since 1997, the IT industry has played a pivotal role in overcoming the financial crisis that struck Korea in late 1997, and in revitalizing the national economy. Production in the IT industry was valued at approximately $120 billion, with a 12.9 per cent of GDP in 2001. The number of IT workers increased from 1.01 million in 1997 to 1.16 million in 2001. As of December 2001, 5073 companies were pursuing IT ventures which accounted for 44.5 per cent of all ventures in Korea (MIC 2002: 12).

## 6. TECHNOLOGY DEVELOPMENTS AND EXPORT

The fourth key objective of CYBER KOREA 21 was to support technology developments by selecting strategic information technology items. Here *The 1999 White Paper* sets out the main points of the government's plan for this objective. The Ministry will be pushing for the early broadcasting of digital TV to foster related industries as strategic export industries in a WTO-consistent manner. This will also help Korea to cope technically with the international trend of convergence between telecommunications and broadcasting of major advanced nations. Korea will provisionally adopt the US standard, the Advanced Television Standard Committee (ATSC), to conduct pilot broadcasting in the year 2000, and to provide full-fledged digital broadcasting in 2001 (MIC 1999a: 51).

By the end of 2001, the share of IT products increased to 26.8 per cent of the total exports (MIC 2002: 12). Among the leading products for export are semiconductors, TFT-LCD (thin film transistor-liquid crystal display), and mobile handsets. Exports of mobile handsets have increased from $446 million in 1997 to $5.5 billion in 2000 (KISDI 2002: 59). However, though domestic sales of digital TVs increased sharply during the period of the 2002 Korea-Japan FIFA World Cup games, it is still too early to assess the effects of digital TV on related industries.

In 2000, the Korean government designated 174 basic core technologies for technology development projects in 2000, investing approximately $125 million in order to gain a technological competitive edge in the areas of the Next Generation Internet, optical telecommunications, digital broadcasting, wireless communications, and computer hardware and software (MIC 2000: 113). With standardization of the 4th generation mobile communications technology, many countries will be undertaking technology development in this field. In response, Korea needs to prepare a technology development plan for next-generation mobile communications by selecting cutting-edge technology focusing on the long term.

## 7. CONCLUDING COMMENTS

Korea has successfully constructed high-speed telecommunications networks to enable the citizens to have access to the broadband Internet services throughout the nation. Despite the careful and extensive government-led efforts, the effects of informatization such as increasing productivity levels and transparency have not yet reached expected levels. This is largely attributable to the incomplete overhaul of social systems and outdated practices and to the incomplete implementation of business process re-engineering. These are certainly massive tasks and cannot possibly be carried out fully overnight. Even so, informatization policies in the future will need to put more emphasis on legal and institutional reforms as well as on increasing the capacity to maximize use of information technologies in all areas of society including government, the private sector and individuals in order to increase the positive effects of the informatization program.

As major social, political and economic functions depend heavily upon information systems and telecommunications networks, the possibility that major information and telecommunications facilities could be attacked by acts of cyber-terrorism increases. As more people are turning to the Internet to obtain information, a foundation for information security needs to be established. Thus, more efforts should be made to secure the safety and reliability of cyberspace.

The CYBER KOREA 21 strategy has been instrumental as a national policy guideline for the informatization of economic, political and social life in Korea. As we have discussed in this chapter, in the first four years since the strategy was adopted, much has been achieved in establishing the infrastructure of information technology. Yet much still remains to be done, recognizing that new technologies are being developed continuously, thus extending the creative potential and the boundaries of information technology. As CYBER KOREA 21 makes clear, IT provides the opportunity for crucial development of the Korean nation and for maximizing the well-being of the Korean economy during this era of great progress in technological development.

## NOTES

1. In June 2002, the Second OECD Broadband Workshop was held in Seoul to discuss Korea's recent informatization policies.
2. According to *The Economist* and PriceWaterhouse and Coopers, Korea ranked fifth from the bottom of 35 countries in national transparency and ranked last in accounting and management transparency in March 2001.

## REFERENCES

Jo, Dong-Gi et al. (2002), *2001 Survey on the Internet Industry in Korea (in Korean)*, Seoul, Korea: Korea Information Society Development Institute (KISDI).

Korea Information Society Development Institute (KISDI) (2002), *IT Industry Outlook of Korea 2002*, Seoul: KISDI.

Ministry of Information and Communication (MIC) (1999a), *The 1999 White Paper: CYBER KOREA 21*, Seoul: MIC.

Ministry of Information and Communication (MIC) (1999b), *Information and Communication: White Paper (in Korean)*, Seoul: MIC.
Ministry of Information and Communication (MIC) (2000), *Information and Communication: White Paper (in Korean)*, Seoul: MIC.
Ministry of Information and Communication (MIC) (2002), *e-Korea Vision 2006*, Seoul: MIC.

# Index